The Many Faces
of Childhood

The Many Faces of Childhood

Diversity in Development

Cecilia M. Shore

Miami University

Boston ■ New York ■ San Francisco
Mexico City ■ Montreal ■ Toronto ■ London ■ Madrid ■ Munich ■ Paris
Hong Kong ■ Singapore ■ Tokyo ■ Cape Town ■ Sydney

Series Editor: Carolyn Merrill
Editorial Assistant: Carolyn Mulloy
Marketing Manager: Wendy Gordon
Production Editor: Paul Mihailidis
Editorial Production Services: Omegatype Typography, Inc.
Manufacturing Buyer: JoAnne Sweeney
Composition Buyer: Linda Cox
Cover Administrator: Kristina Mose-Libon
Electronic Composition: Omegatype Typography, Inc.

For related titles and support materials, visit our online catalog at www.ablongman.com.

Between the time Website information is gathered and then published, it is not unusual for some sites to have closed. Also, the transcription of URLs can result in typographical errors. The publisher would appreciate notification where these occur so that they may be corrected in subsequent editions.

Library of Congress Cataloging-in-Publication Data

The many faces of childhood: diversity in development / [edited by] Cecelia M. Shore.
    p. cm.
   Includes bibliographical references.
   ISBN 0-205-38166-9 (alk. paper)
   1. Child development.   2. Child development—Cross-cultural studies.   3. Individual differences.   4. Children with disabilities.   I. Shore, Cecelia M.

HQ767.9.M28 2004
305.231—dc21

2003043708

Printed in the United States of America

10   9   8   7   6   5   4   3   2   1   08   07   06   05   04   03

Contents

v

Middle Childhood/School Age

Childhood (Across Age Groupings)

Readings by Topic

Readings as They Relate to Factors That Influence Children's Development

Endogenous Factors

Family Characteristics

Subculture: U.S. Minorities

Culture: International

Other

Readings as They Relate to Aspects of Children's Development

Readings by Type

Cognitive Development

Physical Development

Socio-emotional Development

Preface

Diversity is at the heart of development. The long-standing controversy over "nature versus nurture" or "heredity versus environment" has been supplanted by the understanding that development takes place in a biosocial system, as a transaction among many factors that reciprocally influence one another. Every one of us (except for identical twins) begins with a unique set of genetic instructions, which interact with the unique circumstances of one's individual life. As an example, Bronfenbrenner (1979) proposes four nested systems of environmental influence on child development: the family, environments that impact the family such as the parents' workplaces, the community, and the broader society. Because there are so many interacting factors over time, a central fact of development is that developmental pathways become more variable over the lifespan. A good course in child development is necessarily a course in diversity. Developmental processes are revealed not only by developmental universals, but also by the differences among us. These themes, the biosocial system, and the ways that developmental processes are revealed by diversity are outlined by Richard Lerner in Reading 1.

Each of the other readings represents, as Lerner would say, a "reduced model"—a look at how some specific aspect(s) of children's development is affected by the interchange between the child and one or more levels of the environment in which the child is embedded. For example, Readings 11 and 13 focus on how community members such as teachers affect children's development. Readings 4, 5, 8, and 10 examine how culture affects family child-rearing practices and these in turn affect children's behavior. Readings 9 and 20 focus on how broad factors such as socioeconomic status and geography affect children's development by affecting their local social and physical environments. It is important to realize children are not simply passive recipients of environmental impacts. Readings 3, 6, and 15 relate to the theme of bidirectionality of influence—ways that characteristics of the child may affect how others interact with him or her, or may affect the efficacy of later interventions. By examining the similarities and differences among children's development in different contexts, we learn about the mechanisms of development. For example, Readings 2, 14, 17, 18, and 21 all examine questions of developmental universals and "milestones" and whether these occur in the same way in all family structures and cultures. Several readings (7, 12, 16, and 19) focus on the degree to which children's physical, cognitive, and emotional development is resilient even in the face of severe deprivation and trauma.

Because development takes place in multiply nested environments, I believe it is important to represent not only cultural comparisons (a broad level of environment), but also more specific environments, such as the neighborhood, the family, and endogenous factors. Consequently, I have systematically included readings to represent broad level environments, such as cross-cultural comparisons both internationally and within the United States, and also socioeconomic differences (as distinct from race/ethnicity). I have included variations in more focused environments, such as family composition (e.g., children raised by gay/lesbian parents) and school settings. Finally, I have also represented diversity based on physical ability or other endogenous characteristics (e.g., visual impairments or autism).

These many factors influence children's developmental pathways. They influence (and are influenced by) different aspects of the developing person, and the outcomes of these transactions differ at different points in time. The basic outline for the book is chronologically arranged, from birth through toddlerhood, preschool, and middle childhood. The book ends with a group of articles that covers a broad range of the childhood years. Within each of those sections, I have systematically included readings that are targeted toward physical/health outcomes, perceptual-cognitive development, and socio-emotional development.

Another goal for this book is to give students examples of the different kinds of information that developmental psychologists use to think about developmental processes. Since its inception, developmental psychology as a discipline has sustained a dynamic and creative tension between quantitative and qualitative sources of data. We make use of baby diaries on the one hand, and factor analyses on the other. Even if students are not going to be developmental psychologists, they will be professionals who have to interpret many different kinds of information, and who have to make considered evaluative judgments about the utility of different kinds of information. Consequently, I have included empirical journal articles that focus on statistical comparison, empirical studies that rely more heavily on in-depth interview data, research reviews, and personal accounts.

Each of the articles is accompanied by an introduction, which shows how the article relates to the broader themes of the book and provides background that connects it to the typical content of an introductory child development course. Each article also has critical thinking questions. Some of these provide an overview of the general purpose and conclusions of the article, and others focus on the details, and typically examine methodology and analyses.

Childhood has many faces. Nearly every one of us has a unique makeup, and we certainly all have unique life experiences. We each make our way through a unique pattern of risks and resources, challenges and supports. Each of us is a "natural experiment" to see what humankind can become.

I'd like to thank my graduate school advisors, Elizabeth Bates and Inge Bretherton, who introduced me to the two basic ideas in this book, namely that organism and environment mutually define one another, and that individual differences can reveal developmental processes. I'm grateful to Catherine Richter Kell, who previewed the readings and the questions and provided useful feedback about their accessibility to students. I thank all the authors whose work is reproduced here, and the manuscript reviewers, Tasha Howe, Humboldt State University; Deidre Lewin, Manhattenville College; and Larrisa Samuelson, University of Iowa, who gave helpful suggestions for improving this book.

The Many Faces
of Childhood

■ You may be familiar with Bronfenbrenner's (1979) ecological theory of child development. He describes the individual child as being embedded in one or more microsystems of the family and school. The relationships between these microsystems are labeled the mesosystem. The systems that the child doesn't directly experience but which have an effect on him/her, such as parents' workplaces, are called the exosystem. Finally, these systems are embedded in a larger cultural and historical system, labeled the macrosystem. In this article, Lerner elaborates a similar idea, namely that development consists of changes in relationships between the individual child and various levels of surrounding contexts. He explains how this view makes diversity and individual differences a central feature of psychological development.

Overview Questions

1. What is a developmental contextual perspective? From the introduction, summarize a) what new understanding does this perspective give us of the basic process of change, and b) what two conceptual/methodological changes are implied for research?

2. After reading the section on "A revised understanding of the basic process of development," rewrite or paraphrase the second paragraph of that section in your own words. You may find it helpful to look at Figure 1 while you are reading this section.

3. Why does Lerner believe that studying individual differences is important? (Hint: he discusses this in the fifth paragraph of "Revising the research questions . . ." as well as in the section on "Enhancing sensitivity . . .")

Focus Questions

1. Why does Lerner believe that a multidisciplinary approach to the study of development is essential?

2. What are four ways that Lerner argues the model depicted in Figure 1 has been empirically useful? Examine the example that he gives of a "reduced" model that would derive from the big picture and be empirically testable, and then generate your own example.

Changing Organism–Context Relations as the Basic Process of Development: A Developmental Contextual Perspective

Richard M. Lerner

Genes do not by themselves produce structural or functional characteristics. Variables within the organism (e.g., cells, tissues) and extraorganism contextual variables reciprocally interact with genes, making changing organism–context relations the basic process of development. This conception of basic process raises 2 sets of conceptual and methodological alterations for developmental psychology, especially for research pertinent to humans. First, research questions must be formulated that involve intra- and extra-organism contextual relations and that are necessarily multidisciplinary in scope. Second, greater research sensitivity must exist to issues of contextual variability, to diversity in human life and development, and to interindividual differences in the timing of organism–context interactions. Scholars must develop empirically generative models that link integratively developing people with their changing contexts.

Gottlieb (1991b) pointed to compelling evidence that genes do not directly (i.e., in and of themselves) produce any structural or functional characteristics of an organism. That is, Gottlieb indicated that the action of genes (genetic expression) is "affected by events at other levels of the [developmental] system, including the environment of the organism" (p. 5). "All levels of the system may be considered potentially equal" (p. 6), and therefore this is why "genetic activity does not by itself produce finished traits such as blue eyes, arms, legs, or neurons. The problem of anatomical and physiological differentiation remains unsolved, but it is unanimously recognized as requiring influences above the strictly cellular level" (p. 5). Thus, intraorganism variables making up the proximal context of the gene, as well as extraorganism contextual variables, are shown in Gottlieb (1991a, 1991b), as well as in the literature he cites (e.g., Edelman, 1987, 1988; Grouse, Schrier, Letendre, & Nelson, 1980; Kollar & Fisher, 1980; Uphouse & Bonner, 1975; see also Lerner, 1984), to exist in a reciprocally influential relation with genes.

Simply, then, just as genes influence these contexts, the contexts influence genes. Moreover, no less is true of the organism within which genes exist (cf. Ford, 1987). The developmental systems framework of Gottlieb (1991b), termed elsewhere the "developmental contextual" perspective (Lerner, 1986), indicates that all organismic characteristics (e.g., genes, cells, tissues, organs), as well as the whole organism itself, function in a bidirectional, reciprocal, or "dynamic interactional" (Lerner, 1978) relation with the contexts within which the organism is embedded. Gottlieb's (1991b) examples of these dynamic interactions involved, most often, integrated, multilevel exchanges of material (e.g., nutritional, hormonal) or energy (e.g., light) variables. Lerner's (1978, 1979, 1984) examples of these interactions have most often involved integrated, multilevel exchanges of "informational" (i.e., psychological and behavioral) variables (Ford, 1987). Although the two types of examples refer to exchanges having contents which are fundamentally (i.e., qualitatively) different, their structure and function can be integrated within a common model, such as the developmental systems or the developmental contextual model (see Ford, 1987; Tobach, 1981, for other examples).

The depiction of dynamic interactional organism–context relations in such models means nothing less than the fact that developmental psychology as a field must reach a new understanding of what constitutes the basic process of change: Because changes in the organism always occur in dynamic connection with changes in the context (and vice versa), then changes in organism–context relations are the basic change process in development. Moreover, this revised understanding of the basic process of change must be coupled with two rather far-reaching sets of conceptual and methodological alterations for the field of developmental psychology, especially for research pertinent to human development.

First, as a field, we should formulate different research questions: We should ask questions involving intra- and extraorganism contextual relations. For instance, questions about the connection between cognitive and neural functioning, on the one (intraorganism) hand, might be coupled with concerns about the bidirectional connections between person and context that the cognitive–neural relations afford (e.g., see Bullock, 1983; Bullock, Liederman, & Todorovic, 1987). Second, as a consequence of such revised research questions, we must as a field conduct our research with considerably greater sensitivity to issues of contextual variability and diversity in human life and development. Such sensitivity will allow our scientific data base to more adequately reflect, first, the vast array of individual differences in developmental patterns that exist across all of the human life span and, second, the contextual variation (in, for instance, families, communities, societies, cultures, and historical periods) that is both a product and a producer of human diversity across life.

To explain the bases for these two alterations in developmental psychology, I first detail why organism–context relations should be the unit of study in a field devoted to the understanding of systematic change in human life. I then suggest some specific issues (e.g., relating to the timing of interactions) that should be studied as a consequence of a focus on changing organism–context relations, and I indicate some approaches or models that could be used. Finally, I point to implications for the nature of the samples of people we study and for the ways in which we study them.

A Revised Understanding of the Basic Process of Development

Events that impinge on the gene, on the cell, and, indeed, on the whole organism—events related to the gene, to the cell, and to the organism (ie., connected to them) in terms of physical avenues or temporal propinquity—influence the structural and functional outcomes of the developmental system of which genes (or cells or organisms) are only one part (Lerner, 1984). Thus, the most basic process of development is a relational one. Scientists who study only a component of this relational system are appraising, then, only a partial and incomplete subprocess. In other words, in the analysis of basic processes in development, the only approach that suffices is relational analysis. However, by definition, this relation involves change. As Gottlieb (1991b) notes, "Developing systems are by definition always changing in some way [and thus] statements of developmental causality must also include a temporal dimension describing when the experience or organic coactions occurred" (p. 8).

Simply, it is the nature of living matter to alter over time. In addition, this organic matter is bidirectionally related to an inexorably changing physical ecology and a virtually inevitably changing social one. This linkage means that changing organism–context relations constitute the basic process of development. Thus, multilevel, multivariate, and longitudinal views of these relations are absolutely necessary features of "basic research" in developmental psychology; only through such appraisals can we capture accurately the coaction of variables at organismic and contextual levels as they change interdependently across time.

Moreover, because events in both the proximal and distal contexts of the organism influence the structure and function of the cell (e.g., Diamond, 1967; Krech, Rosenzweig, & Bennett, 1963), as well as the structure and function of the gene (e.g., Edelman, 1988; Grouse et al., 1980; Uphouse & Bonner, 1975), the core, superordinate process of development is one involving the changing relations between the organism and its multilevel context. A focus on either element in this relation (in other words, on either, separate level of analysis) is simply inadequate to understand this process. The elements of the relation whose loci lie within the organism (e.g., genes, cells, tissues, organs) can influence the context; the elements of the relation whose loci lie in the multileveled context (e.g., other organisms, features of the physical ecology, proximal social institutions such as the family, more distal social institutions such as those pertaining to politics and social policy) can influence the organism. The presence of this mutuality of influence is why the organism–context relation should be understood as a bidirectional, indeed a reciprocal or "dynamically interactive" (Lerner, 1978, 1979), one. Indeed, it is through this dynamic interaction, this "transactional" (Dewey, 1896) relation, between organism and context that development happens. "The cause of development—what makes development happen—is the relationship of the . . . components, not the components themselves" (Gottlieb, 1991b, p. 7).

Given, then, that multiple levels of the organism (e.g., gene, cell, organ) and multiple levels of the context (e.g., significant other, family, social policies) exist in a dynamically interactive relation, one must approach the study of the organism–context relation using what Schneirla (1957) termed a "levels-of-integration" notion. In other words, to adequately study the basic, relational process of development, one must eschew reductionism; one should recognize the multiple levels of analysis of the organism and the context as qualitatively distinct and yet simultaneously dynamically interactive—and hence as "fused" (Tobach & Greenberg, 1984) or as "synthesized" (cf. Riegel, 1975, 1976)—over the course of the life span.

As a consequence of the integration of these levels of organism structure and contextual organization, one should adopt a multidisciplinary approach to the study of development. It is important to be very clear as to what such an approach actually entails. Obviously, the study of one function of the organism (e.g., cognition) in isolation is not adequate for an analysis of changing organism–context relations; such a focus is not aimed at understanding the basic developmental change process. Rather, no matter how formalized or experimentally elegant such a focus may be, it represents incomplete attention to the core, basic process of life and development. Similarly, the study of this one function would be inadequate if it were approached by a collaboration of scholars from multiple disciplines (e.g., cognitive scientists, linguists, and computer scientists), although such a collaboration would be better than the former, isolationist approach. Only when one studies both intraorganism–context relations (e.g., when cognitive functioning is studied in relation to emotional functioning) and interorganism–context relations (i.e., when the organism is studied in relation to the social group) and does so in a change-sensitive (i.e., multivariate–longitudinal), integrated, and multidisciplinary manner, will knowledge of the basic, relational change process of development be gained. The neurocognitive and contextual modeling involved in adaptive systems research (e.g., Bullock, 1983; Bullock et al., 1987) is an excellent illustration of the sort of research for which I am calling.

Revising the Research Questions Within Developmental Psychology

Given the complexity and enormity of any of the numerous subareas in the field of developmental psychology, no scientist can hope to be a first-rate, productive scholar in any more than a small subset of these subareas. It would seem obvious, then, that the time and motivation needed to maintain expertise in one's chosen subareas would preclude the opportunity to become a credible and productive scholar in a discipline distinct from one's own. I believe that this is almost always the case. Nevertheless, one must overcome such scholarly limits and attempt to work in a collaborative, multidisciplinary milieu if one is to contribute to a better understanding of the basic developmental process.

The means through which to do this do not, however, involve a rejection of a focus on one's disciplinary background and training. Rather, one should work to reorient the approach taken in one's discipline to formulating the questions deemed most important to address. Simply, one should ask change-oriented, relational questions, questions that bridge levels of analysis and that require multidisciplinary collaboration for their answers.

Such an approach is admittedly conceptually complex, methodologically and collaboratively difficult to implement (Nesselroade & Baltes, 1979; Nesselroade & von Eye, 1985), and—in regard to any one program of research—inevitably limited to reflecting only a small portion of the dynamic interactions that integrate intra- and extraorganism levels of analysis. Nevertheless, scholars from all disciplines involved in the study of human development must begin to ask integrative, change-oriented, relational questions if advances are to be made in understanding the temporally varying linkages between developing people and their changing world.

Established scholars must simply begin to reorient their own work. In addition, educators in each of the disciplines involved in the study of human development must begin to train their students differently (Birkel, Lerner, & Smyer, 1989). An appreciation of change, context, and relations must be the cornerstone of future graduate education.

Moreover, because the organismic and contextual components of the causal, dynamic interactions constituting the basis of human development will not occur in the same way or at the same exact ontogenetic time across all people, lawful individual differences in developmental pathways, and not a generic developmental trajectory, characterize human life. Thus, we must instill in future scholars a greater appreciation of the importance of interindividual differences in the timing of causal, dynamic interactions—for the development of human diversity and for the contextual variation that is both a product and a producer of it (Lerner, 1982; Lerner & Busch-Rossnagel, 1981).

Furthermore, it is important to add that university tenure and promotion committees evaluating scientists studying development must be urged to begin to value multidisciplinarily collaborative, and hence multiauthored, publications even more than within-discipline, single-authored products. We cannot train future cohorts of developmental scientists to engage productively in the multidisciplinary collaborations requisite for advancing understanding of the basic process of development and then not reward and value them for successfully doing so. Similarly, if we are to take seriously the need for change-oriented (and hence longitudinal), multilevel (and hence multivariate), and multidisciplinary research, we must recognize the need to educate government agencies and private foundations about the time and financial resources that should be given to such collaborative activities.

Most important, we must begin to attend more to the development of empirically generative theoretical models that link integratively developing people with their contexts across life. For example, the developmental contextual perspective (Lerner, 1986; Lerner & Kauffman, 1985) has been forwarded as one means to understand the reciprocal link between the developing child and his or her developing parent, a relation moderated by the intraindividual interactions (e.g., among biology, cognition, affect, and developmental status) pertinent to each person, as well as by the social networks, the community, societal, and cultural contexts, and the changing historical period within which this dyad is embedded. Figure 1.1 presents an illustration of this developmental contextual perspective.

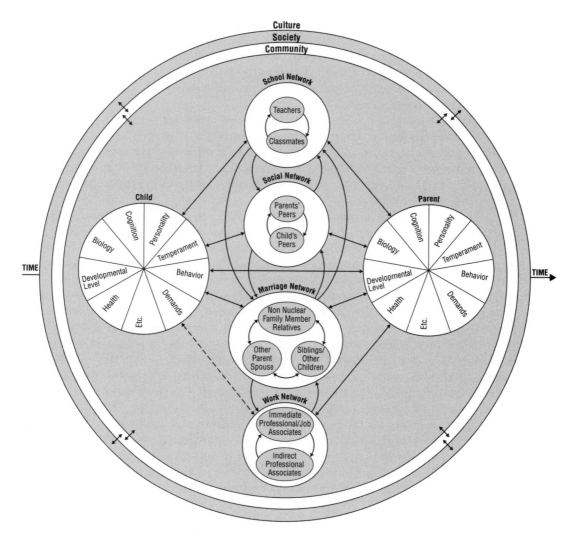

FIGURE 1.1   *A Developmental Contextual Model of Person–Context Interaction (Lerner, 1984, 1986)*

As implied above, the developmental contextual model of person–context relations depicted in Figure 1.1 cannot be studied in one research effort. Nevertheless, this model has proven empirically useful in several important ways. First, it serves as a guide to the formulation of the person–context relational questions that I have argued are critical to forward if knowledge about the basic process of development is to be furthered. Second, the model serves as a limiting frame for the generalizations that a scholar should see as appropriate to make on the basis of any one empirical effort; the model depicts the complexity of the intra- and extraorganism relations that, together, assure human diversity. Thus, this model leads us to question whether or how we can generalize our findings to people developing in distinct familial, community, cultural, or historical settings. Third, the model serves as a guide for the collaboration of scholars from the several disciplines involved in the study of human development; by asking particular relational questions, a developmental psychologist may seek collaboration, in regard to a given research effort, with scholars whose disciplinary bases could range from molecular biology to macrosociology or history. Fourth, the model serves as a general template from which "reduced," more directly empirically testable models may be derived.

One such model would involve the relation between a specific characteristic of the child's organismic individuality (e.g., physical attractiveness or temperament) and a characteristic of the parent pertinent to the characteristic (e.g., expectations, preferences, or demands regarding temperament). These child and parent characteristics would be studied not only in relation to each other, but also in relation to the child's and parent's interactions with contexts (e.g., the school) distinct from the family. Finally, within this reduced model, the person–context relations would be studied within a given community (and hence societal and cultural) context and, because both people and context change over time, all components of the model would be appraised longitudinally.

The empirical utility of such a developmental contextual model has been presented in several articles, chapters, and books (e.g., Lerner, 1987; Lerner & Lerner, 1989) describing the changing person–context relations involved in early adolescents' transition to junior high school. Similarly, other developmental contextual-oriented models—for instance, those of Baltes (1987), Featherman (1985), Ford (1987), (Magnusson, 1988; Magnusson & Ohman, 1987; Stattin & Magnusson, 1990), and Perlmutter (Dannefer & Perlmutter, 1990; Perlmutter, 1988)—have been shown to be empirically quite useful, as have related, developmental ecological models (e.g., Bronfenbrenner, 1979). Indeed, research from several disciplines—appearing in articles, in numerous edited volumes (e.g., Brim & Kagan, 1980; Hetherington, Lerner, & Perlmutter, 1988; Kreppner & Lerner, 1989; Lerner & Foch, 1987; Magnusson & Allen, 1983; Nesselroade & von Eye, 1985; Sorensen, Weinert, & Sherrod, 1986), and in the annual advances series *Life-Span Development and Behavior* (e.g., Baltes & Brim, 1985; Baltes, Featherman, & Lerner, 1988; Featherman, Lerner, & Perlmutter, in press)—has attested to the current empirical value and continued scientific importance of studying the relation between a developing individual and his or her changing context. Indeed, the appreciation of human interindividual variation (or diversity) and of contextual differences that this work has brought to the fore constitutes the second key arena of reorientation required in developmental psychology as a consequence of the recognition that changing person–context relations constitute the basic process of human development.

Enhancing Sensitivity to Human Diversity and Contextual Variation Within Developmental Psychological Research

To this point in the history of developmental psychology, neither human diversity nor contextual variation have been adequately appreciated or understood. Indeed, one might infer from reading the pages of the leading research journals in the field (e.g., *Child Development or Developmental Psychology*) that to understand development it suffices to study, almost exclusively in laboratory–experimental situations, White, middle-class, school-age, American children (Fisher & Brennan, in press; Hagen, Paul, Gibb, & Wolters, 1990). In fact, in an analysis of randomly sampled articles published in *Child Development* over the course of more than 50 years, Hagen et al. (1990) found that, among the studies that informed readers of the demographic characteristics of the children sampled, the preponderant majority of the investigations did indeed appraise groups having these characteristics. However, Hagen et al. (1990) also reported that most of the *Child Development* articles in their sample reported neither the race nor the socioeconomic status of the children. Fisher and Brennan's (in press) analysis of this journal, as well as of other developmental ones, confirmed the findings of Hagen et al. (1990).

Thus, scholars publishing in the best journals in the field of developmental psychology have as a group acted either (a) as if they were studying the "generic child," a child whose context was of such little importance that even mention of some of its general characteristics (e.g., socioeconomic status) was not necessary or (b) as if the only demographics worth mentioning were White, middle-class ones. It may be deemed by some as impolite or impolitic to remind us, as a field, of this shortcoming. However, such lack of sensitivity to human diversity and contextual variation cannot continue. Obviously, the absence of this sensitivity is morally repugnant to many people. In addition, however, such lack of sensitivity is simply bad science. The revised understanding of what constitutes the basic process of human development brings to the fore the cutting-edge importance of continued empirical focus on individual differences, on contextual variations, and on changing person–context relations. Nothing short of these emphases can be regarded as involving scientifically adequate developmental analysis of human life.

Conclusions

The basic, causal process governing human development involves a changing relation between an individually distinct person and the specific features of his or her physical and social context. The substantial evidence supporting the presence of this relational process means that developmental scientists can no longer say "show me the data supportive of the relevance of these organism–context relations for what I study." First, Gottlieb's (1991b) article, and the data from the several sources he cites, provide solid biological and psychosocial evidence for the centrality of these relations in structural and functional developments across life. In addition, there are several data sets that provide evidence converging with that presented by Gottlieb (e.g., see Hetherington et al., 1988; Lerner, 1984; Magnusson, 1988; Magnusson & Ohman, 1987; Sorensen et al., 1986); together, these data sets point compellingly to the importance of changing person–context relations across ontogeny. The presence of this body of information means that "show me" statements such as the one above reflect, at best, an ill-informed knowledge of the nature of the contemporary scientific data base.

Second, it is clear that scientists who have been seeking "the" developmental trajectory in their research or who have been pursuing knowledge of the nature of human development through the study of the acontextualized, generic child have been asking the wrong questions and conducting the wrong sort of research. The data derived from such work cannot be used to argue against the need to bring attention to diversity and context in our future research. It is difficult to find evidence that diversity in developmental patterns is the rule in human life and that context matters when assessment is made only of White, middle-class, American school-age children studied in small-sample, laboratory–experimental investigations. It is hard to demonstrate the importance of sensitivity either to individual differences among humans or to contextual variation when, in the majority of articles published in the field's leading journals, there has been no mention of either the race or the socioeconomic status of the humans being assessed.

Gottlieb's (1991b) article, and the large and rapidly growing biopsychosocial literature of which it is a part, indicated convincingly that diversity and context do matter centrally. They are the core of what human development is all about. As Gottlieb (1991b, p. 7) argued as well, ideas to the contrary "have provided impediments to thinking clearly about the need for conceptual and empirical analysis at all levels of the developmental systems hierarchy." By remaining focused on changing organism–context relations as the basic process of development, our field may begin to overcome these impediments to good science. As our science improves, we will be in an increasingly better position to use developmental knowledge to enhance human life in the full grandeur of its diversity.

References

Baltes, P. B. (1987). Theoretical propositions of life-span developmental psychology: On the dynamics between growth and decline. *Developmental Psychology, 23,* 611–626.

Baltes, P. B., & Brim, O. G., Jr. (Eds.). (1985). *Life-span development and behavior* (Vol. 6). San Diego, CA: Academic Press.

Baltes, P. B., Featherman, D. L., & Lerner, R. M. (Eds.). (1988). *Life-span development and behavior* (Vol. 9). Hillsdale, NJ: Erlbaum.

Birkel, R. C., Lerner, R. M., & Smyer, M. A. (1989). Applied developmental psychology as an implementation of a life span view of human development. *Journal of Applied Developmental Psychology, 10,* 425–445.

Brim, O. G., Jr., & Kagan, J. (Eds.). (1980). *Constancy and change in human development.* Cambridge, MA: Harvard University Press.

Bronfenbrenner, U. (1979). *The ecology of human development.* Cambridge, MA: Harvard University Press.

Bullock, D. (1983). Seeking relations between cognitive and social interactive transitions. In K. W. Fischer (Ed.), *Levels and transitions in children's development* (pp. 97–108). San Francisco: Jossey-Bass.

Bullock, D., Liederman, J., & Todorovic D. (1987). Reconciling stable asymmetry with recovery of function: An adaptive systems perspective on functional plasticity. *Child Development, 58,* 689–697.

Dannefer, D., & Perlmutter, M. (1990). Development as a multidimensional process: Individual and social constituents. *Human Development, 33,* 108–137.

Dewey, J. (1896). The reflex arc concept in psychology. *Psychological Review, 3,* 357–370.

Diamond, M. C. (1967). Extensive cortical depth measurements and neuron size increases in the cortex of environmentally enriched rats. *Journal of Comparative Neurology, 131,* 357–364.

Edelman, G. M. (1987). *Neural Darwinism: The theory of neuronal group selection.* New York: Basic Books.

Edelman, G. M. (1988). *Topobiology: An introduction to molecular biology.* New York: Basic Books.

Featherman, D. L. (1985). Individual development and aging as a population process. In J. R. Nesselroade & A. von Eye (Eds.), *Individual development and social change: Explanatory analysis* (pp. 213–241). San Diego, CA: Academic Press.

Featherman, D. L., Lerner, R. M., & Perlmutter, M. (Eds.). (in press). *Life-span development and behavior* (Vol. 11). Hillsdale, NJ: Erlbaum.

Fisher, C. B., & Brennan, M. (in press). Application and ethics in developmental psychology. In D. L. Featherman, R. M. Lerner, & M. Perlmutter (Eds.), *Life-span development and behavior* (Vol. 11). Hillsdale, NJ: Erlbaum.

Ford, D. H. (1987). *Humans as self-constructing living systems.* Hillsdale, NJ: Erlbaum.

Gottlieb, G. (1991a). Experimental canalization of behavioral development: Results. *Developmental Psychology, 27,* 35–39.

Gottlieb, G. (1991b). Experiential canalization of behavioral development: Theory. *Developmental Psychology, 27,* 4–13.

Grouse, L. D., Schrier, B. K., Letendre, C. H., & Nelson, P. G. (1980). RNA sequence complexity in central nervous system development and plasticity. *Current Topics in Developmental Biology, 16,* 381–397.

Hagen, J. W., Paul, B., Gibb, S., & Wolters, C. (1990, March). *Trends in research on children as reflected by publications in Child Development: 1930–1989.* Paper presented at the biennial meeting of the Society for Research on Adolescence, Atlanta.

Hetherington, E. M., Lerner, R. M., & Perlmutter, M. (Eds.). (1988). *Child development in life-span perspective.* Hillsdale, NJ: Erlbaum.

Krech, P., Rosenzweig, M. R., & Bennett, E. L. (1963). Effects of complex environment and blindness on rat brain. *Archives of Neurology, 8,* 403–412.

Kreppner, K., & Lerner, R. M. (Eds.). (1989). *Family systems and life-span development.* Hillsdale, NJ: Erlbaum.

Kollar, E. J., & Fisher, C. (1980). Tooth induction in chick epithelium: Expression of quiescent genes for enamel synthesis. *Science, 207,* 993–995.

Lerner, R. M. (1978). Nature, nurture and dynamic interactionism. *Human Development, 21,* 1–20.

Lerner, R. M. (1979). A dynamic interactional concept of individual and social relationship development. In R. Burgess & T. Huston (Eds.), *Social exchange in developing relationships* (pp. 271–305). San Diego, CA: Academic Press.

Lerner, R. M. (1982). Children and adolescents as producers of their own development. *Developmental Review, 2,* 342–370.

Lerner, R. M. (1984). *On the nature of human plasticity.* New York: Cambridge University Press.

Lerner, R. M. (1986). *Concepts and theories of human development* (2nd ed.). New York: Random House.

Lerner, R. M. (1987). A life-span perspective for early adolescence. In R. M. Lerner & T. T. Foch (Eds.), *Biological–psychosocial interactions in early adolescence: A life-span perspective* (pp. 1–6). Hillsdale, NJ: Erlbaum.

Lerner, R. M., & Busch-Rossnagel, N. (1981). Individuals as producers of their development: Conceptual and empirical bases. In R. M. Lerner & N. A. Busch-Rossnagel (Eds.), *Individuals as producers of their development: A life-span perspective* (pp. 1–36). San Diego, CA: Academic Press.

Lerner, R. M., & Foch, T. T. (Eds.). (1987). *Biological–psychosocial interactions in early adolescence: A life-span perspective.* Hillsdale, NJ: Erlbaum.

Lerner, R. M., & Kauffman, M. B. (1985). The concept of development in contextualism. *Developmental Review, 5,* 309–333.

Lerner, R. M., & Lerner, J. V. (1989). Organismic and social contextual bases of development: The sample case of adolescence. In W. Damon (Ed.), *Child development today and tomorrow* (pp. 69–85). San Francisco: Jossey-Bass.

Magnusson, D. (Ed.). (1988). *Paths through life* (Vol. 1). Hillsdale, NJ: Erlbaum.

Magnusson, D., & Allen, V. L. (Eds.). (1983). *Human development: An interactional perspective.* San Diego, CA: Academic Press.

Magnusson, D., & Ohman, A. (Eds.). (1987). *Psychopathology: An interactional perspective.* San Diego, CA: Academic Press.

Nesselroade, J. R., & Baltes, P. B. (1979). *Longitudinal research in the study of behavior and development.* San Diego, CA: Academic Press.

Nesselroade, J. R., & von Eye, A. (Eds.). (1985). *Individual development and social change: Explanatory analysis.* San Diego, CA: Academic Press.

Perlmutter, M. (1988). Cognitive development in life-span perspective: From description of differences to explanation of changes. In E. M. Hetherington, R. M. Lerner, & M. Perlmutter (Eds.), *Child development in life-span perspective* (pp. 191–214). Hillsdale, NJ: Erlbaum.

Riegel, K. F. (1975). Toward a dialectical theory of development. *Human Development, 18,* 50–64.

Riegel, K. F. (1976). The dialectics of human development. *American Psychologist, 31,* 689–700.

Schneirla, T. C. (1957). The concept of development in comparative psychology. In D. B. Harris (Ed.), *The concept of development* (pp. 78–108). Minneapolis: University of Minnesota Press.

Sorensen, B., Weinert, E., & Sherrod, L. R. (Eds.). (1986). *Human development and the life course: Multidisciplinary perspectives.* Hillsdale, NJ: Erlbaum.

Stattin, H., & Magnusson, D. (1990). *Pubertal maturation in female development.* Hillsdale, NJ: Erlbaum.

Tobach, E. (1981). Evolutionary aspects of the activity of the organism and its development. In R. M. Lerner & N. A. Busch-Rossnagel (Eds.), *Individuals as producers of their development: A life-span perspective* (pp. 37–68). San Diego, CA: Academic Press.

Tobach, E., & Greenberg, G. (1984). The significance of T. C. Schneirla's contribution to the concept of levels of integration. In G. Greenberg & E. Tobach (Eds.), *Behavioral evolution and integrative levels* (pp. 1–7). Hillsdale, NJ: Erlbaum.

Uphouse, L. L., & Bonner, J. (1975). Preliminary evidence for the effects of environmental complexity on hybridization of rat brain RNA to rat unique DNA. *Developmental Psychobiology, 8,* 171–178.

2

■ Some of the earliest studies of the relationship between nature and nurture were studies of motor development. For example, Dennis and Dennis (1940) examined the locomotor development of infants of the Hopi Native American tribe, who were swaddled on a cradleboard for varying lengths of time, during which they had limited opportunities to practice locomotor skills. Dennis and Dennis found few differences among the infants in the achievement of motor milestones, and concluded that childrearing practices played little role in the development of locomotor skills. More recently, however, Hopkins (1991) observed that parents in different cultures do handle their babies differently, and this treatment relates to infant motor skills. For example, when mothers from Jamaica (residing in Britain) engaged in traditional infant handling routines, such as massage, stretching, and eliciting the stepping reflex, their infants reached motor milestones earlier than a comparison group of white British infants. This raises the question of whether standardized tests of motor abilities are culturally appropriate, comparable to the concerns regarding culture-fairness of standardized intelligence testing (e.g., Helms, 1992). In this article, the authors compare the gross and fine motor skills of Native American toddlers to the performance of the normative sample.

Overview Questions

1. Why is it important to determine whether tests such as the Peabody are culturally appropriate? What is known about the cultural appropriateness of the PDMS to various ethnic groups?

2. Give one or two reasons to believe that standardized tests of motor development may not be suitable for Native American children. How might these authors hypothesize that culture, family environment, individual experience, and neuromuscular development relate to one another?

3. What three practical suggestions do they make for professionals doing assessments? How can practitioners be sensitive to both developmental universals and cultural differences?

Focus Questions

1. Why were the selection criteria important, given the purpose of the study? (Hint: see description of the Denver under "instruments.") Why is it important to have high inter-rater agreement, given the purposes of the study? (Hint: see first paragraph of the introduction.)

2. Z scores tell the relative standing of scores in a group. They measure distance away from the mean in standard deviation units. Positive z scores are above the mean, negative z scores are below the mean. Larger z scores are farther away from the mean and therefore generally rarer (assuming a bell-shaped distribution). From Table 2.2, construct a graph of the mean z scores for each group and gender on the fine motor test and the gross motor test. (Note: some are positive and some are negative, so the zero line will be in the middle of your graph.) Table 2.2 and the third paragraph of the results report

whether each of these groups is significantly different from the normative data. Smaller p values indicate that this mean is more likely to be really different from the norm and less likely to be different by chance. These are also indicated as asterisks in the table. Based on Table 2.2, would you say that younger or older Native American children are more likely to be different from the norm? In what direction? Based on Table 2.2, would you say that fine motor scores or gross motor scores are most likely to be different from the norm?

3. From Table 2.3, show where they get the numbers to support each of their statements about percentages of children who would reach cutoff scores for being labeled "delayed." Why do the authors believe that the problem is something to do with the test, rather than the children? What two specific aspects of the test do they discuss as possible problems?

4. Why do the Kerfeld results support the comments they make about limitations due to sample selection?

Motor Development of Native American Children on the Peabody Developmental Motor Scales

Terry K. Crowe, Catherine McClain, and Beth Provost

Because differences in motor development have been found among various ethnic groups (Cintas, 1995), the cultural relevance of standardized developmental tests must be examined. Such a project is especially important because these tests are used to determine whether a child is developing typically or is in some way delayed, requiring special services (Krefting, 1991). Many states, for example, require the administration of standardized motor assessments to determine whether children qualify for early intervention or special education services. The Peabody Developmental Motor Scales (PDMS; Folio & Fewell, 1983) is frequently selected for this purpose.

The PDMS were normed on 617 children, 85% of whom were white and 15% of whom were nonwhite (either African-American or Hispanic). There are 16 age groups for the Fine Motor Scale and 17 age groups for the Gross Motor Scale. Because only 0 to 6 nonwhite children were included within each of the age groups, white children and nonwhite children within age groups were not statistically compared. Because the performance of the nonwhite children as a group was found well within the normal range, the test authors concluded that the PDMS provides valid scores for African-American and Hispanic children, but "whether this is true for other ethnic and/or cultural groups remains to be determined" (Folio & Fewell, 1983, p. 119).

Motor assessments designed for children of the dominant or mainstream culture are not always appropriate for those from other ethnic backgrounds (Lynch & Hanson, 1992). Developmental norms and expectations as well as life experiences may differ from ethnic group to ethnic group. This is especially true for activities that children have not had the opportunity to practice, such as using scissors or riding tricycles, or for gender-associated and culture-associated tasks, such as ball playing or coloring.

The cultural relevance of a motor assessment for a particular ethnic group can be examined by comparing the scores of children from one ethnic group with the scores of the children on whom the test was normed. Few studies have examined motor development in Native American children. It was found that the scores of Navajo infants on the Wolanski Gross Motor Evaluation (WGME) did not correspond with that of the normed population (Stratman, 1992). This suggests that the WGME is inappropriate for use with Navajo infants. When Kerfeld, Guthrie, and Stewart (1997) compared the scores of 102 Alaska Native children 2 weeks to 6 years of age, on the Denver II with the normative data, they found that many of the Alaska Native children performed skills at earlier ages than did the normative sample, especially skills in the gross motor domain. It was hypothesized that the results may be influenced by differences in child-rearing practices: Unlike the normative sample, Alaska Native children have greater freedom to explore their environment, and caregiving is often turned over to an older sibling. The authors concluded that scores of Native American children on the Denver II should be interpreted carefully to avoid misclassifications of these children, which could possibly lead to overreferrals or underreferrals of children for services.

Results of other studies that explored fine motor and perceptual development in older, school-age Native American children reported mixed results, with one study reporting no significant difference on the Berry Developmental Test of Visual-Motor Integration and the Bender-Gestalt Test (Connelly, 1983) and other studies reporting development below age expectations on the Bender-Gestalt Test and the Minnesota Percepto-Diagnostic Test–Revised (Fuller & Vance, 1995; Price, 1976; Taylor & Thweatt, 1972). No studies were found that examined gross motor ability in older Native American children. This study investigated the cultural relevance of the PDMS by comparing the scores of a sample of 2-year-old Native Americans with those of the normative sample.

Method

Sample

A power analysis indicated that a difference as small as .5 standard deviation or 2 to 3 months in development could be detected with a sample size of 30 for 80% power and an alpha equal to .05. Therefore, a convenience sample of more than 30 was sought. Two-year-old Native American children who were typically developing were recruited for the study from one New Mexico pueblo with the assistance of the Pueblo Early Childhood Program, Child Find, and daycare programs and through recruiting posters placed in public locations around the pueblo. The study criteria were (a) parental report as a full-term, single birth with no significant medical history; (b) parental report of typical development assessed by an investigator-developed parent questionnaire; and (c) a passing score on the fine-motor-adaptive and gross motor sectors of the Denver II (Frankenburg et al., 1990). Of the 48 children recruited, 4 were eliminated after screening on the Denver II.

The 44 children were divided into two groups that were based on PDMS age categories. Group A consisted of 22 children (11 boys, 11 girls) 24 through 29 months of age ($M = 26$ months, $SD = 2$ months), and Group B consisted of 22 children (13 boys, 9 girls) 30 through 35 months of age ($M = 33$ months, $SD = 1.6$ months). Forty-four children completed the Peabody Developmental Fine Motor Scale (PDFMS), and 43 children completed the Peabody Developmental Gross Motor

Scale (PDGMS) because the PDGMS was unscorable for 1 child in Group A because of excessive refusals.

Mothers of children in Group A reported the following educational experience: 45% had attended a university, technical school, or community college; 36% had completed 4 years of high school; 5% had received a general equivalency diploma (GED); and 14% had completed fewer than 4 years of high school. Mothers of children in Group B reported that 40% had attended a university, technical school, or community college; 45% had attended 4 years of high school; 5% had received a GED; and 10% had completed fewer than 4 years of high school. Parents and children received a small financial incentive to participate in the study.

Instruments

A 20-item parent questionnaire was developed to address basic demographic information and indications of typical development. Items included parental education, the child's developmental milestones, and environmental experiences, such as the amount of practice the child has had with stairs or coloring.

The Denver II (Frankenburg et al., 1990) is a normed and standardized developmental screening test, which scores a child as normal, suspect, or untestable. If the score is suspect or untestable, the individual test can be assessed as to which specific sectors (fine-motor-adaptive, gross motor, personal-social, language) contained items that were not passed.

The PDMS is a norm-referenced and standardized motor skill test that consists of a Gross Motor Scale and a Fine Motor Scale (Folio & Fewell, 1983). The normative sample in the 24-month to 29-month age category included 42 Anglo, 5 African-American, and 4 Hispanic children; in the 30-month to 35-month age category, it included 40 Caucasian, 4 African-American, and 2 Hispanic children. The norms on the PDMS for each of its two scales include percentile ranks, age equivalent scores, and normalized standard scores, including z scores and developmental motor quotients (DMQs). The PDMS items are scored 0 when the child's performance does not meet the stated criteria, 1 when the performance partially meets criteria, and 2 when the child's performance meets all of the stated criteria. The more conservative scoring method described by Palisano (1990), which uses scores of 1 less often, was used in this study instead of the more liberal scoring method of Hinderer, Richardson, and Atwater (1989).

Procedure

All children's parents signed a consent form. The developmental testing (including the Denver II and the PDMS) took from 60 min to 90 min, depending on the child's cooperation. At least one parent or relative, who completed the questionnaire, was present. Sometimes other family members, such as grandparents or siblings, also attended the evaluation. All children were tested by an occupational therapist with more than 20 years of experience testing preschool-age children. Children were tested in rooms provided by the Pueblo's Division of Early Childhood Education.

Interrater agreement on the PDMS was assessed between the examiner and one of the authors, a physical therapist with more than 20 years of pediatric experience, including 11 years experience testing preschool-age children for a developmental evaluation program. Before data collection, interrater agreement that was tested on three children ranged from 89% to 97% ($M = 93.8\%$). In addition, interrater agreement was examined periodically during the data collection. Interrater agreement on six children who were tested periodically (two tested each time) ranged from 85% to 97.5% ($M = 92.4\%$).

Data Analysis

Descriptive statistics of the groups (means, standard deviations, and ranges for z scores, percentile ranks, and DMQs) were calculated for the PDFMS and the PDGMS. Data were compared to the normative data by one-sample t tests of the z scores using age groups. Further comparison of z scores by age and gender were done by two-way analysis of variance (ANOVA).

Results

Descriptive data on the PDFMS and the PDGMS for mean DMQ, percentile ranks, and z scores of children in Groups A and B are presented in Table 2.1.

The analysis of z scores by age groups (one-sample t tests) indicated that there was a significant difference between Group A PDFMS z scores and the normative data ($p \leq .0001$) and between Group B PDFMS z scores and the normative data ($p \leq .05$). No significant differences were found in either age group for z scores on the PDGMS.

The two-way ANOVA for gender and age group revealed a significant difference between Group A PDFMS z scores for both boys and girls and the normative data ($p \leq .001$) and for Group B boys ($p \leq .05$) but not for Group B girls (see Table 2.2). There was a significant difference between Group A PDGMS z scores for girls and the normative data ($p \leq .05$) but not between Group B PDGMS z scores for girls and the normative data. There was no significant difference between Group A and Group B boys and the normative data on the PDGMS. A significant ($p \leq .05$) gender effect was found for the PDGMS for the younger 2-year-olds (Group A), with boys having higher scores than girls.

The percentage of children in the study with z scores falling above –1.00, and at or below –1.00, –1.50, and –2.05, are presented in Table 2.3. In the total sample, 36.5% scored at or below –1.5 standard deviations from the normative mean on the PDFMS, and 4% scored at or below –1.5 on the PDGMS.

TABLE 2.1 *Descriptive Data for the Peabody Developmental Fine Motor Scale and Gross Motor Scale for Two Groups*

Scale	Group A	Group B
Fine Motor Scale[a]		
DMQ × (*SD*)	77.1 (11.7)	90.5 (16.5)
Low score/high score	65/109	65/117
Percentile × (*SD*)	11.5 (17.6)	35.5 (28.7)
Low score/high score	1/73	1/87
z score × (*SD*)	–1.5 (0.8)**	–0.6 (1.1)*
Low score/high score	–2.3/+0.6	–2.3/+1.1
Gross Motor Scale[b]		
DMQ × (*SD*)	95.0 (13.7)	99.2 (14.3)
Low score/high score	65/118	79/118
Percentile × (*SD*)	40.1 (27.7)	49.3 (31.6)
Low score/high score	1/88	8/89
z score × (*SD*)	–0.3 (0.9)	–0.04 (0.95)
Low score/high score	–2.3/+1.2	–1.4/+1.2

Note. Significant differences when compared to Peabody Developmental Motor Scale normative data. DMQ = developmental motor quotient. [a]n = 22 for both groups. [b]n = 21 for Group A and n = 22 for Group B.

*$p \leq .05$. **$p \leq .0001$.

TABLE 2.2   *Girls' and Boys' Mean z Scores (SD) by Group*

Scale	Group A	Group B
Fine Motor Scale[a]		
Boys	–1.5 (0.9)**	–0.6 (1.0)*
Girls	–1.5 (.07)***	–0.6 (1.2)
Gross Motor Scale[b]		
Boys	+0.2 (0.6)	+0.3 (0.9)
Girls	–0.8 (1.0)*	–0.5 (0.8)

Note. Significant differences when compared to Peabody Developmental Motor Scales normative data.

[a]$n = 22$ for both groups. [b]$n = 21$ for Group A and $n = 22$ for Group B.

*$p \leq 0.5$. **$p \leq .001$. ***$p \leq .0001$.

TABLE 2.3   *Percentage of z Scores on the Peabody Developmental Fine Motor Scale and Gross Motor Scale by Group and Total*

z Score	Fine Motor Scale[a]			Gross Motor Scale[b]		
	A	B	Total	A	B	Total
> –1.00	23	59	41.0	85	68	77
≤ –1.00 to –1.49	36	9	22.5	5	32	19
≤ –1.5 to –2.04	9	18	13.5	5	0	2
≤ –2.05	32	14	23.0	5	0	2

[a]$n = 22$ for both groups. [b]$n = 21$ for Group A and $n = 22$ for Group B.

Discussion

When assessing development for the purpose of diagnosis or classification, the primary concern for the pediatric clinician is not whether a child achieves the mean score, but whether the score falls within the range demonstrated by the children in the normative sample (Palisano, 1993). The PDMS manual notes that "several school districts and states across the county have adopted 1.0 and 1.5 standard deviations below the mean as the cutoff points for identifying moderate and severe deficits respectively" (Folio & Fewell, 1983, p. 125). Fewer than 25% of the younger 2-year-old Native American children from this one New Mexico pueblo scored greater than –1.0 standard deviations below the mean of the PDFMS. It is distressing to note that if the typically developing Native American children in this study had been referred for developmental testing, more than 50% of them might have been labeled at least "mildly or moderately delayed" in fine motor skills because of z scores less than –1.0, and almost 25% might have been labeled at least "mildly or moderately delayed" in gross motor skills. In addition, 36% of the children might have been labeled "severely delayed" in fine motor skills because of z scores less than –1.50, with close to 25% scoring below –2.05 on the PDFMS.

When children's scores on standardized tests fall less than –1.0 standard deviation below the mean, professionals seek to discover possible reasons for the "delays." There are several possible factors that may have contributed to the lower scores of the children in this study, including scoring factors, test performance factors, gender differences, cultural expectations, and rate of maturation differences.

It should be emphasized that all of the children were judged to be typically developing by their parents and that the children also passed the motor sectors of the Denver II.

The conservative method of scoring the PDMS that was used in this study has been noted to contribute to lower scores of older children on the PDGMS (Green, Deitz, & Brady, 1995), but the extent to which use of the conservative method (Palisano, 1990) versus the more liberal scoring method (Hinderer et al., 1989) would affect the scores of children who are younger is unknown. Aspects of the PDMS 6-month category scoring system also may have contributed to participants' lower scores. Because of the 6-month age categories, participants in each age group (24–30 months, 29–35 months) were scored the same, even though they might have 5 months of developmental difference in their performances. The mean age of Group A was 26 months, and the mean age of Group B was 33 months. The scores of each group might have been higher if the average age was slightly older. However, the mean age in months of the PDMS normative sample was comparable—26 months for the 24-month to 29-month category, and 32 months for the 30-month to 35-month category—suggesting that the mean age was not a major factor influencing the lower scores.

The Native American children in this study may not have demonstrated their true abilities because of test performance factors, such as shyness or caution in a new situation. The tester had many years of experience in making children comfortable, and the tests themselves were conducted within the familiar surroundings of the pueblo's community buildings. However, the tester was not Native American, and the children may have been uncomfortable. Indeed, one child refused too many items to score the PDGMS.

The gender differences found in this Native American sample were not expected on the basis of the findings for the normative sample. Gender differences in children of a specific ethnic group or culture may result from differences in genetically endowed physical aptitude or to differences in cultural expectations and environmental practices. Boys in the two age groups that were examined scored lower than the normative data in fine motor skills but not in gross motor skills. Younger but not older girls scored lower than the normative data on both scales. It is possible that gross motor activities, including ball playing, running, and jumping, may be encouraged, expected, and therefore practiced in young boys of the pueblo, whereas young girls may be less encouraged to engage in these activities. Fine motor activities, such as the use of crayons, may not be encouraged as strongly in the boys and may not be culturally expected or practiced in younger children of either gender at the pueblo.

Comparing the results of our Native American participants with those of Alaska Native children in the Kerfeld et al. (1997) study suggests that there may be performance differences among Native American groups. Another interesting clinical finding from this study is that some children that pass the motor sectors of the Denver II may still score at least 1.0 standard deviation below the mean on the PDMS.

Strengths and Limitations

Sample selection was limited to one tribal group, in order to control for similarity of cultural experiences, and to a sample of 2-year-old children. These limitations do not permit the results to be generalized either to other Native American tribes or to other age groups. Increases in sample size, incorporation of several age groups, and inclusion of more Native American tribal groups in future studies would allow more generalization of results for more appropriate interpretation of standardized motor tests for Native American children.

Conclusion

In general, the results showed several significant differences between the scores of 2-year-old Pueblo Native American children who are typically developing and the normative sample of the PDMS. Both boys and girls in the 24-month to 29-month age group and boys in the 30-month to 35-month age group scored significantly lower than the normative sample on the PDFMS. Girls in the younger age group scored significantly lower than the normative sample on the PDGMS. It is suggested that occupational therapists and other professionals be cautious when they use the published PDMS normative data to judge motor performance of some 2-year-old Native American children who have not been included in the normative sample. If the data are not used carefully, over-referral for intervention services may result. As pointed out by Kerfeld et al. (1997), pediatric evaluators may never have culture-free screening tools or assessments. This limitation indicates that testers need to be sensitive to cultural needs and be able to elicit and include family perceptions about their child's development within their community.

Acknowledgments

We thank the children and families who participated in this study; the staff of the Pueblo Early Childhood Program (especially Rebecca Viers, Program Director) for assistance in recruitment and use of the facilities; and the community of the Pueblo, including the Governor and the Superintendent of Education, for support of this project. We thank especially Ellen (Keri) Ross, OTR/L, for data collection, and Tony Carrillo, Tom Gilbert, and Clifford Qualls, PhD, for data entry and analysis.

References

Cintas, H. L. (1995). Cross-cultural similarities and differences in development and the impact of parental expectations on motor behavior. *Pediatric Physical Therapy, 7*, 103–111.

Connelly, J. (1983). Comparative analysis of two tests of visual-fine-motor integration among young Indian and non-Indian children. *Perceptual and Motor Skills, 57*, 1079–1082.

Folio, M. R., & Fewell, R. R. (1983). *Peabody Developmental Motor Scales*. Allen, TX: DLM Teaching Resources.

Frankenburg, W. K., Dodds, J. B., Archer, P., Bresnick, B., Maschka, P., Edelman, N., & Shapiro, H. (1990). *Denver II screening manual*. Denver, CO: Denver Developmental Materials.

Fuller, G., & Vance, H. B. (1995). A comparison of three Native American groups and a Caucasian group on the Minnesota Percepto-Diagnostic Test-Revised. *Psychology in the Schools, 32*(1), 12–17.

Green, K., Deitz, J., & Brady, K. D. (1995). Comparison of two scoring methods of the Peabody Gross Motor Scale. *Physical and Occupational Therapy in Pediatrics, 14*, 121–132.

Hinderer, K. A., Richardson, P. K., & Atwater, S. W. (1989). Clinical implications of the Peabody Developmental Motor Scales: A constructive review. *Physical and Occupational Therapy in Pediatrics, 9*, 81–106.

Kerfeld, C. I., Guthrie, M. R., & Stewart, K. B. (1997). Evaluation of the Denver II as applied to Alaska Native children. *Pediatric Physical Therapy, 9*, 23–31.

Krefting, L. (1991). The culture concept in the everyday practice of occupational and physical therapy. *Physical and Occupational Therapy in Pediatrics, 11*(4), 1–16.

Lynch, E., & Hanson, M. (1992). Steps in the right direction: Implications for interventionists. In E. Lynch & M. Hanson (Eds.), *Developing cross cultural competence* (pp. 491–512). Baltimore: Brookes.

Palisano, R. J. (1990). Commentary. *Physical and Occupational Therapy in Pediatrics, 10*(1), 1–3.

Palisano, R. (1993). Neuromotor and developmental assessment. In I. Wilhelm (Ed.), *Physical therapy assessment in early infancy* (pp. 173–224). New York: Churchill Livingstone.

Price, T. (1976). Sioux children's Koppitz scores on the Bender-Gestalt given by white or Native American examiners. *Perceptual and Motor Skills, 43,* 1223–1226.

Stratman, S. K. (1992). Gross motor skills in Navajo American Indian children one year or under. *Studies in Human Ecology, 10,* 115–120.

Taylor, H., & Thweatt, R. (1972). Cross-cultural developmental performance of Navajo children on the Bender-Gestalt test. *Perceptual and Motor Skills, 35,* 307–309.

3

This article focuses on the mutual influence between the child's developing cognitive abilities and the immediate social environment. The Russian psychologist Vygotsky emphasized that cognitive development is embedded in the social system to which the child belongs (Vygotsky, 1978). His followers, such as Barbara Rogoff, have elaborated the ways that parents structure situations so that young children can participate and gradually learn the skills that allow them to function independently (Rogoff, 1990). For example, parents gradually give children more responsibility for making purchases, thereby allowing the child to learn skills such as counting money and eventually comparison shopping. These interactions are complex, as parents and children judge moment-by-moment the child's changing level of competence to handle the task. By showing how this interchange takes place in visually impaired children, this article reveals how parents adjust their behavior to characteristics of the child and the ways that children's cognitive and language progress reflect parental behavior. How do parents and children adjust this system when the child has a physical or mental disability? What aspects of the interactions support or impede the child's progress? This article shows us how the child and the environment bidirectionally affect each other.

Overview Questions

1. In general, what differences are there in how parents and children with disabilities interact, compared to typically developing children? Are these differences maladaptive? Are the behaviors of parents and visually impaired children consistent with the general description of interactions with disabled children? What unique features appear because of the visual impairment? What was the aim of the present study?

2. Are their results on the relationship between maternal behaviors and children's development consistent with that of other researchers? What specific behaviors did they find to undermine or support the visually impaired children's language? Why do you think that it was the child's language development (as opposed to the other things they measured) that was so sensitive to maternal control/directiveness? Why do you think that high amounts of goal setting would support exploration of the environment? How do you think it can happen that mothers are high in negative behaviors (amounts of directiveness/control) and also in positive behaviors (quality of control)? Interpret the results on maternal responsiveness from the point of view of attachment theory, which predicts that infants who perceive their caregivers as a "secure base" during times of stress will have the confidence to explore a familiar environment.

3. Why do they say that "direction of causality cannot be interpreted"? Why might poor child language lead to high amounts of maternal control, rather than the other way around? What are some difficulties that pose practical limitations on research with visually impaired children?

Focus Questions

1. What six individual subscale scores did they use to measure the children's development? Why do you think it was important to demonstrate that these sub-scales were internally consistent, and correlated with the Maxfield?

2. What eleven caregiver behaviors are scored by the PCIS? What three aspects of these behaviors are assessed? Which four caregiver behaviors did they actually analyze?

3. Why do you think it was important that they did the data collection at home? Why do you think it was important to establish inter-rater reliability?

4. Which two maternal behaviors were highest and lowest in amount? Which were highest and lowest in quality? Which were highest and lowest in appropriateness?

5. Which two child measures were highest, and which was lowest?

6. The third and fourth paragraphs of the results section are a preview of the next two sections. In the correlational analyses, r values range from -1 to $+1$. Negative correlations mean that high scores on one variable go with high scores on the other. Positive correlations mean that high scores on one variable go with low scores on the other. Interpret in your own words the meaning of the correlations between amount of maternal control and amount of maternal directiveness with children's pragmatic language development. Interpret in your own words the meaning of the correlations between quality of maternal control and quality of maternal directiveness with children's expressive language development. Put in your own words the relationship between quality of maternal responsiveness, and quality of maternal goal setting, with children's sensorimotor development.

7. Make a grid showing the twelve maternal variables (amount, quality and appropriateness of responsiveness, control, directiveness and goal setting) on both the rows and columns. Put an x in the cells where they report significant relationships in the section on chi square data. Summarize in your own words the pattern that you observe. Compare that statement to their summary section.

Characteristics of Maternal Directiveness and Responsiveness with Young Children with Visual Impairments

M. Hughes, J. Dote-Kwan and J. Dolendo

Introduction

The ways caregivers and young children interact exert a powerful influence on children's overall competence. The nature of such interactions is transactional in that caregivers and children are mutually influencing and changing each other's behaviour (Sameroff & Chandler 1975). The interaction patterns and children's development result not only from the unique characteristics of the caregiver and child, but also from the reciprocity that develops as each partner responds and adapts to the other (Barnard & Kelly 1990). Over the past two decades, a substantial amount of experimental research has revealed the importance of the relation of caregiver–child interactions to the developmental outcomes of children with more prevalent types of risks such as mental retardation or global delays (Kogan *et al.* 1969; Cunningham *et al.* 1981; Eheart 1982; Marfo 1982; Crawley & Spiker 1983; Marfo 1984; Rogers 1988; Beckwith 1990). However, few recent studies have explored the relation between caregiver–child interactions and the competence of children with a low incidence disability such as a visual impairment (Preisler 1991; Tröster & Brambring 1992; Behl *et al.* 1996), and even fewer have examined the individual differences that might exist within this type of caregiver–child interaction (Dote-Kwan 1995; Dote-Kwan *et al.* 1997).

For the most part, the majority of past research studies have examined specific isolated qualities of the child or caregiver and found children at-risk or with disabilities as having fewer responses and readable cues, and as being less active and engaged than typically developing children when interacting with their caregivers (Kogan *et al.* 1969; Cunningham *et al.* 1981; Eheart 1982; Marfo 1984; Rogers 1988). In addition, some of the same researchers found that when children were at risk or disabled, the parents dominated the interactions more often, had higher levels of control, and had more difficulty reading their children's cues (Kogan *et al.* 1969; Cunningham *et al.* 1981; Marfo 1984; Beckwith 1990).

Other empirical studies have shown that the characteristics of the interaction of mother–child dyads of children with disabilities or those at risk of developmental delays may not be inherently maladaptive (Marfo 1982; Crawley & Spiker 1983). That is, Crawley and Spiker found that for mothers of young children with Down's syndrome, there was no significant relation between the single behaviours of directiveness or sensitivity to their children's developmental competence. Furthermore, the maternal behaviour, directiveness, did not necessarily preclude or suppress other positive behaviours. They found that when mothers combined sensitivity and directiveness in ways that enhanced stimulation, this positively correlated with children's competence scores. Similarly, Marfo found that mothers who were directive with their young developmentally delayed children also exhibited other more positive behaviours such as warmth, sensitivity, and responsiveness.

In the area of visual impairment, Tröster & Brambring (1992) and Preisler (1991) compared the behaviours observed in caregiver-visually impaired child dyads to those in caregiver-sighted child dyads. In general, these studies reported that infants (under 1 year of age) with visual impairments were found to be vocally and expressively less responsive (Preisler 1991; Tröster & Brambring 1992) and displayed communicative gestures with their bodies and hands (Preisler 1991). When compared with sighted children, the children with visual impairments showed fewer social interactions and required stronger stimulation to focus attention (Tröster & Brambring 1992). In terms of caregiver behaviours, Behl *et al.* (1996) found that mothers of preschool age children with visual impairments were more verbally and physically involved with their children, spoke more often, and demonstrated more control over the activities than the comparison group of mothers. Dote-Kwan (1995) and Dote-Kwan *et al.* (1997) found that a number of specific maternal behaviours such as complying with children's request, repeating or rephrasing children's expressions, and adding new information to children's sounds or words were positively related to children's development.

Thus to date, it appears that the blind-sighted comparisons tend to portray mothers of blind children as a homogeneous group reflecting either a positive or negative type of interactional style, rather than individuals who vary considerably in behaviour. As Crawley & Spiker (1983) report, mothers of children with Down's syndrome who are highly directive can also be highly sensitive when interacting with their children. Therefore, it may not be accurate to assume that caregivers who use a directive style impact the development of their children in a negative manner. Perhaps there are other behaviours that are enhancing development. Moreover, by focusing on group differences, studies have not examined the individual differences that may exist within a group of mothers, and what this ultimately might mean in terms of effective strategies with their children with visual impairments. Therefore, rather than continuing to investigate single behaviours or one facet of behaviour (i.e. quantity) in exclusive ways, there appears to be a need for researchers to explore in a more comprehensive manner the qualities of maternal behaviours and their combined influence on children's development, Hence, the aim of this study was to examine the quantity, quality and appropriateness of maternal directive and responsive behaviours while playing with their children at home, and explore the relation of the children's developmental outcomes.

Methods

Sample

A total of 17 mother–child dyads participated in this study and were recruited from a larger study that was examining the influence of the home environment on children's development. All mother–child dyads were from similar Anglo-Saxon backgrounds. English was the primary language spoken in the homes. The sample of children consisted of 10 boys and seven girls with ages ranging from 20 to 36 months. The children were all legally blind according to the definition of the 1973 American Medical Association with their visual acuity ranging from no light perception to 20/200 (see Table 3.1 for child characteristics).

Instruments

Reynell-Zinkin Developmental Scale

Reynell-Zinkin Developmental Scale for Young Visually Handicapped Children—Part 1: Mental Development (Reynell-Zinkin, Reynell 1979) was used to assess the developmental levels of the children with severe visual impairments. The six areas of development measured were: (1) social adaptation, (2) sensori-motor understanding, (3) exploration of the environment, (4) response to sound and verbal comprehension (receptive language), (5) expressive language, and (6) pragmatic language. There has been no attempt to standardize the Reynell-Zinkin. The age equivalencies were obtained by comparing the raw scores on the Reynell-Zinkin with the age scores on the Social Maturity Scale for Preschool Children (Maxfield & Buchholz 1957). Scattergrams were obtained using these ages in place of chronological ages, and plotting them against raw scores for each child with each subscale. These scattergrams showed developmental progressions and a mean age level equivalent to each score on each subscale. The validity of the Reynell-Zinkin to the Maxfield has been established with a very strong correlation ($r = 0.949$, $p < 0.001$) between the two instruments' total scores (Dote-Kwan 1995). In addition, the correlations between the Maxfield and the Reynell-Zinkin subscales were all highly significant at $\alpha = 0.01$. The internal consistency as measured by Cronbach's alpha for the total scale and subscales ranged from 0.853 to 0.969 for the Reynell-Zinkin.

The Parent Caregiver Involvement Scale

The Parent Caregiver Involvement Scale (PCIS; Farren *et al.* 1986) is an instrument designed to rate 11 caregiver behaviours during a caregiver–child interaction in the home or clinical setting. The scale is comprised of the following behaviours: (1) physical involvement, (2) verbal involvement, (3) responsiveness, (4) play interactions,

TABLE 3.1 *Description of Children*

Gender	Adjusted Age (Months)	Visual Acuity*	Aetiology	Prematurity
M	23.00	20/400	ROP	Yes
F	19.00	20/200	ROP	Yes
M	30.50	LP both eyes	Leber's Amaurosis	No
M	30.75	HM left eye	Septo-optic	No
M	20.25	LP both eyes	Septo-optic	No
M	26.00	NLP	Optic nerve atrophy	No
F	36.25	NLP	Septo-optic	No
M	27.25	NLP	ROP	Yes
M	18.75	LP both eyes	ROP	Yes
F	24.75	20/200	Albinism	No
M	25.75	HM left eye	Brain haemorrhage	No
F	20.75	20/400	ROP	Yes
M	19.25	20/8000	Optic nerve hypoplasia	No
F	20.00	20/560	Bilateral Colobomas	No
M	18.25	LP both eyes	ROP	Yes
F	25.00	20/400	Albinism	No
F	30.50	NLP	Retinopathy	No

ROP = Retinopathy of prematurity; LP = Light perception; HM = Hand movements; NLP = No light perception. *Based on eye examination report; if no acuity was given, then acuity was determined from the U.C. Berkeley Preferential Looking Test.

(5) teaching, (6) control over child's activities, (7) directiveness, (8) relationship among activities, (9) positive emotions or statements, (10) negative emotions or statements, and (11) goal setting.

In addition, the PCIS also measures the amount, appropriateness, and quality of involvement of each of the 11 behaviours. The PCIS has been applied with mothers of children with disabilities (Behl *et al.* 1996; Boyce *et al.* 1991) as well as mothers of typically developing children (Blasco *et al.* 1990; Lussier *et al.* 1994). In addition, revisions of the PCIS have intended to reduce bias toward socioeconomic groups or culture (Wilfong *et al.* 1991). Lastly, a number of studies have shown evidence of reliability across raters (Blasco *et al.* 1990; Wilfong *et al.* 1991; Lussier *et al.* 1994; Behl *et al.* 1996) and time (Boyce *et al.* 1991).

Scoring

The Reynell-Zinkin provided six individual subscale scores for each of the areas of development. No total overall score was used. For subscale analysis, each subscale was converted into a percentage score to eliminate possible interpretation problems due to an unequal number of items within each subscale. The PCIS provided individual subscale scores for each of the 11 behaviours. Summary scores for amount, quality, and appropriateness, collapsed across behaviours, were also determined. Each behaviour was scored using a five-point Likert scale. The odd-numbered points are behaviourally anchored. If a behaviour fell between two anchors then an even number was used. For example, to receive an even rating of 4 the caregiver would have displayed all the behaviours described at point 3 and some of the behaviours at point 5 (Farren *et al.* 1986). Within a subscale, if that behaviour was not observed, the quality and appropriateness scores were not rated for that behaviour.

Procedure

All data collection was gathered in the homes of the families. Initially, when the researchers arrived they spent time talking and developing a rapport with each mother and her child during their daily routine. The first procedure consisted of a mother–child free play interaction. The mothers were instructed to play with their children as they normally would for $\approx$ 15 min. Mothers were given the choice of either using their children's own toys or using developmentally appropriate toys that were provided by the investigators. These interactions were videotaped and coded for later data analyses. The PCIS was used to score the maternal behaviours during the caregiver–child interaction. The second procedure was the administration of the Reynell-Zinkin to the children.

Inter-rater reliability

Two research assistants, who were naïve to the purpose of the study, were trained together using the PCIS training tapes. Adaptations were made to the rating scale to accommodate for the visual impairments of the children (i.e. mother's physical assistance of placing the child's hand on an object was not rated as control). The research assistants then independently rated the same tapes of three blind children of similar age not in the study using the adaptations to the scale. Inter-rater agreement was established between the two research assistants at the 90% level (i.e., within 1 Likert point) during the training phase. The research assistants then coded each of the 17 videotaped caregiver–child interactions independently using the PCIS scale. When there was a disagreement of more than 1 Likert point, the tape was viewed together, discussed, and recoded until agreement was met by the two raters. After the recoding was conducted, the percentage agreement score between the two raters was 88%.

Results

Data analysis

As the primary focus of this study was to examine maternal directiveness and responsiveness, only four of the 11 independent variables coded were analysed and reported. The four maternal behaviours are: (a) directiveness, (b) control of activities, (c) responsiveness, and (d) goal setting. The means and standard deviations for these maternal behaviours as measured by the PCIS are presented in Table 3.2.

The dependent variables in this study were the children's developmental scores as measured by the Reynell-Zinkin. The means and standard deviations of these scores are presented in Table 3.3.

A series of Pearson product moment correlations were conducted to determine the relation between the independent variables (maternal behaviours) and the dependent variables (developmental outcomes). The Pearson product moment correlation for inter-rater reliability for the independent variables ranged from $r = 0.55$, $p < 0.05$ to $r = 0.98$, $p < 0.001$.

Bartlett chi-square tests were used to examine mother's behaviours as rated by the PCIS to determine which maternal behaviours were related to each other during the play session. For example, were mothers who displayed high amounts of control also found to exhibit high amounts of directiveness? Only those independent variables that were significantly related to the child's development, indicated by the Reynell-Zinkin, were used in the chi-square analyses. Both the correlational and chi-square tests revealed significant findings.

TABLE 3.2 *Group Means and Standard Deviations for Parent Caregiver Involvement Scale**

Maternal Variable	M	SD
Directiveness		
Amount	3.24	0.80
Quality	4.20	0.90
Appropriateness	3.82	0.81
Control of activities		
Amount	3.60	1.30
Quality	3.70	0.80
Appropriateness	3.31	1.01
Responsiveness		
Amount	3.90	0.80
Quality	3.53	0.80
Appropriateness	3.60	1.20
Goal setting		
Amount	2.82	1.13
Quality	3.44	0.81
Appropriateness	4.12	1.10

*Each behavior was scored using a five-point Likert scale.

TABLE 3.3 *Group Means and Standard Deviations for Reynell-Zinkin Scale**

Subscales	M	SD
Social adaptation	68.00	16.50
Sensorimotor understanding	57.00	13.70
Exploration of environment	74.00	16.20
Receptive language	34.00	10.94
Expressive language	50.27	15.29
Pragmatic language	7.190	11.80

*The means represent mean group raw scores as a percentage score for each total scale score.

Correlational Data

Many significant associations were found between the subscale scores on the PCIS and measures of developmental outcomes (Reynell-Zinkin percentage scores). The specific maternal behaviour, quality of responsiveness (i.e., the manner in which the caregiver responded to the child) was positively correlated with children's social adaptation, $r = 0.575$, $p < 0.05$, sensorimotor understanding, $r = 0.577$, $p < 0.05$, and exploration of environment, $r = 0.622$, $p < 0.05$.

The amount of control of activities (i.e. the caregiver was continuously organizing the activity) was found to be negatively correlated with pragmatic language development, $r = -0.531$, $p < 0.05$. Whereas, the quality of control, in terms of intensity and flexibility, was positively correlated with receptive language development, $r = 0.602$, $p < 0.05$, and expressive language development, $r = 0.756$, $p < 0.01$.

The amount of directiveness (i.e. number of demands/commands for specific behaviours) made of the child by the caregiver was negatively correlated with pragmatic language development, $r = -0.518$, $p < 0.05$. However, the appropriateness of directiveness, in terms of reasonableness of the demands or commands, was positively correlated with children's receptive language development, $r = 0.601$, $p < 0.05$, and expressive language development, $r = 0.501$, $p < 0.05$.

The various aspects of the caregiver behaviour, goal setting (i.e. degree to which the adult verbally or non-verbally communicated expectations of the child's behaviour) was significantly correlated with a number of developmental subscales. One finding indicated that the amount of caregiver goal-setting behaviour was positively correlated with exploration of the environment, $r = 0.525$, $p < 0.05$. Other findings indicated that the quality of goal setting (i.e. adult's overall flexibility to ensure child success) was positively correlated with sensorimotor development, $r = 0.489$, $p < 0.05$, receptive language development, $r = 0.717$, $p < 0.01$, and expressive language development, $r = 0.503$, $p < 0.05$.

Chi-Square Data

Results found that caregivers who displayed a high degree of one behaviour also exhibited high degrees of other behaviours. That is, caregivers who displayed high amounts of directiveness also tended to display a high amount of control ($p < 0.05$); a high amount of goal-setting behaviour ($p < 0.01$), and a high quality of control ($p < 0.05$). In addition, caregivers who displayed a high quality of control also tended to show a high amount of control ($p < 0.01$) and an appropriate level of directiveness ($p < 0.05$). Lastly, caregivers who showed a high degree of appropriate directiveness also tended to show a high degree in the quality of goal setting behaviour ($p < 0.05$).

Summary

In terms of the correlational data, the results showed that the quality of responsiveness, appropriateness of directive behaviour, and the quality of both control and goal-setting behaviours positively correlated with children's receptive and expressive language, sensorimotor understanding, or exploration of the environment. Whereas, the amount of control, and the amount of directiveness negatively correlated with pragmatic language development in children.

In summarizing the chi square data, the examination of the relationship of mothers' behaviours revealed several patterns of behaviours (i.e. three or more behaviours related to each other) that occurred while playing with their children. One pattern indicated that the amounts of the three maternal behaviours control, directiveness, and goal setting were correlated with each other and the quality of control. In addition, mothers who displayed high amounts of control also exhibited a high quality of control and appropriate directive behaviours.

Discussion

The purpose of this study was to investigate the relation between maternal directive and responsive behaviours and the concurrent development of young children with visual impairments. The maternal behaviours were examined specifically in terms of quantity, quality, and appropriateness.

First, there were a number of interesting findings in this study that indicated both significant positive and negative associations between maternal behaviours and children's developmental outcomes. One group of findings showed that of the three aspects of maternal behaviours, quantity, quality, and appropriateness, the only one that negatively correlated with development was the quantity factor. Specifically, the findings indicated that the amount of control and the amount of directiveness were negatively correlated with pragmatic language development in children. Maternal behaviours such as high frequencies of organization, commands and demands were the types of behaviours observed that appeared to undermine this group of children's language development. This evidence is similar to Marfo's (1982) where the maternal behaviour, intrusiveness, was negatively correlated to the competence level of children with developmental disabilities. Perhaps high amounts of maternal control and directiveness may be comparable with maternal intrusiveness and its documented impact on development. Or perhaps, high amounts of maternal direction leave less time for following the child's lead or taking turns during interactions.

Turn-taking in social interaction is a precursor to the development of dialogue and language exchange. Cunningham *et al.* (1981) revealed that highly reciprocal mother-child interactions related to superior language comprehension skills in children with mental retardation. This may explain why, in this study, the amount of control and directiveness correlated negatively with pragmatic language, but the quality of control and the appropriateness of directiveness positively related to expressive and receptive language. The mothers that were rated high in their quality of control offered their children more of a range of possibilities and choices of activities than the mothers who were rated lower. Furthermore, the mothers that exhibited an appropriate directive style made commands or demands that were reasonable and appropriate to children's competence levels.

Secondly, the findings revealed the importance of examining patterns of maternal behaviours when interacting with their young children with visual impairments. In this study, for example, mothers who were high in the amounts of directiveness, control and goal setting were also high in the quality of control. While the amounts of control and directiveness were negatively correlated with children's language development, the quality of control and the amount of goal-setting behaviours were positively related to language and other areas of development. This might suggest that these mothers may be exhibiting behaviours that positively and negatively correlate with different developmental outcomes at the same time. This evidence is similar to Crawley & Spiker (1983) and Marfo (1982) who also found that mothers of children with disabilities and delays who were highly directive could also be highly sensitive when interacting with their children. Perhaps, directiveness and sensitivity are not mutually exclusive maternal behaviours, and more effective when used in combination with each other.

Another set of findings indicated that the amount of goal-setting behaviours in mothers positively correlated with children's development. Similarly, Rock *et al.* (1994) found that academic stimulation as measured by Home Observation Measurement of the Environment (Bradley *et al.* 1987) positively correlated with the developmental competence of children with visual impairments. It is interesting that the amount of control and directiveness negatively correlated with development in the specific area of pragmatic language, while the amount of goal setting was positively related to a child's ability to interact with his or her environment. These findings may suggest that the development of skills in areas other than language may be facilitated by caregivers or other adults who express clear expectations and have a didactic interactive style in play situations.

The last set of findings in this study indicated that the quality of responsiveness, by the mothers, positively correlated with children's sensorimotor understanding, social adaptation, and exploration of their environment. These three areas of development related to the children's familiarity of objects and other people, and their ability to adapt within an environment. These seemed to be associated with mothers who responded to their children in positive and sensitive ways. Similarly, Bradley & Caldwell (1984) also found that mothers' responsiveness related to development in typical children, and Crawley & Spiker (1983) found that maternal sensitivity positively correlated with development in children with Down's syndrome. Therefore, the findings in this study, as in other studies with typical children and those with disabilities, continue to suggest that mothers who behave towards their children in responsive ways may influence positive developmental outcomes.

Limitations

One important limitation to note is the fact that the direction of causality can not be interpreted from the types of statistical analyses conducted in this study. Therefore, any interpretation of the findings in terms of the cause and effect of the variables examined in this study is not warranted. In addition, as with all research on children with visual impairments, the nature of the participant pool presented a methodological problem. Only about 0.05% of the school age population is classified by the USA federal government as 'visually impaired' (Hallahan & Kauffman 1997). It is therefore, difficult to identify children that are within an obtainable geographical area. Another difficulty is that visually impaired children often have other disabilities. This presents a problem when including children whose only impairment is visual. That is, these characteristics of this population limit the size of the potential sample pool. In addition, the small sample size might present problems with the interpretation of the results. To generalize these results, it would be necessary to replicate this study with a larger number of participants. A final limitation of this study was the fact that it only measured a short videotape of a mother–child interaction, and its relation to children's development in a specific play context. That is, other research has shown that a number of other variables influence children's development such as social economic class (Ramey *et al.* 1979), maternal education (Barnard & Eyres 1979; McGowan & Johnson 1984), family support (Bee *et al.* 1982), and home environment (Dote-Kwan & Hughes 1994; Rock *et al.* 1994). Perhaps examining other distal influences across different contexts and their relations to development continues to be warranted in future studies.

In closing, The Education of Handicapped Act Amendment (Public Law 99-457), federally mandated a family-centred approach to evaluation and planning for children with disabilities or at risk for developmental delays. As families become more involved in programmes, it is essential that service providers (e.g. early interventionists) begin to understand which specific aspects of parental behaviours positively and negatively relate to the development of children with visual impairments. In this study, the results showed that the following specific aspects of maternal behaviours: quality of responsiveness, quality of control, appropriateness of directiveness, and amount and quality of goal setting, were positively related to children's development in the areas of language, sensorimotor comprehension, exploration of environment, and social adaptation. Whereas other findings indicated that the amount of control and the amount of directiveness were negatively associated with children's language. Therefore, in light of the nature of this study and its limitations, more research is warranted to draw conclusions about the influences of maternal behaviours on children's developmental competence.

References

Barnard, K. E. & Eyres, S. J., eds. (1979). *Child health assessment, part 2: The first year of life* (DHEW Publication no. HRA 79–25). US Government Printing Office, Washington, DC, USA.

Barnard, K. E. & Kelly, J. F. (1990). Assessment of parent–child interaction. In: *Handbook of Early Childhood Intervention* (eds S. J. Meisels & J. P. Shonkoff), Cambridge University Press, Cambridge, MA, USA, 278–302.

Beckwith, L. (1990). Adaptive and maladaptive parenting: Implications for intervention. In: *Handbook of Early Childhood Intervention* (eds. S. J. Meisels, & J. P. Shonkoff), Cambridge University Press, Cambridge, 53–77.

Bee, H. L., Barnard, K. E., Eyres, S. J., *et al.* (1982). Prediction of IQ and language skill from perinatal status, child performance, family characteristics, and mother–infant interaction. *Child Development, 53,* 1134–1156.

Behl, D. D., Akers, J. F., Boyce, M. J., & Taylor, M. J. (1996). Do mothers interact differently with children who are visually impaired? *Journal of Visual Impairment and Blindness, 90,* 501–511.

Blasco, P. M., Hrncir, E. J., & Blasco, P. A. (1990). The contribution of maternal involvement to mastery performance in infants with cerebral palsy. *Journal of Early Intervention, 14* (2), 161–174.

Boyce, G. C., Behl, D., & Castro, G. (1991). *A Study of Two Systems That Assess Mother/Child Interaction Involving Young Children with Disabilities.* Poster session presented at the International Early Childhood Special Education Conference, St Louis, MO, USA.

Bradley, R. H. & Caldwell, B. M. (1984). The relation of infants' home environments to achievement test performance in first grade: a follow-up study. *Child Development, 55,* 803–809.

Bradley, R. H., Caldwell, B. M., Rock, S. L., Brisby, J. A., & Harris, P. T. (1987). *Addendum to HOME Manual: Use of the HOME Inventory with Children with Handicaps.* University of Arkansas Center for Research on Teaching and Learning, Little Rock, AR, USA.

Crawley, S. B. & Spiker, D. (1983). Mother–child interactions involving two-year olds with Down syndrome: a look at individual differences. *Child Development, 54,* 1312–1323.

Cunningham, C. E., Reuler, E., Blackwell, J., & Deck, J. (1981). Behavioral and linguistic developments in the interactions of normal and retarded children with their mothers. *Child Development, 52,* 62–70.

Dote-Kwan, J. (1995). Impact of mothers' interactions on the development of their young visually impaired children. *Journal of Visual Impairment and Blindness, 89,* 46–58.

Dote-Kwan, J. & Hughes, M. (1994). The home environments of young blind children. *Journal of Visual Impairment and Blindness, 88,* 31–42.

Dote-Kwan, J., Hughes, M., & Taylor, S. L. (1997). The impact of early experiences on the development of young children with visual impairments: Revisited. *Journal of Visual Impairment and Blindness, 91,* 131–144.

Eheart, B. K. (1982). Motherchild interactions with nonretarded and mentally retarded preschoolers. *American Journal of Mental Deficiency, 87* (1), 20–25.

Farren, D. C., Kasari, C., Comfort, M., & Jay, S. (1986). *The Parent/Caregiver Involvement Scale.* The University of North Carolina at Greensboro, Child Development and Family Relations, School of Human Environmental Sciences, Greensboro, NC, USA.

Hallahan, D. P. & Kauffman, J. M. (1997). *Exceptional Learners. Introduction to Special Education* (7th ed.). Allyn and Bacon, Needham Heights, MA, USA.

Kogan, K. L., Wimberger, H. C., & Bobbitt, R. A. (1969). Analysis of mother–child interaction in young mental retardates. *Child Development, 40,* 799–812.

Lussier, B. J., Crimmins, D. B., & Alberti, D. (1994). Effects of three adult interaction styles on infant engagement. *Journal of Early Intervention, 18* (1), 12–24.

Marfo, K. (1982). Correlates of maternal directiveness with children who are developmentally delayed. *American Journal of Orthopsychiatry, 62,* 219–233.

Marfo, K. (1984). Interactions between mothers and their mentally retarded children: integrated of research findings. *Journal of Applied Developmental Psychology, 5,* 45–69.

Maxfield, K. E. & Buchholz, S. (1957). *A social maturity scale for blind preschool children. A Guide to its Use.* American Foundation for the Blind, New York, NY, USA.

McGowan, R. J. & Johnson, D. L. (1984). The mother–child relationship and other antecedents of childhood intelligence: a causal analysis. *Child Development, 55,* 810–820.

Preisler, G. M. (1991). Early patterns of interaction between blind infants and their sighted mothers. *Child: Care, Health and Development, 17,* 65–90.

Ramey, C. T., Farren, D. C., & Campbell, F. A. (1979). Predicting IQ from mother–infant interactions. *Child Development, 50,* 804–814.

Reynell, J. (1979). *The Reynell-Zinkin Scales: developmental scales for young visually handicapped children-Part 1: Mental development.* Stoelting Co., Chicago, IL, USA.

Rock, S. L., Head, D. N., Bradley, R. H., Whiteside, L., & Brisby, J. (1994). Use of the HOME inventory with families of young visually impaired children. *Journal of Visual Impairment and Blindness, 88,* 140–151.

Rogers, S. J. (1988). Characteristics of social interactions between mothers and their disabled infants: a review. *Child: Care, Health and Development, 14,* 301–317.

Sameroff, A. J. & Chandler, M. (1975). Reproductive risk and the continuum of care-taking causality. In: *Review of Child Development Research* (Vol. 4). (eds. F. D. Horowitz, M. Hetherton, S. Scarr-Salapatek, & G. Siegel), University of Chicago Press, Chicago, IL, USA.

Tröster, H. & Brambring, M. (1992). Early social-emotional development in blind infants. *Child: Care, Health and Development, 18,* 207–227.

Wilfong, E. W., Saylor, C., & Elksnin, N. (1991). Influences on responsiveness: Interactions between mothers and their premature infants. *Infant Mental Health Journal, 12* (1), 30–40.

4

■ Why do infants and caregivers love one another? Attachment theory argues that this emotional bond is a cultural universal, and grows out of our species heritage, in that this bond serves as nature's way of protecting human infants, who are naturally curious, but ignorant of potential dangers (Bowlby, 1969). Infants' desire to stay near the caregiver balances their curiosity and creates a "natural playpen" within which the child can explore safely. Attachment theory predicts that infants who perceive their caregivers as a "secure base" during times of stress will have the confidence to explore a familiar environment. However, attachment theorists also recognize that culture and childrearing practices affect the quality of this bond (Ainsworth, 1967). Thus, similarities and differences across cultures reveal developmental processes of how characteristics of the infant (the balance between desires for security and exploration) are shaped by the social environment.

Overview Questions

1. Explain in your own words the idea of "attachment-exploration balance." How does this idea of complementary systems lead to Hypotheses 1 and 2?

2. What "cultural universals" (or at least similarities between these two Western cultures) did they observe about the attachment-exploration balance?

3. "Securely attached" infants are reasonably confident in exploring an environment when their caregiver is present, while "avoidant" infants show less protest at separation from the caregiver, and take less interest in seeking closeness when reunited (Ainsworth, Blehar, Waters, & Wall, 1978). Using this background, explain in your own words the second paragraph of the discussion and what that might mean for culture-specific patterns of development.

4. What might these authors hypothesize about the relationships among culture, child-rearing behaviors, the child's sense of security, and the child's opportunities to learn about the environment?

Focus Questions

1. In the method section, they provide definitions and examples of each level of exploration. Generate your own examples of each level to help you distinguish among them.

2. List five ways the two samples were similar. What one difference of procedure existed in the two groups? How did they define "novel situation" and "familiar situation"?

3. How did they measure attachment behavior? What is inter-observer agreement, and why is it important to this study?

4. In Table 4.1, "M" is mean and "SD" is standard deviation, a measure of how scattered the scores were away from the mean. Examine the means for the different levels of exploration in, for example, the U.S. infants in the novel situation. Based on these, what level(s) is (are) most age-appropriate for 1-year-olds, and why?

5. Make a graph of the mean total exploration time for each sample in each situation in each culture. Does this support Hypothesis 2? Why or why not? Examining Table 4.1,

how do they get the mean levels of reference to mother (3.7 vs. 2.9) that they report in the results section? Does this support Hypothesis 1? Why or why not?

6. When the correlation between two variables is positive, the higher you score on one, the higher you score on the other. When a correlation is negative, the higher you score on one, the lower you score on the other. Using these definitions, put into your own words the last paragraph of the results section.

Patterns of the Attachment-Exploration Balance of 1-Year-Old Infants from the United States and Northern Germany

Ulrike Zach

Heidi Keller

Evolution has shaped two motivational systems in primates, including human beings: the need to relate to other people ("attachment," cf. Bowlby, 1969; "affiliation," McClelland, 1987), and the drive for exploration ("curiosity," cf. Berlyne, 1960). Ainsworth, Blehar, Waters, & Wall (1978) conceptualized these two motivational systems as complementary in terms of an interdependent hierarchical structure, the *attachment-exploration balance*. If the attachment system is activated, the exploration system is deactivated, and vice versa. The activation of the attachment system is triggered by separation from the attachment figure, fear-inducing novelty, or both (Bowlby, 1969). If the attachment figure is available when the child is exposed to an unfamiliar environment, the appropriate attachment behaviors would comprise seeking physical proximity, visual contact, or both ("social referencing") to reduce the distress. The instigation of specific exploration (e.g., novel toys) constitutes the most prominent mode of exploration during infancy and early childhood. Beyond the situational regulation of the motivational systems, the felt security to refer to an available caregiver promotes exploration of the environment and, thus, facilitates the acquisition of environmentally based knowledge.

Exploration of the environment is achieved with those behaviors that are developmentally appropriate. Belsky and Most (1981) assessed children's exploratory activities from 7.5 months to 21 months and formulated a developmental sequence that also could be confirmed for northern German children (Zach, 1995). According to these results, "simple" and "functional manipulation" (Levels 2 and 3 according to Belsky & Most, 1981) are characteristic of 1-year-old children's exploratory behavior, whereas "mouthing" (Level 1) has almost disappeared, and "relational manipulation" (Level 4) up to "pretense behavior" (Level 8) will be rare. Thus, age-appropriate exploration as expressed in different levels can be differentiated from mere quantity of exploration in terms of total time (Keller, Schneider, & Henderson, 1994).

Although the existence of the motivational systems of attachment and exploration is conceived of as universal, culture-specific modes are acknowledged (Cole, 1992; Van IJzendoorn & Kroonenberg, 1988). Compared with American mother-child dyads, a higher number of northern German children demonstrated independently regulated attachment systems (Ainsworth et al., 1978; Grossmann, Grossmann, Spangler, Suess, & Unzner, 1985; Van IJzendoorn & Kroonenberg, 1988). Thus, the behavioral manifestations of the attachment system especially might vary across cultures (for an overview, see Van IJzendoorn & Sagi, 1999).

From a developmental perspective, we can formulate expectations about 1-year-old infants' regulation of the attachment-exploration balance: Both infants from the United States and northern Germany should refer to their attachment figures more in a novel situation than in a familiar situation (Hypothesis 1). All children also should demonstrate a higher degree of activation of their exploratory behavior as expressed in quantity of exploration in the familiar situation than in the novel situation (Hypothesis 2). Beyond these universal characteristics of the attachment-exploration balance, we expect differences between the two samples with respect to the relation of the children's references toward the mother in a novel situation and their age-appropriate exploration in a familiar situation.

Method

Participants

Cultural subsamples were recruited from a northern German city (Osnabrück, *n* = 19) and from the United States (Washington, DC, *n* = 19). The German subsample was approached through announcements in the local newspaper of Osnabrück and visits in baby exercise classes and mothers' cafeterias. The U.S. subsample was recruited in Bethesda, Maryland, through information in day care and community centers. All women were married, belonged to the middle or upper-middle class (Hollingshead, 1975) and were the primary caregivers. The mean age of the northern German women was 30.4 years (*SD* = 4.16); the U.S. mothers' mean age was 31 years (*SD* = 5.15). The mean age of the northern German infants was 12.37 months (*SD* = 1.06); for U.S. infants, the mean age was 12.18 months (*SD* = 1.0). The developmental status of the infants was controlled (e.g., all infants were able to crawl or walk).

The Laboratory Free-Play Procedure

Mother and child participated in a structured laboratory play session of 10 minutes. The play room in the German study was 7 × 8 meters in size, and that of the U.S. study 3.5 × 4 meters. Both rooms were equipped with a centrally located chair for the mothers; a set of age-appropriate toys (doll, cradle, brush, Legos, wooden blocks, lorry or cart, telephone) was arranged in a fixed order and distance (2 meters) to the mother's chair in both samples. Mothers were instructed to refer to their infants' requests but not to initiate social interaction or to prompt the infants' exploratory behavior. The first 3 minutes after entering the room constitute the novel situation. The last 3 minutes constitute the familiar situation. The whole sequence was videotaped with two remote-controlled cameras.

To address the problem inherent to different room sizes, we examined the intercorrelations between visual references and physical contact of the infants separately for each sample. Within both samples, no significant correlation emerged. Neither in the small nor in the big room did infants exhibit a specific pattern of different modes of referring to their mothers.

Behavioral Assessments

Physical Contact

A 1-year-old infant has several possibilities to establish physical contact with her or his mother: standing close to her, leaning on her, holding her hand, putting her hand onto her lap, touching or grasping any part of her body, or sitting on her lap. Each of these incidents was coded to arrive at a frequency score for the novel and for the familiar situation separately.

Visual References

According to the literature on social referencing (Collins & Jones, 1992), visual references to mother are defined as very quick efforts of the child to catch the mother's eye that do not lead to prolonged episodes of mutual facial exchange. The frequency of these "check backs" to mother were computed for the initial novel situation and for the familiar situation, respectively.

Exploration

Belsky and Most (1981) introduced a coding system to assess children's exploration and play during the first years of life. Whereas in the Belsky and Most study the coding is based on transcripts of a participating observer, we coded the exploratory behavior of the children from videotapes. For both situations, each exploratory act with a toy was classified according to these levels of exploration, and the duration of the activity was recorded in seconds. The levels are defined as follows: Level 1 (Mouthing: putting object into mouth, sucking); Level 2 (Simple manipulation: touching, lifting); Level 3 (Functional manipulation: using one object as intended by the manufacturer, e.g., dialing a telephone, rolling a cart on wheels); Level 4 (Relational manipulation: integrating two objects not according to manufacturer's intention, e.g., setting cradle on phone); Level 5 (Functional-relational manipulation: integrating two objects as intended, e.g., intentionally sticking Legos together, putting doll into cradle); Level 6 (Enactive naming: approximate pretense activity, e.g., raising phone receiver in proximity to ear without making talking sounds); Level 7 (Pretend self: self-directed pretense behavior, e.g., raising phone receiver to ear and vocalizing); Level 8 (Pretend other: pretense behavior directed toward other, e.g., feeding doll with spoon).

The method allows the computation of total time of exploration by summing up the seconds a child explored on each level. Total time of exploration is reported as the percentage of 3 minutes' time for each situation. This score indicates an overall degree of activation of the exploratory system. The age-specific exploration rate was assessed by the time a child explored on Levels 2 and 3. This score also was computed for both situations and is reported as the percentage of Level 2 and 3 of the total time of exploration. Because both scores emphasize different aspects of exploratory performance of 1-year-old infants, we test our assumptions on the basis of both scores.

Interobserver Agreement

All coding is based on videotaped analyses. The behavioral assessment of the infants' references to their mothers and the exploratory performance was conducted by two different pairs of trained observers (advanced students). Interobserver agreement within each pair was assessed for 7 mother-child dyads and reached 75% for visual references, 82% for physical contact, and 85% for assessment of exploration.

Results

Descriptive Data

Descriptive statistics of infants' references toward the mothers and parameters of exploratory activities can be inferred from Table 4.1. Not all children demonstrated Level 8 activities; thus, we combined Levels 4 and 5 and Levels 6 and 7 for an overview.

Means of exploratory activities on Level 1 as well as on Level 4 to Level 8 declined for all children in both situations, with considerable amounts of variance. Thus, we again demonstrated that the best indicator for age-specific exploration is the percentage of time a child explores on Levels 2 and 3.

To test our first hypothesis, we collected all infants' frequencies of visual references and physical contact with mother. The comparison of the mean frequencies of references to mother across the two situations revealed that infants significantly, $t = -5.79$, $df = 37$, $p = .000$, refer more to their mothers ($M = 3.7$) in the novel situation than in the familiar situation ($M = -2.9$). All infants significantly increased their overall exploratory activity, $t = 3.19$, $df = 37$, $p < .005$, in the familiar situation ($M = 56\%$) as compared to the novel situation ($M = 39\%$). There is no effect of situation on the age-specific score of exploration.

The analysis of the correlational pattern between infants' different modes of referencing behavior in the novel situation and their exploration in the familiar situation was conducted for total amount of exploration as well as for the age-specific exploration. Because incidents of physical contact were rather low (cf. Table 4.1) and 10 infants did not demonstrate any physical contact with their mothers at all, children of each sample were assigned to a group of low or high amount of physical contact according to the median-split. The same was done with the variable "visual references." The point-biserial correlations between these dichotomized variables of the novel situation and the age-specific exploration on Levels 2 to 3 in the familiar situation reveal a pronounced pattern (cf. Table 4.2). No significant correlations emerged between the score of total time of exploration and the scores of visual and physical references.

A distinct feature emerged with respect to different modes of contact behavior in the stressful situation and age-specific performance in the familiar situation in the two samples. The U.S. infants' contact behavior in the novel situation is significantly positive related to their age-specific exploratory performance ($r = .58$, $p < .005$). Data from northern German infants reveal a significant negative relation between visually referring to the mother in the novel situation and the age-specific exploration ($r = -.52$, $p < .05$).

TABLE 4.1 *Descriptive Statistics of Attachment and Exploration Behavior of 1-Year-Old Infants from the United States and Northern Germany*

| | U.S. Infants | | | | Northern German Infants | | | |
| | Novel Situation | | Familiar Situation | | Novel Situation | | Familiar Situation | |
	M	SD	M	SD	M	SD	M	SD
References (frequencies)								
Physical	1.6	1.9	2.4	2.8	1.7	1.3	1.0	2.8
Visual	4.2	2.2	3.7	2.4	3.2	1.5	2.1	1.4
Total time of exploration (percentages)	37.6	19.7	55.3	24.3	41.5	19.2	57.1	26.8
Time on level of exploration[a] (percentages)								
Level 1	1.04	3.18	6.45	9.79	5.33	19.07	5.97	20.93
Level 2-3	85.24	25.24	72.10	29.49	73.88	35.48	70.52	25.73
Level 4-5	7.61	14.57	20.06	22.69	8.40	16.40	17.57	19.95
Level 6-7	0.85	3.69	1.39	6.08	1.46	4.10	5.79	20.39
Level 8	—	—	—	—	0.4	1.75	—	—

If the percentage computation was limited due to division through zero (the child did not explore on this level), the zero value was assigned anyway.

TABLE 4.2 *Correlational Patterns Between Referencing Behavior and Exploration*

	Familiar Situation: Age-Appropriate Exploration	
	U.S. Infants	*Northern German Infants*
Novel situation		
Physical contact	.58**	−.25
Visual references	−.05	−.52*

*$p < .05$. **$p < .005$.

Discussion

The results of this study reveal universal as well as culture-specific regulations with respect to the attachment-exploration balance in 1-year-old U.S. and northern German children. As predicted by attachment theory, infants of both cultural subsamples referred more to their mothers in a novel situation and spent more time with exploration in the familiar one.

The results reveal an interesting culture-specific difference with respect to the establishment of the balance. The U.S. infants' behavior conforms with attachment theory prediction. Physical contact in a novel situation (proximity seeking; Bowlby, 1969) as the proposed main mode of distress regulation in 1-year-olds is significantly related to the amount of age-appropriate exploration in the familiar situation. However, northern German infants display a different behavioral pattern. Their age-appropriate exploration is not related to physical contact, but related significantly and negatively to visual references, thus indicating that the more they explore, the less they refer to their mothers. This result could be interpreted as indicating that northern German children regulate their distress in novel situations independently from their mothers. This would be in line with the interpretation of the high amount of the avoidant attachment pattern in northern Germany reported by Grossmann et al. (1985). It can be concluded that cultural regulation and expression of attachment is not only specific with respect to the behavioral mode (physical or visual), but also with respect to the relation between attachment and exploration. Furthermore, culture-specific parenting goals might result in different behavioral strategies already existing in 1-year-olds. The assessment of parenting goals as related to behavioral strategies of infants in further studies might elucidate this relation in more detail.

Focusing on the two aspects of exploratory behavior, it became evident that the features of situation familiarity influence the degree of activation of the exploratory system, but they do not influence the performance of the age-specific activities. The increase in exploration in the familiar situation probably facilitates a diversity of exploratory activities, whereas in the ambivalent condition the necessity for attachment behavior restricts exploratory activity in general. Therefore, it seems necessary to be aware of the different aspects of exploration in further studies (cf. Belsky, Garduque, & Hrncir, 1984). In general, these results support a culture-specific view on early behavioral regulations that is even noticeable in similar Western cultures.

References

Ainsworth, M. D. S., Blehar, M. C., Waters, E., & Wall, S. (1978). *Patterns of attachment: A psychological study of the strange situation.* Hillsdale, NJ: Lawrence Erlbaum.

Belsky, L. Garduque, L., & Hrncir, E. (1984). Assessing performance, competence, and executive capacity in infant play: Relations to home environment and security of attachment. *Developmental Psychology, 20,* 406–417.

Belsky, J., & Most, R. K. (1981). From exploration to play: A cross-sectional study of infant free play behavior. *Developmental Psychology, 17*, 630–639.

Berlyne, D. E. (1960). *Conflict, arousal, and curiosity.* New York: McGraw-Hill.

Bowlby, J. (1969). *Attachment and loss: Vol. 1. Attachment.* New York: Basic Books.

Cole, M. (1992). Culture and development. In M. H. Bornstein & M. E. Lamb (Eds.), *Developmental psychology: An advanced textbook.* Hillsdale, NJ: Lawrence Erlbaum.

Collins, K. L., & Jones, S. S. (1992). The generalizability of social referencing in infancy. *Infant Behavior & Development, 15,* 356.

Grossmann, K., Grossmann, K. E., Spangler, G., Suess, G., & Unzner, L. (1985). Maternal sensitivity and newborns' orientation responses as related to quality of attachment in Northern Germany. *Monographs of the Society for Research in Child Development, 50*(1-2), (No. 209). 233–256.

Hollingshead, A. (1975). *The four factor index of social class.* Unpublished manuscript, Yale University.

Keller, H., Schneider. K., & Henderson, B. (Eds.). (1994). *Curiosity and exploration.* Heidelberg, Germany: Springer.

McCelland, D. C. (1987). *Human motivation.* Cambridge, MA: Harvard University Press.

Van IJzendoorn, M. H., & Kroonenberg, P. M. (1988). Cross-cultural patterns of attachment: A meta-analysis of the strange situation. *Child Development, 59,* 147–156.

Van IJzendoorn, M. H., & Sagi, A. (1999). Cross-cultural patterns of attachment: Universal and contextual dimensions. In J. Cassidy & P. Shaver (Eds.), *Handbook on attachment theory and research.* New York: Guilford.

Zach, U. (1995, March). *Early gaze behavior and later exploratory competence.* Paper presented at the meeting of the Society for Research in Child Development, Indianapolis, IN.

5

■ How children learn language has fascinated parents and scientists for ages, and it seems even more marvelous when they become fluent speakers of more than one language. Children who are growing up with two (or more) languages need to distinguish the two systems from one another and, at the same time, relate each to the objects in the world and meanings in their minds that they want to convey. A common strategy for doing this, the person-language bond, is described in this article. Another feature of becoming bilingual is learning to "code-switch" appropriately, which means changing from one language to another depending on the location, the persons present, the topic, etc.

When most of us think of children learning language, we think of spoken languages. American Sign Language (ASL), like all languages, includes structures that enable its users to express complex and abstract thoughts. Members of the Deaf community are proud of their language and culture. Infants learning ASL as a first language tend to produce their first sign-words and their first sign-sentences at slightly younger ages than children learning to produce spoken words and sentences (Meier, 1991). This article presents the interesting story of a bilingual-bicultural ASL/English family. It illustrates how language-learning processes are similar and different across auditory (English) and visual media (ASL). It also illustrates that children's strategies for learning language are embedded in their immediate social context and in turn in the communities to which their families belong.

Overview Questions

1. Describe the girls' command of English and ASL at each of the following ages: 12 months, 18 months, 2 years, 2–3 years. What advantages does her mother believe Erin has had in schoolwork because of being bilingual? What do you conclude about the similarities and differences between language acquisition in ASL and English?

2. Families are embedded in communities. Give examples, from Ken's life, and from Erin and Kaylee's, of how children's experiences are influenced by the communities around them.

3. According to Finton, what are the key elements of Deaf people's view of themselves? What does this suggest to you in terms of cultural differences and universals in self-image?

Focus Questions

1. How does Grosjean define "bilingual"? Why does Finton prefer "bilingual/bicultural" to a concept of deaf and hearing as opposites?

2. What aspects of Deaf culture were easiest and hardest for Finton to become accustomed to? What about Ken's experiences makes sense of valuing friends or family?

3. What changes in language environments have accompanied raising their daughters? Give examples of code-switching: when do the daughters use ASL versus English? How does this illustrate how language use relates to social context?

4. To what extent does Finton believe that children acquire fingerspelling as individual letters vs. whole shapes in combination? Give examples to support her case. Note the similarity between holistic recognition of fingerspelling and pre-reading children's holistic recognition of commercial logos. Give examples to explain what she means by the "person-language bond." How might this illustrate the idea that children's language-learning strategies interact with their family environment?

Living in a Bilingual-Bicultural Family

Lynn Finton

Thirteen years ago when I married my husband, Ken, I believed the biggest difference between us was that I was Catholic and he was Lutheran. The fact that he was Deaf and I was hearing seemed inconsequential. The idea that we were entering into a bilingual and bicultural marriage and its potential impact on our relationship and future family did not enter our consciousness. Thirteen years and two children later, I have come to appreciate the significance of living in a bilingual-bicultural family.

Only recently have I reflected upon and analyzed bilingualism. When the editor of this book invited me to reflect upon the experience of living in a bilingual-bicultural family and write about it, I hesitated. I felt uncomfortable proclaiming myself a "bilingual." I believed a true bilingual was someone raised from birth with two languages or someone who moved from country to country and developed fluency in two or more languages. I also hesitated to proclaim myself a bilingual since I didn't start learning American Sign Language (ASL) until age eighteen. Although I was fluent in two languages, I didn't fit what I believed to be the definition of bilingualism. In addition, in my field of sign language interpreting, making a claim of bilingualism seemed to belong solely to children of Deaf parents.

The challenge to write about my bilingualism led me to a literature search and a real awakening. In the book *Life with Two Languages: An Introduction to Bilingualism,* François Grosjean (1982) defines bilingualism as "the regular use of two or more languages" (p. 1). That definition allowed me to see myself as a bilingual. I am fluent in two languages and use them on a daily basis both at work and at home. In addition, this book explained for me some of the puzzling experiences my husband and I have had as our daughters developed their two languages. As I read Grosjean's book, I came to realize that these experiences are common aspects of childhood bilingualism. Most importantly, I realized that the experiences of an English/ASL bilingual child are quite similar to the experiences of a Spanish/English or German/French bilingual child. It had never occurred to me to look at the bilingual literature as a source for understanding some of the phenomena that emerged as my daughters developed their languages. It was a wonderful and reassuring revelation to know that what was happening in our family was not unique, that the stages of language development my daughters were going through were typical of bilingual children.

Grosjean's book has also had a significant impact on how I think about Deaf/hearing issues. The terms "Deaf" and "hearing" are on opposite ends of the continuum, they are polar opposites. When Deaf/hearing issues are discussed, it is often in a negative context. Polar opposites and negativity were not, however, the appropriate words that described our Deaf/hearing marriage. The terms "bilingual" and "bicultural" and the positive connotations they carry are much better suited to describe who we are: a bilingual-bicultural couple. With this realization, I gladly accepted the editor's invitation to reflect on living in a bilingual-bicultural family.

This chapter will provide a glimpse of my family and our backgrounds, a look at how our bilingualism-biculturalism is manifest in everyday life as well as at some of the interesting phenomena of raising one's children bilingual-bicultural.

My Background

I am a hearing, native English user. All members of my family are hearing. My initial interest in sign language came about through watching a young Deaf boy communicate in sign language with his family at my church. I was so fascinated! As a result, my best friend and I learned fingerspelling during elementary school so that we could have secret "talks" at church or school. This interest eventually led to my career path in deaf education.

I began learning sign language at age eighteen through a community continuing education course while I was attending college. Having no opportunity to use the language outside of the classroom, I developed minimal fluency. During my junior year I transferred to a college in Sioux Falls, South Dakota, a city with a very active Deaf community. Here I met and began socializing with some Deaf men around my age and only then did I really begin to use the language enough to develop fluency. I remain forever grateful to the Sioux Falls Deaf community for their encouragement and their tolerance of my many cultural faux pas and language errors inevitable in the process of learning a second language. I am particularly indebted to one of those young Deaf men who led me on this journey toward bilingualism-biculturalism—my husband, Ken.

Ken's Background

Ken, who is profoundly Deaf, comes from a predominantly hearing family. He has hearing parents, two hearing siblings and a Deaf sister. Ken was not diagnosed as being deaf until he attended kindergarten in a public school. After this diagnosis, he attended a residential school for the deaf. His younger sister was diagnosed as deaf at approximately the same time and also attended the South Dakota School for the Deaf. Upon learning of the deafness of her two eldest children, Ken's mother began a correspondence course with the John Tracy Clinic, a well-known program for promoting oral education. Through this program, Ken's parents stressed the use of speech and speechreading at home. The program discouraged his parents from learning sign language, even though their children quickly learned sign language while attending the school for the deaf. The family did learn to use fingerspelling, but they only used it when speechreading failed. Ken and his sister lived in the dorms at the school for the deaf. At home, they relied primarily on speech and speechreading to communicate with hearing family members. As a result, Ken and his sister often felt left out of family conversations. Despite their parents' efforts, speech and speechreading failed to provide full access to communication within the family.

Ken transferred from the residential school for the deaf to a public school for his junior high and high school years. Although this decision was not supported by Ken's parents or himself, the residential school promoted it as the best way to challenge Ken academically. He spent these years in school using his residual hearing, speech, and speechreading to communicate. He did not have the benefit of interpreting or note taking services except for the last semester of his senior year. Socially, Ken had little contact with his hearing peers since communication was difficult and thus tended to be superficial. He continued to socialize after school with his friends from the school for the deaf since he felt more comfortable using sign language and interacting with those who shared that language.

Our Mixed Marriage

I attribute our lack of concern in entering a "mixed" marriage to naiveté. Deaf people were only beginning to be recognized as a linguistic and cultural minority back in the late 1970s. I had taken a course or two in American Sign Language, and I did appreciate it as a language separate and distinct from English. I was a fluent signer, not from the course work I took but from frequent interaction with the Sioux Falls Deaf community. Having interacted regularly with Deaf people for several years prior to my marriage, I had an appreciation for the fact that Deaf people were different from hearing people, that they saw things in a different way at times, that their rules of behavior weren't always the same as mine. Beyond that, I gave it little thought.

Over the years Ken and I came to understand these differences and attribute them to our different cultural experiences. It was easy for me to get used to the artifacts of Deaf culture: the TTY, the flashing lights, the caption decoder. It was not that difficult to get used to the typical behaviors Deaf people exhibit: tapping a person to get attention, the importance of eye contact, the lengthy leavetaking. What was most difficult to understand was the different world view that Deaf people have. On one occasion, early in our relationship, the topic of cochlear implants arose. A late-deafened acquaintance of ours had a cochlear implant. It was a relatively new procedure at the time, and she was thrilled with the results, limited as they were. I asked Ken, if he could magically become hearing whether he would do so. His response was an emphatic "No!" He explained that he was Deaf, that he identified with others like him and had no desire to be hearing. Knowing some of the obstacles, discrimination, and occasional frustrations he faced as a Deaf person, I couldn't understand what I perceived as his stubbornness in not wanting to become hearing. It wasn't that I wanted him to become hearing, I just felt that he was displaying a false sense of pride in not being willing to admit that it would be easier to be hearing. I can now greatly appreciate that Ken's identity is tied to his deafness—his language and his culture. Rare is the person who is willing to give up a crucial part of their identity just to have life a little more convenient for them. I realize that there might be certain advantages if I were a male, but I sure have no interest in being one.

Another conflict we faced early on, which was influenced by culture, was the relative importance placed on family versus friends. I come from a very close-knit family with a value system that places family above all else. Ken lived in the dorms at the residential school for the deaf. As is often the case with Deaf people, a familial bonding between peers occurs in this setting. Such was the case with Ken, and although I could intellectually appreciate the concept, at an emotional level I couldn't grasp how friends could be more important than family. I have now come to understand that the Deaf community is very close-knit, and living 1,200 miles from my own family, we now have a group of Deaf friends who truly are our second family.

Another issue we faced was the commonly held belief in the Deaf community that Deaf/hearing marriages don't work. Although common in South Dakota, mixed marriages were rare in Kansas, where we lived during our first year of marriage. I have seen no research data that support or deny the allegation that Deaf/hearing marriages don't work. What I do know is that our marriage is successful. Are there tensions? Sometimes. Are they caused by the fact that Ken is Deaf and I am hearing? No, I don't believe so. Mostly the tensions are because we are both stubborn, we disagree on when and how to spend our money, we have different ideas of child rearing, and so on. Is it difficult to be married to a Deaf person? Sure. He calls to me when I am in the basement and expects me to walk up to see what he wants. It takes him a long time to leave a social gathering. He doesn't want to go to the symphony. Is it difficult for Ken to be married to a hearing person? Sure. I walk all over the house when I talk on the phone. I sing along with the radio, and he thinks he married a nut case because it looks like I'm talking to myself. Are these marriage-shattering issues? Hardly.

Do I interpret for Ken? Sometimes I do, with neighbors, with family members, for the insurance agent and the car salesman. With the availability of captioning and telephone relay services, I interpret much less now than in the beginning of our marriage. Does it bother me when I have to interpret? No. Do I feel as though I am making sacrifices to make this bicultural marriage work? No, I don't! All marriages are a matter of give and take. When conflicts occur, we are not quick to place blame on our hearing status as the cause, but rather we look beyond to the root of the issue. Rarely does the cause lie in the fact that he is Deaf and I am hearing. We have come to accept, appreciate, and respect our cultural differences and perhaps that is the key to our success.

Our Family

Ken and I have two hearing daughters. Erin is seven years old and Kaylee is three. Our family uses American Sign Language and spoken English at home. We socialize with both Deaf and hearing people. We attend a church for the deaf. Ken and I both work at the National Technical Institute for the Deaf, where many people are English/ASL bilinguals. Erin attends a monolingual English school, and Kaylee is presently in a monolingual English home care environment.

Before the children, life in our household was uncomplicated. We used sign language exclusively in our home. Our friends were ASL/English bilinguals, both Deaf and hearing. The birth of our hearing daughters added a new dimension to this existence. We now encounter and interact with many more hearing people who are English monolinguals. Moving into a family-oriented neighborhood brought with it interactions with monolingual English-speaking neighbors. Our daughters found hearing playmates from the neighborhood and school, which brought many hearing monolingual English speakers into the household. Interactions with child-care providers and school personnel, along with our daughters' involvement in extracurricular activities, increased our contacts with hearing monolinguals. We didn't foresee the dramatic increase in the amount of contact with monolinguals before the birth of our children or its impact on our somewhat insular life with English/ASL bilinguals. These changes have resulted in my doing more interpreting for Ken. He has also had to start using his speech and speechreading skills with more frequency.

Language Use in the Home

Because I am married to a Deaf man, people frequently ask what language is used in our home. Until I began reading about bilingualism that question was difficult to answer; language choice is an unconscious process, so I really had to stop and think. My response would be "ASL," qualified with "most of the time." This qualifier refers to all of the influences of language choice and code-switching that goes on with bilinguals.

Because Ken can't hear spoken English, it isn't a fully accessible or comfortable communication option for him. We always sign with him. Whether I speak or sign to my daughters is often dependent on who else is in the environment and the purpose of the communication. For example, when I am with my daughters in public, we often sign. I have not fully determined the reason for this, but my sense is that ASL is the language of privacy for us. After so many years of signing in public without having anyone eavesdrop, it now seems very awkward to talk in public when we can sign and keep our conversation private. I often sign to my daughters in the presence of hearing people to ensure privacy in conversation. It is interesting, though, that I do not feel comfortable speaking with my daughters in front of Deaf people to ensure privacy. Deaf people have been left out of conversations all of their lives because most hearing people can't sign. Because I am bilingual, to deliberately speak in front of a Deaf person without signing seems disrespectful and potentially oppressive.

Ken signs primarily, but at times uses spoken English when reading books, when his hands are otherwise occupied, or sometimes when disciplining. Kaylee signs to Ken and talks to me. Erin signs to me more frequently than ever before, again depending on the environment and the purpose of communication. Erin realizes she has control of two languages and can use them to her advantage. During Erin's kindergarten orientation she didn't say a word to anyone but signed to me throughout. She recognized that no one knew sign language except the two of us and she could communicate her thoughts freely without anyone "overhearing."

Only when it's called to my attention do I realize the amount of language switching and code-switching done in our family. After watching our family interact for about five minutes, a friend once remarked, "your children must be very confused. They never know what language will be coming at them." I would always feel bad after hearing this kind of remark. Although the girls never appeared confused and always answered appropriately, I would feel that maybe we needed to establish a clear communication policy. But that seemed to impose artificial rules on what was happening naturally within our family. After reading about bilingualism, I am comforted to know that we are not just a family with hodgepodge communication. Now my response to these remarks is, "No, they are not confused, they are bilinguals!"

Language Development in Our Children

Ken was adamant that his children be fluent in sign language. While superficial communication was acceptable for acquaintances, it was not acceptable within the intimate confines of the family. So early in our marriage we agreed that our children would be fluent in ASL. Although it would seem natural that a child would become fluent in sign language just by growing up in an environment where sign language is used, unfortunately this is not always the case. We have often seen Deaf parents use sign language with each other but use spoken English with their hearing children. In return, these children speak to their parents. This situation results in children who can comprehend some sign language but gain little mastery in using it themselves. We wanted to make sure that our children had adequate exposure to ASL. Because English is the majority language in American society, we felt assured our children would develop fluency in spoken English. Although the goal of making our children fluent in both English and ASL was clear, the process of achieving it was an unconscious one. We assumed that exposing them to both languages from the cradle would be effective.

It has been fascinating to watch our daughters' language development. I learned ASL as my second language, so I was interested to see how language learning would be different when learning English and ASL simultaneously. As a teacher in an interpreter education program, I frequently see the difficulty that adults endure when attempting to learn ASL as a second language. I was very curious to see how the learning process would be different for my daughters, who were learning two languages in a natural setting, our home.

Both of our daughters seemed to follow a similar pattern of language development. Their first signs were different from their first spoken words. Erin's first signs were MORE, DOG, and AIRPLANE, all appearing around nine to ten months of age. Her first spoken words were "Mommmy" and "Daddy," occurring around age one. Both communicated primarily through sign language, with approximately a fifteen-sign vocabulary but only one or two spoken words, at twelve months. While they could comprehend spoken English, they expressed their needs in sign language. It happened that our child-care arrangements changed when each girl was about one year old. We became concerned about putting them in a new monolingual English environment where their ability to express themselves in sign language wouldn't be understood. In order to prevent frustration, we taught our child-care providers the signs necessary to comprehend our daughters' communications. This seemed to be an effective strategy for the girls until they became more expressively fluent in English.

By eighteen months the girls primarily signed for communication purposes, although they were talking at this time as well. The girls could communicate some things in both languages and some things in just one of the languages. At age two they could communicate fairly equally in the two languages. From age two to three, their use of spoken English increased dramatically and they could communicate more in English than in ASL. As with language development in general, their comprehension of ASL far exceeded their ability to express themselves in that language at this age.

Age two presented some new challenges for us. Nursery rhymes and music became an important part of the girls' childhood. This sound-based entertainment was not part of Ken's cultural experience and is often impossible to translate effectively into sign language. He knew few fairy tales and even fewer nursery rhymes. An unspoken rule that has developed in our house is that I do not interpret between Ken and the girls. They always communicate directly with him. However, for this phase of their childhood it was necessary for me to interpret certain things in order for Ken to appreciate their burgeoning command of English and their recitation of nursery rhymes and songs.

Kaylee, at present, is in a phase in which her ability to express herself in English exceeds her ability to express herself in sign language. This phase can be frustrating for both Ken and Kaylee. She signs to her dad and sometimes just mouths words without voice when she doesn't know a sign for a particular word or concept. She can communicate her basic needs effectively but can't always communicate everything she wants to with him. Speechreading, guesswork, and some interpreting help to alleviate this problem.

When Erin went through this phase, we worried whether she would reach the point where she could express herself equally in both languages. Now, having experienced this phase once before, we are reassured to know that Kaylee will grow out of it, too.

At age three, friends would marvel at the facility with which Erin could switch between ASL and English in a mixed group. She never confused the languages and never used the wrong language with anyone. She could, with total ease and very unconsciously, talk to a hearing person, turn around and sign to a deaf person, and switch right back to English to speak to the hearing person again, never missing a beat!

Erin is now seven. She can communicate equally well in both languages. I believe that her exceptional reading and spelling abilities are, in part, due to her bilingualism. Additionally, her continual exposure to closed-captioning and her interest in using the TTY may have been motivating factors in her wanting to learn to read and spell.

To date, our daughters' experiences as bilinguals have been positive. They have gotten a lot of attention and positive reinforcement for what is perceived as a unique ability. Complete strangers comment frequently and ask such questions as, "When did you start teaching them to sign?" My response is often, "The day they were born!" I go on to explain how children acquire sign language in the same way they acquire any spoken language. Our daughters are good ambassadors for the recognition of ASL as a language. We have educated countless curious people in malls, restaurants, and libraries.

The Use of Fingerspelling

The use of fingerspelling has been one fascinating part of our daughters' acquisition of ASL. It is often believed that fingerspelling is a way to represent English by spelling out words using the manual alphabet. As such, it would appear that fingerspelling would not be appropriate for children until they reach school age. This has not been our experience.

Erin and Kaylee began to comprehend fingerspelling at a very early age. At twelve months, they recognized fingerspelled words such as B-I-B and C-H-E-E-R-I-O-S and would respond appropriately to commands or questions using these fingerspelled words. It appears that children comprehend fingerspellng through the shape or configuration of the letters in combination, not by seeing each individual letter, much the same way a child begins to recognize words in written English.

Ken and I used fingerspelling as a way to communicate privately and prevent our daughters from comprehending. This strategy began to fail us when the girls were around age two. When Kaylee was two I signed to Ken, "AFTER THE KIDS GO TO BED, DO YOU WANT A C-O-K-E?" Kaylee, who had been watching, responded, "Yeah! I want Coke!"

Kaylee now recognizes many fingerspelled words. She can fingerspell words such as P-I-Z-Z-A and Z-O-O. She is unable to spell the words "pizza" and "zoo" out loud because she recognizes them as signs, not as individual letters of the alphabet. She can, however, spell all the names of her immediate family, including those of her maternal grandparents. She recognizes that the fingerspelling of names corresponds with the letters of the alphabet and can spell these names out loud when asked to do so. The concept of spelling was introduced very early to my daughters through the role fingerspelling plays in sign language. Erin and Kaylee could spell their names at age two, an unusual feat among their monolingual hearing friends.

If Kaylee doesn't know a sign for something she wants to communicate, she often does what I call "fingerbabble." She moves her fingers as if she is fingerspelling a word but no distinct letters are evident. To the nonsigner, it may appear as though she is communicating quite effectively. She gets frustrated when Ken can't understand these finger movements. Of course, Ken becomes frustrated too. Erin currently uses a lot of fingerspelling in her use of sign language. It may be that Kaylee sees this and is attempting to emulate that behavior.

Erin began using fingerspelling with much more frequency around age four. Some friends were visiting around Christmas of that year. Erin told us the story of the three wise men. She fingerspelled the words B-E-T-H-L-E-H-E-M and M-A-N-G-E-R. This seemed to us to be an impressive feat for a four-year-old. The spelling was not completely accurate but close enough for the Deaf observers to understand the message. After noting this incident, we began to watch for additional use of fingerspelling. It fascinated us that Erin was fingerspelling these complex words. In addition, the fluency of her fingerspelling made it clear she was not sounding out the words in her head prior to fingerspelling them. We thought perhaps she was fingerspelling words that she had frequently seen fingerspelled and that explained her unique ability. Then we observed her fingerspelling words that she probably had never seen fingerspelled before. When we asked her to spell on paper a word that she had just fingerspelled with amazing accuracy, her response would be, "I dunno how to spell *that!*"

Erin began using fingerspelling with much more frequency in her signing around age five and continues to do this, even at age seven. Even though she knows the correct sign usage, she often chooses to fingerspell words rather than sign them. We have no explanation for this, but the answer may lie in the parallel between her reading development and increased use of fingerspelling.

Person–Language Bond

An interesting phenomenon started to occur with both of my daughters at age two. With my first daughter, Erin, whenever I signed to her rather than spoke, her response would be an emphatic, "Mommy! *talk* to me!" With no explanation for this odd behavior, we were left to guess at the reasons for her rejecting my use of sign language. What I discovered after reading about bilingualism was that a perfectly logical explanation exists for this common phenomenon in bilingual children. The bilingual literature (Grosjean, 1982) identifies it as the person–language bond, where the child associates a particular language with a particular person and expects that person to use that language only. I am the English speaker, Ken is the ASL signer. It was interesting to see how firmly entrenched this was in Erin's mind and her reaction when the person–language bond was broken. Her response was not to answer me unless I used the appropriate language for me—English.

This phenomenon became evident with Kaylee at age two as well. The first time we recognized it, we were sitting at the kitchen table and she wanted my attention. She said "Mommy!" I looked right at her and used the facial expression appropriate in sign language to indicate I was attending. She continued repeating "Mommy" until I said "What?" Even though she responds to Ken in sign language when he uses this facial expression to indicate he is attending, she wanted appropriate spoken English from me. Now, at age three, when I sign, she says, "Mommy, I can't *hear* you."

The person–language bond continued to be strong for Erin at age three. At the dinner table, she would tell me something in English, then repeat the same idea to Ken in sign language. She was repeating everything twice, once in English, once in ASL. Even though I repeatedly reminded her that she could just sign something once and we both would understand her, she continually communicated things in two languages. She would even go so far as to tell me in English what Ken signed to her, as if I didn't understand him!

At age five, the person–language bond was less strong but still quite evident. Sometimes Erin would want to tell me something, and she would start talking to me in the presence of Ken. Upon my reminding her to sign rather than talk so that her father could comprehend, she would do so, but then she would look at Ken as she signed rather than look at me.

Sometimes her response to our request to sign would be, "But I want to tell Mommy!" This translates into: "If I'm telling Mommy something I'll use *Her* language. If I want to tell Daddy, I'll use *His* language." At this age she seemed to have developed more confidence in my ability to comprehend sign language, because the number of times that she communicated everything twice had diminished considerably.

Now at age seven, the person–language bond is much less evident. Erin now signs to me frequently and responds to me in either spoken English or ASL. She can effectively communicate in either language.

Our Children's Biculturalism

Grosjean (1982) defines biculturalism as "the coexistence and/or combination of two distinct cultures" (p. 157). Living in a bicultural environment is the norm for us as a family. It is not something we discuss, it just is. Kaylee knows that in order to communicate with her dad, she has to get his attention by tapping him or banging on the table, something she has been doing since she could crawl. No one told her she had to do this, she just observed these behaviors and copied them. I don't believe she connects these behaviors with the fact that her dad can't hear. The first time Kaylee actually figured out that her dad can't hear was at age two. She was yelling "Daddy, Daddy" while she was in one room and Ken was in another. After getting no response she said to me in yet another room, "Mommy, Daddy can't listen to me!" She now understands that Ken can't hear and takes it upon herself to interpret noises in the house such as the stove timer or the doorbell.

Although we don't talk about what it means to be Deaf, it is always interesting to get a glimpse into our daughters' thinking by verbal comments and behaviors they exhibit. We don't talk about who among our friends is Deaf and who is hearing, but the girls have always figured it out and used the appropriate language. Even when Kaylee plays "telephone," if she is calling a friend who is Deaf, she puts the telephone receiver on the TTY.

One evening at the supper table, when Kaylee was approximately three months old, Erin asked very seriously, "Do you think Kaylee is deaf or hearing?" It was quite evident to me that she was hearing, so I chuckled and replied that of course she was hearing. Erin again replied very seriously, "I don't think so. She doesn't talk." In her world, if you didn't talk, it only meant one thing: you were Deaf.

I recently posed a hypothetical question to Erin to get a feel for her perception of what it means to be Deaf. Because deafness can be viewed from a pathological or cultural perspective and because we never discuss the issue, I was curious about what she had to say. I told her a Martian had just landed on earth and had never encountered a Deaf person before. I asked her how she would describe to this Martian what it means to be Deaf. Her response was enlightening. Erin said, "They sign. They can't talk . . . well . . . they can talk but they don't unless they are at home or with people they know well. They go to church with other Deaf people with a priest who signs like them. They *Can* drive [with sarcasm], they watch TV, all that stuff and they use captioning. That's it!"

I was amazed and thrilled with her response. She describes the cultural definition of Deaf people, the view Deaf people have of themselves. Erin begins her description with the most important and unifying feature of the culture, which is their language. She includes the concept of community when she suggests Deaf people go to a church for Deaf people. Erin goes on to say, "They *Can* drive, they watch TV." She is responding to a common myth about Deaf people that she has been exposed to at some point, that Deaf people can't drive. She is also identifying Deaf people as "normal" people who do "normal" things. Most importantly, she never mentions the fact that Deaf people can't hear. Living in a bilingual-bicultural environment, she realizes that Deaf people can't hear but that the essence of being Deaf isn't the lack of hearing.

Conclusion

I have come to embrace the terms "bilingual" and "bicultural" in describing my family. I am very grateful for having had the opportunity in this chapter to delve into the issues of a deaf/hearing marriage and raising children with two languages. Grosjean's book and the thinking I have done have given me a new way to articulate my perspective on these issues. The positive connotations of the terms "bilingual" and "bicultural" much better describe the positive experience we have had in living in a home with two languages and cultures. Being bilingual and bicultural is an integral part of our family and adds a unique dimension to our lives. My initial perception about the biggest difference between Ken and me is also resolved. He is now Catholic!

Acknowledgments

I would like to thank my family for their encouragement in sharing our story and to thank the many friends and colleagues who read the manuscript and provided feedback.

Reference

Grosjean, F. (1982). *Life with two languages: An introduction to bilingualism.* Cambridge, MA: Harvard University Press.

6

■ Autism is defined as a developmental disorder that includes three primary features (American Psychiatric Association, 1994). First, there is social impairment, such as lacking eye-to-eye gaze, or lack of social-emotional reciprocity. Second, there is communicative impairment, such as delayed language development, or poor ability to initiate or sustain conversation. Finally, there are restricted repetitive and stereotypic patterns of behavior, such as inflexible adherence to specific nonfunctional rituals. Autism is evident before 3 years of age, when children show delayed or abnormal social interaction, language, or symbolic imaginative play. Many theories have been advanced regarding its etiology. In recent years, scholars have become excited by theories suggesting that a deficit in a Theory of Mind module, or in cognitive executive functioning, or in social-orienting skills may underlie this mysterious disorder.

The authors of this article propose that "a developmental and dynamic systems perspective" may be important in understanding the social and communicative deficits in autism. They emphasize throughout the article that the functioning of the developing brain underlies the child's ability to interact with the social environment and is in turn shaped by those interchanges; that these reciprocally influence one another. By observing the deficits that appear when the system breaks down, we can learn about how it normally develops.

Overview Questions

1. What communicative and language skills are impaired in children with autism? What areas of the brain appear to be focal points for these types of social-communicative impairments?

2. What are Theory of Mind and executive functioning? Explain in your own words why some people believe that each of these is responsible for the social and communicative deficits of autism.

3. Explain in your own words how an early disturbance of social orienting could influence the development of a) Theory of Mind and b) executive functioning. With these in mind, explain/give an example in your own words of how "the dynamic interplay between initial biological insult and subsequent transactions with the environment may be crucial to an understanding of autism."

Focus Questions

1. What is metarepresentation, and how is it thought to be responsible for the social deficits of autism? Briefly describe a false belief test and explain why this involves metarepresentation. Give three reasons why the social deficits of autism might be due to a modular (i.e., specialized, neurologically-based) social-cognitive process.

2. Executive functions enable people to do what three things? Why do some people believe that difficulties people with autism have on false belief tasks are due to executive function problems? The left medial frontal gyrus has been linked to what Theory of Mind task and what executive functioning task? What are four problems with executive functioning as an explanation of the social-communicative problems of autism?

3. List four pieces of evidence regarding the joint attention deficits in children with autism. Give four pieces of evidence indicating a social-orienting deficit in children with autism.

On the Nature of Communication and Language Impairment in Autism

Peter Mundy and Jessica Markus

The social and communication disturbance of autism is characterized by a syndrome-specific pattern of strengths and weaknesses, rather than a pervasive lack of responsiveness to others. In children with language, this pattern is manifest as relatively well-developed phonological, syntactic, and semantic facilities, but impaired or deviant pragmatic capacities. In preverbal children, communication for instrumental or attachment functions may be observed, but joint attention, as well as other more purely socially oriented bids, are often lacking. Three neuropsychological models have been proposed that explicitly address elements of this pattern of social communication disturbance in autism. These models differ in the mechanisms of impairment proposed to explain the social-communication disturbance of autism. Nevertheless, these models converge to suggest that the specific pattern of social communication disturbance displayed in autism results from a dysfunction that involves frontal neurological processes. A discussion of the similarities and differences among these models is presented. In the final analysis, this discussion leads to two conclusions. First, it may be necessary to adopt a developmental and dynamic systems perspective to gain a complete understanding of the complexities of the social-communication pathology of autism. Second, the study of autism raises many important observations and hypotheses regarding the ontogeny of the quintessential human capacity for communication and social cognition.

Autism is a pernicious and biologically based disorder that is characterized by impaired social development [Kanner, 1943; Bailey et al., 1996]. It may be more prevalent than once thought, occurring at a rate of 1:1000 [Bryson, 1996]. Also, rather than displaying a "pervasive lack of responsiveness to others" [APA, 1980], it is now understood that people with autism display a *pattern of strengths and weaknesses* in the acquisition of social and communication skills, which changes with development [Mundy and Sigman, 1989a].

In preverbal children, the communication disturbance of autism is exemplified by a robust failure to adequately develop joint attention skills. These skills involve the tendency to use eye contact, affect, and gestures for the singularly social purpose of sharing experiences with others. Prototypical of joint attention behavior is the act of pointing or showing to share one's pleasure in a toy. Alternatively, less impaired is the use of eye contact and gestures to regulate the behavior of others is more instrumental. These behaviors include requesting aid in obtaining objects, or even displaying attachment-reunion behaviors after a caregiver separation [Curcio, 1978; Loveland and Landry, 1986: Mundy et al., 1986; Sigman and Mundy, 1989; Wetherby and Prutting, 1984].

In children with functional speech skills, the processes that enable adequate phonological, syntactic, and semantic usage of language may only be mildly impaired [Volden and Lord, 1991]. Alternatively, a disturbance of the pragmatics of language usage is a prominent feature of autism [Eales, 1993; Happe, 1993; Surian et al., 1996; Tager-Flusberg, 1993]. The pragmatics of language refers to a broad array of skills involved in prosody, appropriate turn-taking, politeness, and topic maintenance in conversation. Pragmatics also involves the critical ability to signal and interpret unspoken premises, as with figures of speech (e.g., metaphor), or with nonverbal behaviors or by relying on the context of a communicative interaction.

This brief synopsis indicates that a comprehensive model of autism will ultimately need to address both linguistic pragmatic difficulties and the very early onset of preverbal social-communication deficits that are characteristic of the syndrome. In the course of debate necessary to develop this model, fundamental issues must be raised and examined. These issues concern not only autism but also the nature of the ontogeny of the human capacity for complex social-communication. Two of these issues will be highlighted in this review.

The first issue concerns the nature of the neurological disturbance that leads to the social-communication disturbance of autism. The current status of the neuroscience of social behavior is not sufficiently well articulated to allow anything but an oversimplified modeling of this neurological impairment. Nevertheless, animal and human lesion studies suggest that neurological functions associated primarily with frontal cortical and medial temporal systems are likely foci for the types of social-communication disturbance displayed by individuals with autism [e.g., Damasio and Maurer, 1978; Bachevalier, 1994; Dawson, 1996; Pennington and Osonoff, 1996; Minshew, 1996; Mundy, 1995]. Of course, there is considerable debate as to whether functional disturbances of these systems are primary in the etiology of autism, or secondary upstream effects of impaired functions in more caudal brain systems [Courchesne et al., 1994; Damasio and Maurer, 1978].

The second issue concerns the functional, or psychological, nature of the neurological disturbance in autism. Three prominent models propose to account for the social-communication disturbance of autism, while sharing a common focus on frontal processes. These include the Theory of Mind model, the Executive Function model, and the Social Orientation model. The Theory of Mind (ToM) model suggests that one aspect of the frontal process may be dedicated to a facility for social cognition necessary to estimating the psychological status of others, such as their beliefs. According to this model, the social-communication disturbance of autism may be understood in terms of an impairment in the functions of this system [Baron-Cohen et al., 1994].

The Executive Function model suggests that social-cognitive and social-communication impairment in autism does not derive from a system dedicated to social cognition. Rather, the social-communication disturbance of autism is viewed as one manifestation of an impairment in frontally mediated executive cognitive structures. The fundamental function of these is to select appropriate goal-directed actions from an array of competing action potentials [Pennington and Ozonoff, 1996].

A critical assumption of a third model is that the earliest forms of social-communication impairment of autism may not be completely understood in terms of either of the cognitive mechanisms espoused in the Theory of Mind or Executive Function models. The Social Orienting model suggests that, prior to the emergence of cognition as the primary regulator of behavior, frontally mediated neuroaffective motivation systems serve to prioritize social information processing in human development. A deficit in these systems is thought to contribute to initial, as well as subsequent, social and cognitive disturbances in autism [e.g., Dawson and Lewy, 1989; Fotheringham, 1991; Hobson, 1993; Mundy, 1995].

Each model provides a different and valuable perspective on the nature of autism, and on social-communication skill acquisition more generally. In the remainder of this essay we will provide an overview of the similarities and differences among these models. We also note that a collective view of these models gives rise to a consideration of how related neurological processes may serve different functions at different stages in the development of autism.

Theory of Mind and Social-Communication Disturbance in Autism

Consider a possible newspaper headline, "IRAQI HEAD SEEKS ARMS" [Pinker, 1994]. Language development alone does not allow for the correct interpretation of this statement. Rather, some cognitive, pragmatic facility that goes beyond neural systems specific to the grammar of language development is assumed to play a role in correctly conveying and recognizing the ambiguous communicative intentions that are frequently embedded in language [Pinker, 1994].

Children with autism display a poor facility for the pragmatics of language [Frith, 1989]. To understand this feature of autism, some have turned to theory and research on the nature of social cognition. The capacity for social cognition may be an important, if not defining, feature of primate, and especially human, neurobehavioral evolution [Cosmides, 1989; Whiten and Byrne, 1988]. In keeping with this evolutionary psychological view, a modular perspective on cognition has been adapted to suggest that the capacity to understand mental states in others follows its own proprietary developmental course, with brain mechanisms responsible for apprehending mental states separate from brain mechanisms related to non-social cognition [e.g., Leslie and Thaiss, 1992; Baron-Cohen, 1995]. This dedicated socioneurocognitive mechanism has various descriptions [Baron-Cohen, 1995], but will be referred to here as the Theory of Mind (ToM) module [Leslie, 1987].

Hypothetically, the ToM module employs a special type of cognition called metarepresentation. Metarepresentational ability allows one to mentally depict the psychological status of others, such as their thoughts and beliefs. It is called metarepresentation because it involves the capacity to cognitively represent the mental representations of others. Metarepresentation also involves a critical "decoupling" mechanism that enables the child to keep cognitive representations organized so that their own thoughts and feelings can be easily distinguished from representations of others' thoughts and feelings [see Leslie, 1987, 1993 for details]. According to the ToM model, a disturbance in this type of representational thought process gives rise to the social and pragmatic deficits of people with autism [Baron-Cohen, 1995; Frith, 1989; Leslie, 1987; Tager-Flusberg, 1993]. The logic here is that, if children with autism have difficulty thinking about others' psychological status, correctly identifying the communicative intent of the author of the headline "Iraqi Head Seeks Arms" would be unlikely. A host of other types of pragmatic errors would also be evident, such as difficulties with understanding figures of speech (e.g., irony), or difficulty in gauging the timing constraints of discourse, or difficulty in gauging the informational needs of others, as well as conventions of topic maintenance. According to the ToM, most if not all of the social deficits of autism may be understood in terms of this type of social-cognitive disturbance [Baron-Cohen, 1995].

Numerous experimental studies support the hypothesis that children with autism have difficulty on theory of mind measures [Baron-Cohen, 1995]. In the prototypical "false-belief paradigm," a child is asked to watch an agent ("Sally") hide an object in one of two hiding places (Place 1 vs. Place 2). Sally then leaves the room and another agent ("Anne") moves the object from Place 1 to Place 2. When Sally returns, the child must answer the question, "Where will Sally look for the object?" To answer this question correctly the child must disregard his/her own knowledge of where the object really is (Place 2) and *think about where Sally thinks* the object is (the putative metarepresentational component of this task has been italicized). Children typically develop the ability to solve this type of problem between 3–5 years of age. However, people with autism manifest robust difficulty with false-belief and related ToM tasks relative to language- and IQ-matched controls. Theoretically, this is because they lack the requisite metarepresentational cognitive functions required to think about others' thoughts [Leslie, 1987].

The argument for the modularity, or the dedicated nature of this type of social-cognitive process, has been made on numerous grounds [Leslie, 1993]. The most important observation may be that representational deficits are more likely to be manifest by children with autism on social-cognitive tasks, rather than analogous nonsocial-cognitive tasks [e.g., Leekam and Perner, 1991; Leslie and Thaiss, 1992; Scott and Baron-Cohen, 1996]. Two other findings are of critical importance. First, ToM-related ability has been directly linked to the degree to which pragmatic skill deficits are displayed among people with autism [Happe, 1993; Surian et al., 1996]. Second, specific neural subsystems may be involved in thinking about the thoughts, beliefs, and feelings of others [Baron-Cohen et al., 1994; Fletcher et al., 1995].

The first of these studies utilized single photon emission computerized tomography (SPECT) data and suggested that the right orbital frontal region may be involved in the processing of mental state turns [Baron-Cohen et al., 1994]. The second study presented actual ToM tasks and employed functional neuroimaging during task engagement [Fletcher et al., 1995]. In this study, six male volunteers were presented with ToM stories in which they were asked to think of the answer to questions about the internal motivations, beliefs, or thoughts of the protagonists. They were also presented with stories that required them to think of the answer to questions about causality of physical events and to answer questions about sequences of unrelated sentences. The results indicated that thinking about the answers to the ToM vignettes involved cortical activity in the left medial frontal gyrus (Brodmann's area 8) to a significantly greater extent than did thinking about the answers to the physical stories or unrelated sentence questions [Fletcher et al., 1995]. Interestingly, the authors observed that this area had been linked in comparative and human studies to facility with conditional learning [Petrides, 1990]. The potential importance of the latter observation will be made clear in the discussion of the Executive Function model.

The ToM model is seminal to the current understanding of language and communication disturbance in autism. It has been directly linked to the significant phenomenon of pragmatic communication disturbance in this syndrome. Moreover, preliminary data on the brain mechanisms that may be specific to ToM functions has also been presented. However, several problems arise with this model. Recent research suggests that ToM tasks deficits may not be as specific to autism as once thought [Peterson and Siegal, 1995; Yirmiya and Shulman, 1996]. It is also debatable whether or not the ToM model can explain deficits in the early forms of social-communication disturbance displayed by children with autism [Leslie and Happe, 1989; Mundy and Sigman, 1989b]. Furthermore, it is not clear if the ToM model can explain a class of phenomena referred to as executive function deficits in autism [Bishop, 1993; Pennington and Ozonoff, 1996]. Alternatively, executive function deficits may contribute to an explanation of difficulties in ToM functions, as well as pragmatic communication disturbance, in people with autism [Hughes and Russell, 1993; Ozonoff, 1995; Pennington and Ozonof, 1996].

Executive Functions and Social-Communication Disturbance

A critical difference between the Executive Function model and the ToM model is that the fundamental disturbance of autism is not considered to be specific to a neurologically dedicated system for social cognition. Rather, a more general cognitive disturbance in so-called executive functions is viewed as central to autism. Executive functions are thought to involve a system of frontal neurological processes that are behaviorally manifest in the related capacities to: 1) initiate behaviors while inhibiting competing responses which may interfere with effective problem solving; 2) regulate attention in order to filter distractions during problem solving and shift attention across relevant stimulus components; and 3) upload and manipulate mental representations to bring them to bear in a task-effective fashion [Pennington and Ozonoff, 1996; Ozonoff, 1995]. Central to the executive functions is the notion of appropriate action selection in the face of competing, but context-inappropriate responses. Action selection is thought to be dependent on the integration of behavioral constraint and activation parameters that flow from memory, perception, and affective or motivation systems [Pennington and Ozonoff, 1996].

Studies indicate that people with autism display difficulties with appropriate action selection in the face of competing response potentials [Hughes and Russell, 1993; see Pennington and Ozonoff, 1996, for review]. Moreover, several researchers have argued that, instead of a disturbance in a ToM module, autistic difficulties on false belief and related social-cognitive tasks may be explained in terms of this type of more general executive function difficulty [Pennington and Ozonoff, 1996; Hughes and Russell, 1993; Frye et al., 1995].

For example, recall that to solve the Sally–Anne false–belief task the child must *disregard their own knowledge* of where the object really is (Place 2), and *think about where Sally thinks* the object is (notice that we have now italicized two operations in this task sequence, the first associated with inhibiting a competing response, and the second associated with metarepresentation). The Executive Function model suggests that children with autism have difficulty with the former, and fail false belief and related social-cognitive tasks because of this difficulty. Similarly, they may be unable to correctly interpret the statement "Iraqi Head Seeks Arms" because they cannot disregard the false literal meaning in favor of the correct nonliteral inference. A key diagnostic feature of autism that involves the singular pursuit of a limited, idiosyncratic set of interests may also be explained in terms of the executive function disturbance of this model [Hughes and Russell, 1993; Ozonoff, 1995].

A recent study has, in fact, suggested that the normal course of ToM development is associated with executive function development. Frye et al. [1995] demonstrated that, in normal 3–5-year-olds, performance on a nonsocial sorting task that measured the ability to select appropriate actions in the face of competing responses was significantly correlated with the development of ToM in the form of false-belief task performance. In addition to being consistent with the Executive Function model, this observation is intriguing for another reason. A link exists between the type of executive function isolated in the work of Frye et al. [1995] and the neurological concomitants of ToM performance. Recall that ToM Performance was linked to activity in left medial frontal circuits (Brodmann's area 8; [Fletcher et al., 1995]). Fletcher et al. [1995] also noted that Petrides [1990] had connected activity in this subsystem to conditional associate learning. The primary task demand of this type of learning is the capacity to inhibit competing responses in order to efficiently solve a problem. Indeed, the task used by Petrides [1990] was very similar to the task employed by Frye et al. [1995]. Thus, the neurological linkage between frontal processes and ToM performance observed by Fletcher et al. [1995] may overlap with frontal correlates of the types of processes that are central to the Executive Function model.

The Executive Function model poses a reasonable alternative to the ToM model of autistic social-cognitive and social-communication pathology. This model, however, may have difficulty explaining the observation that children with autism manage nonsocial representational tasks better than analogous false-belief tasks

[Leslie, 1993]. It may also have difficulty explaining why children with autism display even more basic social-cognitive difficulties, such as more difficulty using mental as opposed to physical state words [Baron-Cohen et al., 1994; Tager-Flusberg, 1993]. Furthermore, while executive function tasks may be correlated with ToM tasks, they do not explain all of the variability in the latter [Frye et al., 1995]. Also, some people with pervasive developmental disorders may display executive function disturbance, but not ToM disturbance [Ozonoff, 1995]. These observations suggest that an executive function disturbance and a ToM impairment may have partially independent paths of effects on the poor social-communication skills of autism. Thus, a combination of the Executive Function and ToM models provides a clearer picture of the social-communication disturbance of autism. It is unlikely, though, that even a combination of these compelling models may provide a complete explanation of the earliest forms of social-communication disturbance observed in autism.

Social Orienting and Social-Communication Disturbance in Autism

Recall that preverbal children with autism display a deficit in joint attention skills, but not in more instrumental social-communication behaviors, such as those involved in requesting or attachment. For example, children with autism will rarely use eye contact and gestures such as showing or pointing to share attention regarding an active wind-up toy. If the toy is moved out of reach, though, they will be as likely to use eye contact and pointing to elicit aid obtaining the object as will comparison children [e.g., Mundy et al., 1994].

This seemingly simple observation may be fundamental to an understanding of autism. Joint attention behaviors reflect the tendency of children to socially orient while engaged in observing an object or event in order to share their experience of the object or event with others [Mundy, 1995]. This capacity normally emerges between 6–12 months. Thus, observations of joint attention impairment in autism suggest that the pathological processes fundamental to this disorder may be manifestly active in the first year of life [Mundy and Sigman, 1989b]. Consistent with this notion, first birthday videotape data suggests that 12-month-old children with autism display evidence of a disturbance in joint attention and social orienting [Osterling and Dawson, 1994]. Measures of joint attention skills have also contributed to the very early identification of autism at 18 months to a sample of 16,000 children [Baron-Cohen et al., 1996].

Several other observations attest to the importance of joint attention deficits. These deficits are observed in young children regardless of IQ, and are related to parents' reports of symptom intensity [Mundy et al., 1994]. Individual differences in joint attention skill development also appear to be singularly powerful in predicting language development among these children [Mundy et al., 1990; Sigman and Ruskin, 1997]. Indeed, joint attention skill development is considered to be integral to language, social, and cognitive development among all children [Tomasello, 1995], not just children with autism. For example, joint attention skills have been observed to predict language development from as early as 6 months of age [Morales et al., 1997], and to predict individual differences in childhood IQ from 13 months of age [Ulvund and Smith, 1996].

Attempts have been made to explain joint attention disturbance in terms of ToM dysfunction [Baron-Cohen, 1995; Leslie and Happe, 1989], or cognitive executive functions [McEvoy et al., 1993]. However, with evidence of the emergence of this domain in the first year of life, it may be less than parsimonious to explain impairments in such an early emerging facet of behavior solely in terms of later developing, complex cognitive functions. Alternatively, several researchers have suggested that joint attention deficits may be understood as part of a fundamental social-approach, or social-orienting impairment [Dawson and Lewy, 1989; Hobson, 1993; Fotheringham, 1991; Mundy, 1995]. These models vary in the hypothesized mechanisms of impairment. Yet they agree that a primary social-orienting impairment may have enormous ramifications for the subsequent development of social, cognitive, and even neurological disturbance in autism. To illustrate this point, consider the basic assumptions of one of these social-orienting models [Mundy, 1995; Mundy and Crowson, in press; Mundy et al., 1993].

Like the ToM and Executive Function models, it is assumed that the social communication pathology of autism, including joint attention disturbance, derives in part from neurological impairment that involves frontal cortical processes. Three studies, using EEG [Card et al., 1997], PET imaging [Caplan et al., 1993], and behavioral measures [McEvoy et al., 1993] have directly linked joint attention development to frontal processes. It is also assumed, though, that frontal systems may play different functional roles at different points in development. In particular, the types of functions proposed by the ToM and Executive Function models are thought to require a degree of cognitive maturation and information acquisition that is not likely to be available in the first 12 to 18 months of life.

Alternatively, in the terminology of the Executive Function model [Pennington and Rogers, 1996], early in life, frontal action selection functions may be more dependent on behavioral constraint and activation parameters that flow from affective and motivational parameters, as opposed to cognitive-memory parameters. That is, prior to the effects of more cognitive constraint parameters, frontally mediated action selection is constrained by a motivational executive system that serves to prioritize perceptual inputs that are most significant to the development of the infant [Derryberry and Reed, 1996; Mundy, 1995; Tucker, 1992]. In particular, this system prioritizes social perceptual input and social information processing, via social orienting, from early on in the development of the child. One mechanism of this prioritization may involve the attribution of positive valence to the perception of social information, possibly by way of temporal/midbrain systems involving the amygdala [LeDoux, 1989], as well as brainstem nuclei (e.g. nucleus ambiguous [Derryberry and Reed, 1996]).

Several studies provide evidence for a basic social-orienting disturbance in autism. Klin [1991] has reported that the typical preference for speech and speech-like sounds, which is usually displayed by infants in the first months of life, was not present in any of the children with autism he observed. It was, however, present in all of the developmentally delayed matched controls observed in this study.

In an even more intriguing study, Dawson et al. [1995a] examined the degree to which children with autism, Down syndrome, or normal development oriented (displayed a head turn) toward social stimuli (clapping hands or calling the child's name) and two nonsocial stimuli (playing a musical jack-in-the-box or shaking a rattle). The results indicated that the children with autism more often failed to orient to both types of stimuli. Their failure to orient to social stimuli, however, was significantly more extreme than their impaired orienting to nonsocial stimuli. Furthermore, individual differences in difficulty with social orienting, but not object-orienting, were significantly related to a measure of joint attention among the children with autism. A disturbance in social orienting among children with autism has also been observed in first birthday videotape data [Osterling and Dawson, 1994]. Finally, individual differences in social orienting have long-term stability and predict the degree to which children with autism process the nonverbal affective information presented by others [Dissanayake et al., 1996]. In addition to providing some support for a social-orienting impairment model, these observations may not be easily explained in terms of current ToM or Executive Function models [see Baron-Cohen, 1995 for an alternative view].

What might the ramifications of an early social-orienting disturbance be? Another assumption of the model is that experience drives a substantial portion of postnatal brain development. This occurs through the competitive enhancement of active neural connections and the culling of less active connections [Huttenlocher, 1995]. We also assume that, to some degree, the human neural behavioral system is self-organizing. One component of this self-organizing system is the aforementioned prioritization of social information processing. This drives the early developing neuroarchitecture along paths that normally emphasize social-cognitive development [Cosmides, 1989]. In the child with autism, however, the lack of this self-organizing feature leads to increasingly deviant development of neurobehavioral systems over time. Thus, autism may be characterized by primary neurobiological deficits, which lead to less than optimal behavioral proclivities in the first months of life (e.g., a lack of early social orienting). These, in turn, lead to a secondary neurological disturbance via a negative feedback system. In this system, the lack of social orienting and social information processing contributes to a dynamic alteration of the typical, experience-driven mechanisms of neural activation and culling. Hence, the lack of early social orienting and processing contributes to subsequent disruptions of neurobehavioral development [Mundy and Crowson, in press].

In this model, joint attention skill measures are viewed as a sensitive index of social-orienting disturbance. Hence, one aspect of autistic social-communication pathology (i.e., joint attention deficits) may be traced directly to this hypothesized social-orienting disturbance [Mundy, 1995]. It is not clear, though, whether all subsequent executive function, social-cognitive, and social-communication deficits flow directly from this early source. Nevertheless, some interesting hypotheses follow from this model.

Frontally mediated social-orienting processes may contribute to the observation that autistic children vary from aloof to active but odd in their social communication style. Dawson et al. [1995b] have reported that variability in frontal activity (EEG power) was related to these social style differences among people with autism. Another observation that the social-orienting disturbance in autism is most severe in the preschool years may be linked to the observation of a transient component of frontal metabolic activity disturbance, which improves between the ages of 6–7 in children with autism [Zilbovicius et al., 1995]. Hence, there may be an early critical period for the process involved in social orienting impairment in autism. This possibility may be important in considering recent reports of positive early intervention effects with autism [Mundy and Crowson, in press].

It is also likely that an early disturbance of social orienting could influence executive function and ToM development. With regard to the former, perhaps the frontal executive motivation system that prioritizes orienting to social stimuli *primes* the development of the more general executive capacity to engage action selection in the face of competing response potentials. Presumably, early in life infants are frequently confronted with a choice between attending to competing social exteroceptive stimuli, nonsocial exteroceptive, and/or proprioceptive stimuli. It may be that the activation of an intrinsically motivated social-orienting system yields, as an important by-product, early practice (hence neuro-organization) associated with selecting an action (social orienting) in the face of exteroceptive and proprioceptive stimuli that compete for attention. Without such practice contributing to adequate neural self-organization, the later-emerging cognitive executive functions of the frontal system may not develop normally in children with autism [see Hughes and Russell, 1993, for an alternative hypothesis].

Similarly, it may be that a relative failure to process social information early on gives rise to a cognitive system that has insufficient information and experience to develop facility with ToM functions and social cognition [Mundy et al., 1993; Mundy, 1995]. Indeed, recent research with sensory-impaired children strongly suggests that sufficient social input is required for typical ToM development as measured on false-belief tasks [Peterson and Siegal, 1995]. Moreover, a disturbance of joint attention development, secondary to a social-orienting impairment, may deprive children with autism of early, critical social interactive experiences. Theoretically, the negative feedback of such a loss during a critical period of cognitive development may distort typical symbolic and social cognitive development [Mundy et al., 1993], as well as contribute to the language delays symptomatic of this syndrome [Mundy et al., 1990; Sigman and Ruskin, 1997]. Finally, we have hypothesized that attenuated social orienting may be associated with a reciprocal augmentation of nonsocial information processing in autism. Such a reciprocal function may assist in explaining the relative success of people with autism in nonsocial problem-solving situations [Mundy, 1995].

Conclusions

Researchers in psychopathology typically agree that models that identify a single cause for abnormal behavior are likely to be incomplete [Cicchetti, 1993]. This is not to say that single-factor models are not valuable. The value of single-factor models, however, may only be truly realized when they are synthesized to yield a more divergent, rather than convergent, perspective on the processes involved in the ontology of pathology. This is clearly the case with respect to the state of research on autism. It is abundantly clear that higher-order cognitive dysfunctions play a critical role in autism [Minshew, 1996]. In particular, at this time both an executive function disturbance and a form of higher-order representational impairment appear to be linked to the social, pragmatic disturbance of communication that is characteristic of the older child with autism [Leslie, 1993; Ozonoff, 1995]. Furthermore, these impairments may be linked to functions of the frontal systems [Baron-Cohen et al., 1994; Fletcher et al., 1995]. A complete understanding of the nature of this linkage, however, may not be clear unless the earliest manifest forms of social-communication disturbance in autism are considered. These joint attention and social-orienting difficulties may also be related to an impairment involving frontal systems. It is unlikely, though, that these ontogenetically primary impairments may be explained simply by way of recourse to the constructs used to explain later-emerging cognitive deficits in autism. Instead, these early-emerging deficits challenge researchers to adopt a more developmental and dynamic systems approach to understanding the nature of autism. Such a perspective reminds us that the behavioral function of a neurological subsystem may change over development. Moreover, a sufficiently powerful disturbance of early behavior may in and of itself lead to subsequent disturbance in neurological and neurobehavioral development. Thus, a consideration of the dynamic interplay between initial biological insult and subsequent transactions with the environment may be crucial to an understanding of autism. It may also be that an understanding of autism will play a critical role in acquiring a better understanding of the complex dance that occurs between neural development and environmental constraint in the ontogeny of the quintessential human capacity for social communication and cognition.

References

American Psychiatric Association. *Diagnostic and statistical manual on mental disorders.* 3rd ed. Washington, DC: APA Press, 1980.

Bachevailer, J. Medial temporal lobe auras and autism: a review of clinical and experimental findings. *Neuropsychologia* 1994;32:627–648.

Bailey A, Philips W, Rutter M. Autism: towards an integration of clinical, genetic, neuropsychological, and neurobiological perspectives. *J Child Psychol Psychiatry* 1996;37:89–126.

Baron-Cohen S. Mindblindness. Cambridge, MA: MIT Press, 1995.

Baron-Cohen S, Ring H, Moriarty J, et al. Recognition of mental state terms: clinical findings in children with autism and a functional neuroimaging study of normal adults. *Br J Psychiatry* 1994; 165:640–649.

Baron-Cohen S, Cox A, Baird G, et al. Psychological markers in the detection of autism in infancy in a large population. *Br J Psychiatry* 1996; 168:158–163.

Bishop D. Annotation: autism, executive functions and theory of mind: a neuropsychological perspective. *J Child Psychol Psychiatry* 1993; 34:279–293.

Bryson S. Brief report: epidemiology of autism. *J Autism Dev Disord* 1996;26:165–168.

Caplan R, Chugani H, Messa C. at al. Hemispherectomy for early onset intractable seizures: presurgical cerebral glucose metabolism and postsurgical nonverbal communication patterns. *Dev Med Child Neurol* 1993;35:582–592.

Card J, Schmidt L, Mundy P. *Frontal EEG social communication to 16-month-old toddlers.* Paper presented at the Society for Research in Child Development. Washington, DC, 1997.

Cicchetti D. Developmental psychopathology: reactions, reflections, projections. *Dev Rev* 1993; 13:471–502.

Cosmides L. The logic of social exchange: has natural selection shaped how humans reason? Studies with the Wason selection task. *Cognition* 1989;31:187–276.

Courchesne E, Chisum H, Townsend J. Neural activity-dependent brain changes in development: implications for psychopathology. *Dev Psychopathol* 1994;6:697–722.

Curcio F. Sensorimotor functioning and cormmmication in mute autistic children. *J Autism Child Schizophr* 1978;8:282–292.

Damasio A, Maurer R. A neurological model of childhood autism. *Arch Neurol* 1978; 35:777–786.

Dawson G. Brief report: neuropsychology of autism: a report of the state of the science. *J Autism Dev Disord* 1996;26:179–184.

Dawson G, Lewy A. *Arousal attention, and the social-emotional impairments of individuals with autism.* In: Dawson G (ed): Autism, nature, diagnosis and treatment. New York: Guilford, 1989:49–74.

Dawson G. Meltzoff A, Osterling J. *Children with autism fail to orient to naturally occurring social stimuli.* Paper presented at the Society for Research in Child Development, Indianapolis, IN, 1995a.

Dawson G, Klinger L, Panagiotides H, et al. Subgroups of autistic children based on social behavior display distinct patterns of brain activity. *J Abnorm Child Psychol* 1995b; 23:569–583.

Derryberry D, Reed M. Regulatory processes and the development of cognitive representations. *Dev Psychopathol* 1996;8:215–234.

Dissanayake C, Sigman M, Kasari C. Long-term stability of individual differences in the emotional responsiveness of children with autism. *J Child Psychol Psychiatry* 1996;36:1–8.

Eales M. Pragmatic impairments in adults with childhood diagnoses of autism or developmental receptive language disorder. *J Autism Dev Disord* 1993;23:593–617.

Fletcher P, Happe F, Frith U, et al. Other minds in the brain: a functional imaging study of "theory of mind" in story comprehension. *Cognition* 1995;57:109–128.

Fotheringham J. Autism: its primary psychological and neurological deficit. *Can J Psychiatry* 1991;36:686–692.

Frith U. A new look at language and communication to autism. *Br J Disord Commun* 1989; 24:123–150.

Frye D. Zelazo P, Palfai T. Theory of mind and rule based reasoning. *Cogn Dev* 1995: 10:483–527.

Happe F. Communicative competence and theory of mind in autism: a test of relevance theory. *Cognition* 1993;48:101–119.

Hobson RP. *Autism and the development of mind.* Hillsdale, NJ: Erlbaum, 1993.

Hughes C, Russell J. Autistic children's difficulty with mental disengagement from an object: Its implications for theories of autism. *Dev Psychol* 1993;29:498–510.

Huttenlocher P. *Synaptogenesis in the human cerebral cortex.* In: Dawson G. Fischer K (eds.): Human behavior and brain development. New York: Guilford, 1994:137–152.

Kanner L. Autistic disturbances of affective contact. *Nervous Child* 1943;2:217–250.

Klin A. Young autistic children's listening preferences in regard to speech: a possible characterization of the symptom of social withdrawal. *J Autism Dev Disord* 1991;21:29–42.

LeDoux J. Cognitive-emotional interactions in the brain. *Cogn Emot* 1989:3;267–289.

Leekam S, Perner J. Does the autistic child have a metarepresentational deficit? *Cognition* 1991; 40:203–218.

Leslie A. Pretense and representation: the origins of "theory of mind." *Psychol Rev* 1987;94: 412–426.

Leslie A. *What autism teaches us about metarepresentation.* In: Baron-Cohen S, Tager-Flusberg H, Cohen D (eds). Understanding other minds: Perspectives from autism. New York: Oxford Publications 1993:83–111.

Leslie A, Happe EF. Autism and ostensive communication: the relevance of metarepresentation. *Dev Psychopathol* 1989;1:205–212.

Leslie A, Thaiss L. Domain specificity in conceptual development: neuropsychological evidence from autism. *Cognition* 1992;43:225–251.

Loveland K, Landry S. Joint attention and language in autism and developmental language delay. *J Autism Dev Disord* 1986:16:335–349.

McEvoy R, Rogers S. Pennington R. Executive function and social communication deficits in young, autistic children. *J Child Psychol Psychiatry* 1993.34:563–578.

Minshew N. Brief report: brain mechanisms in autism: functional and structural abnormalities. *J Autism Dev Disord* 1996;26:205–209.

Morales M, Mundy P, Rojo J. *Gaze following and language development in six- and eight-month-olds.* Paper presented at the Society for Research in Child Development. Washington, DC, 1997.

Mundy P. Joint attention, social-emotional approach in children with autism. *Dev Psychopathol* 1995;7:63–82.

Mundy P, Crowson M. Joint attention and early communication: implications for intervention with autism. *J Autism Dev Disord,* in press.

Mundy P, Sigman M. Specifying the nature of the social impairment in autism. In: Dawson G ed. Autism. New York: Guilford, 1989a:3–21.

Mundy P, Sigman M. The theoretical implications of joint attention deficits in autism. *Dev Psychopathol* 1989b;1:173–183.

Mundy P, Sigman M, Ungerer J. et al. Defining the social deficits of autism: the contribution of nonverbal communication measures. *J Child Psychol Psychiatry,* 1986;27:657–669.

Mundy P, Sigman M, Kasari C. A longitudinal study of joint attention and language development in autistic children. *J Autism Dev Disord* 1990;20:115–128.

Mundy P, Sigman M, Kasari C. The theory of mind and joint attention deficits in autism. In Baron-Cohen S, Tager-Rusberg H, Cohen D eds. Understanding other minds: perspectives from autism. Oxford. UK: *Oxford University Press,* 1993:181–203.

Mundy P, Sigman M, Kasari C. Joint attention, developmental level, and symptom presentation in young children with autism. *Dev Psychopathol* 1994:6:389–401.

Osterling J, Dawson G. Early recognition of children with autism: a study of first birthday home videotapes. *J Autism Dev Disord* 1994:24:247–257.

Ozonoff S. *Executive functions in autism.* In: Schopler E, Mesibov G (eds): Learning and cognition in autism. New York: Plenum Press, 1995:199–220.

Pennington B, Ozonoff S. Executive functions and developmental psychopathology. *J Child Psychol Psychiatry* 1996;37:51–87.

Peterson C, Siegal M. Deafness, conversation and theory of mind. *J Child Psychol Psychiatry* 1995;36:459–474.

Petrides M. Non-spatial conditional learning impaired in patients with unilateral frontal but not temporal lobe excisions. *Neuropsychologia* 1990;28:137–149.

Pinker S. *The language instinct: how the mind creates language.* New York: Harper Collins, 1994.

Sigman M, Mundy P. Social attachments in autistic children. *J Am Acad Child Adolesc Psychiatry* 1989;28:74–81.

Sigman M, Ruskin E. *Joint attention in relation to language acquisition and social skills in children with autism.* Paper presented at the Society for Research in Child Development. Washington, DC, 1997.

Scott F, Baron-Cohen S. Logical, analogical, and psychological reasoning in autism: a test of the Cosmides theory. *Dev Psychopathol* 1996;8: 235–245.

Surian L, Baron-Cohen S, Van der Lely H. Are children with autism deaf to Gricean maxims. *Cogn Neuropsychiatry* 1996;1:55–71.

Tager-Flusberg H. *What language reveals about the understanding of minds of children with autism.* In: Baron-Cohen S, Tager-Flusberg H, Cohen D eds. Understanding other minds: Perspectives from autism. New York: Oxford Publications, 1993:138–157.

Tomasello M. *Joint attention as social cognition.* In: Moore C, Dunham P eds. Joint attention: Its origins and role in development. NJ: Hillsdale, Erlbaum, 1995:103–130.

Tucker D. *Developing emotions and cortical networks.* In: Gunnar M, Nelson C. eds. Minnesota symposium on child psychology, Vo1 24, Developmental behavioral neuroscience. Hillsdale, NJ: Erlbaum, 1992:75–128.

Volden J, Lord C. Neologisms and idiosyncratic language in autistic speakers. *J Autism Dev Disord* 1991;28:109–130.

Ulvund S, Smith L. The predictive validity of nonverbal communication skills in infants with perinatal hazards. *Infant Behav Dev* 1996;19:441–449.

Wetherby A, Prutting C. Profiles of the communicative and cognitive-social abilities in autistic children. *J Speech Hear Res* 1984;27:367–377.

Whiten A, Byrne R. *The machiavellian intelligence hypothesis.* In: Whiten A, Byrne R eds. Machiavellian intelligence: Social expertise and the evolution of intellect in monkeys, apes, and humans. New York: Oxford University Press, 1988:118–137.

Yirmiya N, Shulman C. Seriation, conservation, and theory of mind abilities in individuals with autism, mental retardation and normally developing children. *Child Dev* 1996; 67:2045–2059.

Zilbovicus M, Garreau B, Samson Y, et al. Delayed maturation of the frontal cortex in childhood autism. *Am J Psychiat* 1995;152:248–252.

7

In the 1790s, a boy of about 11 years of age was found wandering in the woods near Aveyron, France. He seemed more like an animal in his behavior than like a human being. His sense of touch seemed more important than sight, he ate rotten food with pleasure, and he seemed insensitive to heat or cold. Though a distinguished scientist, Dr. Itard, dedicated himself to the boy's education, he only learned to speak a few words and to do a few menial tasks, such as setting the table. Dr. Itard's book, *The Wild Child*, like other accounts of such feral children, raises age-old questions about human nature. How much of our humanity is due to inherited patterns and timetables, and how much is due to our early experiences? Children who have experienced severe deprivation are of great interest to developmentalists, because they can help us answer these timeless questions about why we become who we are.

Overview Questions

1. What was the basic goal of the project? What are the two major advantages this study had over previous investigations? Why did they choose an early-adopted within-UK comparison group? How did the two groups of adoptive parents compare in terms of education and occupation?

2. Describe conditions in the institutions in Romania. How many of the 111 children had had less than two weeks of such care?

3. Explain in your own words why they believe that the data from Figure 7.3 suggest the age of entry is more important than malnutrition in determining cognitive scores at age 4. In the discussion, what two qualifications do they add to that conclusion?

4. The idea of "catch-up growth" suggests that there is an inborn timetable for growth, to which children might return, given a supportive environment, after an episode of deprivation. What do the results of this study suggest to you about a) the relationship between nature and nurture, and b) about the importance of early experience?

Focus Questions

1. What was the average age of institutionalization for the Romanian infants? How did they get physical measurements? Why do they believe it was acceptable to use retrospective Denver Developmental Scales?

2. A standard deviation (SD) is the typical distance of scores away from the mean (technically, the average squared deviation from the mean). In a bell-shaped distribution, –1 SD corresponds to the 16th percentile, while a score of –2 SD is above about 2.5% of the scores. List the measures in Table 7.2 where the mean score is greater than the 2.5th percentile. What does this tell you about their general physical condition? How did the non-institutionalized Romanian adoptees compare in Denver score and weight with the institutionalized infants?

3. Why do they believe that the correlation coefficients support the validity of the retrospective Denver scores? What percentage of their Romanian group was *at least* mildly retarded?

4. Explain why it is logically necessary for them to make sure that 1) the within-UK adoptees and the Romanian adoptees were adopted at about the same age, and 2) that the Romanian children admitted to the UK before versus after 6 months were comparable with respect to prior circumstances in Romania and measurements at the time of entry.

5. Since the anthropometric scores are reported in SD units away from the mean, zero is the mean for these measures. How do the within-UK adoptees and the Romanian Adoptees compare to the mean on these measures at age 4? Which group had the lowest cognitive scores at age 4?

6. The beta weights in Table 7.5 are like Pearson's correlation coefficients (range –1 to +1, positive means high scores go with high scores, negative means high scores go with low scores). Complete the following sentences: The higher the child's age at entry to the UK, the ____ the child's cognitive score at age 4. The higher the child's Denver score at entry, the ___ the child's cognitive score at age 4.

7. From Table 7.4, make a graph of the mean McCarthy scores for the three age groups they compared. Based on the information about statistical contrasts provided in the table, write a sentence about how the means for the three groups compared.

8. What three artifacts do they consider as alternative explanations for the deficit seen in late adopted children's cognitive scores, and why do they rule these out?

Developmental Catch-Up, and Deficit, Following Adoption after Severe Global Early Privation

Michael Rutter and the English and Romanian Adoptees (ERA) study team†

Introduction

Over the years, sharply divergent opinions have been expressed about the long-term importance for psychological development of experiences in the first 2 years of life. Some have viewed them as having a critical and lasting impact that is difficult to alter (Pilling & Pringle, 1978). Others have doubted their effects because of infants' limited ability to process their experiences cognitively (Kagan, 1984). Some have emphasized the high potential for radical change after the early years (Clarke & Clarke, 1976), and yet others have seen the long-term consequences as dependent on the cumulative impact of experiences beginning in infancy (Lipsitt,

†Lucie Andersen-Wood, Celia Beckett, Diana Bredenkamp, Jenny Castle, Judy Dunn, Kathryn Ehrich, Christine Groothues, Alexandra Harborne, Dale Hay, Jessica Jewett, Lisa Keaveney, Jana Kreppner, Julie Messer, Thomas O'Connor, David Quinton, and Adele White.

1983). Determination of the specific effects of early experiences, as distinct from those of later experiences, has been difficult because of the strong associations between the two in most ordinary circumstances (Rutter, 1981). There has had to be reliance on the rare cases of individual children rescued after rearing in extremely abnormal circumstances such as being isolated in cellars (Skuse, 1984), follow-up studies of severely abused/neglected children showing growth failure (Money, Annecillo, & Kelley, 1983a, b), or the few follow-up studies of children adopted after early privation (Colombo, De la Parra, & Lopez, 1992; Lien, Meyer, & Winick, 1977; Winick, Meyer, & Harris, 1975). The findings have given rise to the view that it is usual for there to be rapid recovery following "rescue" and provision of a normal rearing environment (Skuse,1984). However some of the samples were very small (e.g. only 16 adoptees in the Colombo et al. study, 1992); the relevant data were sparse; and outcome has often had to be evaluated only in relation to outdated general population norms. The follow-up was often incomplete (for example, a third of the children were not traced in Winick et al.'s study of Korean orphans; and IQ data were available on only just over half of those followed into school). The assessments have also been limited in scope. With the exception of two recent studies of Canadian adoptees from Romania (Ames, 1997; Chisholm, Carter, Ames, & Morison, 1995; Fisher, Ames, Chisholm, & Savoie, 1997; Marcovitch et al., 1997), there are virtually no published data on children's social functioning following severe early privation.

There is a much larger literature on the physical catch-up of children severely malnourished in infancy (see review by Martorell, Kettel Khan, & Schroeder, 1994). The evidence is clear that children who remain in the setting in which they experienced malnutrition and exhibited physical stunting show little or no catch-up in growth later in life. By contrast, major improvements in living conditions (whether by food supplementation or adoption) trigger catch-up growth. This effect is most marked and may be complete if the later life circumstances are really good (as would usually be the case with adoption) and if the change occurs in the first couple of years of life. One study, however, found a reduction in the age of puberty, which may limit ultimate height by curtailing the period of physical growth (Proos, Hofvander, & Tuvemo, 1991 a, b).

The opportunity to examine the psychological effects of early global deprivation more systematically arose from the adoption into English families, following the fall of the Ceaucescu regime, of a large number of children reared in the extremely poor conditions of Romanian institutions; a high proportion of such children are known to show severe developmental retardation as well as growth failure and widespread infections, including intestinal parasites (Johnson et al., 1992; Kaler & Freeman, 1994). Compared with previous studies of institution-reared children, there were two major advantages; (1) that the great majority of the children entered institutional care in early infancy, and (2) that the children's age at placement in U.K. families was largely a function of their age at the time of the fall of the regime. Few children returned from institutions to their biological families in Romania and there were no U.K. adoptions before the regime fell. Accordingly, it was possible to examine whether the degree of recovery was affected by the length of privation experienced. The study involved a dual strategy: first an examination of recovery following the move to the U.K., and consequent radical change in circumstances, allowed an assessment of the degree to which the initial deficits or retardation at the time of entry to the U.K. were a result of a prior depriving environment; and second, the extent to which the continuation of a deficit could be related to some plausible mediating variable (such as duration of privation or degree of malnutrition) provided a means of inferring causal influences on longer-term outcome (Rutter, 1994).

Sample and Methods

The study was drawn from the 324 children adopted from Romania into families resident in England between February 1990 and September 1992, aged below 42 months at the time of entry to the U.K., and dealt with through the legal channels of the U.K. and/or therefore processed by the U.K. Department of Health and Home Office. An unknown number of children entered the U.K. illegally and then were not included in our sampling frame. We also excluded, for practical reasons, those in Scotland, Wales, Ireland, the Isle of Man, and the Channel Isles. Stratified sampling was employed with the aim of obtaining a target number of 13 boys and 13 girls placed between the ages of 0 and 3 months, and 13 placed between 3 and 6 months, and therefore 10 boys and 10 girls in each of the 6-month age bands up to 42 months. Random selection was employed within age bands. In the older age bands, the available numbers fell below target and in these circumstances we took all children into the sample. Eighty-one per cent of the parents approached agreed to participate in the study. Half of the children had received an entirely institutional upbringing, four-fifths had been reared in institutions for most of their life, and only 9% had been reared throughout in a family setting. The great majority had entered an institution in the neonatal period (the mean age at entry was 0.34 months; $SD = 1.26$).

A comparison group of within-country adoptees, placed before the age of 6 months, was selected through a range of local authority and voluntary adoption agencies. Because the adoption agencies provided us with names of within-country adoptions only after they had contacted parents themselves and obtained their agreement, we do not have exactly comparable figures on the participation rate in that sample. However, from the information available to us, it appears that about half of the parents who were approached agreed to take part.

Ideally, several comparison groups would have been useful. Thus, examination of the effects of adoption would have been facilitated by a study of children who remained in Romanian orphanages and who were not adopted. This seemed redundant in view of the extensive evidence that such children fare very badly (Johnson et al., 1992; Kaler & Freeman, 1994). The choice of early-adopted within-U.K. adoptees was made on the basis of wanting a "best scenario" group, controlling for the experience of adoption and of rearing in above-average homes, but differing with respect to an absence of severe early nutritional and psychological privation.

Inevitably, such a group differed ethnically but most of the Romanian adoptees did not physically appear racially different and, although ethnic issues may be important later (Tizard & Phoenix, 1993), it did not seem likely that they would be so in early childhood. Anthropometrically, ethnic variations seem unlikely to be relevant for our samples (Ulijaszek, 1994) and there is no evidence that they will be relevant for cognitive development. Contrasts according to age of adoption are important but it is essential that they control for prior experiences. Accordingly they are best undertaken within the sample of Romanian adoptees, rather than between groups.

The final sample comprised 111 children whose records indicated that they entered England before the age of 2 years; 54 children who entered between 24 and 42 months; and 52 within-country adoptees. The present report is based solely on the first and third groups, both of whom were assessed at age 4 years (and who are currently being reassessed at age 6 years); the second group were assessed only at age 6 years as they were too old at the start of the study for assessment at age 4.

Both groups of adopting parents had educational attainments and an occupational level above general population norms but there were no statistically significant differences between them in these respects. The main difference between the adopting parents of Romanian children and the adopting parents of U.K. children was that the former were somewhat older at the time of placement (a mean age of fathers of 39.0 years vs. 36.0 and of mothers of 36.6 vs. 34.2) and included a considerably higher proportion who already had biological children of their own (34% vs. 2%) and a much lower proportion who had adopted previously (4% vs. 40%). However, the families adopting from Romania were more likely to have adopted more than one child either at the same time or within a year of the first placement (25% vs. 1%). Only a quarter of these pairs of adoptions within a year involved biological siblings. Within the group of families adopting children from Romania, there were no significant differences in family characteristics in relation to the children's age at the time of entering the U.K.

The children's height, weight, and head circumference were assessed on the basis of both the Romanian records and the physical examinations undertaken at the time the children entered the U.K. The Romanian records were rather skimpy and often lacking in detail on the date of the examination but so far as these anthropometric measurements were concerned they agreed reasonably well with those undertaken in the U.K. (Pearson product—moment correlations of .60 for weight and .53 for head circumference) apart from those on height ($r = .12$). The intercorrelations between height and weight were nevertheless reasonably comparable for the two sets of assessments (.45 in U.K. vs. .50 in Romania), as were those between weight and head circumference (.62 vs. .67) and between height and head circumference (.26 vs. .51). There were 14 children for whom we had no measured weight at entry and for 11 of these cases we used the Romanian measurements.

The norms used to derive standard scores for height, weight, and head circumference were based on Buckler (1990). All physical measurements are reported in standard deviation units (Boyce & Cole, 1993). This metric provides a continuous measure of physical development that is not confounded by age. For example, a score of –2.32 for weight indicates that the child's weight is 2.32 standard deviations *below* the U.K. general population norm for a given age. Because extremely low anthropometric measures are likely to index nutritional privation, whereas variations within the normal range may not do so, the data were also dealt with in terms of the proportions below the third percentile on U.K. norms.

Unfortunately, neither the Romanian records nor the assessments at U.K. entry included systematic quantified developmental assessments. Accordingly, it was necessary to rely on parental reporting. The great majority of parents had baby books giving contemporaneous details of developmental milestones and many also had video recordings. The recall task was also much easier than most both because it referred to an especially memorable time period and because parents were being asked to remember the children's actual behaviour at that time and *not* the dates when particular skills were acquired. In order to derive a quantified dimensional score, the parents were asked to complete Denver Developmental Scales (Frankenburg, van Doorninck, Liddell, & Dick, 1986) retrospectively on the children's performance and attainments at the time of entry to the U.K. using whichever contemporaneous records they had available. The Denver Scales are designed to be used by parents to focus on attainments (such as lifting the head, standing whilst holding on, and making meaningful "da-da" sounds) that are readily observable. The scores were transformed into developmental quotients by allocating developmental age according to the age of the item immediately preceding the second failed item, dividing this by the child's chronological age, and multiplying by 100. Especially with retarded babies, such scores can give either a zero quotient because the child is not able to do anything or an unrealistically high quotient because of the effect of one or two passes when dealing with a very small number of items. Accordingly, actual scores were used within the plus and minus 3 *SD* range but, to reduce the effect of extreme outliers, scores above or below these cut-offs were allocated a random score in the 3 to 4 *SD* range. The number of scores that had to be dealt with in this way was substantial, mainly because of the large number ($N = 47$) with scores in the severely retarded range but also the few ($N = 10$) with unusually high scores.

The children's developmental level at age 4 years was assessed using the Denver Scales in the same way plus individual testing of the children on the McCarthy Scales (McCarthy, 1972). The General Cognitive Index (GCI) of the McCarthy Scales has been found to correlate highly (.70s to .80s) with Binet and Wechsler IQs (Keith, 1985; McCarthy, 1972). In the case of the few children ($N = 4$) who were untestable on the complete McCarthy Scales of Children's Abilities, the Merrill Palmer Scale or subtests of the McCarthy were used. Based on findings on those scores, it was decided to allocate each of them a randomly generated McCarthy score between 40 and 50 when dealing with the findings dimensionally. In this paper, the general cognitive index of the McCarthy Scales is used throughout. Details of the patterns of cognitive functioning will be presented separately, as will the findings from other language and cognitive measures. In addition, there were detailed measures of socioemotional and behavioural functioning, also reported elsewhere.

Conditions in Romania

Some of the residential institutions were officially labelled "hospitals" and some "orphanages," but in practice there were few major differences between them in that both provided long-term care for children whose parents had given up looking after them for one reason or another. The conditions in these institutions varied from poor to appalling. In most instances the children were mainly confined to cots; there were few, if any, toys or playthings; there was very little talk from caregivers; no personalised caregiving; feeding of gruel by bottles with large teats, often left propped up; and variable, but sometimes harsh, physical environments. Thus, washing often consisted of being hosed down with cold water. These descriptions closely match those provided by other investigators (Groze & Ileana, 1996; Johnson et al., 1992; Kaler & Freeman, 1994). The home conditions of the few children not in institutions were also usually very poor.

Most of the children who entered institutions in the neonatal period remained there (but with some moves between institutions) until they came to the U.K. Early family experiences were dealt with by subdividing the sample of adoptees from Romania according to their pattern of family or institutionalised rearing in Romania. Out of the sample of 111, only 18 had been reared in a family setting throughout (with less than 2 weeks in an institution), another 5 had had family rearing for up to half of their life in Romania, 36 had been reared in institutions for at least half (but not all) of their life (in almost most cases this amounted to nearly all their life), and the largest group (52) had been reared in institutions throughout. Perhaps surprisingly, the pattern of rearing did not differ significantly between those who entered the U.K. in early infancy (operationally defined as under 6 months) and those who entered the country later. Because there were so few children who experienced small periods of institutional care, the main analyses treated care in terms of a dichotomy according to the presence or absence of institutional rearing for at least 2 weeks. This variable was used as a predictor, in addition to the child's age at the time of entry to the U.K. Of the 58 children who entered the U.K. under the age of 6 months, 12 had not received institutional care compared with 6 out of 53 for those who entered the U.K. when aged 6 months or older, a difference that fell well short of statistical significance.

The children's age at the time of entry to the U.K. was dealt with as a dimensional measure in the first instance because there was no strong a priori reason to expect a nonlinear relationship with outcome. However, because the U.K. adoptees comparison group had all been placed before the age of 6 months, the outcome findings for the Romanian adoptees was also considered separately according to whether or not entry to the U.K. was before the age of 6 months.

Adoption Breakdown

The rate of adoption breakdown in the Romanian sample was extremely low: 1.8% in the group as a whole (i.e. including those who entered the U.K. at up to 42 months of age). This figure is below that found among within-U.K. adoptees of comparable age at adoption (Thoburn, 1993).

Results

Results are presented in three segments. First, the developmental status of Romanian adoptees when they entered the U.K. is discussed. Second, physical growth and cognitive development differences between U.K. and Romanian adoptees and between subgroups of Romanian adoptees are reported. Third, the predictors of cognitive development at the year 4 assessment are described. Where possible, predictor variables were examined both as dimensional and as categorical variables. This analytic strategy contrasts the prediction of individual differences within the normal range to prediction from extreme group membership (see weight, below). Means analyses are based on analysis of variance methods; post hoc comparisons were based on Student–Newman–Keuls test. Regression analyses presented in the third section are based on a simultaneous entry procedure.

Most of the children were in a poor physical state at the time of entry to the U.K. Severe malnutrition was the rule; chronic and recurrent respiratory infections were rife; chronic intestinal infections (including giardia) were common; and many of the children had skin disorders of one kind or another.

As Table 7.1 indicates, at the time of entry to the U.K. the children were severely developmentally impaired on all measures. On both the Romanian and U.K. assessments, the mean head circumference and weight were more than 2 SD below U.K. norms and the mean height was approximately at the minus 2 SD point. Moreover, overall, about half were below the third percentile: 51% (N = 108) on weight; 34% (N = 58) on height; and 38% (N = 61) on head circumference on the U.K. measures.

The findings on the Denver Scale were closely comparable, with the mean of 63 being in the mildly retarded range. Fifty-nine per cent of the children had a developmental quotient below 50 and a further 15% had a developmental quotient in the mildly impaired (50–69) range.

Because any assessment of cognitive catch-up is necessarily crucially dependent on the validity of the retrospective Denver scores, it is necessary to examine this matter in some detail. It was tackled in several different ways. First, reference was made to data on children studied in Romanian institutions. Kaler and Freeman (1994) found a mean Bayley mental age of 9.5 months (SD 7.0) in their sample at a mean chronological age of 35 months; of the 25 children studied, 20 were functioning at levels less than half their chronological age. Second, the Johnson et al. (1992) findings on children from Romania adopted into U.S. families was used as a guide. Only 10% of the 31 children aged over 12 months at the time of evaluation shortly after entry into the U.S. were judged to be developmentally normal. Both sets of data are closely in line with our own. Third, in the minority of cases where they were available, we obtained the medical records taken in the U.K. as soon as possible after entry to the country. Systematic developmental assessments were rarely undertaken but the general descriptions (and specific findings where recorded) were generally in good accord with the parental descriptions. Finally, we used the pattern of correlations (see Table 7.2).

In essence, the main findings are that the Denver score for the child's functioning at the time of U.K. entry showed a moderate positive correlation with the anthropometric measurements at that time (which would be expected if the score

TABLE 7.1 *Circumstances and Conditions of Romanian Adoptees Before and at the Time of Entry to U.K.*

	(N)	Mean	SD
Age at first entry to institutional care	(93)	0.34 mths	1.26
Age at leaving institutional care	(93)	8.38 mths	6.34
Age at entering U.K.	(111)	6.59 mths	5.87
Age-standardised weight as measured in Romania	(98)	–2.44 SD	1.59
Age-standardised weight as measured at U.K. entry	(97)	–2.37 *SD*	1.79
Age-standardised weight as measured at U.K. entry (including subset of cases with weight measured in Romania)	(108)	–2.21 *SD*	1.66
Age-standardised height as measured in Romania	(94)	–1.96 *SD*	1.80
Age-standardised height as measured at U.K. entry	(58)	–1.95 *SD*	1.96
Age-standardised head circumference as measured in Romania	(91)	–2.27 *SD*	1.65
Age-standardised head circumference as measured at U.K. entry	(61)	–2.14 *SD*	1.80
	(N)	DQ	SD
Retrospective Denver Quotient at entry	(98)	62.89	41.24

TABLE 7.2 *Correlations with Denver Quotient (DQ) at Entry and at Age 4 Years*

	DQ at entry		DQ at 4 years	
	Score	(N)	Score	(N)
Head circumference (at entry)	.32*	(58)	.18	(57)
Head circumference (4 years)	.17	(89)	.20	(83)
Height (at entry)	.29*	(55)	.22	(54)
Height (4 years)	.00	(94)	.23*	(90)
Weight (at entry)[a]	.34**	(95)	.11	(90)
Weight (4 years)	.04	(97)	.04	(93)
Denver (4 years)	.45**	(91)	—	—
McCarthy score (4 years)	.34**	(97)	.52**	(93)
Whether reared in institution	–.35**	(98)	–.19	(93)

[a]Weight at entry includes weight as measured at entry into U.K. and subset of cases for which weight in Romania was used.

*p < .05; **p < .01.

constituted a valid estimate), but weak and statistically nonsignificant correlations with the anthropometric measures at age 4 (the opposite of what would be expected on the basis of a hypothesis that retrospective recall was biased by current status). Similarly, the Denver score at 4 years showed a substantial correlation (.52) with the McCarthy GCI score at the same age, suggesting moderate contemporaneous validity, a level that is as high as could be expected with a screening measure. The comparable correlation for the Denver at U.K. entry was lower (.34), again arguing against retrospective bias.

In view of the fact that the Denver is a screening questionnaire, it would not be justifiable to place too much reliance on precise scores. Nevertheless, considered as a whole, the evidence is entirely consistent in indicating that the Romanian adoptees as a group showed major developmental retardation at the time of entry to the U.K., that over half were functioning in the retarded range, and that the Denver scores provide a reasonable, albeit rough and ready, rank ordering of the children's level of developmental functioning.

Differences among Romanian Adoptees According to Experience of Institutional Rearing

The small subsample of 18 children from Romania who had experienced less than 2 weeks of institutional care differed markedly from the remainder in being less impaired at the time of U.K. entry. Thus, their mean initial Denver score was 96.7 (N = 15) compared with 56.8 (N = 83), and their weight 1.28 SD (N = 17) below the U.K. mean compared with 2.38 SD (N = 91) below the U.K. mean—both differences being statistically significant; p = .0004 and .012 respectively. These differences held within both the group admitted to the U.K. below the age of 6 months and those admitted when older. The contrasts on the Denver score were 110.4 (N = 10) vs. 68.3 (N = 41), p < .05 for the former subgroup and 69.3 (N = 5) vs. 45.4 (N = 42), p < .05 for the latter. The comparable figures on weight at entry were −1.9 SD (N = 11) vs. −2.2 (N = 45) (not statistically significant) and −0.15 (N = 6) vs. −2.6 (N = 46), p < .001. It is evident that these family-reared subgroups constitute a useful internal control of children from Romania who were much less developmentally impaired and, hence, who presumably experienced a much milder set of depriving experiences.

Differences among Romanian Adoptees According to Age at U.K. Entry

Our research design is dependent on the validity of two key comparisons. The first involves comparability with respect to age of entry to the adopting family of the within-U.K. adoptees and the Romanian children entering the U.K. before 6 months of age. The two groups were closely similar in that respect (2.5 months vs. 3.5 months). The main control therefore resides in the very deprived early circumstances of the Romanian children.

The second involves comparability within the Romanian sample, according to age of entry to the U.K., with respect to the prior circumstances in Romania and to their anthropometric measurements at the time of entry (see Table 7.3). Good comparability was evident. As already noted, the children admitted to the U.K. before the age of 6 months did not differ from later admitted children in their experience of rearing in a family setting.

The early admitted children, however, had had a significantly shorter period of family care before entering an institution (.07 months vs. .62 months, p = .03), but even in the group entering the U.K. when older, the period of family care was very brief. None of the anthropometric measures differed significantly according to age at entry, although there was a very weak tendency for those admitted when older to be

TABLE 7.3   *Age and Circumstances at Entry to U.K.*

	Under 6 months at entry Mean (SD)	6 months or older at entry Mean (SD)
Weight	–2.1 (1.7)	–2.3 (1.7)
Height	–1.8 (1.6)	–2.2 (2.4)
Head circumference	–2.1 (2.1)	–2.2 (1.3)
Denver quotient	76.5 (48.1)	48.1 (25.4)
Age first in institution[a]	0.07 (0.25)	0.62 (l.7)

[a]Age in months.

slightly more impaired (e.g. weight at entry was –2.3 *SD* as compared with –2.1 *SD*). The children admitted after 6 months of age, however, had a significantly lower initial Denver score (mean of 48.1 vs. 76.5; $p < .001$). In view of the lack of differences on the anthropometric measures, this probably reflects the limitations of the Denver for assessing developmental level in early infancy.

Developmental Catch-up

Physical catch-up by age 4 years was very substantial (see Table 7.4). Compared with the 51% below the 3rd percentile in weight at entry to the U.K., there were only 2% of the Romanian adoptees below the 3rd percentile at 4 years. Similarly, at 4 years, only 1% were below the 3rd percentile on height and only 13% on head circumference. Nevertheless, the Romanian adoptees as a group were slightly lighter, slightly shorter, and had a slightly smaller head circumference than the within-U.K. adoptees. By contrast, however, there were no anthropometric differences within the Romanian group according to the age when they entered the U.K.

The developmental catch-up was equally impressive, but not quite complete in those placed after the age of 6 months. Both the Denver and McCarthy scores of the Romanian children placed before the age of 6 months were closely comparable with those of the within-U.K. adoptees, despite the severe physical and developmental re-

TABLE 7.4   *Anthropometric and Cognitive Measures at 4 Years*

	Within-UK Adoptees		Romanian Adoptees[a]			
			Entry before < 6 mths		Entry at/after > 6 mths	
	Mean	(SD)	Mean	(SD)	Mean	(SD)
Anthropometric Measurements (standard scores)						
Weight $F(2,154) = 4.21$*[b]	0.45	(0.79)	–0.02	(0.92)	0.04	(0.94)
Height $F(2,151) = 6.57$*[b]	0.25	(0.91)	–0.29	(0.89)	–0.36	(1.02)
Head circumference $F(2,144) = 15.59$**[c]	–0.46	(0.84)	–1.10	(0.96)	–1.50	(0.97)
Cognitive Level						
Denver quotient $F(2,128) = 12.03$***[d]	117.7	(24.3)	115.7	(23.4)	96.7	(21.3)
McCarthy GCI $F(2,156) = 15.78$***[d]	109.4	(14.8)	105.9	(17.9)	91.7	(18.0)

[a]Age at entry < 6 months or > 6 months.

[b]U.K. > 0–6, 6–24; [c]U.K. > 0–6 > 6–24; [d]U.K. & 0–6 > 6–24.

*$p <.05$; **$p < .01$; ***$p <.001$.

tardation evident at the time of entry to the U.K. (see earlier). The catch-up in cognitive functioning was not a function of family rearing. The mean McCarthy GO score was 100 for the children who had not experienced institutional rearing and 107 for those who had. The trend within the institution-reared group for those who experienced some family care to score more highly (113 vs. 104) fell well short of statistical significance.

The mean scores of the Romanian children adopted between the ages of 6 and 24 months were only slightly below 100 but, on both the Denver and McCarthy Scales, they were more than a dozen points below those of the within-U.K. adoptee group. The fact that the latter had a mean well above 100 emphasises both the general finding that IQ scores have risen over time (Flynn, 1980) and also that the general population mean is no longer 100 on tests standardised some years ago. If we had relied on test norms instead of having a comparison group, the catch-up would have appeared misleadingly complete.

It is necessary to consider whether the slightly depressed mean cognitive score in the Romanian children adopted after the age of 6 months reflects a general slight shift downwards, or a subgroup of intellectually impaired children, or both. The findings showed that there was both a slight shift downwards in the group as a whole and a small subgroup ($N = 7$) of intellectually impaired children not found in the within-U.K. sample (see Fig. 7.1).

Factors Associated with Cognitive Level at Age 4 Years

The analyses on factors associated with cognitive level at age 4 years were first undertaken with the variables treated as dimensions (see Table 7.5). So far as age at entry to the U.K. was concerned, there was no good a priori reason not to do so. The scattergram shown in Fig. 7.2 indicates little age effect within the first 6 months (a group already found *not* to differ from the within-U.K. adoptees), but an apparently linear effect thereafter. A simultaneous entry multiple-regression analysis (in which the effect of each variable is net of the effect of the other variables) showed that age at entry to the U.K. was much the most powerful predictor of the general cognitive

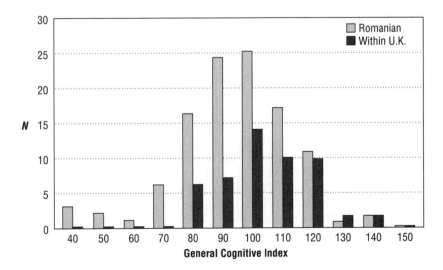

FIGURE 7.1 *McCarthy Scores at 4 Years in Romanian Adoptees and Within-U.K. Adoptees* (Romanian: $N = 108$; within-U.K.: $N = 51$); Romanian adoptees: mean = 99.0 ($SD = 19.2$); within-U.K. adoptees: mean = 109.4 ($SD = 14.8$)

TABLE 7.5 *Prediction of Global Cognitive Index at 4 years from Age of Entry and Early Developmental Indicators*

	beta	R^2
Simultaneous entry predictors ($N = 94$)		
Age at entry	–.41***	
Ever in institution (yes/no)[a]	.07	
Denver score at entry	.27*	
Weight at entry	.14	
R^2		.34***

[a]"Ever in institution" is a dichotomous variable (0 = no, 1 = yes); the other variables are dimensional variables.

*p <.05; ***p <.001.

index at 4 years (a beta weight of –.41; p < .001). There was also a significant, but weaker effect of Denver score at entry (beta weight of .27; p < .05) but no effect of weight at entry (beta weight = .14; p = .2). Because head circumference at entry showed no association (r = .11) with cognitive outcome it was not entered into the regression; the same applied to height at entry (r = .18). Neither family rearing nor the duration of family care prior to institutional admission showed an association with the cognitive score at 4 years in the group as a whole. However, the mean GCI for the tiny subgroup (N = 6) of children entering the U.K. after 6 months who had not experienced institutional rearing was 102 (as compared with 90 for those reared in institutions), and therefore closely comparable with both that for the children entering the U.K. before 6 months (106) and for the within-U.K. adoptees group (109). The inference is that the remaining cognitive deficit was likely to be a consequence of some aspect of institutional rearing.

Because it could be argued that a weight, or head circumference, below the third percentile has a different meaning from variations within the normal range (with only the former reflecting a degree of malnutrition likely to compromise brain growth or impair long-term cognitive functioning), the data were reanalysed in categorical terms (see Table 7.6). The findings for age at entry were essentially the same

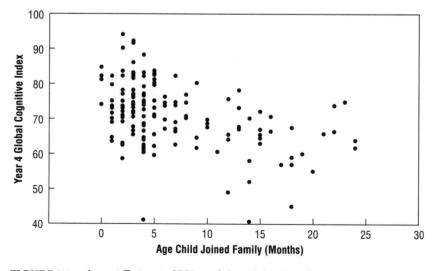

FIGURE 7.2 *Age at Entry to U.K. and Cognitive Level at 4 Years*

as those in the dimensional analysis. Again this was the "initial" variable with the strongest effect. The mean score for those entering before 6 months was 8 points above those entering between the ages of 6 and 12 months, and 19 points above those entering after 12 months (but before 24 months). A weight below the 3rd percentile had only a nonsignificant effect, with just a 6-point difference. A Denver quotient below 50 was associated with a difference of nearly 8 points, an effect that fell just short of statistical significance. There was no appreciable effect of head circumference at entry. There was, however, a weak but statistically significant effect of head circumference at 4 years ($r = .25$) on the cognitive score at the same age. This association applied only in those whose weight at entry to the U.K. was above the 3rd percentile ($r = .31$), being near zero ($r = .08$) in those with a weight below that cut-off.

As Fig. 7.3 shows, the effect of age at entry was greater among the children with a weight above the 3rd percentile (a difference of 22 points) than in those with an initial weight below the 3rd percentile (a difference of 9 points). This strongly suggests that the effect is not simply a consequence of level of malnutrition. Conversely, however, the fact that weight at entry was only weakly (but significantly; $p < .05$) associated with cognitive level at 4 years within a group whose members entered the U.K. before 6 months (a 10-point difference and not at all associated in those admitted later) suggests that variations in degree of malnutrition are not a major determinant of cognitive outcome.

Discussion

Like other studies capitalising on "natural experiments" created by an unusual set of circumstances, this follow-up study of children adopted into well-functioning families after severe global early privation had several unavoidable limitations. First, there were no satisfactory systematic data on the characteristics of the biological parents and, hence, no information on possible genetic influences. Doubtless these played a role in individual differences within the groups of adoptees. On the other hand, it is completely implausible that they could account for the developmental catch-up found. It is equally unlikely that they could play a role in the effects of the children's age at leaving institutional care on outcome. That is because, unlike in pre-

TABLE 7.6 *At Entry Predictors of McCarthy Scores at 4 Years*

Situation at entry	(N)	McCarthy score		Statistical significance
		Mean	(SD)	
Age				
0 < 6 mths	(56)	105.9	(17.9)	$p < .001$ (0–6 mths vs. 6–24 mths)
6 < 12 mths	(23)	98.0	(14.5)	$F (2,105) = 11.48$
12 < 24 mths	(29)	86.7	(19.2)	Contrasts 0–6, 6–12 > 12–24
Weight				
Below 3rd percentile	(54)	97.9	(15.9)	n.s.
Above 3rd percentile	(51)	101.6	(21.3)	$F(1,105) = 2.34$
Head circumference				
Below 3rd percentile	(20)	104.0	(16.7)	n.s.
Above 3rd percentile	(41)	99.6	(20.3)	$F(1,59) = 0.72$
Denver Quotient				
Below 50	(56)	95.5	(16.9)	$p = .055$
Above 50	(41)	103.2	(22.0)	$F(1,95) = 3.77$

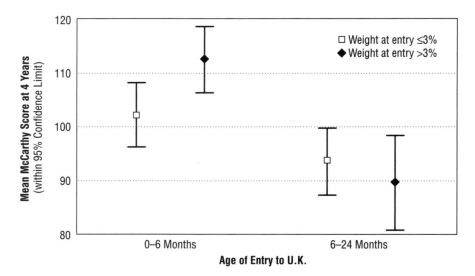

FIGURE 7.3   *McCarthy Scores at 4 Years by Weight and Age at Entry* The means (*SD*) and *N*s for the groups are, from left to right, 102.2 (14.3) *N* = 28;109.7 (20.4) *N* = 28; 91.2 (18.0) *N* = 30; 92.2 (18.9) *N* = 21 [*F*(3,101) = 9.45, *p* < .01]. The second group is significantly greater than the first, third and fourth groups and the first group is greater than the fourth at *p* < .05 based on Student–Newman–Keuls post-hoc contrasts.

vious studies, there is no evidence that children had been placed for adoption or returned to the biological parents before the fall of the Ceaucescu regime. Second, few data were available on the reasons for the children being admitted to institutions. Again, it is implausible that such reasons played any substantial role in our findings; this is because almost all of the children entered the institutions as very young infants. Accordingly, there was no scope for the children to have been placed as a result of their own handicaps. Third, we had no systematic contemporaneous measurements of the children's developmental level at the time of entering the U.K., and hence had to rely on parents' retrospective accounts. Because of this, precise quantification of the degree of cognitive catch-up was not possible. On the other hand, other studies of children in Romania and the parents' own written records (and video tapes in many instances) made clear the very substantial retardation in most cases. Also, as described, we undertook several different types of analyses to detect bias and found no evidence of its presence. The finding that there had been major cognitive catch-up is secure, even if its exact extent remains uncertain. For the reasons given, the effects of the children's age at U.K. entry on cognitive level at 4 years cannot plausibly be attributed to variations in the recall of the children's initial developmental level.

The children adopted from Romanian orphanages were more severely deprived, physically and psychologically, than almost any other sizeable group of children previously studied. At the time of entry to the U.K. just over half had a weight below the third percentile and a similar proportion had a developmental quotient in the retarded range. The conditions in Romanian institutions, in all aspects, were incomparably worse than those in the U.K. or indeed in almost all other industrialised countries. Nevertheless, despite this profoundly unpromising start, the degree of cognitive catch-up by the age of 4 years was spectacular. Thus, in the group as a whole the developmental quotient on the Denver Scales rose from a mean of 63 to a mean of 107, and in the subgroup who experienced institutional rearing and who were admitted to the U.K. after the age of 6 months the mean rose from 45 to 90. This dramatic catch-up following a major change in the circumstances of rearing provides clear evidence that the initial developmental retardation was caused by the profoundly depriving circumstances of their early institutional rearing.

The cognitive catch-up in the Romanian children who entered this country under the age of 6 months following institutional rearing appears to have been virtually complete by the age of 4 years in that no differences from the within-U.K. adoptees, or from the subgroup of children from Romania who did not experience institutional rearing, were found. The respective GCI means on the McCarthy Scales at 4 years were 107, 109, and 100. It is, of course, too early to be sure that there will be no long-term sequelae (and it should be noted that they were still slightly below U.K. norms for physical growth) but the indications so far are very positive.

The situation with respect to those who came to the U.K. after the age of 6 months following institutional rearing was also very positive; their mean McCarthy score of 90 was well within the normal range and a few of the children had scores that were above average. Nevertheless, their mean was a standard deviation below that (109) of the group of within-U.K. adoptees and also below that (102) of the small subgroup of children from Romania entering the U.K. after the age of 6 months but who had not experienced an institutional upbringing. The second follow-up at age 6 years will be important in showing the extent to which there is further catch-up over the age period from 4 to 6, and the 4-year-old findings cannot be seen as providing a picture of the ultimate outcome.

The Canadian study findings are similar. Of the 46 children reared in Romanian institutions and adopted between the ages of 8 and 68 months (median of 19 months), 31 were tested on the Stanford-Binet at 4½ years (Ames, 1997). Their mean IQ was 90 compared with 98 for the 27 Romanian children adopted before 4 months of age, and 109 for a comparison group of 30 non-adopted Canadian children.

The meaning of both the cognitive catch-up in the group as a whole, and the relative cognitive deficit in those entering the U.K. after the age of 6 months, can be inferred from the findings on predictor variables. Much the strongest predictor was the child's age at the time of entry to the U.K. This inevitably reflected both the duration of severe privation in Romania and the span of time in the U.K. adoptive families, the two being colinear and inseparable. Because the minimum period in the U.K. was 2 years, for duration in the adoptive home to be the main causal variable there would have to be a further catch-up of some 19 points during the time after 4 years of age. This seems implausible, and the findings on the children seen so far at age 6 years do not suggest further catch-up of anything approaching that magnitude.

The weakness of the weight at entry as a predictor stands out in contrast. It had no significant predictive power in multivariate analyses when dealt with either as a dimension or categorically in terms of a weight below the third percentile. Also, the finding that head circumference at age 4 years was not associated with the GCI at the same age in those with an initial weight below the third percentile implies a lack of a lasting effect of early subnutrition on brain growth. The implication is that severe malnutrition per se or variations in the degree of undernutrition (in a group most of whom were markedly underweight) had no major continuing effect on cognitive performance after a period of at least 2 years rearing in an adoptive home with dedicated parents of mostly above-average educational background. An important caveat, however, needs to be attached to that inference. It may be that the *duration* of serious malnutrition rather than its degree at any one point in time is what matters with respect to long-term sequelae.

The only sizeable study in the literature that is at all comparable is that by Winick et al. (1975) and Lien et al. (1977). In Winick et al.'s report of U.S.–adopted Korean children renourished before age 2 years and adopted by age 3 years, they found a mean IQ at follow-up of 102 for children initially below the 3rd percentile of weight and height, compared with 106 for those between the 3rd and 24th percentiles (Johnson et al., 1992), and 112 for those at or above the 25th percentile. Lien et al.'s later study of children from the same sample adopted *after* age 2 years showed differences of the same order: 95, 101, and 105, but with appreciably lower means compared with the Winick et al. sample. There was *no* effect of nutritional status for children renourished after age 3 years (in most cases there was a long time period between renourishment in Korea and adoption into a U.S. family). Moreover, in the group as a whole, the age on arrival in the U.S. had an effect on scholastic achievement as great as the effect from nutrition; there was no interaction between the two effects.

The marked difference in level of functioning at age 4 years in our sample as compared with that reported for the Romanian adoptees at the time they joined their adoptive families, together with the dose-response relationship between age at entry and cognitive score at 4 years, strongly suggests that the initial developmental deficit was a function of the children's prolonged experience of grossly depriving conditions, and that the subsequent catch-up was a function of the radical improvement in rearing conditions. Although the Denver developmental quotients cannot be taken as more than a rather crude indicator of level of functioning, all the evidence clearly indicates that most of the children were substantially delayed in their development at the time of coming to the U.K., many severely so. Although, unavoidably, the initial scores were based on retrospective recall, the available evidence supports a substantial degree of validity and provides no indication of bias.

The data available so far do not allow a clear differentiation between the effects of nutritional privation and psychological privation because the great majority of children experienced both. Nevertheless, the findings are striking in showing no independent effect of weight at the time of entry to the U.K. on the cognitive scores at age 4 years. By contrast, there was a major effect of the children's age at entry. It may be concluded that the total duration of privation during the first 2 years of life is more important as a predictor of cognitive outcome than is the extent to which the privation involved subnutrition. The inference, therefore, is that psychological privation constituted an important part of the risk experiences prior to coming to the U.K. Two qualifications, however, need to be added. First, in almost all cases, psychological privation was accompanied by a degree of malnutrition. Accordingly, it may be that the effects of psychological privation are increased by the co-occurrence of malnutrition. Second, the non-nutritional aspects of privation included not only a marked lack of play and communicative experiences but also, in some cases, possible physical and sexual abuse and the use of heavy medication as a means of behavioural control.

The Romanian sample studied does seem to differ from the Korean orphans previously investigated by Winick and Lien in the extreme degree of psychological privation suffered (unfortunately neither of the published reports by Winick et al., 1975, and by Lien et al., 1977 gives satisfactory detail on the conditions of rearing). The degree of psychological privation was also, almost certainly, much more extreme than that in the socially disadvantaged, malnourished children in developing countries who have been studied. Accordingly, the much greater effect found in the Romanian sample for age at leaving institutional care, among children all of whom had left by age 2 years, implies a role for psychological privation. This is also indicated by the major effect of age at entry even in those children whose weight was at or above the third percentile. Currently, we are combining multiple data to derive a summary measure of the degree of psychological privation and its use may clarify the situation. However, the data on the conditions in the institutions as experienced by individual children are extremely sparse, and the range is narrow (all being poor).

Two findings with respect to variations in outcome within the Romanian adoptees appear particularly important. First, we found no measurable deficit in those who came to the U.K. before the age of 6 months. Not only were their cognitive levels well up to U.K. norms, they did not differ from those of the within-U.K. adoptees. This applied to those reared in institutions throughout; also their cognitive resilience was not a function of any lesser degree of malnutrition as judged by height, weight, and head circumference. It is too early to be sure there will be no sequelae but the evidence to date shows a high degree of recovery in a group exposed to an extreme degree of nutritional and psychological privation.

The relative cognitive deficit of about one standard deviation in the group who came to the U.K. after the age of 6 months stands out in contrast. It is too early to know whether the deficit will reduce with an increasing time in the adoptive home but, especially as the deficit was greater than 10 points in those who came to the U.K. after the age of 12 months than it was in those entering between 6 and 12 months, it seems likely that some degree of persisting deficit will remain. Nevertheless, it should not necessarily be assumed that the relative deficit on the McCarthy Scales GCI at age 4 years is measuring a lasting intellectual impairment. Test performance, perhaps especially in the preschool years, is influenced by attentional, motivational, and behavioural features. As described elsewhere, the overall group of adoptees from Romania showed some increase in problems in these domains. The follow-up at age 6 years will be helpful in sorting out how far they influenced cognitive performance.

Possible artefacts need to be considered, but our study has several major advantages over previous research that help rule them out. First, the deficit could be a consequence of handicapped children being placed in institutional care. That seems most unlikely both because the great majority of the children entered institutions as young infants and because no children with diagnosable handicaps were included. Second, as pointed out by Clarke and Clarke (1976), most previous findings on the worse outcome of late-adopted children suffer from the limitation that the children may not have been adopted when younger because they were developing less well. That is not likely to apply to this sample because adoption was not an option prior to the fall of the Ceaucescu regime and the children's age on leaving the institution, therefore, was not a function of their having been rejected earlier for adoption. Third, the deficit could be a consequence of the later-adopted children having a lesser cognitive potential as a result of their genetic background. No usable data on the latter are obtainable but there is no reason to suppose that the children's genetic potential should, or even could, vary according to their age at the time of entry to the U.K. We may conclude that the cognitive deficit is likely to be a valid consequence of gross early privation. The implication is that the sequelae are a consequence of both psychological and nutritional privation, with the former likely to be of greater importance.

Acknowledgements—We are very grateful to the families for their great cooperation during all phases of the study, and to the many other people who have provided us with information. We are also very indebted to Karen Langridge, the study administrator, for help in ways too numerous to detail.

References

Ames, E. W. (1997). *The development of Romanian orphanage children adopted to Canada.* Final report to Human Resources Development, Canada.

Boyce, L., & Cole, T. (1993). *Growth Programme. Version 1 & 2.* Ware, U.K.: Castlemead Publications.

Buckler, J. (1990). *A longitudinal study of adolescent growth.* London: Springer-Verlag.

Chisholm, K., Carter, M. C., Ames, E. W., & Morison, S. J. (1995). Attachment security and indiscriminately friendly behavior in children adopted from Romanian orphanages. *Development and Psychopathology, 7,* 283–294.

Clarke, A. M., & Clarke, A. D. B. (Eds.) (1976). *Early experience: Myth and evidence.* London: Open Books.

Colombo, M., De la Parra, A., & Lopez, I. (1992). Intellectual and physical outcome of children undernourished in early life is influenced by later environmental conditions. *Developmental Medicine and Child Neurology, 34,* 611–622.

Fisher, L., Ames, E. W., Chisholm, K., & Savoie, L. (1997). Problems reported by parents of Romanian orphans adopted to British Columbia. *International Journal of Behavioural Development, 20,* 67–82.

Flynn, J. R. (1980). *Race, IQ and Jensen.* London: Routledge & Kegan Paul.

Frankenburg, W. K., van Doorninck, W. J., Liddell, T. N., & Dick, N. P. (1986). *Revised Denver Prescreening Developmental Questionnaire (R-PDQ).* High Wycombe. U.K.: DDM Incorporated/The Test Agency.

Groze, V., & Ileana, D. (1996). Follow-up study of adopted children from Romania. *Child and Adolescent Social Work Journal, 13,* 541–565.

Johnson, D. E., Miller, L. C., Iverson, S., Thomas, W., Franchino, B., Dole, K., Kiernan, M. T., Georgieff, M. K., & Hostetter, M. K. (1992). The health of children adopted from Romania. *Journal of the American Medical Association, 268,* 3446–3451.

Kagan, J. (1984). *The nature of the child.* New York: Basic Books.

Kaler, S. R., & Freeman, B. J. (1994). Analysis of environmental deprivation: Cognitive and social development in Romanian orphans. *Journal of Child Psychology and Psychiatry, 35,* 769–781.

Keith. T. Z. (1985). McCarthy Scales of Children's Abilities. In D. J. Keyser & R. C. Sweetland (Eds.), *Test critiques* (Vol. 4) (pp. 394–399). Kansas City, MO: Test Corporation of America.

Lien, N. M., Meyer, K. K., & Winick, M. (1977). Early malnutrition and "late" adoption: A study of their effects on development of Korean orphans adopted into American families. *American Journal of Clinical Nutrition, 30,* 1734–1739.

Lipsitt, L. P. (1983). Stress in infancy: Toward understanding the origins of coping behavior. In N. Garmezy & M. Rutter (Eds.), *Stress, coping and development in children* (pp. 161–190). New York: McGraw-Hill.

Marcovitch, S., Goldberg, S., Gold, A., Washington, L., Wasson, C., Krekewich, K., & Handley-Derry, M. (1997). Determinants of behavioural problems in Romanian children adopted in Ontario. *International Journal of Behavioural Development, 20,* 17–32.

Martorell, R., Kettel Khan, L., & Schroeder, D. G. (1994). Reversibility of stunting: Epidemiological findings in children from developing countries. *European Journal of Clinical Nutrition, 48,* S45–S57.

McCarthy, D. (1972). *The McCarthy Scales of Children's Abilities.* New York: The Psychological Corporation/Harcourt Brace Jovanovich.

Money, J., Annecillo, C., & Kelley, J. F. (1983a). Growth of intelligence: Failure and catch-up associated respectively with abuse and rescue in the syndrome on abuse dwarfism. *Psychoneuroendocrinology, 8,* 309–319.

Money, J., Annecillo, C., & Kelley, J. F. (1983b). Abuse-dwarfism syndrome: After rescue. statural and intellectual catch-up growth correlate. *Journal of Clinical Child Psychology, 12,* 279–283.

Pilling, D., & Pringle, M. K. (1978). *Controversial issues in child development.* London: Elek.

Proos, L. A., Hofvander, Y., & Tuvemo, T. (1991 a). Menarcheal age and growth pattern of Indian girls adopted in Sweden. I. Menarcheal age. *Acta Paediatrica Scandinavia, 80,* 852–858.

Proos, L. A., Hovander, Y., & Tuvemo, T. (1991b). Menarcheal age and growth pattern of Indian girls adopted in Sweden. II. Catch-up growth and final height. *Indian Journal of Pediatrics, 58,* 105–114.

Rutter, M. (1981). *Maternal deprivation reassessed* (2nd ed.). Harmondsworth, U.K.: Penguin.

Rutter, M. (1994). Beyond longitudinal data: Causes, consequences, changes and continuity. *Journal of Consulting and Clinical Psychology, 62,* 928–940.

Skuse, D. (1984). Extreme deprivation in early childhood–II. Theoretical issues and a comparative review. *Journal of Child Psychology and Psychiatry, 25,* 543–572.

Thoburn, J. (1993). *Success and failure in permanent family placement.* Aldershot, U.K.: Avebury.

Tizard, B., & Phoenix, A. (1993). *Black, white or mixed race? Race and racism in the lives of young people of mixed parentage.* London: Routledge.

Ulijaszek, S. J. (1994). Between-population variation in pre-adolescent growth. *European Journal of Clinical Nutrition, 48,* S5-414.

Winick, M., Meyer, K. K., & Harris, R. C. (1975). Malnutrition and environmental enrichment by early adoption: Development of adopted Korean children differing greatly in early nutritional status is examined. *Science, 190,* 1173–1175.

8

■ Did you ever, as a teenager, wish your parents were more like those of your friends? There are a number of ways of describing the different disciplinary styles that parents have with their children. Baumrind (1967) defined the authoritarian style as one in which parents expect strict obedience and unquestioning compliance with rules that they unilaterally set. Permissive parents, on the other hand, are friendly with their children, but set few boundaries. Authoritative parents are both firm and flexible, with clear guidelines that children have had an age-appropriate voice in setting. There has been considerable interest in whether different ethnic groups tend to favor one or another of these parenting styles, and whether these parenting styles take on different meaning within the values and relationships of a different culture. In this study, the researchers examined whether culture made a difference in the relationship between children's competence and their mothers' parenting styles. This is an example of how children's development takes place in a multiply-nested environment—child and family embedded within a culture—and how the comparison of cultures reveals meanings that would not be obvious if we only examined one.

Overview Questions

1. What is puzzling about the relationship between parenting style and children's academic performance in Asian American families? Describe the expectations for family relations and self-control in Confucian cultures. Why do these authors think that the Chinese parenting style and socialization for independence seem contradictory?

2. What factors did they try to match between cultural groups, and why? What were the four areas of the child's perceived competence that they measured—which of these were also assessed by teachers?

3. The authors suggest that authority/authoritarian parenting does not mean simply dominance to Chinese parents—what are parents promoting instead? Why do you think authoritarian parenting might be associated with low peer acceptance and low feelings of maternal acceptance?

4. How does this study, taken together with previous studies by Baumrind and Dornbusch, reveal cultural similarities and differences in the relationship between parenting styles and children's academic and social competence?

Focus Questions

1. Examine the distributions of scores in Figure 8.1. Notice for each group, their mean and standard deviation (typical distance from the mean) given in the first paragraph of the results section. How many Chinese mothers scored higher than any Anglo mother did? How many Anglo mothers scored lower than any Chinese mother did? The analysis of variance tests whether the two groups are more different from one another than you would expect, based on the differences within each group. From this graph, would you predict that the analysis of variance would show a significant difference between the groups? Why or why not?

2. Examine Table 8.1. The F column shows the results of the analysis of variance on each item. The bigger the F and the more asterisks beside it indicate lower probability that the difference between the groups is due to chance rather than real differences. (Note that the asterisks have been accidentally omitted from item 31.) Summarize in your own words the general themes of the items that are significantly different.

3. Which of the three perceived competency measures was significantly different between the groups? Did the children's teachers agree with their self-perceptions?

4. When two variables are positively correlated, people with high scores on one variable tend to get high scores on the other variable also. A negative correlations means that high scores on one variable are associated with low scores on the other; r is a measure of this relationship. Summarize in your own words the three significant correlations they report regarding child rearing attitudes and cognitive competence.

Differences in Child Rearing Attitudes Between Immigrant Chinese Mothers and Anglo-American Mothers

Chia-Hui Cindy Wang and Jean S. Phinney

Cultural differences in child rearing attitudes have become a topic of concern among developmental psychologists, because of the importance of such attitudes in a variety of psychological and educational outcomes (Chiu, 1987; Chen and Uttal, 1988; Lin and Fu, 1990; Kelley and Tseng, 1992; Steinberg et al., 1992; Okagaki and Sternberg, 1993). Much interest has been focused on Asians, largely because of the evidence that both Asian and Asian-American students consistently show higher achievement scores than white American students (Stevenson et al., 1986; Sue and Okazaki, 1990; Steinberg et al., 1991). Of the various factors that have been discussed in connection with this difference, the role of parenting style is perhaps the most puzzling. In American samples, authoritarian parenting styles are negatively related to children's and adolescents' competence (Baumrind, 1971, 1989, 1991; Lamborn et al., 1991). Asian-American parents have been shown to be more authoritarian than white American parents, but the academic performance of their children is nevertheless generally superior (Dornbusch et al., 1987; Steinberg, et al., 1991).

Recent reviews and research have begun to explore the complexity of cultural differences and parenting attitudes, and to recognize that simply designating Asian parents as more authoritarian does little to explain actual differences in parent–child relations across cultures. In an important examination of the parenting styles of Chinese parents, Chao (1994) suggested that the concept of authoritarian parenting is somewhat ethnocentric and fails to capture the notion of training in Chinese culture, i.e. teaching children the appropriate or expected behaviors. Teaching of this sort, rather than having the negative connotation that authoritarianism has in American culture, is equated for Chinese with parental concern, caring and involvement.

The research of Chao (1994) calls attention to underlying cultural differences that cannot be captured in a single concept such as authoritarianism. In order to understand child rearing by Chinese mothers, it is necessary to consider the Chinese cultural context, specifically, a culture which is imbued with the spirit of Confucianism (Ho, 1994). A main Confucian doctrine is filial piety, i.e. children must obey their parents unquestioningly, revere their parents' authority, and fulfill their expectations. Compliance with and respect for authority is an integral part of the early socialization process for Chinese children. In turn, the primary responsibility for parents in Chinese society is to nourish and educate their young children. The parents' role is to raise children to be socialized individuals who understand and accept their social obligations, especially filial obligations. If parents do not do a good job in parenting and educating their children, it not only reflects poorly on the parents, but also humiliates the whole family and ancestors (Lang, 1946; Ho, 1981, 1986; Hsu, 1981; Bond and Hwang, 1986; Chen and Uttal, 1988).

Ho (1994) pointed out that Confucian cultures do not simply attempt to teach children obedience to an authority figure. Rather, children are socialized to achieve early mastery of impulse control, so that the child controls his or her own behaviors, rather than being subject to strict discipline and punishment, as is typical of authoritarian parenting in American culture. Other Asian cultures have been shown to share with Chinese culture an emphasis on developing self-control in children. A study of maternal expectations by Hess *et al.* (1980) showed that Japanese mothers tended to expect emotional maturity (self-control), compliance, and social courtesy in their children, in contrast to mothers in the US who expected verbal assertiveness and social skills.

Furthermore, although Chinese culture has often been described as collectivistic, Ho and Chiu (1994) point out that both collectivist and individualist orientations coexist in Chinese culture. They reported that attitudes of self-reliance (individualistic) and cooperation (collectivistic) are positively correlated among Hong Kong university students, i.e. the individualist concept of self-reliance is not antithetical to the Confucian ideal of interdependence. Lin and Fu (1990), in a study of child rearing practices among Chinese, immigrant Chinese, and Caucasian-American parents of young children, found, as expected, that both groups of Chinese parents emphasized achievement, in conformity with the traditional valuing of education. However, contrary to their expectations, the Chinese parents also encouraged children to be independent.

Authoritarian parenting would seem to be at odds with the development of independence and self-reliance. A question of interest then is how Chinese parents socialize children not only to be obedient to authority but also to be independent. Lin and Fu (1990) pointed out the need for further investigation of parental encouragement of independence in different cultures. Ho (1994) has stressed the importance of studying the cultural context in order to understand differences in child rearing across cultures. In pursuit of these goals, the primary purpose of the present study was to explore in depth reported differences in child rearing attitudes between Anglo-American and immigrant Chinese mothers of young children. To go beyond simply documenting global differences in parenting styles, we examined the specific child rearing attitudes endorsed by parents. We expected immigrant Chinese mothers to be generally more authoritarian, but we expected to find evidence of their encouraging independence as well.

In addition to comparing parental attitudes, it is important to examine the relationship of such attitudes to competence in children. Research with predominantly white American samples has consistently shown a negative relationship between authoritarian parenting and academic achievement (Dornbusch *et al.*, 1987; Steinberg *et al.*, 1991). However, Dornbusch *et al.* (1987) found that while Asian high school students rated their parents as more authoritarian, they were performing well academically. Like parental attitudes, school performance needs to be considered within the cultural context. Chinese parents place high value on academic achievement. They strongly believe that education is the best way to be successful in Chinese society. Education is considered to be a means of lifting the individual and all family members to a higher social position (Chao, 1983; Smith, 1989; Ho, 1994). Chen and Stevenson (1989) reported that Chinese children on the mainland and in Taiwan had more homework and spent more time on homework than did American children. In addition, Chinese children obtained more help from family members with their homework than did American children.

Dornbusch *et al.* (1987) pointed out the lack of studies of parenting attitudes and academic achievement across ethnic groups. Much of the existing research on this topic has been with high school students. Thus, a secondary purpose of the present study was to assess the competence of preschool children from both Chinese and Anglo-American backgrounds and to examine the relationship between parental attitudes and children's competence in these two groups.

Method

Participants

The participants were 60 mothers, 60 young children, and 18 children's teachers. There were 30 Anglo-American mothers and their 30 preschool children (18 boys and 12 girls), and 30 immigrant Chinese mothers in the US and their 30 preschool children (16 boys and 14 girls). The criteria for participation for the Anglo-American families were that the mothers were US-born and were identified by the directors of the preschool as Anglo-Americans. The criteria for participation for the Chinese families were that both parents were born in their native countries—Taiwan, Hong Kong, or China, and that the children were born either in the US or in their parents' native country.

The mean age of the Anglo-American children was 4.92 years, and the mean age of the Chinese-American children was 4.96 years. The mean ages of the Anglo-American and immigrant Chinese mothers were 34.37 and 35.40 years, respectively. Maternal characteristics of the two groups were very similar. The subjects were primarily middle to upper middle class and had completed at least a high school education. There were no significant differences between the groups in employment status or the children's birth order. Over 80% of mothers were employed, and over 60% of children were first born.

Of the 30 immigrant Chinese families, 17 families were from Taiwan, 12 were from China, and one was from Hong Kong. The immigrant Chinese families had lived in the US for an average of 9.40 years. With regard to levels of acculturation, over 40% of the immigrant Chinese mothers reported that they spoke only their native language with their children, and an additional one-half spoke predominantly their native language with their children but also used some English. Over 50% of the mothers reported that they participated in all-Chinese gatherings, but an equal proportion preferred that their children have equal number of American and Chinese playmates. About 43% of the immigrant Chinese mothers reported watching more Mandarin than English-speaking television programs, with only few of them (7%) confining themselves to Mandarin or English programs only. The remainder watched more English language programs or both languages equally.

Measures

The measures included a questionnaire of child rearing attitudes completed by the mothers, an interview assessment of children's perceived competence, and ratings of the children's competence completed by the children's teachers.

Attitudes Toward Child Rearing Scale

Parental child rearing attitudes were measured with the attitudes toward child rearing scale (ATCRS) (Croake and Hinkle, 1991). The ATCRS is a 40-item scale containing two sub-scales: a 26-item authoritarian sub-scale and a 14-item democratic sub-scale. Items are responded to on a five-point Likert-type scale, from strongly disagree (1) to strongly agree (5).

On the authoritarian items, a high score indicates agreement, i.e. an authoritarian attitude. The democratic items are reversed in scoring. After reversal of these items, the scores are summed and divided by 40, to obtain the mean. A higher total score reflects more authoritarian attitudes, and a lower total score reflects less authoritarian attitudes. The scale has a 1-week test-retest reliability of 0.91 (Hinkle *et al.*, 1980).

For the present study, the ATCRS was translated into Chinese and then back-translated into English. Internal consistency was assessed for the entire sample by means of Cronbach's alpha. For the authoritarian and democratic sub-scales, alphas were 0.90 and 0.77, respectively (see Table 8.1 for complete scale).

Demographic Information

Background information supplied by the mothers included the mother's age, birth order of children, level of education, employment status, and household income. Immigrant Chinese mothers were asked to answer additional questions to measure their acculturation characteristics: language use, the ethnic make-up in social relations, and Chinese and English media use. This survey was available in English and Chinese.

Children's Perceived Competence

Children's competence was assessed with the pictorial scale of perceived competence and social acceptance for young children (Harter and Pike, 1984). The scale is individually administered and assesses children's self-perception of competence. Competence is rated on 24 items divided into four sub-scales: (1) cognitive competence, including doing puzzles, counting, and knowing numbers, colors, and letters; (2) physical competence, focusing on the child's ability in sports and outdoor games; (3) peer acceptance, assessing the child's competence with peers; and (4) maternal acceptance, measuring the relationship between the child and the mother. Four items were eliminated in the present study because they were inappropriate in terms of the cultural context or school setting. The omitted items in the testing were: getting stars on papers (cognitive competence sub-scale), staying overnight as well as eating dinner at friends' houses (peer acceptance sub-scale), and swinging well (physical competence sub-scale). Scores ranged from 1, indicating low competence or low acceptance, to 4, indicating high competence or high acceptance.

The pictorial scale of perceived competence and social acceptance for young children was translated into Mandarin for use with the Chinese children and did not require back-translation because it was administered verbally by the first author. The reported Cronbach alphas of the sub-scales for Anglo-American and Chinese-American children respectively, were, for cognitive competence, 0.82 and 0.33; for peer acceptance, 0.89 and 0.89; for physical competence, 0.53 and 0.46; and for maternal acceptance, 0.81 and 0.80. Because of the low reliabilities of physical competence scale, this scale was not used in the analyses.

Teachers' Ratings of Child Competence

The teacher rating scale of child's actual competence and social acceptance (Harter and Pike, 1984) was used to verify the children's perceptions of competence. Teachers rated children in only three of the four areas included in the pictorial scale of perceived competence and social acceptance for young children. The three areas were: (1) cognitive

TABLE 8.1 *Means and Standard Deviations for the Attitudes toward Child Rearing Scale Items Grouped by Authoritarian and Democratic Items*

	Anglo M	Chinese M	F
Authoritarian items:			
1. Withholding allowance is a good method of discipline	2.70 (1.21)	3.73 (1.19)	2.96
3. Parents should remind children to say 'Please' and 'Thank you' when they forget	4.43 (0.94)	4.73 (0.45)	2.51
4. Parents should regularly help their children with the homework	3.93 (0.87)	4.60 (0.56)	12.45***
5. It is helpful to frequently remind children of the rules at home	3.73 (1.17)	4.67 (0.48)	16.29***
6. Children should obey the wishes of their elders	3.40 (1.04)	3.97 (0.77)	5.80*
8. In most quarrels between young children, adults should arbitrate	2.67 (0.99)	3.77 (0.94)	19.48***
10. Children should not be allowed to wear clothes that are noticeably dirty	3.60 (0.89)	4.37 (0.62)	14.97***
12. Physical punishment is often the only method of discipline that will work	1.77 (1.07)	2.80 (1.24)	11.88***
13. Parents should demand respect from their children	3.30 (1.47)	4.43 (0.57)	15.59***
14. Parents should make it their responsibility to see how their children are behaving in school	4.50 (0.51)	4.60 (0.68)	0.42
15. Parents should step in if the teacher seems to not understand the behavior of their children	4.07 (0.64)	4.47 (0.57)	6.53*
18. Children should not be allowed to go outside on a cold day without wearing warm clothing	3.93 (0.94)	4.23 (0.57)	2.22
19. If parents really do a good job rearing their children, the children will turn out fine	2.73 (1.11)	4.17 (0.79)	33.08***
21. Parents should try to convince fearful children that there is nothing of which to be afraid	2.87 (1.20)	4.50 (0.51)	47.40***
23. Parents should remind children when it is time to go to bed	4.03 (0.77)	4.27 (0.45)	2.07
25. Parents should praise their children when the children have been good	4.57 (0.68)	4.64 (0.49)	0.19
27. Parents should make sure their children look right in their dress	3.50 (1.01)	4.63 (0.49)	30.64***
28. Children should be paid for doing extra chores around the house	2.80 (1.06)	2.73 (1.08)	0.06
30. Parents should stop a fight between two children if it looks as if one of them will get hurt	4.63 (0.49)	4.53 (0.51)	0.60
31. Children need punishment in order to learn proper behavior	3.03 (1.43)	4.47 (0.51)	26.90
33. Children need to be reminded regularly as to what's right and wrong	3.77 (1.22)	4.67 (0.48)	14.08***
34. Parents should step in if an adult neighbor seems to be unfairly reprimanding their children	3.83 (1.23)	3.77 (0.94)	0.06
36. Parents are morally responsible for how their children behave	3.30 (1.12)	4.40 (0.50)	24.20***
37. Parents should step in if a bully is picking on their children	4.10 (0.61)	4.33 (0.48)	2.73
38. If children receive lots of love and affection they will turn out fine	3.13 (1.07)	4.50 (0.57)	37.82***
40. Parents should point out their children's mistakes	2.90 (1.13)	4.77 (0.43)	72.06***
Democratic items:[a]			
2. Children should be invited to participate in parent–teacher conferences	2.97 (1.07)	3.97 (0.85)	16.13***
7. Children should be able to treat their playthings as they wish, without fear of punishment	2.30 (0.99)	2.67 (1.37)	1.41
9. Children should be able to choose how much of each food they want at a meal	3.40 (1.07)	3.17 (1.09)	0.70
11. Children should participate in a decision about their bedtime	2.47 (1.04)	2.80 (1.10)	1.46
16. Parents should not interfere if an older child seems to be picking on a younger child	1.83 (0.87)	1.73 (0.64)	0.26
17. Children of six can be helpful in deciding whether the family should buy a new car	2.13 (1.17)	3.00 (1.17)	8.22**

TABLE 8.1   *Continued*

	Anglo M	Chinese M	F
20. Parents should assume that their children will do whatever they have agreed to do	2.40 (1.07)	3.90 (0.92)	33.81***
22. Parents who remind their children several times to do a task are training the children in disobedience	2.50 (1.04)	3.47 (1.04)	12.91***
24. All members of family regardless of age should agree on most family decisions	2.50 (1.04)	4.13 (0.68)	51.62***
26. Children should be able to spend their allowance as they choose	3.53 (1.14)	3.27 (1.11)	0.84
29. It is best for parents not to become involved when children are misbehaving	1.57 (0.97)	2.70 (1.32)	14.39***
32. Children should be responsible for putting away their own toys as soon as they learn to walk	2.70 (1.15)	3.97 (0.93)	22.06***
35. To correct children for something that they already know is wrong is not helpful to the children	1.93 (0.79)	3.73 (1.02)	59.05***
39. Parents are disrespectful of their children when they do something their children can do for themselves	2.60 (1.04)	3.40 (1.04)	8.92**

[a]Unreversed scores on the democratic items are presented, so that a high score reflects greater agreement.

*$p < 0.02$, **$p < 0.01$, ***$p < 0.001$.

competence; (2) physical competence; and (3) peer acceptance. The area of maternal acceptance was eliminated because this information may not be known to the teacher. The measure contained six items for each area. Scores ranged from 1, indicating low competence or low acceptance, to 4 indicating high competence or high acceptance.

Procedures

The Anglo-American children were recruited from predominantly white preschools, while the Chinese-American children were recruited from predominantly Asian preschools, all in suburban areas of southern California. If the recruited children met the criteria, their mothers were sent a letter about the study and were asked to review and sign the consent form. The letter and consent forms were available in English and Chinese. Mothers who agreed to participate were asked to complete the background survey and the ATCRS, and to return them to the school's director within 1 week. (Only the Chinese versions of background survey and ATCRS were used with the immigrant Chinese mothers.)

For the child interviews, appointments were arranged with the director of the preschool. All interviews were conducted by the first author. Before the interview, the interviewer was introduced to the child by the teacher and had a warm-up play session to enhance rapport. Each interview was individually conducted and lasted 10–15 min. To facilitate data collection for the Chinese-American children, the interviewer used both languages (predominantly Mandarin, less English) as appropriate.

The teachers of the children were requested to rate the children's competence and mail the evaluation form to the researcher.

Results

Child Rearing Attitudes

An analysis of variance carried out to compare child rearing attitudes of Anglo-American with immigrant Chinese mothers showed a significant difference between the mean ATCRS scores of the two groups, $F(1, 58) = 9.12$, $p < 0.01$. The immigrant Chinese mothers were more authoritarian ($M = 3.71$, S.D. $= 0.22$) than the Anglo-American mothers ($M = 3.51$, S.D. $= 0.28$). In order to illustrate the distribution of scores, individual mean scores were grouped into six clusters defined as being 1, 2, or 3 standard deviations (i.e. 0.3, 0.6 or 0.9) above or below the overall mean (3.60). Figure 8.1 shows the mean ATCRS scores for each cluster on the axis and the frequency of each cluster for the two cultural groups. The Anglo-American mothers had more scores in the lower (less authoritarian) clusters and none in the highest cluster. In contrast, the immigrant Chinese mothers had more scores in the higher (more authoritarian) clusters, and none in the two lowest.

To examine more closely the distinctions between the two groups as measured by the 40 items of the ATCRS, a multivariate analysis of variance (MANOVA) was performed, using ethnic group as the independent variable and all 40 items of ATCRS as dependent variables. The Hotellings test yielded a significant difference between the means of two groups, $T^2 (40, 58) = 11.35$, $p < 0.001$. Follow-up univariate ANOVAs were used to determine which items of ATCRS contributed to group differences. A significance level of 0.02 was used. Results showed that 25 out of 40 items differed significantly between the Anglo-American and immigrant Chinese mothers (see Table 8.1). Of the 25 items that differed significantly between the groups, 16 were derived from the authoritarian items, while the other nine were from the democratic items. The mean score of each of these 16 authoritarian items was significantly higher for immigrant Chinese mothers than for the Anglo-American mothers. An examination of the individual items suggests that the Chinese mothers were more authoritarian in the areas of corporal punishment (e.g. physical punishment) and directiveness (e.g. telling children what to do and demanding children do things) (cf. Robinson *et al.*, 1995).

However, the mean score of each of the nine democratic items that differed significantly between the groups showed *less* authoritarian (or more democratic) attitudes for immigrant Chinese mothers than for the Anglo-American mothers. (In Table 8.1, for purposes of illustration, unreversed scores on the democratic items are presented, so that a higher score reflects greater agreement with the item.) Although the authors of the ATCRS considered these items as democratic, an examination of the individual items suggests that they represent independence training and de-

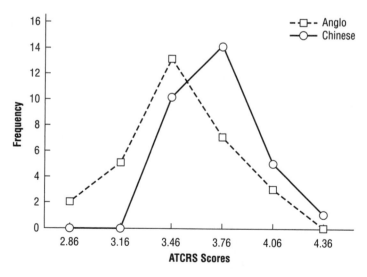

FIGURE 8.1 *Distribution of ATCRS Scores for Anglo-American and Immigrant Chinese Mothers*

mands for maturity. On the basis of these items, immigrant Chinese mothers were more likely to encourage independence and demand maturity from their children.

Competence Scales

Separate analyses of variance for each of the three scales of competence and acceptance showed no significant differences between the Chinese-American and the Anglo-American children in the areas of peer acceptance and maternal acceptance. However, the Chinese-American children scored higher in cognitive competence ($M = 3.88$, S.D. $= 0.18$) than Anglo-American children ($M = 3.58$, S.D. $= 0.48$), $F(1, 58) = 10.20$, $p < 0.01$. This difference should be regarded with caution given the low reliability of the scale for the Chinese. However, the low reliability may be explained by a ceiling effect with the Chinese-American children; 18 out of 30 of these children obtained a perfect score (four points), and eight more received the next highest score (3.8 points). In contrast, only 14 Anglo-American children obtained a perfect score, and one received the next highest score.

Teacher Rating Scale

A series of *t*-tests were carried out separately for each ethnic group to compare children's perceived cognitive competence and peer acceptance with teachers' judgments of these areas. There were no significant differences between the scores of children from either group and their teachers' ratings. Thus, the children's perceived competence was supported by the teacher ratings and appear to be reasonably accurate.

Child Rearing Attitudes and Cognitive Competence

Correlations were calculated separately for Anglo-American and Chinese-American children between the three competence scales and the overall ATCRS as well as the two scales based on the 25 items that differed significantly between the Anglo-American and Chinese-American groups (i.e. the 16 items from the authoritarian sub-scale and the nine items from the democratic sub-scale). There were no significant correlations for either group between the three competence scales and the overall ATCRS scale or the nine items from the democratic sub-scale. However, for the 16 items from the authoritarian sub-scale, for the immigrant Chinese mothers only, there was a positive correlation with cognitive competence ($r = 0.38$, $p < 0.05$), and negative correlations with peer acceptance ($r = -0.42$, $p < 0.05$) and maternal acceptance ($r = -0.47$, $p < 0.01$). Immigrant Chinese mothers with more authoritarian attitudes had children who showed higher cognitive competence but lower peer and maternal acceptance. The 16 items from the authoritarian sub-scale were unrelated to any of the competence scales for the Anglo-American children.

Discussion

The findings of the present study provide new insights into differences in child rearing attitudes between Anglo-American and immigrant Chinese mothers. In accordance with expectations based on previous research (Chiu, 1987; Lin and Fu, 1990; Kelley and Tseng, 1992), immigrant Chinese mothers were more authoritarian than Anglo-American mothers. However, the immigrant Chinese mothers also revealed attitudes that appear contrary to authoritarian attitudes, in that they encouraged children's independence and self-reliance.

Specifically, the immigrant Chinese mothers scored significantly higher or were more authoritarian than the Anglo-American mothers on 16 items from the authoritarian sub-scale of the ATCRS. These items include believing that children should obey their elders, and that they need punishment, including physical punishment, in order to learn; and that parents should demand respect from children, remind children about rules, help with their homework and be responsible for their behavior. These attitudes reflect Chinese cultural values regarding child rearing (Ho, 1986, 1994) that continue to exist among immigrant Chinese mothers in the US.

However, for the nine items of the democratic sub-scale on which the two groups differed significantly, the immigrant Chinese mothers had less authoritarian (or more democratic) attitudes than the Anglo-American mothers. These results reveal another side to Chinese parenting attitudes. These items indicate that immigrant Chinese mothers seek to provide the opportunity and encouragement for their children to develop self-reliance and independence. For example, their attitudes suggest that they are more likely than Anglo-American mothers to favor not doing things for children that children could do for themselves, making children take care of their own possessions, and letting them participate in family decisions. These results are consistent with those of Lin and Fu (1990) who reported that Chinese parents of young children encouraged independence more than American parents did. This encouragement of independence coexists with authoritarian attitudes and suggests that for the Chinese, the concept 'authoritarian' is not equated simply with dominance, as it often is for Americans. Rather, Chinese parents exert authority in order to help children achieve specific goals deemed important in the culture (Chao, 1994).

One of the central values of Chinese child rearing is education. Chinese parents place a high value on education and consider it to be the means to success (Ho, 1981, 1994). Parental authority may thus be directed toward ensuring that children achieve academic goals. In the present study, the Chinese-American children scored higher in cognitive competence than the Anglo-American children, and their cognitive competence was positively associated with more authoritarian parenting. The measure of cognitive competence used in the study included knowing colors, numbers, and letters—abilities which the parents are likely to consider important for future academic success. Many of the Chinese-American children obtained perfect scores on this measure, suggesting that the immigrant Chinese parents are actively involved in promoting the skills needed for early school success. Authoritarian child rearing in Chinese society, as contrasted with the Western society, has a role in promoting educational goals. It appears that rather than dominating the children's behaviors, immigrant Chinese parents are directing children toward academic goals.

On the other hand, parental authoritarian attitudes had a negative impact on the Chinese-American children's competence with peers and their feelings of acceptance by their mothers. These results are consistent with work by Baumrind (1971) with predominantly Anglo-American preschoolers, showing that children of authoritarian parents were less socially competent than those with authoritative parents (see also Hart et al., 1990, 1992). Much of the recent research on parenting styles has focused on school outcomes; the current results suggest the importance of considering social and emotional outcomes as well.

Rogoff and Morelli (1989) reviewed cross-cultural research supporting the idea that human functioning cannot be separated from the contexts of the activities, and that behavior and development vary according to cultural context. In order to understand children from diverse backgrounds, researchers and practitioners must understand the context provided by their cultures of origin. The assumption that authoritarian parenting has the same meaning and the same outcomes in various ethnic cultures as in Anglo-American culture fails to take into account the different values that underlie parenting (Chao, 1994), such as the Confucian values in evidence in the present study.

An awareness of diverse ethnic backgrounds and parenting styles promotes understanding of child development within a given cultural context. This study provides a more complete picture of Chinese child rearing attitudes by showing how values that appear from an American perspective to be inconsistent—exerting control and promoting independence—may co-exist within the Chinese cultural context. Although immigrant Chinese mothers are in some ways more authoritarian than Anglo-American mothers, they nevertheless offer their children leeway in many situations, in order to develop independence. Moreover, at least with young children, their authoritarian approach appears to benefit the acquisition of cognitive skills, while having a negative impact on perceptions of peer and maternal acceptance. Clearly there is need for further research on child rearing attitudes across ethnic groups, in order to clarify the ways in which specific parental values have implications not only for cognitive competence but also for social and emotional outcomes.

References

Baumrind, D. (1971). Current patterns of parental authority. *Developmental Psychology Monograph, 4* (1, part 2).

Baumrind, D. (1989). Rearing competent children. In W. Damon (Ed.), *Child Development Today and Tomorrow.* San Francisco: Jossey Bass, pp. 349–378.

Baumrind, D. (1991). Parenting styles and adolescent development. In J. Brooks-Gunn, R. Lerner and A. C. Petersen (Eds), *The Encyclopedia of Adolescence.* New York: Garland, pp. 746–758.

Bond, M. and Hwang, K. (1986). The social psychology of Chinese people. In M. Bond (Ed.), *The Psychology of the Chinese People.* New York: Oxford University, pp. 213–266.

Chao, P. (1983). *Chinese Kinship.* London: Kegan Paul.

Chao, R. (1994). Beyond parental control and authoritarian parenting style: understanding Chinese parenting through the cultural notion of training. *Child Development, 65,* 1111–1119.

Chen, C. and Uttal, D. (1988). Cultural values, parents' beliefs, and children's achievement in the United States and China. *Human Development, 31,* 351–358.

Chen, C. and Stevenson, H. W. (1989). Homework: a cross-cultural examination. *Child Development, 60,* 551–561.

Chiu, L (1987). Child-rearing attitudes of Chinese, Chinese-American, and Anglo-American mothers. *International Journal of Psychology, 22,* 409–419.

Croake, J. W. and Hinkle, D. E. (1991). Attitudes toward child rearing scale (ATCRS). *The ETS Test Collection Catalog.* Vol. 5. Phoenix, AZ: Oryx Press.

Dornbusch, S., Ritter, P., Leiderman, P. H., Roberts, D. and Fraleigh, M. (1987). The relation of parenting style to adolescent school performance. *Child Development, 58,* 1244–1257.

Hart, C., Ladd, G. and Burleson, B. (1990). Children's expectation of the outcomes of social strategies: relations with sociometric status and maternal disciplinary styles. *Child Development, 61,* 127–137.

Hart, C., DeWolf, D., Wozniak, P. and Burts, D. (1992). Maternal and paternal disciplinary styles: relations with preschoolers' playground behavioral orientations and peer status. *Child Development, 63,* 879–892.

Harter, S. and Pike, R (1984). The pictorial scale of perceived competence and social acceptance for young children. *Child Development, 55,* 1962–1982.

Hess, R., Kashiwagi, K., Azuma, H., Price, G. and Dickson, W. (1980). Maternal expectations for mastery of developmental tasks in Japan and the United States. *International Journal of Psychology, 15,* 259–271.

Hinkle, D., Arnold, C., Croake, J. and Keller, J. (1980). Adlerian parent education: changes in parents' attitudes and behaviors and children's self-esteem. *American Journal of Family Therapy, 8,* 32–43.

Ho, D. (1981). Traditional patterns of socialization in Chinese society. *Acta Psychologica Taiwanica, 23,* 81–95.

Ho, D. (1986). Chinese patterns of socialization: a critical review. In M. Bond (Ed.), *The Psychology of the Chinese People.* Hong Kong: Oxford University Press, pp. 1–37.

Ho, D. (1994). Cognitive socialization in Confucian heritage cultures. In P. Greenfield and R. Cocking (Eds), *Cross-Cultural Roots of Minority Child Development*. Hillsdale, NJ: Lawrence Erlbaum, pp. 285–313.

Ho, D. and Chiu, C. Y. (1994). Component ideas of individualism, collectivism, and social organization. In U. Kim, H. C. Triandis, C. Kagitcibasi, S. C. Choi and G. Yoon (Eds), *Individualism and Collectivism: Theory, Method, and Applications*. Thousand Oaks, CA: Sage, pp. 137–156.

Hsu, F. L. K. (1981). *Americans and Chinese: Passage to Differences*. Honolulu: University Press of Hawaii.

Kelley, M. L. and Tseng, H. (1992). Cultural differences in child-rearing: a comparison of immigrant Chinese and Caucasian American mothers. *Journal of Cross-cultural Psychology, 23*, 444–455.

Lamborn, S. D., Mounts, N. S., Sternberg, L. and Dornbusch, S. M. (1991). Patterns of competence and adjustment among adolescents from authoritative, authoritarian, indulgent, and neglectful families. *Child Development, 62*, 1049–1065.

Lang, O. (1946). *Chinese Family and Society*. New Haven, CT: Yale University Press.

Lin, C. and Fu, V. (1990). A comparison of child-rearing practices among Chinese, Immigrant Chinese, and Caucasian–American parents. *Child Development, 61*, 429–433.

Okagaki, L. and Sternberg, R. (1993). Parental beliefs and children's school performance. *Child Development, 64*, 36–56.

Robinson, C. C., Mandleco, B., Olsen, S. F. and Hart, C. (1995). Authoritative, authoritarian, and permissive parenting practices: development of a new measure. *Psychological Reports, 77*, 819–830.

Rogoff, B. and Morelli, G. (1989). Perspectives on children's development from cultural psychology. *American Psychologist, 44*, 343–348.

Smith, D. C. (1989). *Children of China: An Historical Inquiry into the Relationship Between Chinese Family Life and Academic Achievement*. (ERIC Document Reproduction Service No. ED 305 152).

Steinberg, L., Dornbusch, S. and Brown, B. (1992). Ethnic differences in adolescent achievement: an ecological perspective. *American Psychologist, 47*, 723–729.

Steinberg, L., Mounts, N., Lamborn, S. and Dornbusch, S. (1991). Authoritative parenting and adolescent adjustment across various ecological niches. *Journal of Research on Adolescence. 1*, 19–36.

Stevenson, H., Lee, S. and Stigler, J. (1986). Mathematics achievement of Chinese, Japanese, and American children. *Science, 231*, 693–699.

Sue, S. and Okazaki, S. (1990). Asian–American educational achievements: a phenomenon in search of an explanation. *American Psychologist, 45*, 913–920.

9

■ By the end of the second year, infants show signs of recognizing themselves as distinct entities, for example recognizing their own reflection in the mirror and categorizing themselves by age and gender (Lewis & Brooks-Gunn, 1979). Even this dawning recognition of our individuality takes place within a social environment. Social interaction is important in the child's elaboration of a sense of self. For example, children with high self-esteem are likely to have formed warm secure attachments with parents who relate positively to them (e.g., Verschueren, Marcoen, & Schoefs, 1996). As Cooley (1902) recognized, we see ourselves reflected in how others see us. Consequently, children in different social environments generally come to define themselves in ways that reflect the culture around them. Even within a culture, patterns of self-definition may differ depending on characteristics such as social class or religion. This article describes one familial practice, storytelling, by which families help children construct a sense of who they are. The authors explore how social class affects this practice and may in turn shape children's construction of the self.

Overview Questions

1. Why have developmentalists come to question the idea that an independent self is a universal and normative developmental achievement?

2. These authors make two assumptions about how the self is constructed—what are they, and how does this relate to the term "selfways"? Why do these authors think that it is important to study intra-group variability in European Americans in order to understand the selfways of that culture? Why did these authors choose to focus on observations of cultural practices, rather than parental attitudes? What are two other selfways that may enhance autonomy in European-American children?

3. Although they say that some aspects of the self are present beginning in infancy, these authors focus on the "narrative" or "extended" and "conceptual" selves—what do they mean by these terms? What are the four basic reasons why Wiley et al. chose to focus on co-narrated personal storytelling? (Hint: list two different characteristics of the genre.)

4. Summarize their comparisons of the roles of speaker, initiator, and opponent in the two communities. What conclusions do they draw about the nature and meaning of children's autonomy in Daly Park versus Longwood? What similarities do they note, as both belonging to a broader European-American culture?

5. Reflect on your own experience of personal storytelling in your family. Who gets control over joint narrations? How important is factual accuracy? Is having your own opinion a "right" of the participant? Do others engage in "face-saving" moves to protect one's self-esteem? You might enjoy noticing these patterns at an upcoming family dinner or celebration.

Focus Questions _____

1. Wiley et al. focus on three basic aspects of the child's participation in co-narration: speaker rights, authorship (initiation), and authorship (opponent role). What do they mean by each of these and why do they believe that these roles could differ in the working-class community versus the middle-class community? How do you think that each of these roles could contribute to a sense of the self as autonomous?

2. What are some important similarities and differences between Daly Park and Longwood in terms of geographic location, ethnicity, religion, parent education and employment, and siblings? Why is it important for the purposes of the study that the children in the two samples were of comparable language ability? (A note of explanation: a common convention is to report age as "years,months." Consequently, "2,6" means "two years and 6 months old.")

3. The present study is based on how many hours of videotaped observations of each child? What role did the researchers assume in the family's home? What do you think are the advantages and disadvantages of this form of data collection?

4. What was their definition of "co-narration"? Why was it important for them to be very specific and reliable in identifying the segments of the tape to be coded (the co-narrations) and to provide very explicit and reliable definitions of each of the roles (speaker, initiator, opponent)? What features of each conflict episode did they record? What do you think each of these might have to do with the sense of the self as autonomous?

5. In the results section, "mean" is the arithmetic average, "median" is the score that lies in the middle (half the scores are higher, half lower), and "range" is the lowest to highest score. In Table 9.1, the top row of numbers for each variable represents the means for each of the two communities, the bottom row of numbers shows each individual child's score. For each of the following variables, indicate whether the two communities were the same, or which was higher: number of utterances contributed to co-narrations by child, child initiations, occurrence of conflict episodes (proportion of total co-narrations, lengths), proportion of conflicts in which child is initially opposed, who got the last word in a conflict. What qualitative differences did they observe in style of conflict between the two communities?

Constructing Autonomous Selves through Narrative Practices: A Comparative Study of Working-Class and Middle-Class Families

Angela R. Wiley, Amanda J. Rose, Lisa K. Burger, and Peggy J. Miller

Introduction

Becoming an independent person has been viewed traditionally as one of the culminating achievements of child and adolescent development. The third year of life is often seen as the moment at which children take their first decisive steps toward autonomy. In his classic theory of psychosocial development, for example, Erikson (1963) defined the struggle to defeat shame and doubt and attain increased autonomy from the mother as the chief developmental challenge of the toddler years, a challenge paralleled, at a more advanced level, by the adolescent's struggles to forge an independent identity. However, the assumption that the autonomous self is a "natural" and universal developmental achievement, prefaced by a single normative developmental pathway, is increasingly being questioned in the face of mounting evidence that construals of the self vary substantially within and across cultures (Greenfield & Cocking, 1994; Markus & Kitayama, 1991; Triandis, 1990). Instead, the self that is so familiar to developmentalists—that is, the self as an independent, clearly bounded entity—is now recognized to be but one cultural framework for interpreting the self, a framework deeply rooted in the individualistic ideology and philosophical traditions of much of North America and Europe (Markus & Kitayama, 1994b; Taylor, 1989).

A key question that arises from this new appreciation of the cultural plurality of selves has to do with the process by which these different construals of self get created. How can we explain how children growing up in some cultural communities come to develop autonomous selves (whereas those in other cultural communities come to develop interdependent selves)? This article is intended to illuminate the nature of this process, with particular focus on the third year of life and on children from two European American communities. We examine everyday narrative practices as an arena for the social construction of autonomous selves.

Theoretical Assumptions

Our theoretical stance toward the question of how culture-specific selves get created rests on the twin premises that selves are constructed in interaction with others, and that they develop through participation in sociocultural practices. This is a view upon which several cultural psychologists have begun to converge (Bruner, 1990; Miller, Mintz, Hoogstra, Fung, & Potts, 1992; Miller, Potts, Fung, Hoogstra, & Mintz, 1990; Shweder et al., 1998). It owes a debt to G. H. Mead's (1934) symbolic interactionism and to a variety of recent efforts to extend practice theories, especially sociohistorical theory, beyond cognitive development to encompass the development of self and identity (Goodnow, Miller, & Kessel, 1995; Holland & Valsiner, 1988; Lave & Wenger, 1991; Miller, 1994; Miller et al., 1990). From this perspective, children come to enact certain kinds of selves by virtue of their everyday participation with other people in characteristic self-relevant practices—what Markus, Mullally, and Kitayama (1997) call "selfways." These selfways carry with them shared meanings and are situated in particular institutions, such as the family, the school, and the media.

A major empirical challenge posed by this theoretical perspective is to identify what the relevant selfways are for particular sociocultural groups at particular moments in the lifespan and to discover how children participate in those selfways. Ironically, selfways may be especially difficult to see when the cultural case is well known to us—an instance of what Ochs and Schieffelin (1984) have called "a paradox of familiarity." By focusing on a cultural case—European American—that is pervasively represented in the literature on self development but is rarely scrutinized as a cultural case, we hope to bring to light some of the virtually invisible practices that underlie self development. We want to understand more about how autonomy-promoting developmental pathways get constituted for European American youngsters.

In our view, this goal cannot be fully accomplished without acknowledging intragroup variability in selfways, and hence in autonomous selves. Markus and Kitayama (1994a) review several studies that suggest that marginalized groups within the United States, including women, members of nondominant ethnic groups, the poor, and the unschooled, are less likely to define themselves as autonomous. They say, "These findings suggest that those with power and privilege are those most likely to internalize the prevailing European-American cultural frame . . . and to 'naturally' experience themselves as autonomous individuals" (p. 575). A recent study by Harwood, Miller, and Irizarry (1995) supports this view. These researchers found that both middle-class and working-class Anglo mothers in the United States used a dimension of "self-maximization" to describe qualities that they found desirable in their children. Self-maximization included the interrelated components of independence, self-confidence, and the development of the individual's full potential. Although mothers from both American groups endorsed this ideal, working-class mothers did so less frequently and with an awareness that its attainment might be problematic for their children. This study powerfully demonstrates that there are subtle but important intracultural differences in the meanings that parents attach to key cultural ideals of the self, and suggests that further study of class-based variants of autonomous selves is warranted.

The present study takes up this challenge by comparing young children and their families from two European American communities in Chicago, one working class (Daly Park) and the other middle class (Longwood). We use an approach that is complementary to that of Harwood et al. (1995). Whereas they focused on parental beliefs and values, we examine self-relevant practices on the assumption that there is no better way to uncover the actual processes by which selves are constructed (Miller, 1994; Miller et al., 1992). Cultural psychologists have begun to identify some of the cultural practices that may be relevant to the creation of autonomous selves in early childhood. For example, Rogoff, Mistry, Goncu, and Mosier (1993) report that gradually handing over more and more responsibility for accomplishing a task and praising toddlers' individual efforts are common parental practices in European American families, whereas allowing children to structure their own learning and not overruling them when they refuse or insist are more common in communities in which children are not segregated from adult activities. Sleeping arrangements provide another example: The practice of having children sleep alone at night is thought by middle-class European American adults to encourage children's autonomy (Morelli, Rogoff, Oppenheimer, & Goldsmith, 1992; Shweder, Jensen, & Goldstein,1995). Still another cultural practice that seems particularly worthy of scrutiny as an arena for the construction of autonomous selves is everyday narrative.

Why Focus on Narrative Practices?

We assume that people everywhere have some very basic appreciation of self-other differentiation, an appreciation that is implicit in the biological fact that each person is a distinct organism with his or her own perceptual system. At the same time, we believe that cultures have considerable latitude in the extent to which they create systems of meaning and interpretive frameworks that emphasize, elaborate, and celebrate the individual's separateness from other people. Our focus is on these elaborations.

In European American culture, these elaborations apparently begin very early in life, with such selfways as addressing newborns in proto-conversations. However, our concern in this article is with the period from 2,6 to 3,0 years of age; by this time, children's verbal fluency is well established, and they have become avid narrators of their own experience. We acknowledge that there are senses of self—Stern's (1985) core, subjective, and verbal selves and Neisser's (1988) ecological and interpersonal selves—that emerge earlier in development, but in this article we limit our attention to selves that are verbally expressed and enacted. That is, we focus on what Stern (1989) has called the narrative sense of self and on what Neisser has called the extended and conceptual selves. According to Neisser, the extended self is the self that extends into the past and the future, known primarily through memory, whereas the conceptual self is based on socially established and verbally expressed ideas. Our view is that one of the ways in which conceptual selves begin to get created is by way of children's participation in narrative practices in which family members routinely apply culture-specific interpretations to their past experiences. From this perspective, extended selves and conceptual selves are simultaneously constituted through children's participation in narrative selfways.

The specific narrative practice on which we focus is co-narrated personal storytelling. This practice, in which the child and one or more family members collaborate in narrating an event from the child's past experience, recommends itself for several reasons. First, it is now well established that children are able to recount past experiences in conversation by 2 years of age (Eisenberg, 1985; Fivush, Gray, & Fromhoff, 1987; McCabe & Peterson, 1991; Miller & Sperry 1988; Nelson, 1993; Sperry & Sperry, 1996). Second, studies by our research team suggest that personal storytelling, involving 2-year-olds as participants, occurs routinely as part of everyday life in families from a variety of cultural backgrounds, including working-class and middle-class European American, working-class and middle-class African American, and middle-class Chinese in Taiwan (Miller, 1994; Miller, Fung, & Mintz, 1996; Miller, Wiley, Fung, & Liang, 1997; Miller et al., 1992; Williams, 1994). Thus, this type of narrative practice is robustly available early in life and with sufficient range across diverse communities to permit fruitful investigation.

Additional reasons for studying personal storytelling follow from the nature of the genre itself. In earlier work, we drew upon cultural, sociological, and conversation-analytic perspectives to argue that multiple sources of narrative-self affinity converge in personal storytelling, rendering it an especially important arena for self-construction (Miller et al., 1990). For example, like all narratives, stories of personal experience are organized with respect to time, allowing for the representation of "self-continuity" (Hallowell, 1955), and make use of devices for rendering human action intelligible (Gergen, 1990). In addition to these temporal and causal affinities, there is also an evaluative affinity. Stories, like selves, are inherently evaluative. Because stories of personal experience are expressed from a personal perspective, they are replete with explicit and implicit messages about the self-protagonist (Goffman, 1974; Labov & Waletzky, 1967).

However, most important to our current argument is the fact that personal storytelling occurs in a conversational medium. As such, it is inherently dynamic and interactive, allowing for the enactment of autonomy in the social act of co-narration itself. In this explicitly self-referential practice, claims about the child's past experience are negotiated by the child and others in the course of ongoing talk. A rendition of the child's past experiences emerges from the joint contributions of child and caregiver(s) (Engel, 1986; Fivush, 1994; Miller et al., 1992). At times, child and co-narrator may even assert conflicting versions of the child's own past experiences. A basic premise of this article is that the structuring of young children's participation in personal storytelling affords an important route by which they construct autonomous selves with significant others.

Enacting Autonomous Selves via Speaker, Author, and Opponent Roles

Several studies of children's everyday narrative activity in families have made a distinction between children's rights as speaker versus their rights as author (Blum-Kulka & Snow, 1992; Miller et al., 1990; Ochs & Taylor, 1995; Taylor, 1995). For example, drawing upon Goffman's distinction between speaker and author roles, Miller et al. (1990) described a narrative practice in which young children

contributed verbally to narrations of their past experiences—that is, they participated as speakers—but caregivers intervened in ways that overrode the child's version of what had happened, thereby limiting the child's rights to author or exercise
control over his or her own experience. In this article we elaborate this speaker/
author distinction by way of distinguishing among several levels of narrative autonomy in Daly Park and Longwood.

We defined the first level of narrative autonomy in terms of the speaker role:
To what degree are young children in the two communities granted speaker rights
in narrating their past experiences? We expected that youngsters from both communities would participate as speakers, but that children from working-class Daly
Park would have more opportunities to participate, compared with their middle-
class counterparts in Longwood. This expectation was based on past research that
showed that personal storytelling is highly valued and avidly practiced by adults in
working-class communities (Bauman,1986; Labov & Waletzky, 1967; Miller, 1994),
and that children participate from an early age (Heath, 1983; Miller, 1994; Miller &
Sperry, 1988).

The second level focused on authorship. To what degree are young children in
the two communities granted rights of authorship in narrating their past experiences? There are a number of ways in which "authorship" could be assessed. We
chose to define authorship in two ways—in terms of initiation of stories, and opposition in stories. Ochs and Taylor (1995) have dubbed the co-narrator who opens a
narrative the "introducer." We are in agreement that the person who introduces or
initiates a story exercises pivotal narrative control, proposing topics that are elaborated into co-narrations. In a study of dinner table narrations (which may or may not
have referred to the child's own experience), Blum-Kulka and Snow (1992) found that
in working-class families most stories were initiated by adults, and the child's participation was structured by questions from the adult; in middle-class families a "display" mode predominated in which the child initiated stories and remained the
primary narrator throughout the narration.

Whether there are disputes between children and co-narrator(s) concerning the
child's past experience and how such disputes are managed is also clearly important in determining the degree of authorship exercised by the child. Are children's
contributions challenged, and, if so, how do children defend their claims? Do children challenge others' contributions? Although conflicts in young children's co-
narrations have not been studied, it is well established that young children engage
in here-and-now conversational conflicts (Dunn & Munn, 1987; Eisenberg & Garvey,
1981; Shantz, 1987). Conflict practices have been shown to vary across groups in
accordance with cultural beliefs and values (Corsaro & Rizzo, 1990; Garvey &
Shantz,1992; Wiley,1997). For example, in their study of the working-class community of South Baltimore, Miller (1986) and Miller and Sperry (1987) found that
mothers deliberately and routinely engaged their young daughters in teasing interactions, a form of playful disputing, on the belief that such experiences were necessary preparation for the harsh realities of life. No such practices have been reported
in middle-class communities. This led us to expect that conflict style would differ in
Daly Park and Longwood.

In sum, by investigating young children's everyday participation in personal
storytelling, we hope to shed fresh light on the actual process by which European
American children begin to construct selves that bear the imprint of an autonomous cultural framework. Because we believe that such frameworks do not
operate uniformly, we have chosen to study variation among European American
families, focusing on working-class families in Daly Park and middle-class families
in Longwood. By examining the ways in which young children participate as
speakers, authors, and opponents, it will be possible to create a nuanced picture of
two versions of narrative autonomy.

Method

Research Sites

This research was conducted in Daly Park and Longwood (pseudonyms), both of which are predominantly Catholic communities located in the city of Chicago. Daly Park is a working-class neighborhood originally supported by the stockyards and meat packing plants. Since hitting its peak population in the 1920s, Daly Park has shown a gradual decline in the number of residents. In recent years many residents have struggled with factory closings and other economic hardships. Most families live in modest homes or apartments. Until about 15 years ago, the neighborhood was homogeneous, consisting almost entirely of the descendants of Polish, German, and Irish immigrants. Although they still comprise the minority, the number of Hispanic residents has increased dramatically. Many residents of Daly Park are active in the local churches and send their children to the parochial schools located in the neighborhood.

Longwood is a middle-class neighborhood of spacious single-family dwellings situated on quiet, tree-lined streets. The neighborhood is known locally for the beauty of its streets and homes, several of which are on the National Register of Historic Places. Civic organizations have worked actively to preserve the special character and small-town ambiance of the neighborhood. Most of the residents are Irish Catholic, with strong intergenerational roots in the community and extended family members living nearby. Like Daly Park, many residents are active in local churches and send their children to the local parochial schools. Traditional values and family patterns are the norm (see Miller et al., 1996, for a more detailed description of Longwood).

Participants

For this report we focused on six children and their families from each of the two communities. Each sample was balanced by gender. The focal children were 2,6 at the first observation session and 3,0 at the second session. All of the children lived in two parent households. Daly Park parents were high school graduates. Fathers were employed in a variety of blue-collar jobs, including truck driving, grave digging, and construction work. Several of the mothers worked part-time as secretaries, cashiers, or bookkeepers. Four of the children had siblings, and two were only children. Longwood parents were college educated. Fathers' occupations included businessman, lawyer, and salesman. The mothers had worked as teachers or social workers but had chosen not to work outside the home after their children were born. All of the Longwood children had at least one sibling.

Mean length of utterance, a widely used measure of language level, was computed according to the procedures provided by Brown (1973). At 2,6 MLUs ranged from 2.26 to 4.04 with a mean of 2.95 in Daly Park, and from 2.54 to 3.68 with a mean of 3.21 for Longwood. At 3,0 MLUs ranged from 2.66 to 3.64 with a mean of 3.19 for Daly Park, and 2.82 to 3.66 with a mean of 3.10 for Longwood.

Procedures

This study is part of a larger comparative project designed to investigate how families use personal storytelling to socialize young children in a variety of socioculturally distinct communities (Miller, 1996; Miller et al., 1992, 1996, 1997). Ethnographic fieldwork was combined with extensive audio and video recording of naturally occurring talk in the family context. Researchers spent at least 2 years in the field and collected longitudinal observations at 2,6, 3,0, 3,6, and 4,0 years. This report is based on observations at 2,6 and 3,0. At each data point, 4 hr of video-recorded home observations were collected, usually consisting of two 2 hr sessions on successive days. This study is thus based on a total of 96 hr of observations, 48 in each community. Observation sessions were scheduled at the families' convenience and usually occurred on weekday mornings or afternoons. As the primary caregivers in all the families, mothers were always present during the observation sessions, whereas fathers were usually at work during these times. In other words, although our sample of narrative talk is skewed toward mothers and away from fathers, this skewing reflected the usual social ecology in these homes on weekdays.

The researcher visited the home on several occasions prior to the first taping session to enhance rapport with adults and children. The families were told that we were interested in how children learn to communicate in the context of ordinary family life. During the taping sessions, the researchers tried to behave in a way that was least disruptive to the communicative norms of the family (Miller & Hoogstra, 1992). They aimed not to be invisible or silent nor to "lead" the conversation but to observe and participate in a relaxed, low-key way, joining in the conversation when appropriate, following up on narrative topics when appropriate. This stance on the part of the observer was intended to maximize the ecological and cultural validity of the samples of narrative talk (see Miller, 1996, and Miller et al., 1996, for further discussion of the researcher's role).

Transcription and Identification of Co-Narrations

The video recordings were examined for co-narrations of personal experience, and all speech by the focal child and by other speakers that occurred within the co-narration was transcribed verbatim. Gestures, actions, and paralinguistic information were also described where relevant. Each transcript was checked at least three times by two different transcribers. A co-narration of personal experience was defined as an episode of talk involving three or more utterances, addressed to an interlocutor, describing a particular past event or a class of past events in which the child portrayed himself or herself as a protagonist. Co-narrations had to include at least two substantive on-topic utterances by the focal child. Episodes in which the child's participation was limited to yes/no or other nonsubstantive utterances were excluded. A past event was defined as an event that occurred prior to the observation session. In most cases the child provided some temporal ordering of the information. If not, the episode was included only if the co-narrators provided temporal ordering.

Miller et al. (1992) showed that co-narrations could be reliably identified in naturally occurring family talk. The same procedures for establishing intercoder reliability were adopted in the present study. A two step procedure was followed. First, two coders independently identified all co-narrations of personal experience in eight 30 min transcription segments. These segments were randomly selected from four children (two at 2,6 and two at 3,0) from Daly Park and four children (two at 2,6 and two at 3,0) from Longwood. The percentage of agreement was 97% (n = 31 conarrations). Second, a more stringent estimate of intercoder reliability addressed the boundaries of the co-narration: The coders independently identified the first utterance and the final utterance of each narration. The first utterance was defined as the first utterance, whether by the focal child or by an interlocutor, that referred to the past event. The final utterance was defined as the last utterance, whether by the focal child or by an interlocutor, relevant to the past event. The percentage of agreement under these conditions was 87% (n = 62 boundary utterances in 31 co-narrations).[1]

---

1. For establishing intercoder reliability for this coding and the following coding, percent agreement, rather than Cohen's kappa, is the appropriate statistic. Cohen's kappa corrects for chance agreement when there are a predetermined number of instances to be coded and a mutually exclusive set of codes. In terms of locating an utterance (such as an initiating utterance) from many hundreds of utterances, coding each utterance is not a practical approach, and there is little need to correct for chance. In addition, Cohen's kappa could artificially boost our agreement score compared to percent agreement because Cohen's kappa takes into consideration agreements on the many hundreds of utterances which are not initiating utterances as well as agreement on those few which are. See Bakeman and Gottman (1986) for more details.

Coding of Autonomy in Co-Narrations

The following codes, which rest on the distinction between speaker and author, were designed to capture different levels of autonomy. Both quantitative and qualitative analyses were undertaken. For each of the autonomy codes, intercoder reliability estimates were based on two coders' independent coding of one-third of the data (i.e., data from two randomly chosen children at 2,6 and 3,0 from each community). Percentage of agreement ranged from .87 to 1.00. Periodic reliability checks showed that the coders remained reliable throughout the coding process.

Child as Speaker

Because the focal child was, by definition, a speaker in co-narrations, this analysis simply involved computing the frequency of co-narrations and the length of co-narrations in the two communities. Length was determined for both total number of utterances within co-narrations and total number of child utterances within co-narrations. Means, medians, and ranges were determined for each of these measures.

Child as Author: Initiator

The initiator of the co-narration was defined as the person who made the initial reference to the past event. To compare children with different numbers of total co-narrations, an initiation proportion score was computed for each child. This score was the number of co-narrations that the child initiated divided by the total number of co-narrations initiated by the child and mother. Means, medians, and ranges were determined for this measure.

Child as Author: Opponent

A conflict episode within a co-narration was defined as a sequence that begins with an opposition and ends with a resolution or dissipation of conflict. Following Eisenberg and Garvey (1981), an opposition was defined as any negating response, including disagreements, conflicting claims, contradictions, denials, and refusals. For example, in response to the child's assertion, "We went to the Brookfield zoo," the mother opposed by saying, "We didn't go to the Brookfield zoo. [pause] Lincoln Park." (Note that conflict episodes did not necessarily include mutual opposition; that is, opposition by one co-narrator was not necessarily followed by opposition by a second co-narrator.) To compare the amount of conflict in co-narrations, a conflict in co-narration proportion score was computed for each mother and child by dividing the number of conflicts by the number of co-narrations for that dyad. Conflict length was determined in terms of both utterances and oppositions. Means, medians, and ranges were computed for each of these measures. Conflicts in co-narrations were further coded as follows:

Topic of conflict. This refers to what was at issue in the conflict. There were two possibilities: a narrator could oppose some aspect of the act of narration itself (e.g., whether to narrate, appropriateness of topic of narration) or assertions about what happened in the past event. Proportional frequencies were computed for each community.

Initial opposition. In determining how the opponent role was defined, it is important to ask who launched the conflict, that is, who made the initial oppositional move. Because most conflicts involved mothers and children, we compared how frequently mothers versus children contributed the first opposition. Proportional frequencies were computed for each community. Means, medians, and ranges were determined for this measure.

Ending of conflict. Two types of endings were coded, resolutions and last words. A resolution occurred when both parties came to an agreement about the disputed issue. For example, the child announces, "I fall down in the street," to which the mother responds, "You did? No, didn't you fall off the slide?" The child ends the conflict by agreeing. Proportional frequencies of resolutions were computed for each community. When no resolution occurred, the participant who made the final un-challenged claim was coded as having the last word. For example, Child: "Last time, I had a turn with that [the researcher's camera]." Mother: "Last time you had a turn with that, I don't think so." Child: "Yeah, I did." In this example, the dispute over whether the child had a turn with the camera is not resolved, but the child gets the last word. Proportional frequencies in which mother got the last word were computed for each community. Means, medians, and ranges were determined for each of these measures.

Oppositional style. The final conflict analysis focused on qualitative differences in the manner in which conflicts were conducted, including such stylistic dimensions as indirection and insistence on veridicality.

Data Analysis: Comparisons between Communities

Comparisons were made by community (Daly Park versus Longwood) for all of the previously listed codes. For each code, we examined both averages and variability within each distribution to determine the extent of differentiation or overlap between the communities. We did not expect age differences on these measures over the brief interval from 2,6 to 3,0, and preliminary analyses did not reveal any such differences. Therefore, data from the two data points were collapsed, yielding 8 hr of observation per child, a particularly large and stable sample of observed co-narrations for each child.

Results

Child as Speaker

A total of 278 co-narrations were observed in Daly Park, compared to 112 in Long-wood. Co-narrations occurred at average rates per hour of 5.79 for Daly Park and 2.33 for Longwood. On average, families in Daly Park produced many more co-narrations, *M* = 46.33, *median* = 47, *range* = 11–71, than families in Longwood, *M* = 18.67, *median* = 13.5, *range* = 9–34.

Combining across the total number of co-narrations, there were more co-narrative utterances in Daly Park than in Longwood. Families in Daly Park produced over twice as many utterances in co-narrations, *M* = 870.33, *median* = 968, *range* = 147–1,280, than the families in Longwood, *M* = 371.17, *median* = 347.5, *range* = 188–540. The children in Daly Park also contributed over twice as many utterances in co-narrations, *M* = 290.50, *median* = 337.5, *range* = 36–445, than did Longwood children, *M* = 105.67, *median* = 87.5, *range* = 53–177.

The means and participant distributions by community for this and all further community comparisons are presented in Table 9.1. Note that for total number of co-narrations, total number of utterances, and total number of child utterances, the overlap in the distributions of Daly Park and Longwood is minimal.

Child as Author: Initiator

Compared to their mothers, the Daly Park children initiated .37 (*median* = 31) of all co-narrations, whereas Longwood children initiated .50 (*median* = 55.5). The distributions of child initiations in the two communities (Daly Park, *range* = .20-.60; Longwood, *range* = .00-.80) indicate that the patterns are similar.

TABLE 9.1 *Summary of Community Comparison Results: Means and Distribution of Scores for All Participants by Community*

	Daly Park	Longwood
Child as speaker:		
Average no. of co-narrations	46.33 (11, 34, 44, 50, 68, 71)	18.67 (9, 13, 13, 14, 29, 34)
Average no. of utterances across all co-narrations	870.33 (147, 654, 928, 1008, 1205, 1280)	371.17 (188, 264, 283, 412, 540, 540)
Average no. of child utterances across all co-narrations	290.50 (36, 180, 323, 352, 407, 445)	105.67 (53, 80, 61, 114, 149, 177)
Child as author: initiator:		
PROPORTION OF CO-NARRATIONS INITIATED BY CHILDREN VERSUS MOTHER	**.37 (.20, .28, .31, 31, .55, .60)**	**.50 (.00, .29, .43, .68, .78, .80)**
Child as author: opponent:		
Proportion of co-narrations with conflicts	.18 (.00, .03, .14, .16, .34, .39)	.32 (.12, .15, .29, .38, .41, .36)
Mean length of conflict (utterances)	4.38 (3.00, 3.87, 4.53, 4.86, 5.64)	4.34 (3.30, 3.50, 4.18, 4.33, 4.50, 6.20)
Mean length of conflict (oppositions)	2.02 (1.00, 1.57, 2.26, 2.42, 2.86)	1.93 (1.25, 1.50, 1.75, 1.80, 2.25, 3.00)
Proportion of conflicts in which child is initially opposed	.93 (.68, .96, 1.0, 1.0, 1.0)	.71 (.25, .60, .60, .83, 1.0, 1.0)
Proportion of conflicts resolved	.57 (.35, .36, .43, .71, 1.0)	.52 (.20, .40, .50, .75, .75)
Proportion of conflicts in which mother got the last word	.34 (.00, .29, .43, .43, .57)	.08 (.00, .00, .00, .00, .20, .25)

Note: The distributions for Daly Park involving features of conflicts include only five scores because one child in Daly Park had no conflicts.

Child as Author: Opponent

A total of 98 conflicts occurred in the co-narrations, 66 in Daly Park and 32 in Longwood. There was a tendency for conflicts to occur less frequently in Daly Park, where they occurred in .18 (*median* = 1.5, *range* = .00–.39) of co-narrations, compared with .32 (*median* =.34, *range* =.12–.56) in Longwood. However, the distributions for individual families in these communities revealed a great deal of overlap.

The length of conflict episodes was similar in both communities, whether computed in terms of utterances (Daly Park *M* = 4.38, *median* = 4.53, *range* = 3.00–5.64; Longwood *M* = 4.34, *median* = 4.26, *range* = 3.30–6.20) or oppositions (Daly Park *M* = 2.02, *median* = 2.26, *range* = 1.00–2.86; Longwood *M* = 1.93, *median* = 1.78, *range* = 1.25–3.00).

Although there was little difference between the two communities in the *proportional* rate and length of conflicts in co-narrations, it is important to note that because Daly Park children participated in many more co-narrations than their Longwood counterparts, they received twice as much experience of narrative conflicts.

Topic of Conflict

The vast majority of conflict topics in both communities centered on assertions about what happened in the past event (over .90 in each). For example, topics at issue included whether the focal child had dropped or thrown a toy bank, whether the child cried or not when he got a shot, and whether the child threw up yesterday or a while ago. Conflicts that revolved around the act of narration were rare. For example, the mother wanted the child to tell a story and the child was reluctant to do so, or the child wanted to narrate about a topic (dog shit on his bed) that his mother found unacceptable.

Initial Opposition

In conflicts in both communities, children were initially opposed more than were mothers. Children in Daly Park were initially opposed in a conflict somewhat more frequently, $M = .93$, median = 1.0, range = .68–1.0, than children in Longwood, $M = .71$, median = .72, range = .25–1.0. However, there was a great deal of overlap in the distribution of individual scores in Daly Park and Longwood.

Ending of Conflicts

Most conflicts ended with an agreement between the parties about the disputed issue. Further, these resolutions occurred at similar rates in both communities. In Daly Park, .57 of narrative conflicts ended in resolution, median = .43, range = .00-.57, compared to .52 in Longwood, median = .50, range = .20-.75.

The proportion of conflicts in which mothers got the last word revealed a notable community difference. Mothers in Daly Park were found to get the last word in an average of .34, median = .43, range = .00–.57, of the conflicts, whereas mothers in Longwood were found to get the last word in only .08, median = .00, range = .00–.25, of the conflicts. There is minimal overlap in the distributions of the two communities. Closer examination revealed that whereas only one of the five Daly Park mothers never got the last word, four of the six Longwood mothers never got the last word.

Oppositional Style

Daly Park and Longwood also differed qualitatively in the way in which oppositions were framed and conflicts were conducted. In Daly Park, mothers tended to contradict their children's claims in a direct and matter-of-fact manner. This is illustrated in the following excerpted episodes, all of which begin with the mother's opposition (in italics) to the child's answer to her question.

Example 1 (David 2,6)

Mother: What did we buy in the store yesterday for you?

Child: Batman, da-na-na-na.

Mother: *No, we didn't buy Batman.*

Child: Batman [unintelligible]!

Mother: No, what are you, what'd we buy yesterday in the store?

Example 2 (Colleen 2,6)

Mother: What is the game you play?

Child: Somersault.

Mother: *Not with the dog, you do somersaults by yourself.* What, what game do you play with the dog?

Child: Um.

Mother: Do you have uh something round?

Child: [nods]

Mother: What is the round thing?

Child: It's got, um it's got [unintelligible].

Mother: Do you throw something over the fence?

Child: Balls.

Mother: Balls, and what does Boston do? [episode continues]

Example 3 (Colleen 3,0)

Mother: What was the surprise for?

Child: Me!

Mother: *No, it wasn't for you.* Why did you get your picture taken? You and all those other kids?

Child: Because I wanted to.

Mother: You wanted to? Did you um, give that picture, a big picture like this to someone for Christmas?

Child: Sara!

Mother: No.

Child: Yeah I did.

Mother: Grandma and Pop.

Child: Poppy.

Mother: Poppy and Gram.

Those conflicts that proceeded beyond the initial exchange, as did these examples, un-folded in two ways. Mother and child exchanged a series of oppositions (Example 1) or mothers prompted children until they produced the answers that they considered to be "correct" (Example 2). In some cases, mothers used both strategies (Example 3). When prompting children, mothers were sometimes quite stringent in their defini-tions of what counted as a correct response. Opposition exchanges were often quite lengthy, as in the following example, which involves eight turns of opposition.

Example 4 (David 3,0)

[Preceded by discussion about some stickers that David had yesterday]

Child: I can't find two of them [stickers].

Mother: I think you only had one. I think it only came with one.

Child: No, Ma, it came with two and I can't find two of them.

Mother: No, it only came with one.

Child: No, it came with two.

Mother: Where did I buy it from?

Child: [unintelligible] it came with two.

Mother: One.

Child: Two!

This kind of conflict, in which the child received experience defending his or her claims against a determined opponent, occurred rarely in Longwood. Instead, mothers went to considerable lengths to avoid saying "no" or overtly contradicting their children. Examples 5 and 6 parallel examples 1 through 3 from Daly Park in that the initial opposition takes the form of mother opposing the child's answer to her question. However, Longwood mothers conveyed their opposition by interpreting the child's answer as "different" rather than "wrong." (The initial opposition is italicized.)

> *Example 5 (Megan 2,6)*
>
> *Mother:*   Who brought you the sunglasses?
> *Child:*   Santa Claus.
> *Mother:*   *Santa Claus? Does Santa Claus come at Easter?*
> *Child:*   Yeah.
> *Mother:*   Oh, I'm confused.

> *Example 6 (Tommy, 3,0)*
>
> *Mother:*   What was Megan dressed as?
> *Child:*   Um, um a pine cone.
> *Mother:*   *Oh pine cone . . . you wanna know what it rea[lly] . . . what another name
>   for it is?*
> *Child:*   Yeah.
> *Mother:*   Unicorn, Megan was a unicorn because she had one horn coming out
>   her nose, right? She was a unicorn.
> *Child:*   She was a unicorn fish!

In these examples the mother used rhetorical questions ("Santa Claus? Does Santa Claus come at Easter?") to hint that the child might want to reconsider his or her claim or tactfully suggested an alternative to the child's response ("you wanna know what it rea[lly] . . . what another name for it is?"); in comparable situations, Daly Park mothers would have challenged the children's claims more directly: "No, Santa Claus doesn't come at Easter," or "Not a pine cone. Megan was a unicorn." In those infrequent instances in which Longwood mothers did use explicit opposition, either they tended to do so only after using more mitigated forms, or they marked the episode as nonserious. Both strategies are used in the following example. The mother initially challenges the child's claim by asking a rhetorical question ("I did?"). When the child sticks to his original claim, she overtly challenges his claim ("No, I didn't") and then explicitly frames the child's opposition as "goofy."

> *Example 7 (Steve 3,0)*
>
> *Mother:*   Who cut your hair?
> *Child:*   You.
> *Mother:*   I did?
> *Child:*   [nods]
> *Mother:*   No, I didn't.
> *Child:*   [nods again]
> *Mother:*   You're goofy [laughing].

Although Longwood children often ended up affirming their original claims (as in Examples 5 and 7), their behavior did not feel "oppositional" because their mothers refused to define it as such. By contrast, the role that Daly Park children played in narrative conflicts was both more frankly oppositional (when they stuck to their original claims) and more frankly cooperative (when they acceded to their mothers' version of the "correct" answer).

Discussion

This comparative study of working-class and middle-class families in two European American communities in Chicago contributes to our understanding of the process by which autonomous selves develop by describing children's participation in one frequently recurring selfway. It provides a multifaceted picture of how young children begin to construct autonomous selves through the medium of co-narrated personal storytelling. Taking advantage of the fact that children's participation in personal storytelling is structured in culture-specific ways, we determined how young children's narrative autonomy was actually enacted. Results indicate that similarities combined with differences to form subtly distinctive configurations of autonomy in the two communities.

Elaborating a distinction between the participant roles of speaker and author, we identified three levels of narrative autonomy. At the most basic level, we found that young children, aged 2,6 and 3,0, exercised autonomy by participating as speakers in co-narrations of their past experiences. This finding may seem obvious, but it is important to keep in mind that speaker rights are not necessarily granted to young children in every culture (Ochs & Schieffelin, 1984; Schieffelin & Ochs, 1986). To have the right, at such an early age, to speak of one's past experiences in conversations with a parent is to be affirmed as a social actor of some weight. As expected, children in both communities participated routinely as speakers. Also as expected, working-class youngsters from Daly Park participated far more frequently and at greater length in co-narratives than did their middle-class counterparts. At 3 years of age, personal storytelling occurred at an average rate of 6.3 per hour for Daly Park youngsters, compared with 2.3 for Longwood youngsters.

The second level of analysis focused on the initiation of co-narrations as an index of the degree to which children authored their past experiences and enacted autonomous selves. Results indicated no difference between the communities in the extent to which children versus mothers initiated stories about the child's past experience. During the latter half of the third year of life, both working-class and middle-class children took the initiative to bring up their own topics from the past, and these topics were attended to and elaborated on by others, chiefly their mothers. Children launched narratives at average rates as high as .50, implying a substantial but still limited degree of autonomy in narrative initiations.

The third level of analysis focused on the ways in which children enacted autonomous selves by opposing what their co-narrators said and by responding to their co-narrators' oppositions. The pattern of findings with respect to conflict in co-narratives points to similarities between the communities in the rate, length, and topic of conflict. In addition, in both communities, the initial opposition tended to be made by mothers, rather than children, and conflicts were resolved at similar rates. At the same time, conflicts differed in important ways. Mothers were more likely to get the last word in Daly Park than in Longwood. Qualitatively different oppositional styles were enacted in the two communities. Also, although there was little difference in the rate at which conflict occurred in co-narratives, Daly Park children received much more experience of conflict because they participated in many more co-narrations compared with their Longwood peers.

The mosaic of convergent and divergent patterns of story participation in these two communities leads to the conclusion that each community has its own distinct way of structuring children's autonomy. In the Daly Park version of autonomy, children were integrated into the storytelling practice with very little overt accommodation. In the context of jointly narrated stories of the child's past experiences, children participated freely and thus had extensive speaker rights but were expected to achieve their own authorship by engaging in the practices as a near equal. The best illustration of this is the mothers' insistence on accurate reporting. Like any other story participant, the child was expected to give a factual accounting. If this did not occur, a conflict ensued and continued until the child produced or agreed to the expected answer or the mother got the final word. Mothers were unlikely to soften their oppositions or to give in quickly. In this manner, the children gained experience in the presentation and defense of their claims in the face of quite resolute opposition. This pattern is consistent with the use of teasing as a survival tool in working-class communities, a way of teaching young children to stand up for their rights in the face of repeated threats and affronts (Heath, 1983; Labov, 1972; Lein, 1975; Miller, 1986). In this working-class community, then, narrative autonomy is a prize that young children have to work to obtain. To have one's own view and to express it is not a natural right guaranteed to all, but something to be earned and defended.

Autonomy was enacted somewhat differently in Longwood; although children were less likely to participate as speakers in personal storytelling, they were allowed more latitude to express their own views. Mothers were more likely to accommodate their storytelling practices for the less skilled child-participant. Oppositions to children were typically mitigated; instead of treating children as near equals, mothers scaffolded their participation in the adult practice. Accuracy was less important in two ways. Correct responses were either not required at all, or the mothers quickly and discreetly provided correct answers. When children contributed obviously incorrect information, mothers frequently either provided gentle, indirect cues as to the correct response or allowed the topic to end after wryly marking the situation as odd or humorous. Mothers seemed willing to sacrifice accuracy rather than infringe on the child's right to articulate his or her view of the past experience. The version of autonomy constructed in Longwood is thus one where children are given autonomy, in small increments, as a gift from the adults around them. To express one's views is a natural right, rather than something that has to be earned or defended. The caregiving practice of accepting the child's view and downplaying one's own opposing view is consistent with other practices in this community, such as narrating experiences that cast the child in a favorable light and avoiding invidious comparisons between siblings, that seem to reflect the mothers' commitment to protect and promote their children's self-esteem (Miller et al., 1996, 1997).

Although these subtle differences are important, they should not overshadow the similarities between the two communities. In parallel with the findings of Harwood et al. (1995), these subtly different configurations are best viewed as class-based variants on a theme. In both communities, young children were not only allowed extensive rights to speak of their past experiences but were also granted limited rights to author their experiences in the context of a social activity that was not a rare or isolated occurrence but a recurrent feature of everyday family life. We suggest that the repeated enactment of speaker, initiator, and opponent roles in the routine practice of personal storytelling helps to constitute an early step along a developmental pathway toward the construction of autonomous selves in European American communities.

An important task for future research will be to identify pathways that lead in other directions, toward other construals of self, including interdependent construals. As mentioned earlier, cultures vary in the degree to which young children are granted rights to speak. In the case of the Gusii of Kenya, for example, caregivers want their children to be respectful, quiet, obedient, and undemanding, and they spend more time holding than vocalizing to infants (LeVine, 1990). One would expect that adults in this group would be less likely to encourage young children to speak of or author their own past experiences when interacting with their elders, although they might tolerate such talk when it is directed to the child's peers. Similarly, in Western Samoa, young children are not considered appropriate conversational partners for parents. Although they have the right to "speak," often their speech is directed by a higher-status person to a lower-status person and thus is not "authored" by the child (Ochs, 1988). In the Taiwanese families that we studied, parents participated frequently in co-narrated personal storytelling with their young children, thereby granting them rights to speak, but they were more likely than their American counterparts to invoke a voice of authority and to insist that the child accept the caregiver's version of the past experience (Miller et al., 1996, 1997). These several examples point to a variety of ways in which cultural groups limit young children's rights to express their own views of their past experience, promoting instead a deference to the views of others, especially those in authority. Also relevant to the constitution of developmental pathways leading toward interdependent selves are narrative practices that create interpersonal bonds and promote group harmony. For example, the Kwara'ae of the Solomon Islands use narrative to restore harmonious relations among family members (Watson-Gegeo & Gegeo, 1990), and Taiwanese parents say that it is important to share their recollections of their past experiences with their children so that the children not only will come to appreciate the parents' lives but will also learn vicariously from their example (Sandel, Liang, Fung, & Miller, 1997).

Another important task for future research will be to delineate later steps along a developmental pathway toward the construction of autonomous selves in European American families. In an earlier study, we found that 5-year-olds, unlike 2½-year-olds, were beginning to explicitly portray themselves as independent when co-narrating their past experiences with family members (Miller et al., 1992). This implies that using an autonomous cultural framework to interpret the content of one's past experience is a later developmental step. We speculate that still later in development children will take more extensive control over the narration of their own past experiences and will become sensitive to infringements on their storytelling rights (see Shuman, 1986). For example, we have heard older children object to parental efforts to intervene in their stories.

In looking beyond the preschool years, it is also worth speculating about the educational implications of the class-based variants of narrative autonomy discovered here. Many educational practices (e.g., show and tell or sharing time) that are commonly used in kindergartens and first grades rest on the pedagogical intuition that personal storytelling can serve as a meaningful bridge from home to school (see Miller & Mehler, 1994). Finding such bridges is especially important for children from working-class and minority backgrounds. The remarkable frequency with which personal storytelling occurred in the working-class families in this study corroborates other research that shows that this kind of talk is highly valued and avidly practiced with young children in a range of working-class communities (Heath, 1983; Miller, 1994; Miller & Sperry, 1988; Sperry & Sperry, 1996); by 3 years of age, telling stories of personal experience seems to be second nature to many working-class children.

Although these findings suggest that personal storytelling may have a positive role to play on behalf of working-class children, easing their transition to school, other research indicates that the narrative style that characterizes show and tell in many classrooms is a middle-class style that is incompatible with the style that is familiar to children from non-mainstream backgrounds (Michaels, 1991). The findings of the current study point to another way in which working-class children's version of personal storytelling may depart from the middle-class model. Tobin (1995) has argued that many early childhood educational practices, including show and tell, embody an implicit middle-class ideal of self-expression that is insensitive to class and cultural differences within American society. In many of his examples of classroom practice, teachers participate in ways that are similar to the ways in which the middle-class mothers in our study participated; for example, in show and tell sessions teachers created a protective space in which the child's feelings and point of view could be affirmed without challenge. Thus, although being able to defend one's own perspective or experience in the face of resolute opposition—the version of autonomy promoted by the working-class families in our study—would seem to be a hallmark of self-expression, there may be little room in the early grades for working-class children to express themselves in this way.

We conclude with two further suggestions for future work. The first follows from the small sample size employed in this study. Obviously, it will be important to verify these findings with larger samples. However, as Miller et al. (1997) have argued, intensive study of small numbers of children under everyday conditions can contribute insights that cannot be obtained by other methods, insights that are crucial to a full understanding of the actual process by which children become cultural beings. There is no way to discover just how frequently families co-narrate young children's past experiences or whether young children initiate such stories without resorting to the labor-intensive method of observing the naturally occurring flow of social life. The loss in number of participants is thus repaid in the depth of empirical grounding in the concrete particulars of lived experience. This approach thus affords an appreciation of subtle patterns of similarities and differences within and across cultural groups, an appreciation that is essential if we are to move beyond dichotomous comparisons of sociocultural groups.

A final area for future work follows from the fact that this study focused on a single selfway, namely, personal storytelling. Future work should cast a wider net and examine how children enact and express autonomous selves across a range of practices, including other discursive practices. Ultimately, it will be necessary to integrate patterns of discursive practices with patterns from other selfways, such as those described by Rogoff et al. (1993) and Shweder et al. (1995), and with articulated ideals of the self (Harwood et al., 1995; Markus & Kitayama,1994b) to achieve a comprehensive understanding of the process by which autonomous selves are constructed.

Acknowledgments

This research was supported, in part, by a grant from the Spencer Foundation awarded to the last author. We wish to thank the families who participated in this study. We are grateful to the editor and the anonymous reviewers for their constructive feedback.

References

Bakeman, R., & Gottman, J. M. (1986). *Observing interaction: An introduction to sequential analysis.* Cambridge: Cambridge University Press.

Bauman, R. (1986). *Story, performance, and event: Contextual studies of oral narrative.* Cambridge: Cambridge University Press.

Blum-Kulka, S., & Snow, C. (1992). Developing autonomy for tellers, tales and telling in family narrative events. *Journal of Narrative and Life History, 2,* 187–217.

Brown, R. (1973). *A first language: The early stages.* Cambridge, MA: Harvard University Press.

Bruner, J. (1990). *Acts of meaning.* Cambridge, MA: Harvard University Press.

Corsaro, W., & Rizzo, T. (1990). Disputes in the peer culture of American and Italian nursery school children. In A. Grimshaw (Ed.), *Conflict talk* (pp. 21–66). Cambridge: Cambridge University Press.

Dunn, J. M., & Munn, P. (1987). Development of justification in disputes with mother and sibling. *Developmental Psychology, 23,* 791–798.

Eisenberg, A. R. (1985). Learning to describe past experiences in conversation. *Discourse Processes, 8,* 177–204.

Eisenberg, A. R., & Garvey, C. (1981). Children's use of verbal strategies in resolving conflicts. *Discourse Processes, 4,* 149–170.

Engel, S. (1986). *Learning to reminisce: A developmental study of how young children talk about the past.* Unpublished doctoral dissertation, The City University of New York.

Erikson, E. (1963). *Childhood and society.* New York: Norton.

Fivush, R. (1994). Constructing narrative, emotion, and self in parent-child conversations about the past. In U. Neisser & R Fivush (Eds.), *The remembering self: Construction and accuracy in the self-narrative* (pp. 136–157). Cambridge: Cambridge University Press.

Fivush, R., Gray, J. T., & Fromhoff, F. A. (1987). Two-year-olds talk about the past. *Cognitive Development, 2,* 393–409.

Garvey, C. S., & Shantz, C. U. (1992). Conflict talk: Approaches to adversative discourse. In C. U. Shantz & W. W. Hartup (Eds.), *Conflict in child and adolescent development* (pp. 93–121). Cambridge: Cambridge University Press.

Gergen, K. J. (1990). Social understanding and the inscription of self. In J. W. Stigler, R. A. Shweder, & G. Herdt (Eds.), *Cultural psychology: Essays on comparative human development* (pp. 569–606). Cambridge: Cambridge University Press.

Goffman, E. (1974). *Frame analysis.* Cambridge, MA: Harvard University Press.

Goodnow, J. J., Miller, P. J., & Kessel, F. (Eds.). (1995). *Cultural practices as contexts for development.* New directions for child development, No. 67. San Francisco: Jossey-Bass.

Greenfield, P. M., & Cocking, R. R. (1994). *Cross-cultural roots of minority child development.* Hillsdale, NJ: Erlbaum.

Hallowell, A. I. (1955). *Culture and experience.* Philadelphia: University of Pennsylvania Press.

Harwood, R. L., Miller, J. G., & Irizarry, N. L. (1995). *Culture and attachment: Perceptions of the child in context.* New York: Guilford.

Heath, S. B. (1983). *Ways with words: Language, life and work in communities and classrooms.* Cambridge: Cambridge University Press.

Holland, D. C., & Valsiner, J. (1988). Cognition, symbols, and Vygotsky's developmental psychology. *Ethos, 16,* 247–272.

Labov, W. (1972). *Language in the inner city: Studies in the Black English vernacular.* Philadelphia: University of Pennsylvania Press.

Labov, W., & Waletzky, J. (1967). Narrative analysis: Oral versions of personal experience. In J. Helm (Ed.), *Essays in the verbal and visual arts* (pp. 12–44). Seattle: University of Washington Press, American Ethnological Society.

Lave, J., & Wenger, E. (1991). *Situated learning: Legitimate peripheral participation.* Cambridge: Cambridge University Press.

Lein, L. (1975). "You were talkin though, oh yes, you was": Black American migrant children: Their speech at home and school. *Anthropology and Education Quarterly, 6,* 1–11.

LeVine, R. A. (1990). Infant environments in psychoanalysis: A cross-cultural view. In J. W. Stigler, R. A. Shweder, & G. Herdt (Eds.), *Cultural psychology: Essays on comparative human development* (pp. 454–474). Cambridge: Cambridge University Press.

Markus, H. R., & Kitayama, S. (1991). Culture and the self: Implications for cognition, and motivation. *Psychological Review, 98,* 224–253.

Markus, H. R., & Kitayama, S. (1994a). A collective fear of the collective: Implications for selves and theories of selves. *Personality and Social Psychology Bulletin, 20,* 568–579.

Markus, H. R., & Kitayama, S. (1994b). The cultural construction of the self and emotion: Implications for social behavior. In S. Kitayama & H. R. Markus (Eds.), *Emotion and culture: Empirical studies of mutual influence* (pp. 89–130). Washington, DC: American Psychological Association.

Markus, H. R., Mullally, P. R., & Kitayama, S. (1997). Self-ways: Diversity in modes of cultural participation. In U. Neisser & D. Jopling (Eds.), *The conceptual self in context.* New York: Cambridge University Press.

McCabe, A., & Peterson, A. (1991). *Developing narrative structure.* Hillsdale, NJ: Erlbaum.

Mead, G. H. (1934). *Mind, self, and society from the standpoint of a social behaviorist.* Chicago: University of Chicago Press.

Michaels, S. (1991). The dismantling of narrative. In A. McCabe & C. Peterson (Eds.), *Developing narrative structure* (pp. 303–351). Hillsdale, NJ: Erlbaum.

Miller, P. J. (1986). Teasing as language socialization and verbal play in a white, working-class community. In B. B. Schieffelin & E. Ochs (Eds.), *Language socialization across cultures* (pp. 199–212). Cambridge: Cambridge University Press.

Miller, P. J. (1994). Narrative practices: Their role in socialization and self-construction. In U. Neisser & R. Fivush (Eds.), *The remembering self: Construction and accuracy in the self-narrative* (pp. 158–179). Cambridge: Cambridge University Press.

Miller, P. J. (1996). Instantiating culture through discourse practices: Some personal reflections in socialization and how to study it. In R. Jessor, A. Colby, & R. A. Shweder (Eds.), *Ethnography and human development: Context and meaning in social inquiry* (pp. 183–204). Chicago: University of Chicago Press.

Miller, P. J., Fung, H., & Mintz, J. (1996). Self-construction through narrative practices: A Chinese and American comparison of early socialization. *Ethos, 24,* 1–44.

Miller, P. J., & Hoogstra, L. (1992). Language as a tool in the socialization and apprehension of cultural meanings. In T. Schwartz, G. White, & C. Lutz (Eds.), *New directions in psychological anthropology* (pp. 83–101). Cambridge: Cambridge University Press.

Miller, P. J., & Mehler, R. (1994). Personal storytelling, socialization, and self-construction at home and in kindergarten. In A. Hass-Dyson & C. Genishi (Eds.), *The need for story: cultural diversity in classroom and community* (pp. 38–54). Urbana, IL: National Council of Teachers of English.

Miller, P. J., Mintz, J., Hoogstra, L., Fung, H., & Potts, R. (1992). The narrated self: Young children's construction of self in relation to others in conversational stories of personal experience. *Merrill-Palmer Quarterly, 38,* 45–67.

Miller, P. J., Potts, R., Fung, H., Hoogstra, L., & Mintz, J. (1990). Narrative practices and the social construction of self in childhood. *American Ethnologist, 17,* 292–311.

Miller, P. J., & Sperry, L. L. (1987). The socialization of anger and aggression. *Merrill-Palmer Quarterly, 33,* 1–31.

Miller, P. J., & Sperry, L. L. (1988). Early talk about the past: The origins of conversational stories of personal experience. *Journal of Child Language, 15,* 293–315.

Miller, P. J., Wiley, A. R., Fung, H., & Liang, C. (1997). Personal storytelling as a medium of socialization in Chinese and American families. *Child Development, 68,* 557–568.

Morelli, G. A., Rogoff, B., Oppenheimer, D., & Goldsmith, D. (1992). Cultural variations in infants' sleeping arrangements: Question of independence. *Developmental Psychology, 28,* 604–613.

Neisser, U. (1988). Five kinds of self knowledge. *Philosophical Psychology, 1,* 35–39.

Nelson, K. (1993). Events, narratives, memory: What develops? In C. A. Nelson (Ed.), *Memory and affect in development: Minnesota symposia on child psychology* (Vol. 26, pp. 1–24). Hillsdale, NJ: Erlbaum.

Ochs, E. (1988). *Culture and language development: Language acquisition and language socialization in a Samoan village.* Cambridge: Cambridge University Press.

Ochs, E., & Schieffelin, B. (1984). Language acquisition and socialization: Three developmental stories and their implications. In R. Shweder & R. LeVine (Eds.), *Culture theory: Essays on mind, self and emotion* (pp. 276–320). Cambridge: Cambridge University Press.

Ochs, E., & Taylor, C. E. (1995). The Father knows best dynamic in dinnertime narratives. In K. Hall & M. Bucholtz (Eds.), *Gender articulated: Language and the socially constructed self* (pp. 97–120). New York: Routledge.

Rogoff, B., Mistry, J., Goncu, A., & Mosier, C. (1993). Guided participation in cultural activity by toddlers and caregivers. *Monographs of the Society for Research in Child Development, 58*(8, Serial No. 238).

Sandel, T. L., Liang, C-H., Fung, H., & Miller, P. J. (1997, August). *Storytelling across generations: Continuity and change in Taiwanese families.* Paper presented at the Second Annual Conference on the History and Culture of Taiwan, New York.

Schieffelin, B., & Ochs, E. (1986). Language socialization. *Annual Review of Anthropology, 15,* 163–246.

Shantz, C. U. (1987). Conflicts between children. *Child Development, 58,* 283–305.

Shuman, A. (1986). *Storytelling rights: The use of oral and written texts by urban adolescents.* Cambridge: Cambridge University Press.

Shweder, R. A., Goodnow, J., Hatano, G., LeVine, R., Markus, H., & Miller, P. J. (1998). The cultural psychology of development: One mind, many mentalities. In W. Damon (Ed.), *The handbook of child psychology* (pp. 865–937). New York: Wiley.

Shweder, R. A., Jensen, L. A., & Goldstein, W. M. (1995). Who sleeps by whom revisited. In J. J. Goodnow, P. J. Miller, & F. Kessel (Eds.), *Cultural practices as contexts for development.* New directions for child development, No. 67, pp. 21–39. San Francisco: Jossey-Bass.

Sperry, L. L., & Sperry, D. E. (1996). The early development of narrative skills. *Cognitive Development, 11,* 443–465.

Stern, D. N. (1985). *The interpersonal world of the infant: A view from psychoanalysis and developmental psychology.* New York: Basic.

Stern, D. N. (1989). Crib monologues from a psychoanalytic perspective. In K. Nelson (Ed.), *Narratives from the crib* (pp. 309–319). Cambridge, MA: Harvard University Press.

Taylor, C. (1989). *Sources of the self. The making of the modern identity.* Cambridge, MA: Harvard University Press.

Taylor, C. E. (1995). *Child as apprentice-narrator. Socializing voice, face, identity, and self-esteem amid the narrative politics of family dinner.* Unpublished doctoral dissertation, University of Southern California.

Tobin, J. (1995). The irony of self-expression. *American Journal of Education, 103,* 233–258.

Triandis, H. C. (1990). Cross-cultural studies of individualism and collectivism. In J. Berman (Ed.), *Nebraska Symposium on Motivation, 1989* (pp. 41–133). Lincoln: University of Nebraska Press.

Watson-Gego, K. A., & Gegeo, D. W. (1990). Shaping the mind and straightening out conflict: The discourse of Kwara'ae family counseling. In K. A. Watson-Gego & G. M. White (Eds.), *Disentangling: Conflict discourse in Pacific societies* (pp. 161–213). Stanford, CA: Stanford University Press.

Wiley, A. (1997). Religious affiliation as a source of variation in childrearing values and parental regulation of young children. *Mind, Culture and Activity, 4,* 86–107.

Williams, K. (1994). *The socialization of literacy in black, middle class families.* Unpublished doctoral dissertation, University of Chicago.

10

■ There is a common saying that "it takes a village to raise a child." But what if the surrounding physical and social environments pose serious hazards for children's successful development? In such situations, children need someone to create a bridge that will lift them over the local conditions to the wider world. Once again, we see that the child's environments are multiply nested. In this article, Jarrett explores how "community-bridging" parents guard their children from pitfalls, recruit compensatory resources, and provide a sheltering environment that emphasizes building the skills the child will need to succeed in the larger society beyond the immediate surroundings. Studies of resilient children, those who have managed to thrive despite all odds, often find that one such person can literally be a life preserver for youth in stormy seas (Werner & Smith, 1992). The strategies used by successful parents in high-risk neighborhoods show similarities and differences to parents in many situations.

Overview Questions

1. What are features of social relations and survival skills on inner city streets? Why is this life appealing?

2. Describe the strategies used by "community-bridging" parents to monitor their children's lives. What are two major types of resource-seeking strategies used by effective inner city parents? What are direct and indirect methods used by community-bridging parents to promote academic skills?

3. To summarize, community-bridging parents guard their children from pitfalls, recruit compensatory resources, and provide a supportive environment for skill acquisition. In what ways are these parenting activities similar to and different from those of middle-class parents?

4. What do you think about the author's argument that community-bridging parents are "subsidizing local institutions" and that they are doing more than their fair share, going more than halfway to meet local institutions? Can/should the broader society be of more help to community-bridging parents?

Successful Parenting in High-Risk Neighborhoods

Robin L. Jarrett

Like other Americans, low-income African-American parents aspire that their children will grow up and lead mainstream lives. However, youths growing up in impoverished, inner-city neighborhoods face obstacles to conventional development.[1,2] Many African-American adolescents are caught up in the subculture of "the streets" and, in the transition to adulthood, risk becoming school dropouts, premature parents, marginally employed adults, welfare recipients, and struggling family members. Some may become drug dealers and users, and the perpetrators and victims of violence.[3–6] Yet, while neighborhoods with multiple risks and limited opportunities impose developmental boundaries on the youths who reside there, their effects are not deterministic. Some local parents rear adolescents who become high school (if not college) graduates, gainfully employed adults, and stable family members.[5,7,8] Some become superstars whose extraordinary achievements belie their modest backgrounds.

No one recognizes better than inner-city parents how pervasively the neighborhood around them shapes the lives of young people. This article uses qualitative studies of low-income African-American families to identify effective parenting strategies in impoverished neighborhoods.[9] A well-developed set of urban ethnographies describes everyday family life in poor African-American neighborhoods.[10,11] A review of these detailed case studies, summarized briefly here, identifies three parenting strategies—youth-monitoring strategies, resource-seeking strategies, and in-home learning strategies—that facilitate conventional adolescent development.

The Neighborhood Context for Development

Inner-city neighborhoods provide limited economic, institutional, and social resources for the families and adolescents living there. In the absence of basic assets, "the streets" in impoverished African-American communities become the major lifestyle contender and developmental niche for many young people.[3,5,12–14] Social relations on the street are characterized by an individualistic, competitive, and predatory ethos, where "hustling" and "getting over" are valid ways of securing scarce resources. Participants in the "street" lifestyle learn key survival skills in a setting where violence is not uncommon and where peers are critical for creating and endorsing a valid identity. The personal characteristics valued by street companions, however, are not consistent with the demands of success in the broader environment.[3,5,14]

One ethnographer observed the appeal of the street lifestyle this way: "The ghetto street culture can be glamorous and seductive to the adolescent, promising its followers the chance of being 'hip' and popular with certain 'cool' peers who hang out on the streets or near the neighborhood school. . . . But also important is the fact that the wider culture and its institutions are perceived, quite accurately at times, as unreceptive and unyielding to the efforts of ghetto youths."[15]

Most inner-city parents reject the street subculture. Despite their best efforts, however, some of their teens do not resist the lifestyle. Walter's mother expresses a typical concern: "I know he is out there [on the streets] when I'm at work. I don't have any other way right now to have someone watch my children. . . . I hope and pray that I taught Walter the right things, though. He knows, too, that when I'm home he better be straight. The Lord only knows, I have to believe that what I taught him, the good I taught him, will bring him through and make him a good man."[16]

Adolescents whose parents are not as overwhelmed by survival issues as Walter's mother may not become casualties of "the streets." They owe much of their success to the vigilant efforts of their parents.

Effective Parenting Strategies in Inner-City Neighborhoods

Qualitative accounts of poor African-American families and youths illuminate parenting strategies that promote conventional youth development. To combat the deleterious effects of living in an inner-city neighborhood, effective parents (1) use stringent monitoring strategies, (2) seek out local and extralocal resources, and (3) utilize in-home learning strategies. The term *community bridging* can be used to describe this complex of strategies because these parental actions link adolescents to mainstream opportunities and institutions.[17]

Youth-Monitoring Strategies

Community-bridging parents protect their adolescents from negative neighborhood influences by closely supervising their time, space, and friendships.[8,13,18,19] One researcher profiled the active monitoring strategies of some local parents: "The parents are known in the community as 'strict' with their children; they impose curfews and tight supervision, demanding to know their children's whereabouts at all times. [T]hese parents scrutinize their children's friends and associates carefully, rejecting those who seem to be 'no good' and encouraging others who seem to be on their way to 'amounting to something.' "[20]

Significantly, "strict" parents take a two-pronged approach in their monitoring efforts. On the one hand, they discourage untoward friendships, while on the other hand, they replace these friendships with prosocial ones.

Another commonly used monitoring strategy is chaperonage—the accompaniment of children on their daily rounds in the neighborhood by a parent, family friend, or sibling.[16,21,22] While community-bridging parents explicitly chaperon young children, they use more subtle forms of monitoring with adolescents. One ethnographer described the pattern of sibling chaperonage: "[Seventeen-year-old] James Earl [Treppit] has begun visiting his girlfriend weekdays from 6:00 P.M. until the 11:00 P.M. parentally imposed curfew. . . . Since he wants to visit outside the home, Mrs. Treppit had decided to allow him to do it as long as he agrees to take his 16-year-old brother, Johnny, with him wherever he goes. In this way, Mrs. Treppit feels she still may exercise some control over James Earl's activities. Johnny is reliable in reporting all of his older brother's activities to his parents."[23]

Clearly, Mrs. Treppit acknowledges her son's growing need for autonomy, but she maintains oversight by enlisting her younger son—a peer to his brother—as a chaperon.

When monitoring strategies such as intensive supervision and chaperonage become ineffective, some community-bridging parents resort to extreme measures. Field researchers identified a pattern of "exile" in which concerned parents removed their teens from the local neighborhood altogether. Johnnie, a promising teen, states: "[My mother sent me to live with my uncle in California so] I won't get in trouble. . . . She wanted me to come out here because she always said if I go to

California—every time I come out, I go to school, I do real good. When I go there [St. Louis] I do really bad."[24]

In cases such as Johnnie's, parents are willing to be geographically separated from their teens to promote conventional development.

Resource-Seeking Strategies

In addition to insulating their adolescents from neighborhood dangers, community-bridging parents garner resources to promote their development by seeking out the well-functioning local institutions and organizations that exist even in poor African-American communities.[25,26] They target churches that sponsor scouting and tutoring programs, parochial and magnet schools that promote academic achievement, and athletic programs that support physical mastery and discipline.[14,21] For instance, Tina reports to an interviewer that: "My mother . . . has made sure I've gotten a head start in life. She got me a scholarship to Dalton. She was connected to people who helped young African-American women get on the right track. She has always networked with the right people."[27]

Tina's mother is a resourceful and competent woman who devotes large portions of time and energy to finding opportunities for her daughter.

Well-connected parents also take advantage of resources for their teens that exist outside of the local community. Kinship networks of grandparents, older siblings, godparents, and other biological and fictive kin can provide broader opportunities for youths.[11,25,28–30] When kin are better off economically, youngsters gain access to resource-rich communities that offer a wider array of institutional, informational, and economic assets, including well-functioning schools. Field worker observations highlight the importance of kinship ties: "Johnnie's family and history are not contained in a single geographical area but rather in a kinship centered in two neighborhoods differentiated by social class and culture. . . . Johnnie's mother, a beautician, lives in an inner-city St. Louis neighborhood. . . . Johnnie's uncle, who works for the FBI, lives in the suburban middle-class area that surrounds Huntington High School [where Johnnie attends]."[31]

Kinship connections, such as those in Johnnie's family, expand adolescents' resource bases beyond the local neighborhood.

In-Home Learning Strategies

At home, community-bridging parents directly promote their adolescent's development of academic skills and competencies. Field observations of Sheila Johnson, a high achiever, revealed that she and her mother regularly played word games, unscrambling blocks of letters that spelled words found in a word list at the top of each puzzle page.[32] Reflecting a long-term pattern of in-home literacy activities begun in childhood, Mrs. Johnson's current efforts promote Sheila's language development.

Community-bridging parents who lack the literacy skills necessary to assist their teens may turn to indirect strategies for promoting learning. For instance, the parents in the Harrison family offer their teens encouragement for school achievement: "Like many ghetto parents Lincoln and Lillie place a great value on education for their children. . . . [T]he Harrisons have translated their concern into several positive steps aimed at encouraging their children to stay in school and excel. This is one area in which the use of positive emotional rewards is most apparent. Both parents make it a deliberate point of complimenting and praising each effort of their children—'good' report cards, special honors, even satisfactory homework assignments are celebrated."[33]

Supportive learning strategies, such as those practiced in the Harrison family, keep youths attached to school authority, classroom routines, teacher directives, and conventional peers.

The Future of Inner-City Youths

Community-bridging parents use monitoring strategies, resource-seeking strategies, and in-home learning strategies to enhance the likelihood that their adolescents will develop conventionally, despite neighborhood impoverishment. Unlike so many of their neighbors, these parents are able to mediate the deleterious effects of growing up in inner-city neighborhoods. They create insulated and enriching developmental niches for their adolescents in the midst of neighborhood decline.

The fact that some parents foster positive adolescent development under adverse conditions demonstrates their tenacity and competence, but their efforts entail personal costs as well. Achieving conventional development in impoverished neighborhoods requires adults to concentrate single-mindedly and single-handedly on the welfare of their teens, often at the expense of personal needs and goals. Adolescents whose safety, if not survival, depends on the constriction of their social worlds may forgo a broader range of developmental experiences. Moreover, as the most capable families withdraw from local neighboring relations, the prospect of revitalizing inner-city neighborhoods is further discouraged. As individuals, community-bridging families should be commended for their efforts, but an examination of their experiences draws disturbing attention to the larger social, economic, and political conditions that create inner-city ghettos and the need for such exacting adaptive responses.

Efforts are needed to change the neighborhood conditions that compromise the developmental trajectories of poor African-American youths and place great burdens on their parents. More well-functioning youth-serving institutions are needed, including good-quality schools, youth programs, libraries, parks, and other organizations that provide enriching developmental contexts for youths. Increased job and economic opportunities for residents would provide an alternative to the street lifestyle, and economically stable neighbors could serve as mentors, role models, and supportive coparents to local youths. Such institutional and individual changes would lessen the need for the demanding parenting efforts described here and might allow local parents to become more active members of the larger community.

Community-bridging parents in effect subsidize local institutions by fulfilling functions that are typically shared with well-functioning schools, churches, and other youth-serving institutions. Inner-city neighborhoods with limited social, economic, and institutional resources demand that parents be "super-parents" to ensure conventional development for their adolescents. Supportive neighborhood environments should, at the very least, meet parents halfway. When they do, there is a greater likelihood that both extraordinary and ordinary parents can ensure a promising future for their adolescents.

Members of the Social Science Research Council's Working Group on Communities and Neighborhoods, Family Processes, and Individual Development, and the MacArthur Research Network on Successful Pathways through Middle Childhood, made helpful comments on an earlier draft.

References _____

1.   Brooks-Gunn, J., Duncan, G., and Aber, J. S., eds. *Neighborhood poverty, Vol. 1: Context and consequences for children.* New York: Russell Sage Foundation, 1997.

2.   Jencks, C., and Mayer, S. E. The social consequences of growing up in a poor neighborhood. In *Inner-city poverty in the United States.* L. Lynn and M. McGeary, eds. Washington, DC: National Academy Press, 1989, pp. 111–86.

3.   Anderson, E. *Streetwise: Race, class, and change in an urban community.* Chicago: University of Chicago Press, 1990.

4.   Prothrow-Stith, D. *Deadly consequences.* New York: Harper Collins, 1991.

5.   Williams, T., and Kornblum, W. *The Uptown kids: Struggle and hope in the projects.* New York: Putnam and Sons, 1994.

6.   Wilson, W. J. *The truly disadvantaged: The inner city, the underclass, and public policy.* Chicago: University of Chicago Press, 1987.

7.   Clark, R. M. *Family life and school achievement: Why poor black children succeed or fail.* Chicago: University of Chicago Press, 1983.

8.   Jarrett, R. L. Growing up poor: The family experiences of socially mobile youth in low-income African-American neighborhoods. *Journal of Adolescent Research* (1995) 10:111–35.

9.   The literature review focuses on qualitative studies published between 1960 and 1997, which describe parenting behaviors and family characteristics that influence child and youth social mobility outcomes. See note no. 8, Jarrett.

10.   Jarrett, R. L. Resilience among low-income African-American youth: An ethnographic perspective. *Ethos* (1997) 25:1–12.

11.   Jarrett, R. L. African-American children, families and neighborhoods: Qualitative contributions to understanding developmental pathways. *Applied Developmental Science* (1998) 2:2–16.

12.   Merry, S. *Urban danger: Life in a neighborhood of strangers.* Philadelphia: Temple University Press, 1981.

13.   Sullivan, M. *Getting paid: Youth crime and work in the inner city.* Ithaca, NY: Cornell University Press, 1989.

14.   Williams, T., and Kornblum, W. *Growing up poor.* Lexington, MA: Lexington Books, 1985.

15. See note no. 3, Anderson, quote on p. 91.

16.   Burton, L. M. Caring for children. *The American Enterprise* (1991) 2:34–37.

17.   The converse of community-bridging strategies, "community-specific" patterns, represent adaptations to the local inner-city community. For a detailed discussion of "community-bridging" and "community-specific" parenting strategies, see note no. 8, Jarrett. See also, Jarrett, R. L. *A comparative examination of socialization patterns among low-income African-American, Chicano, Puerto Rican, and white families: A review of the ethnographic literature.* New York: Social Science Research Council, 1990.

18.   Fordham, S. *Blacked out: Dilemmas of race, identity, and success at Capital High.* Chicago: University of Chicago Press, 1996.

19.   Puntenny, D. L. The impact of gang violence on the decisions of everyday life: Disjunctions between policy assumptions and community conditions. *Journal of Urban Affairs* (1997) 19:143–61.

20.   Anderson, E. Sex codes and family life among inner-city youths. *Annals of the American Academy of Political and Social Studies* (1989) 501:59–78.

21.   Furstenberg, F. F., Jr. How families manage risk and opportunity in dangerous neighborhoods. In *Sociology and the public agenda.* W. J. Wilson, ed. Newbury Park, CA: Sage, 1993, pp. 231–58.

22.   Ladner, J. *Tomorrow's tomorrow: The black woman.* New York: Anchor Books, 1971.

23.   See note no. 7, Clark, quote on p. 53.

24.   Davidson, A. L. *Making and molding identity in schools: Student narratives on race, gender, and academic engagement.* Albany, NY: State University of New York Press, 1996, quote on p. 164.

25.   Aschenbrenner, J. *Lifelines: Black families in Chicago.* New York: Holt, Rinehart, and Winston, 1975.

26.   Macleod, J. *Ain't no makin' it: Aspirations and attainment in a low-income neighborhood.* Boulder, CO: Westview Press, 1995.

27.   See note no. 5, Williams and Kornblum, quote on p. 59.

28. Jarrett, R. L. A family case study: An examination of the underclass debate. In *Qualitative methods in family research.* J. Gilgun, G. Handel, and K. Daley, eds. Newbury Park, CA: Sage, 1992, pp. 172–97.

29. Martin, E., and Martin, J. *The black extended family.* Chicago: University of Chicago Press, 1978.

30. Zollar, A. C. *A member of the family: Strategies for black family continuity.* Chicago: Nelson-Hall, 1985.

31. See note no. 24, Davidson, quote on p. 153.

32. See note no. 7, Clark, quote on p. 92.

33. Tatje, T. A. Mother-daughter dyadic dominance in black American kinship. Unpublished doctoral dissertation, prepared for the Department of Anthropology, Northwestern University, 1974, quote on pp. 185–86.

11

■ For a variety of reasons, families sometimes pull up their roots in one country and culture, and make a new life in a new land. They must then determine the kind of embeddedness they will have in the new environment. Some members of the family may choose to cling to the familiar culture and to interact primarily with other immigrants from the "old country." This strategy has been labeled "separation" (Berry, Kim, Power, Young, & Bujaki, 1989). By contrast, "assimilation" occurs when an individual wishes to attain a new cultural identity and seeks daily interactions with the dominant surrounding culture. Immigrants who wish to maintain their original culture and yet participate in the new community are said to have an "integration" strategy, while those who have little interest in either the old or the new ways are said to be "marginalized." Often, when we think of the agents who help socialize children, we think primarily of parents. Immigrant families may serve to highlight the roles that others play as well—older siblings, teachers, and community members who can serve as "cultural brokers," those who serve as bridges between the old and new worlds for immigrants and their children who wish to seek a future in the larger social network of the new country.

Overview Questions

1. Why are these researchers especially concerned about the elementary school years for Latino youth? Do children of Mexican immigrants have career aspirations comparable to non-Hispanic youth? What barriers do they see to reaching their goals?

2. What three examples did the authors give of things that teachers can do to act as "cultural brokers"? What are five ways community program staff can provide support for Latino youth?

3. What do Latino immigrant parents see as their primary role in promoting their children's achievements? What limitations do they generally face? How do older siblings help younger siblings with schoolwork? When and why does this break down?

4. What do you think about how the roles of family members, teachers, and community program staff are similar and different for children of immigrants versus children born in this country?

Cultural Brokers: Helping Latino Children on Pathways Toward Success

Catherine R. Cooper, Jill Denner, and Edward M. Lopez

Elementary school represents a critical time in the lives of Latino students. It is during these school years that they begin to follow either *el buen camino* (the good path toward responsible adulthood) or a path leading to high-risk behaviors. Recent studies show that by the third grade, large gaps emerge between Latino children and national norms in reading, written language, and math. These early gaps widen in subsequent years.[1] In 1995, some 30% of Hispanic young people were school dropouts, compared with only 9% of non-Hispanic white youths and 12% of non-Hispanic black youths.[2] Thus Latino youths come to be underrepresented in college-prep classes and overrepresented in the juvenile justice system.[3]

A college education is not the only definition of success in life, but conversations with children of Mexican immigrants reveal that they begin school with high hopes, dreaming of becoming doctors, lawyers, sports heroes, teachers, and firefighters.[4] Parents who work in strawberry fields, hotel kitchens, and factories dream that their children will become doctors, teachers, and lawyers.[5] A key period of vulnerability occurs, however, as students move from elementary to junior high or middle school. This is a time when students must coordinate their family relationships and responsibilities with increasingly salient relationships with peers. Yet many Latino parents, most of whom have less than a high school education, lack the knowledge of U.S. schools to guide their children to college and careers.[5]

This article discusses ways in which teachers, family members, and young adult staff in community programs can serve as culture brokers for Latino students by helping them to feel safe in home, school, and community, to find educational experiences beyond the classroom, and to remain on pathways that lead to personal and academic success. Families, schools, peers, and communities represent both resources and challenges for children. They can help Latino children stay in school and can act as intermediaries as children bridge their worlds. This article draws on new research to illuminate the conditions under which Latino children attempt to achieve their dreams, focusing on immigrant families from Mexico because they represent the largest group of immigrants in the United States.[6]

The Aspirations of Latino Youth

What do Latino children want to be when they grow up? What challenges do they face and what resources do they see for achieving their dreams? A recent study analyzed the essays written by 116 Mexican-descent sixth graders applying for a program offering scholarships to the local community college.[4] Most children described dreams of becoming doctors, lawyers, nurses, and teachers, as well as secretaries, police officers, firefighters, and mechanics, although many of their parents worked as agricultural field workers or held service jobs. The challenges the children saw to their achievement of their dreams included not having enough money to pay for school, as well as the expectations of key people in their lives such as family members ("my parents wanted me to work in the field") and peers ("friends who will pressure me to take drugs"). The children saw their greatest resources in their families, including parents, siblings, and cousins; their schoolteachers, counselors, and coaches; their friends; and themselves ("never giving up, looking for help by asking people, and studying a lot"). Children also named the program staff and scholarships as resources in their essays.

During the transition from elementary to middle school, children begin to look ahead in their own lives and look up to older siblings, peers, and adults. Some children's pathways lead them toward college and adult responsibilities, while others lead toward school dropout and the risks of "underground" occupations. Consequently, these years are a critical time to ensure that children find help moving toward the goals that they and their families hold.

Bridges and Barriers, Resources and Challenges

Schools and Mexican-immigrant parents share the ideal that all children will be safe—both physically and emotionally—and have an equal chance to learn and succeed. Even so, factors in schools, families, and communities help some children to move along academic pathways, while others slip away.[7]

Schools as Gatekeepers and Brokers

Teachers act as institutional gatekeepers when they assess students against standardized benchmarks of achievement that determine eligibility for college-prep classes or placement in vocational or remedial classes.[8,9] When elementary school-teachers disproportionately place Latino students in special education classes and in low reading and math ability groups, they send these students toward remedial tracks in middle and high school.[10]

Teachers—from any ethnic background—can also act as cultural brokers who help Latino children to succeed in school and to achieve their dreams. Some review the assessments of Spanish-speaking students to ensure that they are not wrongly placed in special education due to language differences.[11] Teachers can also encourage the dreams and goals of Latino children. For instance, in a rural elementary school in California, fourth graders wrote a children's book in English and Spanish that discussed the links between career dreams and going to college, defined grade point averages and scholarships, and explained practical college issues, like dormitories, that would be meaningful to school-age children.[12] In Arizona, university researchers collaborate with teachers to bring Latino parents into the school as sources of valued expertise.[13,14] When school staff members find ways like these of working with Latino children and parents, they link children's home and school in ways that nourish children's aspirations for the future.

Parents Promoting "The Good Moral Path"

The transition from childhood to adolescence triggers both hopes and fears for parents who want to promote their children's school achievement but also want to protect them from drugs, violence, and early pregnancy. In one study, Latino parents in Los Angeles, who were primarily Mexican immigrants, described their children as nearing the crossroads between the good moral path (*el buen camino*) and the bad path (*el mal camino*).[15] The parents considered moral guidance of their children as their primary role and sought to protect their children from negative peer influences (*malas amistades*). To these parents, a strong moral upbringing includes and supports academic achievement.

Mexican-immigrant parents, however, often face the dilemma of holding high aspirations for their children's school success while they lack the knowledge of educational institutions needed to guide their children. For example, one study interviewed parents in 36 Mexican-immigrant families with children in third, fifth, and seventh grades.[5,16] Most of the parents worked as farm laborers or in canneries and had left school in their Mexican villages at age eight. By fifth grade, the children from these families exceeded their parents' schooling, making it difficult for parents to help with homework. The parents hoped their children would become doctors, lawyers, or teachers, but some did not know that these goals required a college education. Others understood the importance of college, but could offer little assistance because they did not know of application procedures or financial aid. Parents tried to help their children indirectly by making homework a priority over chores and by holding up their own lives of physical labor as examples of what not to do.

On moral topics, however, the parents saw themselves as experts. They taught their children respect, honesty, and responsibility. One parent said, "We are people who are very poor, but we don't give them (our children) bad examples about anything. We behave well, hoping that they will learn to behave." As children approached adolescence, parents' hopes of education as the way out of poverty were challenged by their fears of drugs, neighborhood violence, and negative friends. Some families moved to other neighborhoods or sent their children back to Mexico.[16] Their dreams of college and professional work dimmed to hopes that children would finish high school and find steady jobs.

Siblings as Mentors

In many Latino families, older siblings are more able than parents to orient students to school, help with homework, and model positive school behavior. One study of sibling pairs in California families of Mexican descent revealed that older siblings taught reading, math, and school expectations to younger brothers and sisters.[17] These contributions are crucial when their immigrant parents have low levels of schooling and are unfamiliar with U.S. schools. Because Latino families often value close family ties, older siblings' companionship and emotional support at school can enhance students' motivation and achievement.

The study also found, however, that as children reached junior high school, a number of older siblings slipped out of the mentor role, because they were not doing as well in school as their younger siblings or they had left school altogether. Therefore, resources beyond schools and families are needed to support Mexican-heritage youths in early adolescence.

Program Staff as Culture Brokers

The young adults encountered by Latino children in community programs can play key roles in helping them feel confident and safe in their neighborhoods; learn alternatives to violence; gain educational experiences; and acquire the bicultural skills needed for success in school. Young adult staff can also give children a chance to talk and write about their dreams for careers, education, families, and their communities.[18] In Latino communities, young adults from a range of ethnic backgrounds work in programs for school-age children and often act as culture brokers. They value children's home communities, and many share a common language and sometimes a family history with the children. Yet many have learned to be bicultural and can help children become so as well, by passing on their understanding of how to retain community traditions while entering and succeeding in schools, colleges, or local gov-

BOX 11.1 • *A Latina Comadre Promotes Student Success*

One program director described a *comadre's* (godmother's) brokering between her family and school: "My parents immigrated from Mexico to Los Angeles in search of a better life for their children. They made sure we did our homework and maintained frequent contact with school, and nine of their thirteen children completed college. Most of my peers dropped out before they reached high school. Their parents also came to the United States to give their children a better life, with dreams for their children to obtain a college degree. But like many noneducated immigrant parents, they did not feel comfortable helping their children with school because they did not understand the system. My parents had a *comadre* who took them under her wing, explained how U.S. schools function, and reassured them their participation was demanded for us to be successful."

Source: Domínguez, E. E. Proyecto Mano á Mano: A model for parental involvement. Unpublished M.A. thesis in Education, University of California at Santa Cruz, 1995, p. 3.

ernment. These staff members build on Latino traditions of *comadres* and *compadres* (godmothers and godfathers) who help parents in guiding their children in school and life (see Box 11.1).[19]

An interview study found that, like Latino parents, young adult staff members working with Latino children in after-school programs defined success in life in moral and academic terms.[4] In guiding youths, the staff drew on positive and negative aspects of their past experiences. When reflecting on the sources of their own success, three young men credited mentors they had and programs they had attended, but they lamented the scarcity of positive role models in the communities of the children with whom they worked. Though sensitive to the difficulties children faced, staff members understood that others would judge the children on criteria like school grades and so they helped the children with homework and other tasks. Staff also felt that some children in their programs were growing up in families where the pressure of scarce family resources meant that it was up to the program staff to create the conditions for the children's success.

The young adult staff in community programs have supportive attitudes toward children, similar to those of family members, but they also offer children a broader view of schools, college, and other mainstream institutions. They can help children link their worlds of family, school, street, and community with their personal dreams and fears for the future.[20] Community and business mentoring programs bring successful adults into contact with youths,[21] but interviews with students suggest that some prefer mentors who are closer to them in age.[22,23]

Cultural Partnerships for Latino Youth

Families, schools, and communities can join together to create bridges for Latino children, working together to support their safety, school achievement, and emotional and social well-being. (Their efforts echo the community-bridging strategies adopted by the African-American families described in the article by Jarrett in this journal issue; and the relationships between young adult staff and youths resemble those created in the Bridges to Success program described in the article by Dryfoos in this journal issue.) In times of rapid cultural change, parents do not know all that their children need to learn to survive and flourish, so sources of guidance must be found beyond the family;[24] yet strong ties with family elders sustain access to wisdom and cultural traditions, including moral values. This article has emphasized the role that older siblings or young adult staff in community programs can play in helping Latino children to find pathways to success in the eyes of their families, their communities, and mainstream American schools.

In schools, community-based programs, and neighborhoods, links across generations can be forged across senior staff, young adults, and the parents and children they serve. These loosely knit networks can also foster new generations of leadership with the cultural skills that today's children need to succeed in an increasingly diverse world. Although programs like Head Start focus on the transition into school, and Upward Bound helps high school youths find their way to college, new research suggests that close attention should be paid to the middle years, when few adults may take children's dreams seriously.

References

1.   Gándara, P. The challenge of Latino education: Implications for social and educational policy. In *Latino politics in California*. A. Yánez-Chávez, ed. San Diego: Center for U.S. Mexican Studies, University of California, San Diego, 1996, pp. 51–75.

2.   Center on National Education Policy. *The good—and the not-so-good—news about American schools*. Washington, DC: Center on National Education Policy, 1996.

3.   California Youth Authority. *Summary fact sheet*. Sacramento, CA: CYA, 1996.

4.   Denner, J., Cooper, C. R., Lopez, E. M., and Dunbar, N. D. Mexican-American youth negotiating risk and opportunity: Obstacles and strategies for reaching career goals. Paper presented at the Annual Meeting of the American Educational Research Association. Chicago, 1997; Orellana, M. F., Denner, J., and Cooper, C. R. Community program staff: Brokering home-school relationships for Latino youth. Paper presented at the Annual Meeting of the American Educational Research Association. Chicago, 1997.

5.   Azmitia, M., Cooper, C. R., Garcia, E. E., and Dunbar, N. The ecology of family guidance in low-income Mexican-American and European-American families. *Social Development* (1996) 5:1–23.

6.   Latinos in the United States include people whose families come from Mexico (64%), Central and South America (14%), Puerto Rico (11%), Cuba (4.7%), and other points of origin (6.3%). See Shartrand, A. *Supporting Latino families: Lessons from exemplary programs*. Vol. I. Cambridge, MA: Harvard Family Research Project, 1996. According to the Immigration and Naturalization Service, immigrants from Mexico far outnumbered those from the next most numerous nations, which from 1981 to 1996, were the Philippines, China, the Dominican Republic, and India. See Immigration and Naturalization Service. *Statistical yearbook of the Immigration and Naturalization Service*. Washington, DC: U.S. Department of Justice, 1996.

7.   Stanton-Salazar, R. D., Vasquez, O. A., and Mehan, H. Engineering success through institutional support. In *The Latino pipeline*. A. Hurtado, ed. Santa Cruz, CA: University of California, Santa Cruz, 1996, pp. 100–36.

8.   Erickson, F., and Shultz, J. *The counselor as gatekeeper: Social interaction in interviews*. New York: Academic Press, 1982.

9.   Heinz, W. R., ed. *Institutions and gatekeeping in the life course*. Weinheim, Germany: Deutscher Studien Verlag, 1992.

10.   Catsambis, S. The path to math: Gender and racial-ethnic differences in mathematics participation from middle school to high school. *Sociology of Education* (1994) 67:199–215.

11.   Olson, L., Chang, H., De la Rosa Salazar, D., et al. *The unfinished journey: Restructuring schools in a diverse society*. San Francisco: California Tomorrow, 1994.

12.   Stonebloom, K., and McCue, L. *Introducing kids to college: A curriculum guide for intermediate grades to accompany "kids around the university."* Santa Cruz: University of California at Santa Cruz, 1998.

13.   Moll, L. C., Velez-Ibanez, C., and Gonzalez, N. *Funds of knowledge*. Santa Cruz: National Center for Research on Cultural Diversity and Second Language Learning, 1991.

14.   See note no. 6, Shartrand.

15.   Reese, L., Balzano, S., Gallimore, R., and Goldenberg, C. The concept of educación: Latino family values and American schooling. *International Journal of Educational Research* (1995) 23:57–81.

16.   Cooper, C. R., Azmitia, M., García, E. E., et al. Aspirations of low-income Mexican-American and European-American parents for their children and adolescents. In *Community-based programs for socialization and learning: New directions in child development*. F. A. Villaruel and R. M. Lerner, eds. San Francisco: Jossey-Bass, 1994, pp. 65–81.

17.   Azmitia, M., Cooper, C. R., Lopez, E. M., and Rivera, L. M. Older siblings' participation in Mexican-descent students' academic achievement. Paper presented at the American Educational Research Association. San Diego, CA, 1998.

18.   Heath, S. B., and McLaughlin, M. W., eds. *Identity and inner-city youth: Beyond ethnicity and gender*. New York: Teachers College Press, 1993.

19.   Hurtado, A. Figueroa, R., and García, E. E., eds. *Strategic interventions in education: Expanding the Latina/Latino pipeline*. Santa Cruz: Regents of the University of California, 1996.

20.   Phelan, P., Davidson, A. L., and Yu, H. C. Students' multiple worlds: Navigating the borders of family, peer, and school cultures. In *Cultural diversity: Implications for education*. P. Phelan and A. L. Davidson, eds. New York: Teachers College Press, 1991, pp. 52–88.

21.   Public/Private Ventures. *Mentoring: A synthesis of P/PV's research: 1988–1995*. Philadelphia: P/PV, 1996.

22.   Gándara, P. *High School Puente evaluation executive report number 3*. Davis, CA: University of California, Davis, 1997.

23.   Gándara, P., Larson, K., Mehan, H., and Rumberger, R. *Capturing Latino students in the academic pipeline*. Report #1. Sacramento, CA: Chicano/Latino Policy Project, 1998.

24.   Weisner, T. Ecocultural niches of middle childhood: A cross-cultural perspective. In *Development during middle childhood: The years from six to twelve*. W. S. Collins, ed. Washington, DC: National Academy Press, 1984, pp. 335–69.

12

Some children face overwhelming odds. Poverty, malnutrition, lack of education, a disorganized family, physical illness, or other factors can combine to make it very difficult for them to survive, let alone succeed. Yet some children manage to steer a course through these obstacles. What protective factors support these resilient children? By examining the lives of children such as those described in this article, researchers have been able to identify some common elements that may support children's development in spite of difficult conditions. One such factor may be personal resources, such as intelligence, sociability, or communication skills, while another may be social support, either within or outside the family (Garmezy, 1991).

Overview Questions

1. Ekwenye opens and closes the article talking about how teenage girls in homeless families become surrogate mothers. Cite a few examples of how Ada carries out this role in her family. Do you find counter-examples of her mother being clearly "in charge"?

2. In the last paragraph, Ekwenye characterizes Ada as being honest and strong and as being able to delay gratification, to organize, and to manage. Give examples of each of these from the case study.

3. Think about how Bronfenbrenner's model of four nested systems of environmental influence (the family, environments that impact the family such as the parents' workplace, the community, and the broader society) applies to Ada's situation. Can you identify factors at several levels that have a negative impact on Ada's life?

4. What examples of protective factors in Ada's life, such as personal resources and/or social support, can you identify?

Beggar Children in Nigeria: Strength in an Out-of-Order Existence

Chi E. Ekwenye

"As mothers become less assured of their abilities and opportunities to mother, children appear to become less confident and assured of their present and increasingly ambiguous about their future. . . ." (Boxill & Beaty, 1990, p. 62).

As cities across the world experience dramatic increase in the number of homeless families, concern and interest has grown in the complexity and dynamics of this phenomenon. Boxill and Beaty (1990) in their participation and observation in a public night shelter in Atlanta, Georgia, noted what they called "unraveling of the mother role." They observed teenage girls taking the leadership in preparing sleeping spaces, doing laundry, or caring for younger siblings. In essence, these children became surrogate mothers as they disciplined, fed, bathed, and bedded younger siblings. According to these researchers, "in an unkind and often assaulting world, mothers were comforted by their children's special acts of assistance and caring" (p. 59).

In far away Nigeria, where homeless mothers and children are called beggars or vagrants, 10-year-old Ada trudges the busy and chaotic streets of her town as she labors to bring some order to her family's out-of-order existence. Based on field notes from a study of beggar children in Nigeria, the following is a snapshot of one family. Ada looks about ten, even though she thinks she is six. She is the first of three siblings. Her younger sister is about eight, and her baby brother is about two. A fourth sibling is on its way.

Ada is shy. Even though she is the older of the two sisters, she is the least talkative, deferring to her younger sister and only speaking when she is addressed. Like her mother and baby brother, her name does not reflect her "obvious" tribe. She and her family appear to be living away from their tribe of origin. With an accent, they speak the language of the tribe among whom they beg, suggesting that they are not of this tribe. Ada's younger sister's name is more in consonant with her accent and their real tribe. They know this but have adopted major attributes of this tribe. Ada's reason for doing this is that "it is easier." However, even though they have tried to "fit in," the people of this tribe are not fooled. "They still call us names," Ada laments.

Ada does not remember her father. She was about four when he died, back in their village. They used to have a mud house with a thatch roof, however, when the rains came, and her mother could not keep up with the roof, the house fell. They lived for a while with their "Aunty," a woman from her mother's home town. When they could not bring in money for food, Aunty asked them to leave. Ada says her paternal grandmother died in a fire. She remembers her, but not very well. Both her maternal grandparents are dead.

Their village is about 50 miles away from where they live now. They visit their village whenever they have enough money to pay their way. They stay with Aunty for as long as they have money. When they run out of money, they return to the city.

Today, Ada's "body is not well." She coughs long and hard and at frequent intervals. She coughs up thick yellow phlegm and spits it into the busy street. She has tears in her eyes and looks like she is crying, but she says she is not. Her body is very warm, suggesting that she is running a temperature. She says she has already taken medicine, "panadol," an analgesic. She has had the cough for a long time and "takes medicine" everyday, but the cough is "a bad one" and just won't go away. Ada spends part of her earnings each day on medicine for her cough. Today, she could not beg much because her body didn't feel very well. She is not very happy about this situation and wants to feel well so she can beg actively like other beggar children. Besides, if she does not beg enough during the day, then she and her family will have less money for food.

Ada's mother says Ada and her sister are in school. She says the children beg only when schools are on holidays. Ada and her sister both say they are in elementary one, the first year of elementary school, but they do not know the names of their teachers or of anybody else in their school. On further examination, they both start laughing, hinting that they may not be telling the truth about being in school.

Talking about school is not always a laughing topic for Ada and her sister. They both get very angry when the issues of school and school children come up. They get particularly upset about school children "who won't mind their business." These school children, while being driven to school by their parents gawk at Ada and her family. They stare at Ada, pointing at her, and referring to her and her family as "mad people." Ada hates this. She often tells the children to mind their business, and then she calls them mad too! Ada's sister gets even more upset about this situation. She adds: "I hate them, and I ask [invoke] thunder to fire them and their Mama and their Papa. Yes I do! I also throw stones at them. That way they think twice before they look at me or call me mad."

Ada and her family pass their days begging on the busy streets of Aba, a teeming commercial city in Southeastern Nigeria. They pass their nights at the corridors of an old colonial office building close to where they beg during the day. They put out plastic sheets on the concrete floor and use their spare clothes and rags as pillows. Ada sleeps next to her sister at one end of the corridor, while their mother sleeps with the baby nearby. Their mother lends them one of her wrappers (thin cotton fabric) as cover sheet. Ada's greatest problem sleeping under this condition is overnight low temperatures and the early morning dew that makes their surroundings damp and cold. Also, cars start passing too early in the morning; long before Ada is ready to get up. "But then, that is good," she adds. The cars help wake her up so she does not oversleep. When she hears the cars passing at frequent intervals, she knows it is time to get up even though it may still be dark.

Her day and that of her family begins "before it is light." She and her sister draw water in a plastic bucket from a nearby public pump. They bathe, wake up their brother, bathe him, and then draw some more water for their mother's use. Their mother too must bathe before it is light. Whatever they do, they must be dressed, packed, and gone from their night shelter before seven o'clock. If not, they run the risk of losing the only home they have. They will not be allowed to return if workers show up and they are still around. When Ada is dressed and ready for the day, she packs her family's belongings in two separate bags, sends her sister and the baby off with one bag, leaves the remaining bag with her mother, wishes her goodbye, and then goes off on her own.

Ada's regular post is the "Hiace Park," a commercial motor station about half a mile from their night shelter. Her sister and baby brother sit on a plastic mat by "Bata Shoe Company" at the intersection of two industrial parkways. They sit with their bag next to them and a little blue bowl in front of them. Their mother sits by herself, some distance across from her two youngest children. She too has a bowl, a brown one in front of her. From where she sits, she sees her daughter and son clearly and knows what is going on with them. However, she acts like she doesn't know them. They must do this so they can cover more area, and most likely get more money or material things from the giving public. In Ada's own words, "when we divide, we get more."

The Hiace Park is often Ada's first port of call. Sometimes, she spends most of her day here. She begs from the commercial motor drivers, the park authorities, and the passengers. She may stop near sitting vehicles, may run after slowly moving ones, those stuck in traffic (a common occurrence), or she may accost pedestrians. Usually she holds out her hand and addresses her would-be benefactor in the local language. She uses a range of placatives: soothing, pleading, appealing, and flattering; depending on how she has judged the mood of her target. She is not always successful. In fact, she is unsuccessful more often than not. She summarizes this experience like this: "They tell me, 'go and work, nothing is wrong with you.' "Go and sell ice-water like other children.' They tell me other things too." She does not mind being told "things," she says. She ignores her tormentors, holds onto their hands if she has to, or clings to their trousers or skirts as the case may be. Sometimes, they give her money even after telling her to go get a "job." At other times, she knows they are not going to, no matter what she does, so she moves on.

Sometimes, Ada runs into other beggar children. Some of these are "good children and don't make trouble, while others are bad and full of trouble." At other times, she runs into adult beggars who drive her away, and tell her she is in their "territory." At times like these, she wanders off to more friendly locations. Business is not always good. Some days she makes enough money to return to her mother and siblings for lunch. On days she hasn't made any money by lunch time, she still returns to her family at a designated time during the day. That way she can share in the proceeds of the others or so the others can share in hers if she made enough. Ada and her sister buy all their meals from food vendors nearby. They will find a convenient place nearby to eat and retire for about half an hour or more.

After a meal, their mother and the baby may nap while Ada and her sister watch over their belongings. Sometimes they too are tired and sleepy, but they try to keep awake to allow their mother time to rest. "You have to be awake and watchful when you live on the streets," Ada cautions. Her baby brother was nearly killed when he was less than one-year-old. He got knocked down by a car because they let him wander too close to a moving vehicle. Now they all try to be alert and careful, especially when crossing streets or following moving vehicles. The dangers of living on the streets are many, as Ada recalls: "Sometimes they [motorists] try to jam us if we come too close to them. They push us away, and call us mad. Other children call us mad too. Maybe we are mad. If we are not mad, we won't be on the street. We are mad here [in the city], but in my village, we are not mad, only here."

When lunch is over and Ada's mother is up from her nap, Ada returns to her personal post. Her sister does the same, always with the baby. Their mother remains by her post. Ada may choose to return to the Hiace Park or just wander off somewhere where she knows there will be plenty of civil servants. Civil servants are her best "customers." On Saturdays when workers do not work, she has a "bad day." However, if it is a workday, she spends her afternoons doing the same thing she did in the morning hours. She begs until it is about 5 p.m. She then returns to her mother and siblings again. She counts her money and hands it over to her mother. On good days, she brings back an average of 40 to 50 U.S. cents. She hands this over to her mother, and so does her sister. If they received anything else other than money, they also surrender these to their mother. Their mother then gives them money for food for the night. If business was good, they buy enough food for all four of them. If not, they buy a little, not enough for four. This means that the baby gets most of it, leaving the rest of them hungry and upset.

Dinner does not mean the end of day for Ada and her family. They go by the light of the day. Ada stays out to beg for as long as it is light. When the light of day fades, she knows it is time to go "home." She and her family leave for their night shelter at the corridors of the office building. Today, Ada has a friend with her. Kodi is a young runaway beggar girl. She looks about 16 and is about five months pregnant.

Ada's mother is not upset that she has brought somebody home without telling her first. All she wants to know is where Kodi is headed. When Kodi tells them, they tell her she can't go there. Where Kodi is headed is dangerous; "bad things" happen to beggar people there, they warn. They invite her to spend the night with them and to stay until she finds her own place. Kodi is obviously relieved and thankful for the company and protection.

When they get home, and having already eaten dinner, Ada changes into warmer clothes for the night. She changes her baby brother, and makes sure that her sister does the same. Then they sit around and talk or sing songs in the dark. Then they lie down for the night. Sometimes they are able to go to sleep immediately. At other times, they are not able to. "Bad" people may come to bother them, try to steal their things, or just plain harass them. It may just be mad people or drunks fighting near by and keeping them awake for a very long time. At other times, vehicles seem to run till late into the night. Rainy nights are the worst for Ada and her family. Gusty winds blow the rain on them and make them change position several times during the night. On such nights, they may get up and huddle together at a dry corner. When none of these things happen, it could be just the baby waking up and crying for food. On nights when they had a good day, they will have something for him to eat. If they had a bad day, then there will be nothing to eat and the baby will cry for a long time before he goes back to sleep. Nevertheless, Ada manages to get some sleep most nights.

Today, however, is not a typical day for Ada and her family. Besides Kodi, this researcher has been visiting them for the past three days. Ada is sicker than she has been in the past and is less talkative than usual. She is cautious in what she says, especially to strangers. She is particularly careful about what she says to this researcher, and cross checks her answers with her mother most of the time. She cross checks her responses with her mother in their dialect, which she knows the researcher does not understand. Then she responds to the researcher in the local dialect. Her sister will give more direct answers, most often without checking with her mother. Ada also serves as the interpreter for her mother and the researcher. She does this in between chores: changing clothes for the night, changing her brother, laying out their sleeping places, and taking her medicine for the night. Today, she makes an extra sleeping place for Kodi and informs her that that will be her sleeping spot. As Ada gets her family ready for the night, her sister sets out bowls for the tea and bread the researcher brought for them. Her mother shares the bread, making sure everybody gets a piece, including Kodi and the researcher. As everybody eats, the children tell the researcher what to bring next time she visits. They need blankets and sweaters for cold nights, medicine for Ada's cough, a change of clothes, shoes, and school books.

Reflecting on his work with homeless and marginalized people, Kozol (1995) spoke of the clarity and honesty of children in the South Bronx. Ada's honesty appears to come mostly from her naïve acceptance of her way of life. Certainly, she knows that other children lead lives that are very different from hers, but this is her life and she lives it, for now, without questions. What is unknown is whether her strength, her ability to delay gratification, to organize, and to manage will lead her out of this existence, or whether, like her mother, she will welcome the opportunity to be cared for by her own children.

To echo Kozol (1988), perhaps someday there will be no beggar children on the streets of Aba or anywhere else in Nigeria. Perhaps someday, but not yet—not for children like Ada who are living now and will have no chance to live their childhood again. Perhaps this article will bear witness to the toll that street begging and vagrancy take upon the children of the dispossessed. Perhaps this article will "pay tribute to the dignity, the courage, and the strength with which [children like Ada] manage to hold up beneath the many terrifying problems they confront" (Kozol, 1988, 185).

References _____

Boxill, N. A. & Beaty, A. L. (1990). Mother/Child interaction among homeless women and their children in a public night shelter in Atlanta, Georgia. In N. A. Boxill (Ed.), *Homeless children: Watchers and Waiters*: 49–64. New York. Haworth Press.

Kozol, J. (1995). *Amazing Grace. The lives of children and the conscience of a nation.* New York: Harper Perennial.

Kozol, J. (1988). *Rachel and her children: Homeless families in America.* New York: Crown Publishers.

13

■ On a family trip to France, we watched small children playing in a park with their parents and effortlessly conversing in French—such a contrast to my struggle for months with grammar books and language tapes! It is no accident that children come to speak the same language as their parents; social interaction plays an important role in children's language acquisition. One important feature of the language learning environment is the parent's tendency to talk about things in the immediate environment in which the child shows an interest (Harris, 1992). Not surprisingly, children's first words are generally names of objects that they can move or that move by themselves, that is, capture attention (Nelson, 1973). Although learning one's "mother tongue" is different from learning a language via formal instruction, comparing these two situations underscores some similarities in fundamental language learning processes; note in Gersten's article the importance of interest, attention, and motivation.

Overview Questions

1. What was the new policy statement by the Secretary of Education, and how does it relate to scholarly opinion? Describe in your own words how the debate over bilingual language relates to Bronfenbrenner's (1979) model of four nested systems of environmental influence on child development (the family, environments that impact the family such as work and school, the community, and the broader society).

2. According to August and Hakuta, as well as Kirst, what problems exist in the research on the optimal age for a child to be taught academic content in English?

3. Describe the historical sequence of practices in teaching students about the English language (ESL, ESOL, ELD): prior to 1980, in the 1980s, and in the 1990s. Summarize the seven principles that Gersten advocates for merging ELD with content learning. Choose three of these and describe how they involve basic learning processes such as attention and motivation.

The Changing Face
of Bilingual Education

Russell Gersten

The past year or so has brought a virtual avalanche of dramatic events in the field of bilingual education, portending a significant shift in how English language learners are taught in the United States.

In April 1998, Secretary of Education Richard Riley announced a major shift in policy, calling for a goal of English language proficiency in three years for virtually all English language learners. Riley asserted that "new immigrants have a passion to learn English, and they want the best for their children" (p. 2). A survey of 420 randomly selected members of the Association of Texas Educators (both inside and outside the field of bilingual education) found that the majority agreed with the secretary. They believed that children spend too much time in native language instruction (Tanamachi, 1998). Traub (1999) also argues that Latino students spend far too much time in native language instruction, concluding that, in its current form, "bilingual education seems to be hurting" Latino students the most—"the one group it was initially designed to help" (p. 33).

This view stands in stark contrast to the position of several noted scholars in the field, who feel that English language learners should be taught all academic subjects in their native language for no fewer than five, and preferably seven, years (for example, Cummins, 1994). These scholars believe that extensive academic instruction in the native language is necessary for students to benefit from mainstream classrooms.

Recent events indicate that some large school districts (for example, New York and Denver) and some states (for example, California) are seriously rethinking how they educate English language learners. Invariably, the initiatives call for students to enter English language academic instruction at a much earlier age, and they propose a significant reduction in academic instruction in native languages. An article in the New York Times reports that "in response to years of criticism of the city's bilingual education programs . . . New York City plans to dramatically increase the amount of time devoted to English language development" (Archibold, 1998). The article concludes with a summary of major lawsuits. Lawsuits or threatened litigation in Sacramento, Denver, and Albuquerque convey the emotional tenor of the debate.

Increasingly, parents and teachers (most notably Jaime Escalante and Gloria Tuchman) have begun to question the small amount of time devoted to English language development in many bilingual education programs in the primary grades. Advocacy groups have consistently raised such issues as parental choice in the amount of English language instruction each child receives, how early a child is introduced to substantive English language instruction, and when a child should exit classrooms that use a great deal of native language instruction.

It seems reasonable to expect that after so much attention, controversy, and discussion, research would provide answers to questions such as these:

- At what age is it best to introduce academic instruction in English to young students?
- To what extent—if any—does native language instruction benefit students' cognitive and academic growth?
- Which are the best instructional methods for developing English language proficiency?

Unfortunately, research findings have stubbornly failed to provide answers to the first two questions. Ironically, we have more research-based information on the third—and least emotional—of these guiding research questions.

Searching for Answers

An unbiased review of research addressing the first question indicates that we do not have adequate information to determine the optimal time for a child to be taught academic content in English.[1] This is not to say that researchers have not passionately debated the issue or that they have not developed and disseminated a vast array of complex theories. This issue has been debated extensively and serves as the basis of some of the aforementioned lawsuits.

The cornerstone of most contemporary models of bilingual education is that content knowledge and skills learned in a student's primary language will transfer to English once the student has experienced between five and seven years of native language instruction. Yet absolutely no empirical research supports this proposition. Methodological problems so severe that the question cannot be adequately answered plague the research on the subject (August & Hakuta, 1997). These problems appear to be most severe in some of the larger studies intended to "answer" major policy questions.

The recent report released by the National Academy of Sciences, *Improving Schooling for Language Minority Children* (August & Hakuta, 1997), offers a laundry list of complaints concerning these studies:

> The major national-level program evaluations suffer from design limitations, lack of documentation of study objectives, poorly articulated goals, lack of fit between goals and research designs and excessive use of elaborate statistical designs to overcome shortcomings. (P. 138)

In addition, the report concludes that "it is difficult to synthesize the program evaluations of bilingual education because of the extreme politicization of the process" (p. 138). The report makes clear that the prevalence of writings by "advocates who are convinced of the absolute correctness of their positions" (p. 138) presents serious barriers to attempts to improve the quality of instruction for English language learners.

Trying to unravel the issues behind these conflicts and debates can be frustrating. Even the National Academy of Sciences report is of little immediate help. It is as filled with contradictions as most other writing in the field. For example, the authors savagely critique the research on effective schooling and classroom processes, yet report the findings from these seriously flawed studies as if they represented solid facts. Similarly, the authors indicate that there is no empirical support for the effectiveness of native language instruction in the early grades, yet still advocate its use. However, the report also demonstrates an awareness of the contradictory nature of the database by noting:

> It is clear that many children first learn to read in a second language without serious negative consequences. These include children who successfully go through early-immersion, two-way, and English as a second language (ESL)-based programs in North America. (P. 23)

---

[1]An unpublished meta-analysis by Jay Greene (1998) has been occasionally cited as support for native language instruction. However, when we examined his data, we found that his results show no benefits of native language instruction for Latino students in the elementary grades. We also noted numerous methodological problems in his meta-analysis (Baker, Gersten, & Otterstedt, 1999). Thus we conclude that there is no empirical evidence of benefits to extensive native language instruction.

Michael Kirst of Stanford University (Schnaiberg, 1998) recently provided some valuable insight into the problems within the bilingual education knowledge base. In discussing California, he noted:

> From its inception . . . in the 1970s, bilingual education has been oriented toward inputs, process and compliance . . . . The assumption was if you have this input, the outputs would take care of themselves. So . . . [we monitor] . . . whether you mounted the program, *and not its results.* (P. 16, [emphasis added])

Although Kirst was discussing California, similar problems have been noted in states such as Texas and Massachusetts. This concern with compliance as opposed to learning outcomes helps explain why the bilingual education knowledge base is so inadequate—which in turn contributes to many of the current problems in the field.

Increasingly, researchers argue that we need to focus on aspects of instruction that lead to improved learning outcomes as opposed to political labels that at best crudely describe complex instructional interventions. Several years ago, my colleagues and I received support from the U.S. Department of Education to begin to articulate these components. Our charge was to synthesize the knowledge base on effective classroom practices that simultaneously promote English language development and academic learning. We intentionally eschewed the ongoing political debates. Our goal was to delineate specific techniques that teachers could use to simultaneously promote learning and English language development.

English Language Development

Although questions about optimal age remain unanswered, at some point all English language learners begin academic instruction in English. The initial transition is often called "content area ESOL," "structured immersion," or "sheltered content instruction." The common feature is teachers' use of English designed for students who are not proficient in the language. In sheltered instruction, teachers modulate their use of English so that it is comprehensible to the student and base their degree of support on their knowledge of that student. In some cases, teachers use native language to help a child complete a task, to clarify a point, or to respond to a question.

Almost invariably, sheltered content instruction is coupled with instruction geared toward building the student's knowledge of the English language. In years past, this component has been referred to as ESL or ESOL. Increasingly, educators are using "English language development" (ELD). Historically, teachers focused on the formal structure of language (for example, grammar and mechanics). Critics routinely attacked this approach, however, because it failed to capitalize on the communication function of language, did not generate student interest, and resulted in very limited generalization.

The 1980s brought more "natural" conversational approaches to teaching English. These also attracted criticism, primarily because they did not necessarily help students learn the highly abstract, often decontextualized language of academic discourse. A movement began about 10 years ago to merge English language learning with content acquisition. The rationale is that students can learn English while learning academic content and that this type of learning will build academic language (Cummins, 1994)—that is, the abstract language of scientific, mathematical, or literary discourse. However, too often teachers merely "hope that language occurs [during lessons]. These is a risk during content instruction of neglecting language development" (Gersten & Baker, in press).

The erratic quality of ELD instruction is at the root of the growing dissatisfaction with current practice. Inadequate attention has been devoted to curriculum development, pragmatic teacher training and professional development, and applied research. In a recent professional work group that I conducted in California for the U.S. Department of Education (Gersten & Baker, in press), an educator from the district bilingual education office articulated the problem: "It's important for teachers to be clear about objectives and goals . . . yet an explicit statement of goals does not exist [in district or state curricular materials]."

I would argue, however, that we have made definite progress in understanding what instructional goals are feasible for this group of students and what specific classroom practices are likely to help meet these goals. In our two-year research synthesis project (Gersten & Baker, in press), we concluded that the beginning of an empirical knowledge base on effective instructional practices for English language learners exists. It is important to emphasize, however, that this knowledge base is emerging and should be the topic of controlled, high-quality classroom research.

Principles for Merging ELD with Content Area Learning

ELD programs must include the development of oral and written proficiency, the development of basic conversational English and academic language, and the systematic proactive teaching of conventions and grammar (Saunders, O'Brien, Lennon, & McLean, 1998; Fashola, Drum, Mayer, & Kang, 1996). As they undertake these tasks, teachers should keep in mind the following instructional principles derived from the limited research in this area:[2]

- Avoid oversimplifying with contrived, intellectually insulting material when teaching academic content in English. Subjects such as science and math can be excellent venues for merging English language development because all students are learning a new technical vocabulary and there is great potential to use concrete objects (Chamot, 1998).
- Use visuals to reinforce verbal content when teaching in English (Saunders et al., 1998; Reyes & Bos, 1998).
- Use both oral and written modalities frequently (Saunders et al., 1998).
- Employ strategic use of synonyms. Word choice and sentence structure need to be consistent and concise during second language learning. Pay attention to use of metaphors and similes and other highly culture-specific phrases and expressions (Gersten & Jiménez, 1994).
- Focus on approximately five to eight core vocabulary words in each lesson. Some strategies include (1) carefully selecting words (evocative words that stimulate instruction, key words for understanding a story), (2) linking words or concepts to words known in the native language, (3) showing new words in print, and (4) using visuals (for example, concept maps) to depict concepts or word meanings (Saunders et al., 1998).
- Use native language during ELD strategically. At times, it might be helpful to use both native language and English during instruction; however, be aware of the risk of overreliance on simultaneous translations.

[2]For a more complete description see Gersten, Baker, and Marks (1998). The practices are embedded in programs such as Instructional Conversations (Echevarria & Graves, 1998), Bilingual CIRC (Calderon, Hertz-Lazarowitz, & Slavin, 1998), Cognitive Academic Language Learning Approach (Chamot, 1998), collaborative strategic reading (Klingner, Vaughn, & Schumm, 1998), Peer-Mediated Instruction (Arreaga-Mayer, 1998), and the Effective Strategies for Studying Literature model used successfully in Los Angeles schools by Saunders and colleagues (1998).

- During the early phases of language learning, modulate and be sensitive when providing feedback and correcting language usage; however, during later stages, identify errors and provide specific feedback to students (Reyes, 1992).

To date, much has evolved from grassroots experimentation and attempts by researchers to describe practices that appear to engage students and enhance their learning. Nonetheless, it is becoming increasingly clear that a set of practices exists that teachers can use to persistently, but sensitively, encourage students to learn content while expressing their ideas in a new language. This information may be particularly helpful as the shift toward greater emphasis on instruction in English takes effect.

References

Archibold, R. C. (1998, June 21). Crew plans an overhaul of bilingual education. *New York Times*, p. 27.

Arreaga-Mayer, C. (1998). *Language sensitive peer mediated instruction for culturally and linguistically diverse learners in the intermediate elementary grades.* In R. R. Gersten & R. Jiménez (Eds.), Promoting learning for culturally and linguistically diverse students: Classroom applications from contemporary research (pp. 73–90). Belmont, CA: Wadsworth.

August, D., & Hakuta, K. (Eds.). (1997). *Improving schooling for language-minority children.* Washington, DC: National Academy Press.

Calderon, M., Hertz-Lazarowitz, R., & Slavin, R. (1998). Effects of bilingual cooperative integrated reading and composition on students making the transition from Spanish to English reading. *Elementary School Journal, 99*(2), 153–165.

Chamot, A. U. (1998). *Effective instruction for high school English language learners.* In R. Gersten & R. Jimenez (Eds.), Promoting learning for culturally and linguistically diverse students: Classroom applications from contemporary research (pp. 187–209). Belmont, CA: Wadsworth.

Cummins, J. (1994). *Primary language instruction and the education of language minority students.* In Schools and language minority students: A theoretical framework (2nd ed.). Los Angeles: California State University, National Evaluation, Dissemination and Assessment Center.

Echevarria, J., & Graves, A. (1998). *Sheltered content instruction: Teaching English-language learners with diverse abilities.* Des Moines, IA: Allyn & Bacon.

Fashola, O. S., Drum, P. A., Mayer, R. E., & Kang, S. (1996). A cognitive theory of orthographic transitions: Predictable errors in how Spanish-speaking children spell English words. *American Educational Research Journal, 33*, 825–844.

Gersten, R., & Baker, S. (in press). *The professional knowledge base on instructional interventions that support cognitive growth for language minority students.* In R. Gersten, E. Schiller, S. Vaughn, & J. Schumm (Eds.), Research synthesis in special education. Mahwah, NJ: Erlbaum.

Gersten, R., Baker, S., & Marks, S. U. (1998). *Productive instructional practices for English-language learners: Guiding principles and examples from research-based practice.* Reston, VA: Council for Exceptional Children.

Gersten, R., Baker, S., & Otterstedt, J. (1999). *Further analysis of "A meta-analysis of the effectiveness of bilingual education," by J. P. Greene (1989).* Technical Report No. 99–01. Eugene, OR: Eugene Research Institute.

Gersten, R., & Jiménez, R. (1994). A delicate balance: Enhancing literacy instruction for students of English as a second language. *The Reading Teacher, 47*(6), 438–449.

Greene, J. P. (1998). A meta-analysis of the effectiveness of bilingual education. Unpublished technical report. Austin, TX: University of Texas & the Thomas Rivera Policy Institute.

Klingner, J. K., Vaughn, S., & Schumm, J. S. (1998). Collaborative strategic reading during social studies in heterogeneous fourth-grade classrooms. *Elementary School Journal, 99*(1), 3–22.

Reyes, M. (1992). Challenging venerable assumptions: Literacy instruction for linguistically different students. *Harvard Educational Review, 62*(4), 427–446.

Reyes, E., & Bos, C. (1998). *Interactive semantic mapping and charting: Enhancing content area learning for language minority students.* In R. Gersten & R. Jiménez (Eds.), Promoting learning for culturally and linguistically diverse students: Classroom applications from contemporary research (pp. 133–152). Belmont, CA: Wadsworth.

Riley, R. W. (1998, April 27) Helping all children learn English. Washington, DC: U.S. Department of Education, Office of Public Affairs.

Saunders, W., O'Brien, G., Lennon, D., & McLean, J. (1998). *Making the transition to English literacy successful: Effective strategies for studying literature with transition students.* In R. Gersten & R. Jiménez (Eds.), Effective strategies for teaching language minority students: Classroom applications from contemporary research (pp. 99–132). Belmont, CA: Wadsworth.

Schnaiberg, L. (1998, April 29). What price English? *Education Week,* pp. 1, 16.

Tanamachi, C. (1998, July 18). Educators poll: Set bilingual time limit. *Austin American Statesman,* p. B1.

Truab, J. (1999, January 31). The bilingual barrier. *The New York Times Magazine,* pp. 32–35.

14

■ "If at first you don't succeed, try, try again." How do we explain our failures? Are they due to lack of effort, as this old saying implies? Or are they due to lack of ability? Dweck and Leggett (1988) propose that our beliefs about success and failure are closely related to achievement motivation. If failure is due to lack of effort, we should be motivated to persevere and master the challenge. But if we failed due to lack of ability, we are likely to believe that our efforts are futile. Efforts are worthwhile if we believe that our ability can be improved with effort—"practice makes perfect"—but effort is useless if we believe that our ability is fixed, unchangeable, and inadequate to the task. What we believe about effort and ability can make the difference between rising to meet a challenge versus giving up in despair.

The fact that we have old sayings that encourage persistence suggests that, for some skills at least, we have a cultural belief that success is due to effort. Yet, we can all think of students who have to study very hard to perform at the same level as others who don't seem to study at all. How do children resolve this apparent contradiction? Are there universal developmental trends in children's understanding of the relationship between effort and ability, or does this understanding develop in culturally-specific ways?

Overview Questions

1. Why is the research on achievement motivation in Chinese students puzzling? What two different beliefs might Chinese students hold about the relation between effort and ability? Which of these is prescribed by the culture? Give two examples of the Chinese cultural norm to exert effort.

2. Some Western research shows age differences in children's beliefs regarding effort and ability. What do younger versus older children typically believe? However, other research shows individual differences—describe how these are related to learning goals.

3. Why does the work by Salili and Hau on Chinese children's attributions of effort and ability contrast with that of Barker and Graham in Western culture? Which belief about this relation is expected to show more individual differences? If students hold this belief, what does the author predict about their motivation and performance? If teachers hold this belief, what is predicted about their teaching strategies?

4. How do the results of this study answer the puzzle about Chinese students introduced at the beginning of the article? Reflect on how you would have answered the questions they posed the students and teachers. Does this article give you any insight about your own academic experiences and history?

Focus Questions

1. The standard deviation tells the "typical" distance of scores from the mean. Compare the standard deviations for belief in a postitive relationship between ability and effort with those for belief in a compensatory relationship between ability and effort. Do these support the author's prediction; why or why not? Pearson's r measures how much two variables correlate; it ranges from -1 to $+1$, with 0 meaning that one cannot

predict scores on one variable by knowing the individual's score on the other. How *strong* do you believe the relationship is between belief in the compensatory rule and motivation and performance?

2. Why, in the second study, did the researcher use a scenario, rather than simple questionnaire items, as in Study 1, to assess beliefs about effort and ability? The researcher used the pattern of teacher responses to two questions regarding "Students A and B" to assess beliefs; do you agree with the author's interpretation of the AA, BB, and BA choices?

3. In a chi square analysis, one constructs a grid such that you simultaneously categorize responses in two ways, for example, compensatory rule endorser and ability versus effort attributor. If there is no relationship between these, responses should be randomly and equally distributed across these cells (e.g., 25% in each of the four cells). The test assesses whether the observed pattern is probably non-random, that is, it indicates a true relationship between the variables. Explain in your own words how you would interpret the results of the chi square analysis on compensatory beliefs and attributions regarding poor performance.

4. Draw a graph of the comparison of mean beliefs in malleable intelligence in teachers who preferred effort versus ability attributions for poor performance. Explain in your own words why one would have predicted belief in malleable intelligence to be related to compensatory versus positive beliefs in effort-ability.

5. The smaller the *p* value of a statistical test, the less likely that the results are due to chance, and probably due to a real difference. By convention, statistical tests are considered "significant" if $p < .05$. Which of the results in the section on teaching methods should be considered the strongest?

Chinese Students' and Teachers' Inferences of Effort and Ability

Ying-yi Hong

> Li Bai, a great poet in Tang Dynasty, was said to be lazy in studying when he was young. One day, when he was playing at a riverbank, he saw an old woman rubbing a metal rod against the rocks. Li was curious and asked the woman what she was doing. The old woman explained that she wanted to make a needle out of the metal rod. Li looked at the woman with disbelieving eyes. The old woman explained that "If you are hard-working and persevering enough, a metal rod can be made into a needle." Li was inspired. From that day on, he studied very hard and became one of the greatest poets in Chinese history.

Most Chinese children know this story and, like Li, they know that effort and hard work are important if one wants to achieve anything.

Much research in America has shown that effort attribution is linked to a more mastery oriented achievement pattern, especially in the face of failures. Might the effort attribution emphasized in Chinese culture render Chinese students more motivated in learning and less vulnerable to helpless achievement patterns? Research findings pertaining to this question are equivocal. While there are many indications of superior academic learning by Chinese students (e.g., Stevenson, Stigler, Lee, Lucker,

Kitamura, & Hsu, 1985) there are also indications that Chinese students tend to feel less competent, less task oriented and more anxious than their Western counterparts. These findings suggest that the link between effort attribution and learning motivation may not be straightforward in Chinese culture. This paper thus aims at examining the meaning of effort in an achievement situation in Chinese culture. We proposed that the unique achievement pattern found among Chinese students might in part be understood with reference to how the relationship between effort and ability is construed in Chinese culture. We examined this issue first from the perspective of students and then from the perspective of teachers.

We argue that, first, exertion of effort is a Chinese cultural norm. Second, within this cultural context, people could still hold two seemingly contradictory beliefs about the relationship between effort and ability. Specifically, the present paper sought to demonstrate that many Chinese people may, on the one hand, believe that effort is instrumental to success, and on the other hand, believe that people with high ability need not work hard to succeed. The former belief, being the culturally prescribed belief, might be held by most people in the culture. The latter belief is a relatively more personal belief, and thus could be differentially held by individuals in the culture. Among students, the beliefs in the relation between effort and ability might be associated with their learning motivation and academic performance. Among teachers, the beliefs might be associated with the ways they understand students' learning problems and what teaching methods they would use to help students with poor performance.

Exertion of Effort Is a Cultural Norm

Hard work is highly valued in Chinese culture. Perseverance and hard work are believed to be crucial to success. Chinese children are socialized to value hard work, perseverance and academic excellence (Yang, 1986). In modern Chinese societies, children are trained to study hard not only in school, but also after school. For example, it is very common for children in Hong Kong and Taiwan to go to private tutoring classes after school. To work hard and excel in academic performance are considered to be the primary obligations of children and adolescents (Tao & Hong, in press). Students also consider studying hard a moral obligation. For example, we found in our study (Hong & Lam, 1992) that Hong Kong students would feel guilty if they failed in examinations. These students thought that they had not fulfilled their obligations and felt they were responsible for causing their families to lose face.

Not surprisingly, effort is a salient or accessible cause many Chinese use to explain achievement outcomes. Indeed, Stevenson and his associates (e.g., Stevenson & Lee, 1990; Stevenson & Stigler, 1992) have shown that Chinese parents and students are more likely than their American counterparts to make effort attributions in achievement situations. Other researchers also argue that Chinese culture with its emphasis on hard work seems to encourage effort attributions and mastery of task (Hau & Salili, 1990; Hess, Chang, & McDevitt, 1987; Salili & Mak, 1988). In this cultural context, how do people conceive of the relation between effort and ability?

Beliefs in the Relationship Between Effort and Ability

Research in Western Cultures

Research findings on students' inferences of effort and ability are equivocal. There has been some controversy over the developmental course of judgments of ability in relation to effort. Basically, in this research children of varying ages are given information about an actor's level of performance and effort and they are asked to judge the actor's level of ability (e.g., Barker & Graham, 1987; Kun, 1977; Nicholls, 1978, 1989). For instance, Barker and Graham (1987) showed children of different ages a video in which a teacher was giving feedback to two students. After watching the video, the children were asked to judge the ability and effort of the two students in the video. The researchers varied the performance of the students and the teacher's feedback to create four experimental conditions—(a) success accompanied by praise to one student, (b) success accompanied by neutral feedback to the other student, (c) failure in conjunction with blame directed toward one student, and (d) failure and neutral feedback toward the other student. The children can judge ability to be unrelated to effort (and solely a function of performance), inversely related to effort (greater effort implies lower ability), or positively related to effort (greater effort implies greater ability). Results revealed that among the 5-year-olds, the correlation between their effort and ability judgments was .84 for success and .86 for failure. This suggests that young children view that effort and ability are strongly positively related in both outcome conditions. For the middle-elementary-age group (8 to 9-year-olds), the correlation was positive but relatively moderate ($r = .24$ for success and .55 for failure). In contrast, among the 11-year-olds, the correlation between effort and ability judgments was strongly negative ($r = -.79$ for success and $-.82$ for failure), indicating that the 11-year-olds believed in a compensatory relation between effort and ability.

Similarly, Nicholls (1989) has shown that young children (at ages younger than 11) usually view ability and effort as positively correlated, whereas older children (at ages 11 and older) often view effort and ability as compensatory. That is, young children usually believe that people who accomplish with greater effort have higher ability. Older children, in contrast, believe that a high ability person would need less effort to attain a certain level of achievement, relative to someone with lower ability. Nicholls explains that young children hold a positive belief because they cannot differentiate ability (as a cause of outcomes) from effort, whereas older children are able to conceive of ability as capacity and understand that the effects of effort on performance relative to others are limited by capacity.

This interpretation, however, is contrary to the results revealed in some other studies (e.g., Dweck & Elliott, 1983; Leggett & Dweck, 1986; Surber, 1984), which have shown individual differences in the judged relationship between ability and effort. For example, Surber (1984) found that, among a group of adult participants, some judged ability and effort to be positively related, whereas others judged ability and effort to be negatively related. Leggett and Dweck (1986) also reported that some eighth graders (14-year-olds) believe in a positive effort-ability relationship, whereas others believe in a compensatory one. They further showed that such individual differences were systematically related to the students' goals in academic settings. Specifically, students who were concerned about performing well and showing off their ability (i.e., held performance goals) viewed effort as a measure of (lack of) ability, and were likely to believe in a compensatory relation between effort and ability. In contrast, students who were concerned about mastery of the task (i.e., held learning goals), instead, viewed effort as a means of increasing ability and were likely to believe in a positive relation between effort and ability. In sum, these studies have shown that, rather than universal developmental differences in the judgments, there appear to be individual differences in the judged relationship between effort and ability, which may be systematically linked to the individual's other concerns and belief systems.

Research in Chinese Culture

Salili and Hay (1994), using the procedures similar to those used in Barker and Graham (1987), examined how Chinese children (between 7 to 15 years old) view the relation between ability and effort. In their study, they presented children with a story about two students: Student A and Student B. Both students got the correct answer on a question. However, Student A received a neutral feedback from a teacher who said, "Yes, 15 is the correct answer." Student B, however, received praise (positive feedback) from the teacher, "You have done very well, 15 is the correct answer." Then, the children were asked to rate Student A and Student B's ability and effort. In the failure condition, children were presented with a story about two students: Student C and Student D. This time both students got the wrong answer. However, Student C received a neutral feedback from a teacher who said, "10 is incorrect." Student D, however, received negative response, "What have you done there, 10 is incorrect!" Again, students were asked to rate Student C and Student D's ability and effort. Results revealed a positive correlation between children's ability and effort ratings. That is, the children thought that the more hardworking students were always more able, and vice versa. This positive relationship was strong even among 11 year-olds ($r = .60$ for the positive feedback condition, and $r = .57$ for the negative feedback condition). Although the correlation was weaker for older children, it was never negative. This pattern of result is in contrast to the negative correlations Barker and Graham (1987) found from 11 year-old American children ($r = -.79$ in the positive feedback condition, and $r = -.82$ in the negative feedback condition). Salili and Hau (1994) suggested that Chinese students, unlike their American counterparts, perceived great similarity (or positive relationship) between effort and ability. "For Chinese students, people working hard have higher ability and those who have high ability must have worked hard." (Salili & Hau, 1994, p. 233)

Using Nicholls' framework, the positive relationship found seems to imply that Hong Kong Chinese children are incapable of differentiating capability from effort. This explanation seems to be unlikely, as there is no evidence of any deficiency among Chinese children in forming achievement related concepts. One possible alternative interpretation, like that proposed by Salili and Hau (1994), is that the positive relationship found could be a manifestation of the emphasis on effort in Chinese culture. That is, students may believe that someone with high ability should work hard since working hard is both their responsibility and a means to succeed. However, more importantly, the positive relationship found may not fully reflect students' beliefs in the relationship between effort and ability. That is, people affected by the cultural norm may believe that effort can facilitate the application of ability. However, at the same time, they may also believe that people with high ability do not need to make as much effort as people with low ability to succeed. Such belief in a compensatory relationship is reflected in a popular Chinese saying that "hard work may compensate for ineptitude." In sum, the positive and compensatory beliefs, even though seemingly contradictory, may co-exist in Chinese culture.

My main postulation thus is, inasmuch as exerting effort is a cultural norm, most Chinese students and teachers may believe to some extent that effort enhances ability. Hence, a belief in the positive rule (effort is positively related to ability) should be prevalent in Chinese culture. However, this cultural norm might not have preempted a belief in the compensatory rule (effort is inversely related to ability). One may still reason that an individual with high ability does not need to work as hard as someone who has lower ability to achieve success. Accordingly, they may conclude that effort implies a lack of ability. However, because the compensatory rule is not a culturally prescribed belief, individuals in the culture might not uniformly hold it. In other words, unlike the positive rule, there should be great individual differences in the endorsement of the compensatory rule. Furthermore, even more important, the belief in compensatory rule should be meaningfully related to students' learning and teachers' teaching. The two studies reported in this chapter were designed to address this issue.

Study 1 sought to test empirically if (a) Chinese students hold the positive and compensatory inferences of ability and effort at the same time, and (b) there are greater individual differences in the students' endorsement of compensatory rule than that of the positive rule. Furthermore, if the compensatory belief held is an integral part of the Chinese students' achievement process, it should also be related to other components of the achievement process. Specifically, as noted, a belief in compensatory rule has been found to be associated with performance goals (to document one's ability) rather than learning goals (to master new skills) (Leggett & Dweck, 1986). I therefore predicted that a belief in a compensatory relationship between ability and effort would be associated with a lower motivation to learn and thus a lower level of academic achievement.

Study 2 examined teachers' beliefs in the relationship between effort and ability and how the beliefs relate to the ways they understand students' learning problems and what teaching methods they would use to help students with poor performance. Again, I predicted greater individual differences in the teachers' endorsement of the compensatory rule than that of the positive rule. Teachers' compensatory rule endorsement should also predict greater emphasis on evaluating students' ability (vs. effort) and preference for teaching methods that bolster performance outcomes rather than a thorough mastery of the materials.

Study 1: Students' Beliefs about Effort and Ability and Their Correlates

Two samples were recruited as participants. The first sample consisted of 79 Hong Kong university students (40 males, 38 females, and one student whose gender was not reported). Their age ranged from 19 to 22 with the average age being 20.26. The second sample consisted of 175 Form 1 students in a Band 5 secondary school in Hong Kong (94 males and 81 females). Their age ranged from 12 to 15 with an average age of 13.05. Form 1 is equivalent to Grade 7 in the U.S. In Band 5 schools, most of the students had the lowest scores in public examinations. These two groups of students were recruited because of convenience of sampling.

We asked both groups of students the extent to which they would agree to the items that depict a positive relation between ability and effort: "If you are really good at some subjects, working hard would help you to have a thorough understanding of the subjects." "You must work hard to solve problems in order to utilize your ability on the subjects." Students were asked to rate their degree of agreement on a scale from 1 ("absolutely disagree") to 10 ("strongly agree"). As predicted, both college students ($M = 8.01$, $SD = 1.69$) and high school students ($M = 7.65$, $SD = 1.88$) subscribed strongly to the view that working hard is necessary for the application of ability. In this sense, effort and ability are believed to be positively related. That is, the more effort one exerts, the more ability one can develop.

The same students were also asked to respond to two other items that convey a compensatory relation between ability and effort: "If you need to work really hard to solve some problems, this means that you are not very good at that subject," and "If you are really good at a certain subject, you don't need to work hard to get good results in examination." Again, subjects were asked to rate their degree of agreement on a scale from 1 ("absolutely disagree") to 10 ("strongly agree"). The mean endorsement of these items, as predicted, unlike that of the positive relationship items, fell on the mid-point of the scale with quite a lot of individual variations in both samples ($M = 5.84$, $SD = 1.88$ for the college sample and $M = 5.49$, SD 2.08 for the high school sample).

Interestingly, the correlations between the agreement to the positive relationship items and the compensatory relationship items were virtually zero ($r = .03$ for the college sample, and $r = -.07$ for the high school sample). This suggests that, as predicted, the positive view and the compensatory view are not necessarily related or do not preclude each other.

Compensatory Rule and Deep Motivation

In the college sample, we also asked the students to respond to Biggs' Study Process Questionnaire (1992). The questionnaire consists of 42 items and we were particularly interested in the deep motivation and surface motivation subscales. Examples of the deep motivation items are "I find that studying gives me a feeling of deep personal satisfaction," and "I become increasingly absorbed in my work the more I do." Examples of the surface motivation items are "I chose my present courses largely with a view to the job situation when I graduate rather than because of how much they interest me," and "I am discouraged by a poor mark on a test and worry about how I will do on the next test." Students were asked to rate from 1 ("never like me") to 5 ("always like me"). As predicted, results revealed a negative association between the endorsement of compensatory rule and deep motivation to learn ($r = -.25, p < .05$). That is, the stronger the belief in the compensatory rule, the lower the deep motivation. However, the association between the endorsement of compensatory rule and surface motivation was not significant ($r = .11, p > .05$).

The endorsement of the positive rule, in contrast, was not significantly associated with the level of deep motivation.

Compensatory Rule and Academic Achievement

In the Form 1 student sample, we also collected the students' grades on Chinese, English, and Mathematics in the final examination. The final examination was conducted about a month after we assessed students' beliefs in ability and effort. As predicted, findings revealed that students' endorsement of the compensatory rule was negatively associated with their average scores on the three subjects ($r = -.29, p < .001$). That is, the stronger the belief in the compensatory rule, the lower the achievement.

Again, the endorsement on the positive rule was not significantly associated with the level of academic achievement.

Discussion

Findings from this study suggest that some students might believe that effort could facilitate the application of ability (the positive rule) and at the same time believe that people who have a high level of ability would not need much effort to succeed (the compensatory rule). More importantly, these students also showed a lower level of deep motivation to learn and a lower academic performance than did those who disputed the compensatory rule. These findings may shed light on the vulnerability of Chinese students. The pervasive belief in the positive rule may lead Chinese parents and teachers to pressure students (especially those who perform poorly) to work hard. In fact, this is consistent with the findings by Salili et al. (this volume) that Hong Kong students spent on average more time studying (16 to 20 hours per week) than did European Canadian students (i.e., Canadian students of European ancestry) (11 to 15 hours per week). However, the grades Hong Kong students received in school were significantly lower than those of the European Canadian students. This suggests that teachers in Hong Kong on average were more stringent in grading and set higher standards than did teachers in Canada. Moreover, studying time is negatively correlated with examination results for Hong Kong students ($r = -.20, p < .01$), but positively correlated ($r = .41, p < .001$) for European Canadian students. Furthermore, Salili et al. classified the students into high and low achievers according to their actual performance. They found that for European Canadian students, regardless of whether they were high or low achievers, studying time was positively correlated with performance results. This suggests that studying hard does indeed link to better grades in school in Canada. However, they found that among high achievers in Hong Kong, the time spent on studying was not related to performance results. More strikingly, the time spent on studying was negatively correlated with academic performance among low achievers in Hong Kong! In other words, in real life, low achievers often work harder than do high achievers. This, by itself, is forceful evidence that supports the compensatory rule. It is ironic that an emphasis on studying hard among low performing students might lead students to believe more in the compensatory rule. Furthermore, the frustration resulting from the lack of positive outcomes after working hard might in turn negatively affect students' learning motivation, which then may further dampen the students' performance. This vicious circle, which is set up by Chinese people's beliefs in the relation between effort and ability, might be a key to understanding the vulnerability of Chinese students, which few researchers have realized.

Study 1, however, is limited in that only students' responses to four statements were used as predictors. The findings that most students endorsed the positive rule could be subject to alternative interpretations. A major one is that the two statements in the questionnaire that measured positive rule were phrased in socially desirable ways. Thus most participants agreed rather than disagreed with the statements. This alternative explanation is hard to rule out. However, if the positive rule is indeed widely held in Chinese culture, as we argued, it would be quite impossible to have statements that, on the one hand, directly convey the concept of the positive rule, and on the other hand, do not invite social desirable responding. To overcome such limitation, indirect measures were designed in Study 2 to assess participants' endorsements of the positive versus compensatory rule.

Study 2: Teacher's Beliefs about Effort and Ability

Because teachers and students are close partners in learning situations, what students believe may reflect what teachers believe. That is to say, teachers and students may share similar beliefs in learning and achievement. Thus, we predicted that many of the teachers, like their students, also believe in the compensatory rule and the positive rule at the same time. Furthermore, if the compensatory belief held is an integral part of the teachers' system of beliefs about achievement, it should also be linked to their understanding of students' learning problems and the method they use to help students with learning problems. Previous research has shown that, among students, a stronger belief in the compensatory rule is associated with stronger endorsement of performance (vs. learning) goals (Leggett & Dweck, 1986). In this study, we tested if, among teachers, a stronger belief in the compensatory rule is associated with a greater tendency to evaluate students' ability and thus a greater tendency to make ability (vs. effort) attributions. Furthermore, we examined if teachers believing in the compensatory rule would encourage the students with (learning problems to focus on getting a pass in examinations rather than learning the materials.

Participants were 78 primary school (i.e., grade school) and 50 secondary school (i.e., high school) teachers in Hong Kong (35 males and 85 females; the average age was 30.31, $SD = 7.85$). On average, they had taught for 3.79 years ($SD = 2.51$). They were asked to fill out a set of questionnaires in which items measuring the compensatory and positive rules were embedded. Because of the limitations we observed in Study 1, we did not use direct statements but instead used a scenario to assess teachers' beliefs. The teachers were presented with the following scenario: "Student A and B ranked the first and the tenth in a class test, respectively. Student A was a diligent student; every week he studied what was taught. Student B only studied before the test."

The teachers were asked to indicate which student they thought was more intelligent. We reasoned that teachers who viewed effort as an indication of lack of intelligence (i.e., compensatory rule) should be more likely to choose B than A.

Then, the teachers were asked to indicate which student they thought would receive better grades at graduation. We reasoned that participants, who viewed B as smarter and believed that smartness, more than effort, determines performance outcomes should be more likely to choose B than A again.

In sum, teachers who chose Student B on both items were likely to believe in the compensatory rule and think that intelligence, more than effort, determines performance. In contrast, teachers who chose Student A on both items were likely to hold a belief in the positive rule and believe that effort facilitates intelligence and performance. Teachers who chose Student B on the first item and Student A on the second item might hold mixed beliefs: On the one hand, they believed that Student B who used less effort but performed well was smarter, suggesting that they believed in the compensatory rule. On the other hand, they predicted that Student A who worked hard would receive higher grades at graduation, indicating that they also believed in the positive rule. If teachers hold both positive and compensatory rules at the same time, they would choose Student B on the first item and Student A on the second item. 60.40% of the teachers chose the Student B-Student A option, whereas only 25.74% and 13.86% of teachers chose the Student A-Student A option and Student B-Student B option, respectively. (Student A-Student B option was an illogical option and only 1 participant chose it.) Thus, most teachers subscribe to both the positive and compensatory rules.

How might teachers' beliefs of the relationship between effort and ability relate to their attributions and teaching strategies?

Attributions of Students' Poor Performance

The teachers were presented with the following scenario: "Ming received average grades when he was in Form 1. However, his grades became poorer when he got into Form 2. In the examination of the first term, he ranked 36 in the class. In the examination of the second term, his grades were the poorest in the class. His class master met with Ming's parents and found that nothing special had happened in his family in the past year. As usual, Ming went to school everyday and went home to study after school. There was no indication that he had been negatively influenced by peers or addicted to drugs. How would you account for Ming's decrease in performance?" Participants were given four options: (a) he has low intelligence and thus could not cope with difficult materials, (b) he lost interest in learning, (c) his studying methods were inadequate, and (d) he was not diligent enough. Participants were asked to rank the four options according to their likelihood as causes. We were particularly interested in whether the teachers thought intelligence or effort was more likely to be the cause. Thus, we classified the teachers into two groups: Teachers who preferred ability (option a) to effort (option d), and those who preferred effort (option d) to ability (option a). Then we examined the association between these attributions and the teachers' beliefs in the relationship between effort and ability.

A chi-square analysis revealed a significant association between teachers' attributions and beliefs in the relationship between effort and ability ($X^2 = 6.06$, $p < .05$). Specifically, 50% of the teachers who believed in the compensatory rule (i.e., those who chose the Student B-Student B option) also preferred ability attributions. In contrast, only 34.62% of the teachers who believed in the positive rule (the Student A-Student A option) and 19.67% of those who chose the mixed rule (Student B-Student A option) preferred ability attributions.

Implicit Theories of the Malleability of Intelligence

Carol Dweck and her associates have identified two types of implicit theories people hold about the malleability of intelligence: Some people believe that intelligence is relatively fixed, whereas others believe that intelligence is relatively malleable (see Dweck, 1999; Dweck & Leggett, 1988; Dweck, Chiu, & Hong, 1995 for reviews). Furthermore, recent studies have shown that Hong Kong college students as well as American college students who believed in fixed intelligence were less likely to make effort attributions in the face of setbacks (Hong, Chiu, Dweck, Lin, & Wan, 1999). Might we find a similar pattern of association among Hong Kong teachers? As noted, we found an association between attributions and beliefs in the relationship between effort and ability. Might we also find associations between these two variables and the implicit theories? To test these predictions, the teachers were asked to respond to the Implicit Theories of Intelligence Measure developed by Dweck and Henderson (1988), which consists of three items: "You have a certain amount of intelligence and you really can't do much to change it;" "Your intelligence is something about you that you can't change very much;" and "You can learn new things, but you can't really change your basic intelligence." Participants were asked to show their degree of agreement with each item on a 6-point Likert scale, from 1 ("strongly agree") to 6 ("strongly disagree"). Thus, the higher the participants' scores the less they believe that intelligence is a fixed entity. Both the reliability and validity of this measure have been tested extensively and found to be high (see review in Dweck et al., 1995). The internal reliability of the measure found for the present sample was high as well ($\alpha = .90$).

There was a significant correlation between implicit theories of intelligence and attributions ($r = .30$, $p < .001$). As found among students in Hong et al. (1999), teachers who preferred effort attributions believed to a greater extent intelligence is malleable (mean score on the Implicit Theories Measure = 4.33, $SD = .90$) than did teachers who preferred ability attributions ($M = 3.72$, $SD = .88$), $F(1, 122) = 11.87$, $p < .001$.

However, teachers' implicit theories of intelligence were not related to their beliefs about the effort-ability relationship. Such a result is unexpected, and thus needs replication to validate its robustness.

Teaching Methods in Helping Students with Poor Performance

How might teachers' beliefs and attributions relate to the ways they help students with poor performance? To examine this question, the teachers were asked to respond to the following question, "If there is a student in your class who has been working hard but still performs poorly in class, how likely would you use the following ways to help him?" Seven alternatives were provided: (1) "Lower your requirements to the level of his ability," (2) "Do not give him challenging schoolwork so as not to give him further frustration," (3) "Train him to memorize materials that will allow him to cope with examinations, but do not require him to understand these materials," (4) "Look for some inspiring materials to stimulate his thinking and promote his analytical ability," (5) "Encourage him to try different studying methods to increase his learning ability," (6) "Encourage him to study with students with good grades and learn from them ways of thinking," (7) "Advise him not to be discouraged by his low learning ability, and encourage him to develop in other areas that he is good at (e.g., music, sports)." The participants indicated their likelihood of using each alternative on a 10-point scale from 1, "very unlikely," to 10, "very likely."

Table 14.1 lists the mean endorsements on the seven alternatives. Alternatives 4, 5, 6, and 7 had high mean endorsements and small standard deviations. Alternatives 1 and 2 had moderately high mean endorsements. Alternative 3, which em-

TABLE 14.1 *Mean Endorsements of the Seven Alternative Ways To Help the Low Achieving Student*

Teaching Method	Mean (SD)
Lower your requirements to the level of his ability.	6.30 (1.86)
Do not give him challenging schoolwork so as not to give him further frustrations.	6.18 (1.96)
Train him to memorize materials that will allow him to cope with examinations, but do not require him to understand these materials.	4.07 (2.14)
Look for some inspiring materials to stimulate his thinking and promote his analytical ability.	7.88 (1.31)
Encourage him to try different studying methods to increase his learning ability.	8.31 (1.26)
Encourage him to study with students with good grades and learn from them ways of thinking.	8.33 (1.33)
Advise him not to be discouraged by his low learning ability, and encourage him to develop in other areas that he is good at (e.g., music, sports).	7.88 (1.94)

phasizes rote learning, was the only alternative which had mean endorsement below the mid-point (i.e., 5.5). This alternative was also related to teachers' implicit theories and attributions.

Correlation analysis revealed that the likelihood of recommending rote learning was significantly associated with teachers' implicit theories of intelligence ($r = -.30$, $p < .001$) and marginally associated with teachers' attribution ($r = -.17$, $p = .06$). That is, teachers who believed in malleable intelligence were less likely than those who believed in fixed intelligence to recommend rote learning to students with learning problems. Teachers who preferred effort attributions were also less likely ($M = 3.88$) than those who preferred ability attributions ($M = 4.67$) to recommend rote learning, $F(1, 124) = 3.57$, $p = .06$. Beliefs about the effort-ability relationship, however, were not associated with the likelihood of recommending rote learning.

Implications and Conclusion

The main results in the present research are that while most students in Chinese culture believe in a positive relationship between effort and ability, some of them also believe in a compensatory relationship between effort and ability. These students were likely to be the ones who had low academic performance and levels of deep motivation in learning. Analogous results were found among teachers. Over half of the teachers in the sample endorsed both the positive and compensatory beliefs at the same time. Teachers who endorsed a compensatory belief were more likely to attribute students' poor performance to ability than effort. This attributional style, in turn, was related to the teachers' beliefs in the malleability of intelligence. Compared to those who believed in malleable intelligence, teachers who believed in fixed intelligence were more likely to attribute students' poor performance to ability than effort and to encourage rote learning among students who showed learning problems.

Previous research has shown that compared with their Western counterparts, students, teachers, and parents in Chinese culture are more likely to attribute students' poor performance to effort, which should make Chinese students more mastery-oriented and thus more free of learning problems. However, previous research has also shown that many Hong Kong Chinese students suffer from learning problems, such as lower confidence in their ability and higher test anxiety, which are typically associated with ability attributions. To understand these seemingly contradictory findings, we may need to understand the meaning of effort and its sequel in Chinese culture. Because the culture emphasizes the virtue of hard work, most Hong Kong Chinese students work very hard and on average spend many hours on studying (Salili et al., this volume). However, problems might occur if the effort spent does not pay off. Students who study hard but still get low grades may have no alternative but to blame their ability.

These students' belief in a compensatory relationship between effort and ability may be a reflection of their experiences in the achievement situation. When teachers are dealing with students with low performance, they may encourage students to work hard but at the same time believe that their poor performance indicates their lack of ability. If teachers also believe that intelligence is fixed and cannot be improved through learning, among the many ways they use to help the students, they might encourage students to memorize materials without requiring them to fully understand the materials. Although motivated by good intentions, these teachers' actions might communicate to the students that their teachers do not expect them to be competent enough to master difficult materials. Indeed, this is parallel to the previous findings that students believing in fixed intelligence have little faith in the effectiveness of effort (Stipek & Gralinski, 1996; Sorich & Dweck, in press). That is, students holding fixed intelligence belief may think that even with great effort, people who do not have ability cannot achieve high performance. The present research suggests a similar pattern of reasoning among teachers. That is, teachers who believe in fixed intelligence, compared to those who believe in malleable intelligence, think that even with great effort, students with low ability might not benefit much from their teaching. Also, within a fixed intelligence framework, the long hours that Chinese students put into studying may only be a means to fulfill role obligations rather than motivated by the expectation that effort can enhance ability.

In sum, Chinese students' success has been explained by their higher effort attributions. However, few researchers have realized that the cultural emphasis on effort could be a mixed blessing to Chinese students. On the one hand, the emphasis on effort has led parents and teachers to put pressure on students to study for long hours, and might have to some extent fostered among students perseverance in studying difficult materials. On the other hand, in Chinese culture, endorsement of a positive view on the relationship between effort and ability may co-exist with a belief in a compensatory view. This belief combination could bring along negative effects on learning and teaching. In studying achievement, it is important to be sensitive to the nuances in the meanings of the effort-ability relationship within the cultural context.

References

Barker, G. P., & Graham, S. (1987). Developmental study of praise and blame as attributional cues. *Journal of Educational Psychology, 79*, 62–66.

Biggs. J. B. (1992). *Why and how do Hong Kong students learn? Using the learning and study process questionnaires.* Education Paper 14, Faculty of Education, University of Hong Kong. Hong Kong.

Dweck, C. S. (1999). *Self-theories: Their role in motivation, personality and development.* PA: Psychology Press.

Dweck, C. S., & Elliott, E. S. (1983). Achievement motivation. In P. Mussen and E. M. Hetherington (Eds.), *Handbook of child psychology* (pp. 643–692). New York: Wiley.

Dweck, C. S., & Henderson, V. L. (1988). *Theories of intelligence: Background and measures.* Unpublished manuscript.

Dweck, C. S., & Leggett. E. L. (1988). A social-cognitive approach to motivation and personality. *Psychological Review, 95,* 256–273.

Dweck, C. S., Chiu, C., & Hong, Y. (1995). Implicit theories and their role in judgments and reactions: A world from two perspectives. *Psychological Inquiry, 6,* 267–285.

Hau, T., & Salili, F. (1990). Examination result attribution, expectancy and achievement goals among Chinese students in Hong Kong. *Educational Studies, 16,* 17–31.

Hess, R. D., Chang, C. M., & McDevitt. T. M. (1987). Cultural variations in family beliefs about children's performance in mathematics: Comparisons among Peoples Republic of China, Chinese-American, and Caucasian-American Families. *Journal of Educational Psychology, 79,* 179–188.

Hong, Y., & Lam, D. J. (1992). Appraisal, coping, and guilt as correlates of test anxiety. In K. A. Hagtvet (Ed.), *Advances in test anxiety research* (Vol. 7, pp. 277–287). Lisse, Netherlands: Swets and Zeitlinger.

Hong, Y., Chiu, C., Dweck, C. S., Lin. D. M., Wan, W. (1999). Implicit theories, attributions, and coping: A meaning system approach. *Journal of Personality and Social Psychology, 77,* 588–599.

Kun, A. (1977). Development of the magnitude-covariation and compensation schemata in ability and effort attributions of performance. *Child Development, 48,* 862–873.

Leggett, E. L., & Dweck, C. S. (1986). *Individual differences in goals and inference rules: Sources of causal judgments.* Unpublished manuscript.

Nicholls, J. G. (1978). The development of the concepts of effort and ability, perception of academic attainment, and the understanding that difficult tasks require more ability. *Child Development, 49,* 800–814.

Nicholls, J. G. (1989). *The competitive ethos and democratic education.* Cambridge, MA: Harvard University Press.

Salili, F., & Hau, T. (1994). The effect of teachers' evaluative feedback on Chinese students' perception of ability: A cultural and situational analysis. *Educational Studies, 20,* 223–236.

Salili, F., & Mak, P. H. T. (1988). Subjective meaning of success in high and low achievers. *International Journal of Intercultural Relations, 12,* 125–138.

Sorich, L., & Dweck, C. S. (in press). Mastery-oriented thinking. In C. R. Snyder (Ed.), *Coping.* New York: Oxford University Press.

Stevenson, H., W. & Lee, S. Y. (1990). Contexts of achievement: A study of American, Chinese, and Japanese children. *Monographs of the Society for Research in Child Development, 55,* 1–116.

Stevenson, H. W., & Stigler, J. W. (1992). *The learning gap.* New York: Summit.

Stevenson, H. W., Stigler, J., Lee, S., Lucker, G., Kitamura, S., & Hsu, C. (1985). Cognitive performance and academic achievement of Japanese, Chinese, and American children. *Child Development, 56,* 718–734.

Stipek, D. J., & Gralinski, H. (1996). Children's beliefs about intelligence and school performance. *Journal of Educational Psychology, 88,* 397–407.

Surber, C. F. (1984). Inferences of ability and effort: Evidence for two different processes. *Journal of Personality and Social Psychology, 46,* 249–268.

Tao, V., & Hong, Y. (in press). A meaning system approach to Chinese students' achievement goals. *Journal of Psychology in the Chinese Societies.*

Yang, K. S. (1986). Chinese personality and its change. In M. H. Bond (Ed.), *The psychology of the Chinese people.* Hong Kong: Oxford University Press.

15

Sadly, family violence is a feature of many children's lives. A national survey in the 1990s indicated that 11 percent of children had been attacked by their parent in the past year, including being hit, kicked, bitten, hit with an object, beaten up, burned, or threatened/attacked with a knife or gun (Wolfner & Gelles, 1993). Children who have been abused generally experience socio-emotional problems and academic difficulties (Trickett & McBride-Chang, 1995). Among the problems these children experience is Post-Traumatic Stress Disorder. PTSD, according to the American Psychiatric Association (1994), includes persistent re-experiencing of the event (e.g., recurrent dreams or memories, flashbacks). It also involves numbing or avoidance of the trauma (e.g., feelings of detachment; efforts to avoid activities, places or people associated with the trauma; or sense of foreshortened future). PTSD patients also show symptoms of increased arousal (e.g., irritability, difficulty concentrating, or exaggerated startle response). In this article, the authors compare the cognitive functioning of abused children with children who have not suffered such abuse, to make inferences about the brain areas that have been compromised by PTSD. Here, we can see the deleterious effects of family experiences on the brain and cognitive functioning of children. These, in turn, are believed to affect the child's responses to environmental interventions in the future. Thus the abuse that the child experiences may set in motion a chain of reciprocally-influencing events which may have long-term consequences.

Overview Questions

1. What areas of cognitive functioning show deficits in adults with PTSD? What brain changes are associated with PTSD in children?

2. In what two ways are the results they obtained consistent with the expectations based on adults and the neuroimaging studies? (Hint: review question 1.) In what ways are they inconsistent?

3. In their introduction, what do the authors say about why they believe that it is particularly important to examine the neuropsychology of PTSD in children? Given their findings, what "developmental ramifications" would you predict to result from the specific cognitive deficits they observed?

Focus Questions

1. What factors did they attempt to match between the comparison sample and the PTSD sample? Why was it important to administer the neuropsychological battery blind to group membership? Why was it important to exclude subjects from the study for the reasons they listed? List the six cognitive domains they assessed.

2. In Table 15.1, the p value of a z or t test tells how likely it is that the two samples were randomly selected from the same population. Choose any one of the attention or abstract reasoning/executive function measures where the p value was $\leq .05$, indicating that the two groups are probably really different from one another. Draw a bar graph representing the two means for the groups. Use a vertical line to show one standard

deviation above and below each mean. Standard deviation shows how far people typically scored away from the mean. The Bonferroni correction gives a more conservative
estimate of which differences are likely to be real.

Neuropsychological Function in Children with Maltreatment-Related Posttraumatic Stress Disorder

Sue R. Beers and Michael D. De Bellis

Posttraumatic stress disorder (PTSD) is now widely recognized in children. Although findings are equivocal (1), studies of adults have reported cognitive problems
in individuals with PTSD, particularly in the areas of concentration, learning, and
memory (2). In contrast, cognitive function indexed by performance on standardized
neuropsychological instruments has not been extensively evaluated in children with
PTSD. It is particularly important to characterize the neuropsychological deficits associated with childhood PTSD because they are likely to have broad developmental
ramifications, affecting both response to therapy and school performance.

Unlike studies in adults with PTSD, neuroimaging studies indicate that PTSD
in children is associated with diffuse CNS effects (i.e., smaller cerebral volumes and
corpus callosum areas) but no anatomical changes in limbic structures (3). Functional
imaging procedures indicate that medial prefrontal cortical dysfunction may be associated with both adult and pediatric PTSD (4). The neuropsychological consequences of these brain alterations have not been extensively studied.

In this pilot study, we examined cognitive functioning using a battery of neuropsychological instruments measuring language, attention, abstract reasoning/
executive function, learning and memory, visual-spatial processing, and psychomotor functioning in maltreated children with PTSD and sociodemographically similar
comparison children who had not been maltreated and who did not have PTSD. The
tests, described by Spreen and Strauss (5), are listed in Table 15.1. On the basis of neuroimaging research (3, 4), we hypothesized that the children with PTSD would perform more poorly on cognitive measures, particularly in the domains mediated by
the prefrontal cortex.

Method

We recruited 14 medication-naive children with PTSD secondary to maltreatment
who were psychiatric outpatients and 15 healthy comparison children who had not
been maltreated and who were similar to the PTSD patients in age, race, socioeconomic status, and IQ. The mean age of the PTSD patients was 11.38 years (SD=2.60)
and that of the comparison children was 12.17 (SD=1.75). Six of the PTSD patients
were girls and eight were boys; seven of the comparison subjects were girls and eight
were boys. In the PTSD group, 10 patients were white, two were African American,

TABLE 15.1 *Neuropsychological Test Scores of 14 Maltreated Children With PTSD and 15 Healthy Comparison Children Who Had Not Been Maltreated*

Cognitive Domain and Measure	Score				Analysis		
	Comparison Children		Children With PTSD				
	Mean	SD	Mean	SD	t or z	df	p
Language							
Clinical Evaluation of Language Fundamentals							
Concepts and Directions	10.85	3.65	10.83	2.55	t=0.01	23	0.99
WISC-III Vocabulary	11.20	2.24	10.57	1.95	t=0.80	27	0.43
Attention							
Stroop Color and Word Test							
Word	48.79	8.52	49.70	9.96	t=−0.24	22	0.81
Color	45.86	8.73	42.10	7.92	t=1.08	22	0.29
Color/word	53.00	9.00	42.00	11.23	t=2.66	22	0.01[a]
Interference	53.36	6.72	45.90	8.70	t=2.37	22	0.03
Digit Vigilance Test							
Total time	490.13	149.82	490.36	159.42	t=−0.004	24	0.99
Omission errors	6.87	4.55	17.36	12.31	t=2.71	24	0.006[a]
WISC-III Digit Span	10.38	2.81	9.08	1.93	t=−1.14	24	0.25
Abstract reasoning/ executive function							
Wisconsin Card Sorting Test							
Categories	5.45	0.69	3.50	2.07	t=2.52	21	0.01[a]
Perseverative responses	14.36	7.43	38.33	36.82	t=−1.63	21	0.10
Controlled Oral Word Association Test							
Animal Naming	20.00	4.04	14.11	5.30	t=3.02	21	0.007[a]
Total Words	31.79	11.58	23.20	6.37	z=−1.94	22	0.05
WISC-III Similarities	12.47	1.46	10.50	2.95	t=2.24	27	0.04
Trail Making B	31.60	18.25	30.40	13.19	z=0.25	23	0.80
Learning and memory							
California Verbal Learning Test							
List A: Total Words, trials 1–5	54.40	8.41	49.38	10.93	t=1.37	26	0.18
List B	6.00	1.41	5.31	2.14	z=−1.63	26	0.10
Short delay free recall	11.27	2.09	9.46	3.33	t=1.74	26	0.09
Long delay free recall	11.67	2.02	9.92	2.56	t=2.01	26	0.05
Discriminability	97.93	2.22	94.64	6.38	z=−1.59	27	0.11
Rey-Osterrieth Complex							
Figure recall	16.57	5.87	11.69	7.62	t=1.91	26	0.07
Visual-spatial function							
Rey-Osterrieth Complex							
Figure copy	31.20	4.26	22.93	10.74	z=−2.36	26	0.02
Money Road Map	24.62	7.07	23.30	6.17	z=−0.72	26	0.47
WISC-III							
Block Design	11.93	2.74	10.00	2.35	z=−1.76	27	0.08
Object Assembly	11.07	2.81	10.50	3.08	t=0.52	27	0.61
Judgment of Line Orientation	22.60	5.67	17.71	5.89	t=228	27	0.03
Psychomotor speed							
Trail Making A	13.53	6.52	14.75	4.22	z=1.30	25	0.19
Grooved Pegboard Test							
Dominant hand	69.07	7.12	83.36	22.12	z=1.71	27	0.09
Nondominant hand	77.80	10.84	80.93	17.00	z=0.11	27	0.91
WISC-III Coding	10.31	4.13	9.46	3.55	z=0.56	21	0.58

[a]After Bonferroni corrections, $p < 0.01$.

and two were biracial (white and African American); in the comparison group, 12 subjects were white, one was African American, and two were biracial. In the PTSD group, the mean socioeconomic level according to the Hollingshead Four-Factor Index of Socioeconomic Status (6) was 39.21 (SD=11.28); in the comparison group the mean was 39.60 (SD=7.69). The mean fullscale IQ (estimated by the WISC-III four-factor score [7]) was 105.71 (SD=11.89) in the PTSD group and 113.20 (SD=11.69) in the comparison group.

After complete description of the study was given to the children and their parents, written informed consent was obtained. All of the children assented to their participation. Subjects received monetary compensation for participation.

A board-certified child psychiatrist (M.D.D.) conducted psychiatric interviews of all subjects and their legal guardians using a detailed trauma interview described elsewhere (8). A masters-level clinician, blind to clinical status, completed a modified version of the Schedule for Affective Disorders and Schizophrenia for School-Age Children—Present and Lifetime Version (9). The diagnosis of the children with chronic PTSD was based on DSM-IV. The traumata they experienced included sexual abuse (N=7), physical abuse (N=2), and witnessing domestic violence (N=5). Comorbid disorders included major depressive disorder (N=5), dysthymic disorder (N=2), separation anxiety disorder (N=2), oppositional defiant disorder (N=6), and attention deficit hyperactivity disorder (inattentive subtype) (N=1). Comparison subjects had no lifetime history of any axis I diagnosis.

Inclusion criteria for the PTSD group were "reported and indicated" child maltreatment experiences noted by child protective services before this investigation, the availability of one nonabusing caregiver who could cooperate with this protocol, and a stable home environment (i.e., the child had not been in danger from the perpetrator[s]) for at least the previous 3 months). Exclusion criteria for all subjects included birth complications; substantial medical illness; head injury associated with wounds requiring sutures, emergency room treatment, or loss of consciousness; gross obesity (i.e., weight greater than 150% of ideal body weight) or growth failure (i.e., height less than the third percentile); Wechsler full-scale IQ less than 80; history of treatment with psychotropic medications: anorexia nervosa, pervasive developmental disorder, schizophrenia, adolescent-onset alcohol or substance abuse or dependence; prenatal exposure to alcohol and/or other substance use greater than twice a month during the 3 months before discovery of pregnancy; and mother's use of controlled substances during the known period of pregnancy.

Subjects completed a comprehensive neuropsychological battery administered blind to whether the child did or did not have PTSD. Instruments are described in Spreen and Strauss (5) and listed in Table 15.1.

We evaluated the distribution of our data for normality using Shapiro and Wilks's W statistics. When no transformation normalized the data, we applied nonparametric tests. Student's t test, or Wilcoxon/Kruskal-Wallis rank sums were used to assess between-group differences on cognitive results. Two-tailed alpha equaled 0.05; analyses were completed with Statistical Discovery Software (SAS Institute Cary, N.C.).

Results

Children with PTSD performed more poorly on measures in four of the six cognitive domains (Table 15.1). In the domain of attention, PTSD subjects performed more poorly on two measures of freedom from distractibility, Stroop Color and Word Test color/word and interference. The PTSD group made significantly more omission errors on a measure of sustained visual attention (Digit Vigilance Test).

On measures of problem solving and abstract reasoning/executive function, PTSD subjects completed fewer categories on the Wisconsin Card Sorting Test. On two measures of semantic organization, the Controlled Oral Word Association Test Animal Naming and the Total Words, children with PTSD generated fewer category members and named fewer words beginning with target letters (i.e., F, A, S). Significant differences were also identified on WISC-III Similarities; again, the children with PTSD scored lower than the comparison subjects.

Children with PTSD performed more poorly on one test of learning and memory, the California Verbal Learning Test long delay free recall. Finally, on measures of visual-spatial function, children with PTSD completed a poorer copy of the Rey-Osterrieth Complex Figure and made more errors on the Judgment of Line Orientation.

No significant differences between groups were found on any tests of language or psychomotor speed. After a Bonferroni correction for multiple comparisons was applied within each of the cognitive domains, only results within the domains of attention (i.e., Stroop color/word and Digit Vigilance Test omission errors) and abstract reasoning/executive function (i.e., Wisconsin Card Sorting Test categories and Controlled Oral Word Association test Animal Naming) remained significant.

In the PTSD group, variables that remained significant between groups were correlated with the number of clinical symptoms grouped by PTSD clusters (i.e., cluster B, intrusive symptoms; cluster C, avoidant symptoms; and cluster D, increased arousal symptoms) by applying Spearman's rank-order correlation. After Bonferroni corrections for multiple correlations, no significant correlations were seen between clinical symptoms and cognitive variables.

Discussion

Children with maltreatment-related PTSD demonstrated significant deficits within the domains of attention and abstract reasoning/executive function when compared with sociodemographically similar healthy children who had not been maltreated. The children with PTSD were more susceptible to distraction and demonstrated greater impulsivity, making more errors on a task of sustained attention. Children with PTSD also demonstrated deficits on two tests designed to measure frontal lobe function (10)—the Wisconsin Card Sorting Test, an instrument requiring hypothesis testing and problem solving, and the Controlled Oral Word Association Test, a measure of semantic organization. These findings are consistent with neuroimaging studies showing CNS changes in the frontal cortex in PTSD (4). In contrast, after corrections to protect from experiment-wise error, PTSD children did not perform differently from comparison children on measures of language, memory and learning, visual-spatial abilities, or psychomotor skills.

Memory problems associated with PTSD are commonly identified in adults (2). We were unable to replicate the findings of Moradi et al. (11) of general memory deficits associated with childhood PTSD. However, the small number of subjects in our study may have obscured significant findings in this domain. Our findings suggest deficits in long-term memory for verbal information.

The study reported here must be considered preliminary because of the lack of a comparison group of children who had been maltreated but did not have PTSD. Therefore, we do not know if our results are related to maltreatment or the presence of an anxiety disorder. Additionally, these findings may be explained by the presence of comorbid psychiatric disorders, particularly mood disorders, in the children with PTSD. Although it is tempting to assert that psychiatric symptoms may account for neuropsychological deficits, further research is necessary to ascertain how psychiatric symptoms interact with neuropsychological deficits.

References

1. Barrett, D. H., Green, M. L., Morris, R., Giles, W. H., Croft, J. B.: Cognitive functioning and posttraumatic stress disorder. *Am J Psychiatry*, 1996; 153: 1492–1494.

2. McNally, R. J.: Experimental approaches to cognitive abnormality in posttraumatic stress disorder. *Clin Psychol Rev*, 1998; 18: 971–982.

3. De Bellis, M. D., Keshavan, M., Clark, D. S., Casey, B. J., Giedd, J., Boring, A. M., Frustad, K., Ryan, N. D. AE Bennett Research Award: developmental traumatology, part II: brain development. *Biol Psychiatry*, 1999; 45: 1271–1284.

4. De Bellis, M. D., Keshavan, M. S., Spencer, S., Hall, J.: N-Acetytaspartate concentration in the anterior cingulate of maltreated children and adolescents with PTSD. *Am J Psychiatry*, 2000;157: 1175–1177.

5. Spreen, O., Strauss, E.: *A Compendium of Neuropsychological Tests*, 2nd ed. New York, Oxford University Press, 1998.

6. Hollingshead, A. B.: *Four-Factor Index of Social Status*. New Haven, Conn, Yale University, Department of Sociology, 1975.

7. Sattler, J. M.: *Assessment of Young Children*, 3rd ed, revised. San Diego. J. M. Sattler, 1992.

8. De Bellis, M. D.: Posttraumatic stress disorder and acute stress disorder, in *Handbook of Prevention and Treatment With Children and Adolescents*. Edited by Ammerman, R. T., Hersen, M. New York, John Wiley & Sons, 1997, pp. 455–494.

9. Kaufman, J., Birmaher, B., Brent, D., Rao, U., Flynn, C., Moreci, P., Williamson, D., Ryan, N.: Schedule for Affective Disorders and Schizophrenia for School-Age Children—Present and Lifetime Version (K-SADS-PL): initial reliability and validity data. *J Am Acad Child Adolesc Psychiatry*, 1997; 36: 980–988.

10. Levin, H. S., Culhane, K. A., Hartman, J., Evankovich, K., Mattson, A. J.: Developmental changes in performance on tests of purported frontal lobe functioning. *Dev Neuropsychol*, 1991; 12:377–395.

16

■ War is one way in which the broader socio-political environment can affect children's daily lives and development. Children in a war zone, and those who become refugees in another land, often have experienced horrors. Research on the psychological impact of these experiences has tended to concentrate on Post-Traumatic Stress Disorder (PTSD). Post-Traumatic Stress Disorder (PTSD) includes persistent re-experiencing of the event, numbing or avoidance of the trauma, and symptoms of increased arousal (American Psychiatric Association, 1994). Berman's article emphasizes the ways in which the socio-political context can serve to disrupt children's family relationships, causing emotional distress. She also suggests ways that children's developmental level and gender socialization may affect their responses to trauma, reminding us that children's experience of war will be filtered through the lenses of their developmental histories.

Overview Questions

1. According to research done at the time of WWII, and contemporary research, what is the single most traumatic war experience for children? Describe how the number and type of war stressors is related to psychological symptomatology. Give an example of how children can become habituated to an ongoing state of war.

2. Give an example of the impact of separation from family after moving to a new country. List Berry's four modes of acculturation—which of these are best and worst for psychological adjustment? When parents and children acculturate at different rates, what are some possible consequences?

3. List and give examples of Garmezy's three protective factors that can shield children from the effects of trauma. What are two contradictory hypotheses about whether older versus younger children are more at risk? How might gender socialization play a role in how children react to traumatic events? From the implications section, what does Berman believe is necessary for children to heal from their traumatic experiences?

Focus Questions

1. List five rights that the 1989 UN Convention on the Rights of the Child accords to children. What is the primary mandate of the UNHCR? What consequences have arisen from the misperception that refugee flows are localized, non-recurrent and isolated?

2. What evidence is there that PTSD persists over time?

3. Why is the original description of PTSD events as "outside the range of usual experience" problematic for children of war? What features of children's experience are overlooked if one focuses on checklists of PTSD symptomatology? Why does Berman criticize the available measures of PTSD as giving a "distorted measure of the degree of distress"? Give two examples of how ideology may serve as a buffer for the effects of war.

Children and War: Current Understandings and Future Directions

Helene Berman

Of course, I'm "young" and politics are conducted by "grown-ups." But I think the "young" would do it better. We certainly would not have chosen war.

—*Zlata Filopovic, 11 years old Sarajevo* (Filopovic, 1994, p. 103)

Childhood and adolescence are developmental stages that are fraught with many challenges, even under the best of circumstances. Vandenberg (1971) described the early years as a time for "becoming at home in the world" (p. 1). The way in which young people learn to become at home in the world varies across social and cultural contexts, and is influenced by ideological and moral assumptions about the nature of childhood. The dominant image which has prevailed throughout the twentieth century, however, is one in which childhood is depicted as a time of innocence and vulnerability. Consistent with this image, children and adolescents are not supposed to experience or witness violence, and are certainly not supposed to partake in it. This image is embodied in the 1989 United Nations Convention on the Rights of the Child, which states that all children have the right to a life that includes more than physical survival. All children have the right to intellectual, spiritual, and moral development in a family and a society conducive to such growth; to protection from physical and mental harm; to an education; to adequate health care; and the time and space to play. The Convention further stipulates that children are entitled to their own identity—not only to have a name and a nationality, but to have privacy, dignity, and a voice in decisions that concern their lives. According to the Convention articles, children have the right to live in a world at peace (Vittachi, 1989).

In reality, many of these fundamental rights are denied to millions of children growing up in war zones throughout the world. Even after hostilities end, or alternatively—the children obtain asylum in another country—long-term physical and emotional traumas haunt them. Refugee youths have often directly or indirectly encountered trauma before and during escape from their homeland. Many have witnessed the torture or murder of relatives. Multiple losses are defining features of the refugees' experiences as they are uprooted from their family, friends, culture, and everything that is familiar to them (Berman, 1996).

The Office of the United Nations High Commission for Refugees (UNHCR) was established at the Geneva Convention in order to assist the large numbers of refugees created in the aftermath of World War II. The primary mandate of the UNHCR is to provide refugees with international protection and, at the request of the host government, to assist them towards durable solutions to their problems. When the UNHCR was first established, there were approximately 1.5 million refugees and displaced persons throughout the world. Today, religious, ethnic, and political strife all combine to leave no continent without refugees. Although numbers vary and depend upon one's definition, it is estimated that there are about 14 million refugees and displaced persons, 75% of whom are women and children (U.S. Committee for Refugees [USCR], 2000). Regardless of the definition used, it is clear that large portions of humanity are on the move.

Traditionally, refugee movements have been regarded as localized, nonrecurring, and isolated flows (Stein, 1981). As a result of this misperception, efforts to respond to the problems confronted by each group have been undertaken on an ad hoc basis, few comprehensive programs have been developed, and little research has been conducted, particularly with refugee children and adolescents. In recent years, however, there has been growing recognition that the stressors imposed by premigration and postmigration events have the potential to jeopardize all aspects of health and many investigators have begun to examine the effects of war on health and well-being. Among the published studies, findings are often inconclusive and contradictory. While several investigators have documented a multitude of physical and emotional health problems, including post-traumatic stress disorder (PTSD), others have observed that many refugee children demonstrate remarkable resilience, strength, and motivation. As Beiser, Dion, Gotowiec, Hyman, and Vu (1995) have noted, such seeming inconsistencies imply that, while premigration and postmigration stressors have the potential to result in adverse health sequelae, a range of mediating variables and protective factors likely interact to mitigate harmful effects.

Within nursing, the heightened interest in the health of refugee groups is evident in the growth of research and publications addressing various aspects of the experiences of refugees and immigrants (Fox, Cowell, & Montgomery, 1994; Frye & Avanzo, 1994; Lipson, Hosseini, Kabir, & Edmonston, 1995; Meleis, Arruda, Lane, & Bernal, 1994; Muecke & Sassi, 1992). Still, research with refugee children and adolescents, both within nursing as well as within other health and social science disciplines, remains sparse. Despite this gap in theoretical scientific knowledge, nurses, psychologists, social workers, educators, and physicians are attempting to meet the needs of this population in many settings. The purpose of this article is to examine current knowledge and understandings related to the effects of war on refugee children and adolescents. Critical comments regarding the phenomenon of PTSD and its use as an organizing framework for understanding the experiences of this population will be presented. Finally, implications for nurses and directions for future research will be posited.

Premigration Stress

The premigration experiences of refugee children vary considerably, but many have either witnessed or directly experienced trauma prior to escape from their native countries. Many have witnessed the torture or murder of relatives. In addition to the trauma associated with premigration exposure to violence, including the loss of loved ones and separation from family, by the time these young people arrive in North America, many have endured years of deplorable living conditions in refugee camps.

Some of the earliest understandings of children's responses to war are based on studies with children and adolescents during and after World War II (Freud & Burlingham, 1943; Henshaw & Howarth, 1941; Stoltz, 1951). Many children were forced from their homes, separated from their families, and resettled in unfamiliar surroundings with caregivers whom they did not know. A consistent finding from these studies was that separation from parents and siblings was perceived as more distressing to the children than the air raids or bombings. Those children who were able to remain with their parents, carry on with their usual daily routines, and had parents who conveyed a sense of hope and optimism, were thought to be protected, or "buffered," from potentially harmful effects. Still, some children who were afforded such protection demonstrated an array of emotional and behavioral difficulties, including anxiety, hostility, and aggression, which persisted for many years. Although these studies are widely cited in the literature, it is not clear whether the children who remained with their families had, in fact, personally confronted death or destruction. Thus, the impact of trauma cannot be fully assessed solely on the basis of this body of work (Athey & Ahearn, 1991).

The results of studies based on children's responses to war in the contemporary world are similar to those of the early studies and highlight the importance of family and community ties (Fox et al., 1994; Laor et al., 1997; Rumbaut, 1991; Thabet & Vostanis, 2000). The children in Berman's (1999) research, who came to Canada from Bosnia, Burundi, Somalia, and Liberia, repeatedly identified separation from their families during the war as the single most frightening aspect of living in a war zone.

Nature and Duration of War Stress

In recent years, several investigators have begun to examine whether it is the totality of exposure to war-related stress that is harmful to children, or whether their responses depend upon the nature, type, and duration of exposure to stress (Athey & Ahearn, 1991; Goldstein, Wampler, & Wise, 1997; Jensen & Shaw, 1993). This field of study represents an important research direction because children who grow up in war zones are typically exposed to multiple stressors including physical harm, intimidation or other forms of psychological trauma, loss, deprivation, malnutrition, bereavement, or abuse. Although stress is common to any wartime situation, the degree and nature in which it is experienced varies greatly in each context.

Chimienti, Nasr, and Kalifeh (1991) noted that children in Lebanon exposed to shelling, death, and forced displacement were 1.7 times more likely to manifest regression, depression, and aggression than those who were not similarly exposed. Macksoud and Aber (1996) examined the relationship between the number and type of war traumas and psychosocial development among Lebanese children, 10 to 16 years of age. Using the War Trauma Questionnaire, these investigators examined 10 categories of war exposure. As predicted, the number and type of traumatic exposures were positively related to PTSD symptoms. Children exposed to multiple traumas, who were bereaved, or had witnessed violent acts showed more PTSD symptoms than those who had not witnessed these acts. In addition, depressive symptoms were more evident among children who had experienced separation from their parents than those who remained with their parents.

Consistent with this line of investigation, several researchers have examined the effects of prolonged exposure to war-related violence in order to evaluate whether children become inured to war, or get used to it over a period of time. For children growing up in parts of the world where war is all they have ever known, including such places as Northern Ireland, Mozambique, South Africa, and Beirut, where they have never lived in peace, this is a significant question.

Greenbaum, Erlich, and Toubiana (1993) described the phenomenon of habituation in their research with Israeli children living for years during the *intifada*, the Palestinian resistance to Israeli military occupation following the Six Day War in 1967. These researchers examined the effects of prolonged exposure to stress as a result of the intifada, and relatively short exposure to stress as a result of the Gulf War. Although the children in this research expressed concern about the war and the intifada, traffic accidents were of greater concern 4 months after the end of the Gulf War. Thus, the intifada, which has been going on for a long period of time, and the war, which did not expose the children to prolonged or particularly intense trauma, receded in importance in the everyday lives of the children. The authors suggested that a combination of successful coping and habituation enabled Israeli children in this region to function with low levels of anxiety.

Postmigration Stress

The experience of migration is typically accompanied by many stressors. For refugees, there is often little time to prepare for escape thus, it may be difficult to attend to practical issues that might facilitate the resettlement process. For children and adolescents, uprooting often necessitates loss of homes, friends, possessions, and in some cases, parents or siblings. Coehlo and Ahmed (1980) have noted that many experience significant threats to their sense of well-being, particularly if they do not feel that the adults in their lives are able to protect them. Poverty and separation from family are common, and attitudes of racism toward newcomers have been documented (Beiser et al., 1988; Noh, Beiser, Kaspar, Hou, & Rummens, 1999). Although many adult refugees are well-educated and had been employed in professional occupations in their native countries, their credentials are typically not recognized in North America. Thus, many refugees are forced into marginalized positions where they experience financial strain and downward mobility (Anderson, Waxler-Morrison, Richardson, Herbert, & Murphy, 1990).

Separation from Family

Separation from family members after migrating to a new country has consistently been identified as a threat to the health and well-being of refugee youth (McCloskey & Southwick, 1996; Porte & Torney-Purta, 1987; Rumbaut, 1991; Servan-Schreiber, Le Lin, & Birmaher, 1998). According to Kinzie, Sack, Angell, Manson, and Rath (1986) and Kinzie, Sack, Angell, Clarke, and Rath (1989), neither the amount or type of trauma witnessed, nor the child's age or gender were clearly predictive of PTSD in their research with Cambodian refugees. Psychiatric effects, however, were strongly related to the presence of a nuclear family member. Although these refugees had lost an average of three family members, those who had been able to reestablish family contact with at least one family member reported fewer adjustment problems than those without family contact.

Even when children are not separated from their families, there is some evidence that other stressors within the family adversely affect outcomes. Hjern, Angel, and Jeppson (1998) conducted research on the mental health of Chilean and Middle Eastern refugee children in exile and observed that important family life-events, including the birth of a sibling, divorce among parents, or parental psychiatric disorders, play a significant role in the mental health of the child refugee.

Acculturation Stress

Interest in the effects of acculturation on the health of refugee populations is reflected in a variety of studies (Gil, Vega, & Dimas, 1994; Rumbaut & Ima, 1988; Salgado de Snyder, Cervantes, & Padilla, 1990). According to Williams and Berry (1991), acculturation is defined as the process of mutual cultural exchange resulting from contact between cultures, during which each culture influences the other. Typically, the dominant culture contributes more to the flow of cultural elements to the smaller and weaker groups (Rick & Forward, 1992). Berry (1991) identified four distinct patterns, or modes, of acculturation: (1) assimilation, closely linked to the melting pot idea; (2) integration, whereby the group's cultural identity is maintained in conjunction with efforts to become an integral part of the larger society; (3) separation, depicted by little contact with the dominant culture; and (4) marginalization, characterized by alienation from both the dominant and traditional cultural groups.

The relationship between acculturation style and psychological adjustment has been the focus of several studies (Phinney, Lochner, & Murphy, 1990; Vega, 1993; Waheit, Zimmerman & Apospori, 1993). A positive relationship between an integration acculturation style and self-esteem was reported by Phinney, Chavira, and Williamson (1992). According to Berry and Kim (1988), it is generally agreed that marginalization is the least satisfactory outcome.

One of the distinct postmigration challenges faced by refugee youth and their families is differential rates of acculturation (Williams & Westermeyer, 1983). Because refugee children and adolescents are exposed to the dominant culture's values when they attend school, they typically adopt language and behaviors from the host country more quickly than their parents. Resulting intergenerational conflicts have been described (Rick & Forward, 1992). As children and adolescents become skilled in the language and customs of the new country, their parents may need to depend on their children for help with language and social skills. The resulting role reversal is seen as a threat to the parents' authority.

PTSD

During the past 10 years, a small but growing number of investigators have documented the occurrence of PTSD in refugee youth from El Salvador and Nicaragua (Arroyo & Eth, 1985); Cambodia (Kinzie et al., 1989; Sack et al., 1993); Afghanistan (Mghir, Freed, Raskin, & Katon, 1995); the Gaza Strip (Thabet & Vostanis, 2000); Iran (Almqvist & Brandell-Forsberg, 1995); South Africa (Magwaza, Killian, Petersen, & Pillay, 1995); Bosnia (Weine et al., 1995); Croatia (Ajdukovic & Ajdukovic, 1993); and Tibet (Servan-Schreiber et al., 1998). In one survey conducted with children in Bosnia, Goldstein et al. (1997) reported that almost 94% of their sample met the criteria for PTSD.

The studies by Kinzie et al. (1986, 1989) represent some of the few efforts to evaluate the persistence of PTSD over many years. These researchers examined the effects of massive trauma on 40 Cambodian refugees who had been imprisoned for up to 2 years in concentration camps during the Pol Pot regime. All of the refugees endured separation from family, forced labor, and starvation, and many had witnessed killings and other forms of torture. Four years after leaving Cambodia, 50% developed PTSD. Mild, but prolonged, depressive symptoms were evident in 38%. Results of a 3-year follow-up study with 30 of the original subjects revealed that, although depression had diminished, 48% still fit the criteria for PTSD, adding to the idea that traumatic symptoms endure over time.

Saigh (1991) administered the Children's PTSD Inventory to 840 Lebanese children, ages 9 to 12 years, in Beirut. Although the nature of traumatic exposure varied among the children, with some directly confronting violence and others confronting violence in more indirect ways, no comparable differences were observed in the PTSD scores. In all, 230 (27%) respondents met the DSM-III PTSD criteria. The results of this research lend support to the view that children can be traumatized in a variety of ways.

Protective Factors and Resilience

As these studies demonstrate, the effects of childhood exposure to war are variable. While some children who grow up in dangerous environments experience a multitude of long-term problems, including PTSD, others show no outward clinical problems and appear to be more resilient in the face of adversity. Garmezy (1983) has called attention to the importance of protective factors thought to shield children from the harmful effects of traumatic events. Based on an extensive review of the literature on children's responses to stressful situations, Garmezy (1983) described a triad of protective factors that emerged from the existing research. These factors are: (1) dispositional attributes of the child, including the child's ability to respond to new situations and positive self-esteem; (2) support within the family, such as a positive relationship with at least one parent and; (3) environmental supports, including peers, teacher, nurse, and relatives.

Age and Gender

The importance of age and gender has received some attention, but like other aspects of this research, results have been inconsistent and there is currently no widespread agreement that certain groups are at greater risk than others on the basis of either age or gender. Some researchers have suggested that younger children are better able to handle their experiences; others have reached opposite conclusions (Berman, 1996; Elbedour, Bensel, & Bastien, 1993). Eth and Pynoos (1985) have suggested that, although the manifestation of post-traumatic symptoms may differ according to age, the general pattern of responses is similar. These authors have described a variety of responses that correspond to children's cognitive and developmental abilities at different stages and have concluded that children's efforts to cope with traumatic stress are a function of maturity. In contrast, Terr (1990), who studied 26 children who had been kidnapped and buried alive in a bus in Chowchilla, California, observed that, while children's responses to trauma differ on many dimensions from those of adults, no notable differences were noted among children between the ages of 5 and 14 years old.

Bodman (1941) described the experience of 44 children who were being treated at a hospital when a bomb exploded. For the older children, the event was retold much like one recalls an adventure. Opposite results were described by Berman (1999) who observed that the younger children in her qualitative study were more apt to describe their experiences with a sense of bravado and generally seemed less cognizant of the dangers they faced. For example, one 10-year-old boy who had fled his home in Somalia 3 years earlier, enthusiastically told about the time he had outrun a soldier who was in pursuit. Although this child had just witnessed the soldier shooting someone, this fact seemed to be a peripheral detail. His story was about himself and the soldier, not about someone being shot. Other young participants described, with similar panache, events which occurred while they and their families were on the run during escape from their homelands. In contrast, the older participants had greater difficulty speaking about the wars in their native countries. As one female participant noted, because she was older, it was more difficult for her to forget what had occurred, an idea that was repeated by several other participants.

The notion that older children and adolescents may be at greater risk than younger ones has some intuitive appeal. Adolescents are more capable of hypothetical and abstract thought. They are typically able to consider the possibilities, and thus, more fully grasp the potentially harmful consequences of living in a war zone. The importance of age, however, could be considered from a different perspective. As Jensen and Shaw (1993) noted, older children and adolescents have developed a more sophisticated array of coping abilities than younger children. In fact, it could be speculated that younger children may be at greatest risk, not only because they have not yet mastered the cognitive skills of their older counterparts, but also because they commonly attribute egocentric explanations to events and are typically less able to talk about distressful experiences. An alternative, and more likely interpretation, is that age can provide some clues as to how children respond to exposure to violence, but by itself, provides only a partial picture.

Like the research related to age as a determinant of children's responses to exposure to war, the research related to gender has also yielded inconsistent results. Several investigators have suggested that boys exposed to violence experience higher stress levels than girls and that males are more vulnerable to traumatic stress than females (Elbedour et al., 1993). On the other hand, two separate studies with children exposed to the Gulf War (Greenbaum et al., 1993; Klingman, 1992) found that females showed a higher frequency of stress reactions than males. Similarly, Berman (1996) reported that the female children of war in her study had significantly higher PTSD scores than their male counterparts.

Several issues regarding differences among male and female children merit consideration. The first issue pertains to the differential socialization, child-rearing processes, and expectations on the basis of gender. Typically, girls are socialized to openly express their fears, anxiety, and other emotions, whereas boys are generally discouraged from such open display of emotions and are more likely to conceal, deny, or repress difficult feelings and emotions (Gilligan, 1982). Thus, the level of distress among both groups might be similar, but differences in PTSD scores may reflect differences in cultural expectations governing the display of emotion, with girls therefore showing higher scores than boys. It is also possible that males and females use different protective strategies when confronted with potentially traumatic events. While males are more inclined to repress their feelings, and are more likely to take action, females are more apt to acknowledge their feelings and concerns more openly, resulting in higher scores.

Limitations of Prevailing Approaches

As these studies collectively indicate, much of the current knowledge about children's responses to wartime trauma is based on research in which PTSD is the primary outcome measure. Using a variety of models derived from the stress, coping, and resilience literature, researchers have examined the role of the various protective factors suggested by Garmezy (1983) thought to protect children from harm. Two important limitations are evident in these approaches. The first pertains to concerns about the conceptualization of PTSD. The second relates to limitations in the dominant stress and coping frameworks and the failure to incorporate broader social, structural, and political contexts.

Constraints Implicit in PTSD

Each of the studies presented throughout this article contributes some to a general understanding of the stressful nature of early exposure to violence. The conceptualization of PTSD, the way in which it has been defined, measured, and used as an organizing construct for understanding children's responses to political violence, however, raises several significant questions. As first articulated by the American Psychiatric Association (1987), traumatic events were defined as those events that were "outside the range of usual human experience." This definition has been challenged by several writers (Brown, 1991; Herman, 1992). The essence of the criticisms is that, because violence is such a common part of the everyday lives of many women and children, it cannot be construed as being outside the range of normal. Considering the large number of people affected by war over the last century, military trauma must also be recognized as a common part of human experience.

For many young people who grow up amid violence, trauma is not a single or isolated event. Garbarino, Kostelny, and Dubrow (1991) wrote about the experience of children in war zones around the world and in the "war zones of Chicago." As these authors observed, when children are repeatedly forced to confront violence, the trauma becomes a central condition of their lives; there is no "post" trauma period. Even if they are fortunate enough to escape from immediate harm, the task goes beyond getting over a horrible experience. Rather, the challenge is to find ways to make sense of a world in which terrifying experiences are a part of everyday reality. Herman (1992) has persuasively argued for the need to recognize "complex PTSD" to reflect this more chronic form of trauma. Reflecting this concern, the revised DSM-IV criteria no longer includes the original "outside the range of usual experience" proviso.

While this change represents a significant improvement, other limitations remain. By attending to a group of symptoms as the primary measure of children's responses, it is easy to pathologize and individualize the problem of violence (Richman, 1993). Similarly, the current emphasis on identification of a "disorder" perpetuates the tendency among researchers to highlight weaknesses and deficits, and to simultaneously overlook the strengths and resources that enable children to grow and thrive in the face of seemingly overwhelming challenges.

An additional issue concerns the limited scope of PTSD as it is currently defined. The symptoms that comprise PTSD are only one dimension of the reactions to traumatic experiences. The effects of violence on the lives of children are complex and may not be captured through the various checklists of symptoms on the PTSD instruments. For example, children who have been exposed to war often describe feelings of loss and betrayal; separation from family, friends, and countries; and racism in their new countries (Berman, 1999). None of these issues are captured through the available instruments. While the information derived from the PTSD instruments may contribute to an understanding of children's responses to traumatic exposure, this information is only one aspect of the multitude of complex responses.

According to Richman (1993), the available instruments may provide a somewhat distorted measure of the degree of distress because they do not provide a qualitative understanding of how children are affected by their experiences. For example, we may learn that children who have grown up amid war experience flashbacks, intrusive thoughts, nightmares, or try to avoid painful memories of their experiences, but the instruments do not help us to understand the intensity of these responses, or the degree to which they interfere with the children's sense of well-being and everyday life. As Sack et al. (1993) and Mollica, Poole, Son, Murray, and Tor (1997) have shown in their studies with Cambodian refugees, many of those who met the criteria for PTSD continued to function well, both socially and academically.

Conceptually, there are other concerns about ethnocentric biases underlying the conceptualization of PTSD. As Bracken, Giller, and Summerfield, (1995) have noted, the diagnostic category of PTSD is based on a western notion that assumes the centrality of the individual, a notion that is not universally agreed upon. Further, these authors suggest that there is a mistaken assumption of universality of PTSD, and that this assumption has resulted in a tendency to obscure differences. Although many of the same signs and symptoms may be evident among individuals exposed to trauma, the meaning of these varies across cultural contexts. Given these issues, it would seem incumbent upon those interested in understanding the responses of children exposed to potentially traumatizing circumstances to acknowledge the centrality of issues of context with respect to social, political, and cultural realities.

Meaning of the Event: The Missing Link

Based on her work with Palestinian children living in refugee camps under Israeli occupation, Punamaki (1989) reported that seemingly protective factors such as age, gender, and family supports, made little difference in children's responses; that exposure to political violence had a direct negative effect on the mental health of mothers and children regardless of age, gender, or "happy family life"; and that mothers' efforts to act as a buffer between the traumatic environment and her children's well-being contributed to a secondary stress for the mothers. Punamaki (1989) concluded that children's responses cannot be understood by focusing only on individual mediating factors, and suggested that the way in which social, political, and ecological contexts act as mediators needs to be considered.

In her research with children living in the West Bank and Gaza Strip, Punamaki (1996) concluded that ideological support for the conflict may buffer some of the stresses of war. Despite the constant threat of danger, the children derived strength from their ideological and political commitment to their country's struggle. Similar patterns were observed among those imprisoned and tortured in German concentration camps during World War II. Individuals who held strong political and ideological beliefs were more able to endure the horrors that surrounded them. Though these contexts are different in many respects, in both situations, it was clear who the enemy was and why the war was necessary.

Implications and Future Research Directions

Elie Wiesel (1984) wrote that once you have been in a situation of constant danger, you never feel fully safe again. Although this observation was made in reference to the horror of the Holocaust, it fits the experience of many children who have grown up in environments where violence is woven into the fabric of daily life. Implicit in his remark is the idea that we are forever changed by our experiences.

Children who live in any of the vast number of war zones throughout the world are deeply affected by their experiences in a multitude of ways. For some of the children, violence poses a direct threat to their health and well-being. For others, the effects of growing up in violent environments are more subtle and insidious. Though it would not appear that all children who grow up amid violence are irreparably harmed by their exposure to dangerous circumstances, they are all affected by it.

In nursing, the body of research in the area of violence has grown tremendously in the last 10 years. Few nurse researchers, however, have attended to the problems and challenges faced by refugee youth. Future research efforts are needed that will contribute to the development of sound theoretical and empirical knowledge that can be used to guide nursing care with children and their families who have fled homes and countries as the result of war. In order to elicit comprehensive understandings regarding the effects of wartime exposure, culturally meaningful and relevant research approaches that incorporate both stories and numbers are appropriate. While numbers may be more persuasive in the legislative and political arena, stories put a face on the numbers and allow participants to gain new insights into the circumstances of their lives, to name their reality, and to devise strategies to bring about action and change. Together, stories and numbers have the potential to contribute to new understandings in a way that neither approach alone can achieve (Berman, Ford-Gilboe, & Campbell, 1998).

Instead of the dominant biomedical view of children as recipients of trauma, a more meaningful approach would be one in which an understanding of how children actively construct their experiences of violence, its meaning to them, and the process by which they strive to make sense of traumatic events, is emphasized. Within such a framework, the social conceptualization of violence is accorded a central role in understanding its effects.

Because public health nurses encounter individuals at critical and varied points in their development, we are ideally and strategically positioned to intervene with children who have been witnesses to, or have directly experienced, war trauma. Before intervening, however, we must collectively raise our own consciousness and develop intervention approaches that enable and empower children to critically reflect on the experiences in their lives, and about the nature and meaning of the violence they have suffered, endured, and survived.

The horrors of war are not new. Emmy Werner (1998) recently wrote about the experiences of children who had grown up during the American Civil War. Through the voices of these children, the reluctant witnesses, we learn about courage and determination, about hope and despair, and about struggle and survival. The stories they tell are remarkably similar to those told by children who have survived any of the atrocities of the modern world, including the Holocaust, the killing fields of Cambodia, the disappearances of untold numbers in Guatemala, the mass genocide of hundreds of thousands in Rwanda and Burundi, or most recently, the genocide commonly referred to as ethnic cleansing in Bosnia or Kosovo. Although the details differ, and there are as yet many gaps in research and knowledge, several aspects of the experience are shared and can provide some direction for nursing practice.

A common response to trauma is to deny and repress painful memories, rather than confront than. While such a response may enable young people to cope with disturbing events, at least in the short term, it does not allow them to heal. Children need opportunities to talk openly and safely about what occurred to them, to their families and loved ones, and to their homes and countries. As Werner (1998) wrote with respect to children in the Civil War, recounting past events was often more than the retelling of exciting tales, but may have been a strategy used by the children to mend themselves and "to put together the pieces of their shattered lives."

The ultimate goal of primary prevention is the creation of a world where peace becomes a reality. As nurses who interact with children and families in the community, we must work in conjunction with policymakers, educators, social service workers, and community leaders to articulate clear stands against war and all other forms of violence.

References

Ajdukovic, M., & Ajdukovic, D. (1993). Psychological well-being of refugee children. *Child Abuse and Neglect 17*, 843–854.

Almqvist, K., & Brandell-Forsberg, M. (1995). Iranian refugee children in Sweden: Effects of organized violence and forced migration on preschool children. *American Journal of Orthopsychiatry, 65*(2), 225–237.

American Psychiatric Association (1987). *Diagnostic and statistical manual of mental disorders* (rev. ed.). Washington, DC: Author.

Anderson, J., Waxler-Morrison, N., Richardson, E., Herbert, C., & Murphy, M. (1990). Delivering culturally sensitive health care. In N. Waxler-Morrison, J. Anderson, & E. Richardson (Eds.), *Cross-cultural caring. A handbook for health professionals in Western Canada* (pp. 245–267). Vancouver: University of British Columbia Press.

Arroyo, W., & Eth, S. (1985). Children traumatized by Central American warfare. In S. Eth & R. S. Pynoos (Eds.), *Post-traumatic stress disorder in children* (pp. 103–120). Washington, DC: American Psychiatric Press.

Athey, J. L., & Ahearn, F. (1991). The mental health of refugee children: An overview. In F. Ahearn & J. Athey (Eds.), *Refugee children: Theory, research, and services* (pp. 3–19). Baltimore, MD: Johns Hopkins University Press.

Beiser, M., Barwick, C., Berry, J., da Costa, G., Fantino, A., Ganesan, S., Lee, C., Milne, W., Naidoo, J., Prince, R., Tousignant, M., & Vela, E. (1988). *After the door has been opened: Mental health issues affecting immigrants and refugees.* Ottawa, ON: Ministries of Multiculturalism and Citizenship, and Health and Welfare.

Beiser, M., Dion, R., Gotowiec, M., Hyman, I., & Vu, N. (1995). Immigrant and refugee children in Canada. *Canadian Journal of Psychiatry, 40*(2), 67–72.

Berman, H. (1996). Growing up amid violence: A critical narrative analysis of children of war and children of battered women (Doctoral dissertation, Wayne State University, 1996). *Dissertation Abstracts International, 57* (12B), 9715809.

Berman, H. (1999). Stories of growing up amid violence by children of war and children of battered women living in Canada. *Image: Journal of Nursing Scholarship, 31*, 57–63.

Berman, H., Ford-Gilboe, M., & Campbell, J. (1998). Combining stories and numbers: A methodological approach for a critical nursing science. *Advances in Nursing Science, 21*(1), 1–15.

Berry, J. (1991). Refugee adaptation in settlement countries: An overview with an emphasis on primary prevention. In F. Ahearn & J. Athey (Eds.), *Refugee children: Theory, research, and services* (pp. 20–38). Baltimore, MD: Johns Hopkins University Press.

Berry, J., & Kim, U. (1988). Acculturation and mental health. In P. R. Dasen, J. W. Berry, & N. Sartorius (Eds.), *Health and cross-cultural psychology.* Newbury Park, CA: Sage.

Bodman, F. (1941). War conditions and the mental health of the child. *British Medical Journal, 2,* 486–488.

Bracken, P. J., Giller, J. E., & Summerfield, D. (1995). Psychological responses to war and atrocity: The limitations of current concepts. *Social Science Medicine, 40,* 1073–1082.

Brown, L. S. (1991). Not outside the range: One feminist perspective on psychic trauma. *American Imago, 46,* 119–133.

Chimienti, G., Nasr, J., & Khalifeh, I. (1991). Children's reactions to war-related stress: Affective symptoms and behavior problems. *Social Psychological Psychiatry Epidemiology, 24,* 282–287.

Coehlo, G. V., & Ahmed, P. I. (1980). *Uprooting and development: Dilemmas of coping with modernization.* New York: Plenum.

Elbedour, S., Bensel, R. T., & Bastien, D. (1993). Ecological integrated model of children of war. Individual and social psychology. *Child Abuse and Neglect, 17,* 805–819.

Eth, S. & Pynoos, R. (1985). Developmental perspective on psychic trauma in childhood. In C. Figley (Ed.), *Trauma and its wake: The study and treatment of post-traumatic stress disorder* (pp. 36–52). New York: Brunner/Mazel.

Filipovic, Z., Pribichevich-Zoric, C., & Di Giovanni, J. (1994). *Zlata's diary: A child's life in Sarajevo.* New York: Penguin Books.

Fox, P., Muennich Cowell, J., & Montgomery, A. (1994). The effects of violence on health and adjustment of Southeast Asian refugee children: An integrative review. *Public Health Nursing, 11,* 195–201.

Freud, A., & Burlingham, D. (1943). *War and children.* New York: Medical War Books, Ernst Willard.

Frye, B. A., & Avanzo, C. D. (1994). Cultural themes in family stress and violence among Cambodian refugee women in the inner city. *Advances in Nursing Science, 16*(3), 64–77.

Garbarino, J., Kostelny, K., & Dubrow, N. (1991). *No place to be a child: Growing up in a war zone.* Lexington, MA: D. C. Heath (p. 130).

Garmezy, N. (1983). Stressors of childhood. In N. Garmezy & M. Rutter (Eds.), *Stress, coping and development in children* (pp. 43–84). New York: McGraw-Hill.

Gil, A. G., Vega, W., & Dimas, J. (1994). Acculturative stress and personal adjustment among Hispanic adolescent boys.

Gilligan, C. (1982). *In a different voice.* Cambridge, MA: Harvard University Press.

Journal of Community Psychology, 22, 43–54.

Goldstein, R., Wampler, N., & Wise, P. (1997). War experiences and distress symptoms of Bosnian children. *Pediatrics, 100,* 873–878.

Greenbaum, C. W., Erlich, C., & Toubiana, Y. H. (1993). Settler children and the Gulf War. In L. A. Leavitt & N. A. Fox (Eds.), *The psychological effects of war and violence on children* (pp. 109–130). Hillsdale, NJ: Lawrence Erlbaum Associates.

Henshaw, E. M., & Howarth, H. E. (1941). Observed effects of wartime conditions on children. *Mental Health, 2,* 93–101.

Herman, J. L. (1992). *Trauma and recovery.* New York: Basic Books.

Hjern, A., Angel, B., & Jeppson, O. (1998). Political violence, family stress and mental health of refugee children in exile. *Scandinavian Journal of Social Medicine, 26*(1), 18–25.

Jensen, P., & Shaw, J. (1993). Children as victims of war: Current knowledge and future research needs. *Journal of the American Academy of Child and Adolescent Psychiatry, 32,* 697–708.

Kinzie, J. D., Sack, W., Angell, R., Clarke, G., & Rath, B. (1989). A three-year follow-up of Cambodian young people traumatized as children. *Journal of the American Academy of Child Psychiatry, 28,* 501–504.

Kinzie, J. D., Sack, W. H., Angell, R., Manson, S. M., & Rath, B. (1986). The psychiatric effects of massive trauma on Cambodian children: I. The children. *Journal of the American Academy of Child Psychiatry, 25,* 370–376.

Klingman, A. (1992). Stress reactions of Israeli youth during the Gulf War. A quantitative study. *Professional Psychology: Research and Practice, 23,* 521–527.

Laor, N., Wolmer, L., Mayes, L., Gershon, A., Weizman, R., & Cohen, D. (1997). Israeli preschool children under scuds: A 30-month follow-up. *Journal of the American Academy of Child and Adolescent Psychiatry, 36*, 349–356.

Lipson, J., Hosseini, T., Kabir, S., Omidian, P., & Edmonston, F. (1995). Health issues among Afghan women in California. *Health Care for Women International, 16*, 279–286.

Macksoud, M., & Aber, J. (1996). The war experiences and psychosocial development of children in Lebanon. *Child Development, 67*, 70–88.

Magwaza, A., Killian, B., Petersen, L., & Pillay, Y. (1995). The effects of chronic violence on preschool children living in South African townships. *Child Abuse and Neglect, 17*, 795–503.

McCloskey, L., & Southwick, K. (1996). Psychosocial problems in refugee children exposed to war. *Pediatrics, 97*, 394–397.

Meleis, A., Arruda, E., Lane, S., & Bernal, P. (1994). Veiled, voluminous, and devalued: Narrative stones about low-income women from Brazil, Egypt, and Colombia. *Advances in Nursing Science, 17*(2), 1–15.

Mghir, R., Freed, W., Raskin, A., & Katon, W. (1995). Depression and posttraumatic stress disorder among a community sample of adolescent and young adult Afghan refugees. *Journal of Nervous and Mental Disease, 183*(1), 24–30.

Mollica, R., Poole, C., Son, L., Murray, C., & Tor, S. (1997). Effects of war trauma on Cambodian refugee adolescents' functional health and mental health status. *Journal of the American Academy of Child Psychiatry, 36*, 1098–1106.

Muecke, M., & Sassi, L. (1992). Anxiety among Cambodian refugee adolescents in transit and resettlement. *Western Journal of Nursing Research, 14*, 267–285.

Noh, S., Beiser, M., Kaspar, V, Hou, F., & Rummens, J. (1999). Perceived racial discrimination, depression, and coping: a study of Southeast Asian refugees in Canada. *Journal of Health and Social Behavior, 40*, 193–207.

Phinney, J., Chavira, V., & Williamson, L. (1992). Acculturation attitudes and self-esteem among high school and college students. *Youth and Society, 23*, 299–312.

Phinney, B., Lochner, B., & Murphy, R. (1990). Ethnic identity and psychological adjustment. In A. Stiffman & L. Davis (Eds.), *Ethnic issues in adolescent mental health* (pp. 53–72). Newbury Park, CA: Sage.

Porte, Z., & Torney-Purta, J. (1987). Depression and academic achievement among Indochinese refugee unaccompanied minors in ethnic and nonethnic placements. *American Journal of Orthopsychiatry, 57*, 536–547.

Punamaki, R. (1989). Factors affecting the mental health of Palestinian children exposed to political violence. *International Journal of Mental Health, 18*, 63–79.

Punamaki, R. (1996). Can ideological commitment protect children's psychosocial well-being in situations of political violence? *Child Development, 67*, 55–69.

Richman, N. (1993). Annotation: Children in situations of political violence. *Journal of Child Psychology and Psychiatry, 34*, 1286–1302.

Rick, K., & Forward, J. (1992). Acculturation and perceived intergenerational differences among Hmong youth. *Journal of Cross-Cultural Psychology, 23*, 85–94.

Rumbaut, R. G. (1991). The agony of exile: A study of the migration and adaptation of Indochinese refugee adults and children. In F. Ahearn & J. Athey (Eds.), *Refugee children: Theory, research, and services* (pp. 53–92). Baltimore, MD: Johns Hopkins University Press.

Rumbaut, R. G., & Ima, K. (1988). *The adaptation of Southeast Asian refugee youth: A comparative study*. Washington, DC: U.S. Office of Refugee Resettlement.

Sack, W., Clarke, G., Him, C., Dickason, D., Goff B., Lanham, K., & Kinzie, D. (1993). A 6-year follow-up study of Cambodian refugee adolescents traumatized as children. *Journal of the American Academy of Child and Adolescent Psychiatry, 32*, 431–437.

Saigh, P. A. (1991). The development of posttraumatic stress disorder following four different types of traumatization. *Behavioral Research Therapy, 29*, 213–216.

Salgado de Snyder, N., Cervantes, R. C., & Padilla, A. (1990). Gender and ethnic differences in psychological stress and generalized distress among Hispanics. *Sex Roles, 22*, 441–453.

Servan-Schreiber, D., Le Lin, B., & Birmaher, B. (1998). Prevalence of posttraumatic stress disorder and major depressive disorder in Tibetan refugee children. *Journal of the American Academy of Child and Adolescent Psychiatry, 37*, 874–879.

Stein, B. N. (1981). The refugee experience: Defining the parameters of a field of study. *International Migration Review, 15*, 320–330.

Stoltz, L. (1951). The effect of mobilization and war on children. *Social Casework, 32,* 143–149.

Terr, L. (1990). *Too scared to cry.* New York: Harper Collins.

Thabet, A., & Vostanis, P. (2000). Post-traumatic stress disorder reactions in children of war: A longitudinal study. *Child Abuse and Neglect, 24,* 291–298.

U.S. Committee for Refugees (USCR). (2000). World refugee survey, 2000. Washington, DC: USCR.

Vandenberg, D. (1971). *Being and education.* Englewood Cliffs, NJ: Prentice Hall.

Vega, W., Gil, A., Warheit, G., Zimmerman, R., & Apospori, E. (1993). Acculturation and delinquent behavior among Cuban American adolescents: Toward an empirical model. *American Journal of Community Psychiatry, 21,* 113–125.

Vittachi, A. (1989). *Stolen childhood: In search of the rights of the child.* Cambridge, UK: Polity Press.

Weine, S., Becker, D., Becker, D. F., McGlashan, T. H., Vojvoda, D., Hartman, S., & Robbins, J. P. (1995). Adolescent survivors of "ethnic cleansing": Observations on the first year in America. *Journal of the Academy of Child Adolescent Psychology, 34*(9), 1153–1159.

Werner, E. (1998). *Reluctant witnesses: Children's voices from the civil war.* Boulder, CO: Westview Press.

Wiesel, E. (1984). The refugee. *Cross Currents, 34,* 385–390.

Williams, C., & Berry, J. (1991). Primary prevention of acculturative stress among refugees. *American Psychologist, 46,* 632–641.

Williams, C., & Westermeyer, J. (1983). Psychiatric problems among adolescent Southeast Asian refugees. *Journal of Nervous and Mental Disorders, 171,* 79–85.

17

Researchers and clinicians often think in terms of the "family life cycle": children grow up in the care of a married couple, gradually separate and find their own spouses, give birth to their own children, and eventually launch them to start families of their own (Duvall, 1977). This model generally overlooks the experiences of gays and lesbians, for whom legal marriage is generally unavailable, and for whom bringing children into the family may involve the practical and emotional complexities of artificial insemination or adoption. In meeting the challenges of raising their children, they cannot fall back on the gender-based divisions of labor that were probably modeled by their own heterosexual parents. They are likely to face prejudice from the surrounding society as an additional stressor. Despite these additional complications, or perhaps because of them, such families may have particular strengths: the children are generally very much wanted and welcomed, and parents are often very consciously reflective about their role and how to do it well. In this article, the authors examine the research on whether children who are raised by lesbian mothers are similar to or different from those who are raised by heterosexual parents. Such a comparison can help us learn whether the ways that families support children's development depend on having parents of different genders.

Overview Questions

1. According to those who believed that children of lesbian mothers were at risk for psychological problems, what was the chain of circumstances that was believed to bring about these problems?

2. Do children in lesbian families evidence gender identity confusion or inappropriate gender role behavior? What did the authors suggest might account for these findings? Are children of lesbian mothers more likely to identify as homosexual than children from heterosexual families?

3. Do these authors conclude that lesbian versus heterosexual families are more alike or more different in terms of the impact on children's development? What do they believe is important about family life for children's adjustment?

Focus Questions

1. The earliest studies of lesbian families used divorced mothers—why? What control groups have been used in later studies? In general, how do these groups compare on measures of social competency, adjustment, and psychological problems? What, in the conclusion, do they point out as an ongoing criticism of the methods of these studies?

2. Which two theories of gender development place most emphasis on the role of parents? Which two place the least, and what do they think instead is the most important in gender socialization?

Children of Lesbian Mothers: From the 1970s to the New Millennium

Julie Mooney-Somers and Susan Golombok

Introduction

In both the popular and academic media, lesbian and gay parenting is the issue of the moment. Recent examples include the case of two gay men fathering twins with a surrogate mother in the US; the results of a study of gay fathers by Gill Dunne at the London School of Economics (Guardian, 12 January, 2000); and comments from Dame Elizabeth Butler-Sloss, President of the Family Court, on the appropriateness of lesbian women and gay men as adoptive or foster parents (Guardian, 16 October, 1999). These examples show that current debates focus on gay fathers, assisted reproduction and fostering/adoption. Does this mean that the concerns first raised in child custody disputes in the 1970s—that children raised in lesbian mother families would be at risk for psychological problems and atypical gender development—have been laid to rest?

Psychological Problems

Concerns about the psychological well-being of children of lesbian mothers were based on the widely accepted view that some childhood experiences carry a risk of psychiatric disorder. This is predominately an argument about social acceptance; because lesbianism is not socially acceptable, the children of lesbian mothers will experience social disapproval. Thus, they will be likely to experience teasing and bullying by peers, which in turn may cause them to become socially withdrawn. Ultimately, it has been argued, the child will be unable to form and maintain friendships, an ability that has been shown to be important for self-esteem and psychological well-being in later life.

The principal British study of lesbian mother families (Golombok, Spencer & Rutter, 1983), initiated in the late 1970s, addressed this issue by investigating a volunteer sample of lesbian mothers and a matched comparison group of single heterosexual mothers, all with school age children. The two types of family were alike in that the children were raised by women without the presence of a father, but differed in the sexual orientation of the mother. This allowed the consequences of the mothers' sexual orientation on their children's development to be examined without the potentially confounding effect of the presence of a father in the family home. As in the custody cases, all of the children in the study had been born into a heterosexual household, and later experienced parental separation. It was found that the children of lesbian mothers were no more likely to be teased or bullied, or to experience psychological difficulties, than those of single heterosexual mothers. In addition, no differences were found between children from the two family types with respect to the quality of their friendships.

In the US, at around the same time, several studies of children of divorced lesbian mothers were also carried out. The earliest was Green's (1978) investigation of 37 children aged 3–20 years old. Following this, controlled studies were published by Green, Mandel, Hotvedt, Gray & Smith (1986) who looked at 58 children aged 3–11 years, and Kirkpatrick, Smith & Roy (1981) who examined 20 children aged 5–12 years. The findings of the US and UK studies were strikingly similar, leading to the conclusion that growing up in a lesbian family did not have an adverse effect on children's social or emotional development.

Nevertheless, a shortcoming of this body of research was that the long-term effects of being raised in a lesbian mother family were not examined, and it was argued by some that children of lesbian mothers would experience psychological problems when they grew up. In order to address these potential 'sleeper effects', the children in the UK study were followed up 14 years later, at an average age of 23½ years. It was found that these young adults continued to have good mental health, and were no more likely to have sought professional help for anxiety, depression or stress-related problems than their counterparts from heterosexual homes (Tasker & Golombok, 1997).

Whereas the early studies examined lesbian mothers who had their children while married, more recent studies have looked at the outcomes for children raised in a lesbian family right from the start, i.e. children born to women who had come out as lesbian before becoming mothers. Many of these children had been conceived by donor insemination. The first study of children born to lesbian mothers was conducted by Steckel (1985, 1987) in the US, who found that children of lesbian and heterosexual mothers were more similar than different. Subsequent studies, also carried out in the US, produced comparable findings: Patterson (1994) showed that the 37 4–9 year old children in her study all performed within the normal range for behavioural adjustment; Flaks, Ficher, Masterpasqua & Joseph (1995) found no differences in cognitive functioning or behavioural adjustment in their comparison of 15 lesbian families with 15 heterosexual families; and in an investigation of 55 families headed by lesbian mothers, Chan, Raboy & Patterson (1998) demonstrated that parental sexual orientation was unrelated to children's performance on measures of social competence and behavioural adjustment.

Two investigations of children raised by lesbian mothers from birth have also been conducted in Europe. In the UK, Golombok & Tasker (1994) studied a group of 30 children aged between 3–8 years (most of whom had been conceived through donor insemination) in comparison with matched samples of 42 single heterosexual mother families and 41 two-parent heterosexual families with a child conceived through donor insemination. The children in the lesbian mother families were found to have good psychological adjustment, and to be no more likely to experience emotional or behavioural problems than children from the other family types. In addition, there was no difference between the different groups of children in how accepted they felt by their mother or by peers, although the father-absent children were slightly less confident about their physical skills and cognitive abilities. Similar findings were reported by Brewaeys, Ponjaert, Van Hall & Golombok (1997) in a comparison between 30 lesbian mother families with a child conceived by donor insemination and 68 heterosexual two-parent families in Belgium. Thus it seems that there is no additional risk to children's psychological adjustment of being raised in a lesbian family from the start.

Gender Development

Concerns about the gender development of children of lesbian mothers are based on the premise that in order to develop appropriate gender identity and gender role behaviour, a child must have a male and a female role model. These role models must also display the appropriate gender role behaviour for their sex. A commonly expressed view is that children of lesbian mothers will grow up to be confused about their gender identity, show behaviour that is inappropriate for their gender, and possibly identify as homosexual, an outcome that is often considered undesirable by courts of law. This begs the question, "To what extent can parents influence the gender identity and gender role behaviour of their child?"

The answer is contingent on which psychological perspective is taken (see Golombok & Fivush, 1994). From a psychoanalytic perspective, the significant process is the resolution of the Oedipal conflict, and it is only after this occurs that healthy psychological development can be achieved. In contrast, classical social learning theory proposes that the key processes at work are differential reinforcement and modelling, whereby gender appropriate behaviour is reinforced by the parents and the child also models the behaviour of the parent of the same sex. However, contemporary social learning theorists argue that rather than modelling the same-sex parent, children model the gender stereotypes that are pervasive in their social world. The cognitive developmental approach places even less emphasis on the role of parents in their children's gender development, proposing that children actively seek out gender-related information for themselves, and adopt behaviours that they perceive to be appropriate for their sex. It is gender stereotypes rather than parents that are the source of this information, and thus the socio-cultural environment is considered to have primacy.

According to both psychoanalytic and traditional social learning theorists, the absence of a male parent, and the presence of female parents who do not conform to the traditional female role, is likely to result in atypical gender development for the child. However, both contemporary social learning theorists and cognitive developmental theorists place greater weight on the role of gender stereotypes than on the role of parents in children's development of gender identity and gender role behaviour. From this perspective, children's gender development may be affected only to the extent that having a lesbian mother results in greater exposure to non-traditional stereotypes.

Empirical investigations of the gender development of children raised by lesbian mothers have largely focused on the gender identity and gender role behaviour of school age children. The early British study (Golombok, Spencer & Rutter, 1983) found no evidence of gender identity confusion for any of the children studied; none of the children wished to be the other sex, or consistently engaged in cross-gender behaviour. In terms of gender role, no differences were found between children in lesbian and heterosexual families, for either boys or girls, in the extent to which they showed behaviour that was typical of their sex. Daughters of lesbian mothers were no less feminine, and the sons no less masculine, than the daughters and sons of heterosexual mothers. Similarly, in the US, both Kirkpatrick *et al.* (1981) and Green *et al.* (1986) found no evidence of gender identity confusion among children of lesbian mothers, and no differences in gender role behaviour as assessed by toy, television character and game preferences when the sons and daughters of lesbian and heterosexual mothers were compared.

One interesting, and possibly related, finding is that lesbian mothers are often particularly careful to ensure that there are male role models in their child's life. Brewaeys *et al.* (1989) points to various studies showing that lesbian mothers encourage their children to develop relationships with men (Kirkpatrick *et al.*, 1981), or actively seek male role models (Mandel & Hotvedt, 1980; Lewin, 1981 (as cited in Brewaeys, 1989)). Indeed, Hare & Richards (1993) found that 90% of children of divorced lesbian mothers had contact with their fathers, and Golombok *et al.* (1983) showed that children of divorced lesbian mothers had more contact with their fathers than children of divorced heterosexual mothers.

By following up the children in the original British study, it was possible to examine the sexual orientation of these young people in adult life (Golombok & Tasker, 1996; Tasker & Golombok, 1997). Young adults who grew up in a lesbian family were more likely to have experienced a sexual relationship with someone of the same gender than those raised by heterosexual mothers. However, in terms of sexual identity as heterosexual, bisexual, lesbian or gay, the large majority (92%) of young adults raised by lesbian mothers identified as heterosexual. It seems, therefore, that mothers' sexual orientation has little impact on the sexual orientation of their daughters and sons.

Conclusion

The evidence from 25 years of research suggests that a mother's sexual orientation is not, in itself, an important variable in determining the psychological well-being, or gender development, of her children. It seems that whether their mother is lesbian or heterosexual matters less for children's psychological adjustment than the quality of relationships in the family home and, contrary to the assumptions of traditional psychoanalytic and social learning theories, parents have little influence on the gender development of their children.

So is there any more to be said about this issue as we enter the new millennium? One outstanding criticism of the existing research is that, with the exception of Brewaeys *et al.'s* (1995) investigation of children born to lesbian mothers by donor insemination, only volunteer samples have been studied. Thus it may be the case that mothers whose children are experiencing difficulties are under-represented in the research. Two ongoing studies of general population samples, one of teenage children in the US by Charlotte Patterson and colleagues, and the other by the present authors in collaboration with the Avon Longitudinal Study of Pregnancy and Childhood in the UK, will confirm whether the findings of research carried out to date can be extended to the general population of lesbian mother families. If so, these results will have important implications for the development of social policy relating to child custody, fostering and adoption, and access to assisted reproduction procedures.

References

Brewaeys, A., Devroey, P., Helmerhorst, F. M., Van Hall, E. V., & Ponjaert, I. (1995) Lesbian mothers who conceived after donor insemination: a follow up study, *Human Reproduction*, 10, pp. 2731–2735.

Brewaeys, A., Olbrechts, H., Devroey, P,. & Van Steirteghem, A. V. (1989) Counselling and selection of homosexual couples in fertility treatment, *Human Reproduction*, 4, pp. 850–853.

Brewaeys, A., Ponjaert, I., Van Hall, E. V., & Golombok, S. (1997) Donor insemination: child development and family functioning in lesbian mother families, *Human Reproduction*, 12, pp. 1349–1359.

Chan, R. W., Raboy, B., & Patterson, C. J. (1988) Psychological adjustment among children conceived via donor insemination by lesbian and heterosexual mother, *Child Development*, 69, pp. 443–457.

Dyer, C. (1999) Gays can bring up children—judge. *The Guardian*, 16 October.

Flaks, D. K., Ficher, I., Masterpasqua, F., & Joseph, G. (1995) Lesbians choosing motherhood: A comparative study of lesbian and heterosexual parents and their children, *Developmental Psychology*, 31, pp. 105–114.

Gold, K. (2000) A better breed of dad. *The Guardian*, 12 January.

Golombok, S. & Fivush, R. (1994) *Gender Development*, (New York, Cambridge University Press).

Golombok, S., Spencer, A. & Rutter, M. (1983) Children in lesbian and single parent households: Psychosexual and psychiatric appraisal, *Journal of Child Psychology and Psychiatry*, 24, pp. 551–572.

Golombok, S. & Tasker, F. (1994) Children in lesbian and gay families: theories and evidence, *Annual Review of Sex Research*, 5, pp. 73–100.

Golombok, S. & Tasker, F. (1996) Do parents influence the sexual orientation of their children? Findings from a longitudinal study of lesbian families, *Development Psychology*, 32, pp. 3–11.

Green, R. (1978) Sexual identity of 37 children raised by homosexual or transsexual parents, *American Journal of Psychiatry,* 135, pp. 692–697.

Green, R, Mandel, J. B., Hotvedt, M. E., Gray, J., & Smith, L. (1986) Lesbian mothers and their children: A comparison with solo parent heterosexual mothers and their children, *Archives of Sexual Behaviour,* 15, pp. 167–184.

Hare, J. & Richards, L. (1993) Children raised by lesbian couples: does the context of birth affect father and partner involvement? *Family Relations,* 42, pp. 249–255.

Kirkpatrick, M., Smith, C., & Roy, R. (1981) Lesbian mothers and their children: A comparative survey, *American Journal of Orthopsychiatry,* 51, pp. 545–551.

Patterson, C. J. (1994) Children of the lesbian baby boom: behavioural adjustment, self-concepts, and sex-role identity, in: B. Greene & G. Herek (Eds.), *Comtemporary Perspectives on Lesbian and Gay Psychology: Theory, Research and Application,* pp. 156–175 (Beverly Hills, CA, Sage).

Steckel, A. (1985) Separation-individuation in children of lesbian and heterosexual couples. Unpublished doctoral dissertation, Wright Institute Graduate School, Berkley, CA.

Steckel, A. (1987) Psychosocial development of children of lesbian mothers, in: F. W. Bozett (Ed.), *Gay and Lesbian Parents,* pp. 75–85, (New York, Praeger).

Tasker, F. & Golombok, S. (1997) *Growing Up in a Lesbian Family* (New York, Guilford).

18

■ Abigail Lovett (1998), President of Adoption Forum, said, "Moses, Oedipus, King Arthur, the Ugly Duckling, Superman, and Luke Skywalker all have something in common: they were all adopted. They are also some of our culture's major self realization archetypes: without the search there would have been no story." We all struggle with the challenge of discovering who we are, but this search for identity is particularly complex and poignant for adopted children. In this article, Silin examines similarities and differences between how adopted and non-adopted children negotiate typical "developmental tasks."

Overview Questions

1. What are some differences between pregnant and adoptive couples in terms of challenges to self-esteem, time frame, and social support?

2. In what way is attachment similar for birthparents and adoptive parents? In what three ways are they different?

3. What feature needs to be added to the narrative of the adoption as children reach school age? What changes typically arise between 8–11 years in children's attitudes about being adopted? In what ways can being adopted complicate children's self-esteem and identity?

4. What features of adolescence lead to desire for connection to the birth mother? How does adoption feature in adolescents' growing awareness of their sexuality? How does Silin suggest that these issues be handled?

Focus Questions

1. What myth shaped the adoptive process in the 1940s? How did this affect parental behavior and children's experience?

2. What do studies suggest regarding the length of time it takes for an infant to adjust to adoptive parents? Why is finalizing the adoption a psychological landmark, in addition to a legal one?

3. What does Silin believe is the basic message that parents should convey to adopted toddlers? How does she believe parents should handle toddlers' fantasies about being in the adoptive mother's tummy?

The Vicissitudes of Adoption for Parents and Children

Marilyn W. Silin

Introduction

Psychological reactions to the adoptive process are experienced in many ways by children and parents throughout their lives. Children's feelings, questions and ideas about their adoption are interwoven into the normal developmental phases of childhood while parents experience a magnitude of reactions to the adoption situation. When parents are comfortable with their feelings and are able to listen receptively to their children's fantasies and thoughts an atmosphere is created for meaningful communication within the family. The following excerpt from an interview with a nine-year-old boy describes his inner feelings about the adoption and his growing identity.

> "My parents wanted to adopt a baby boy, and one day they got a phone call from someone who asked if they would like a little Indian boy. They said they would *love* one, and so that's how they got me. They had to sign a lot of papers and then they became my parents. I was five months old at the time. My real mother wasn't able to provide for me, and she thought that the most loving thing she could do for me was to place me with a family who could take care of me. . . .
>
> "I might like to meet my Indian parents someday, but I don't think about it all that much. I usually have other things on my mind, like doing my homework or meeting a friend, and I imagine they're probably busy too doing other things.
>
> "I do wish my skin color was a little bit lighter. I don't like getting a tan in May while school is still going on, because the kids tease me and call me names like 'Brownie' and 'Chocolate Chip' and this hurts my feelings. If they're my age I either punch them or tell my parents, but if they're younger, I let it go. The first time, it made me cry, but my sister Beth was with me and she helped me to feel better. She told me to try and ignore them. Most of the time, though, they don't tease me. In fact, they make me feel special and proud to be the only full Indian in my school. . . . I know a lot more about Indians than my friends do, about my overall past, but I don't know much about my individual history. I know it sounds funny to say, but even though I'm adopted and on top of that a completely different race from my parents and sisters, it just never occurs to me that they're not my real family!" (Krementz[3], (1982) p. 33–35.)

History

Adoption is much harder and more diverse than it was thirty years ago. In the 1940s agencies stated that they could find a home for any child who needed a family. At that time, social workers tried to match the biological characteristics of the child, usually an infant, with the biological characteristics of the biological family. The wished-for blending encouraged a belief that there were no differences between biological and adoptive parenthood.

Parents tried to maintain that myth by not using the word "adoption" at all, or by telling the child an abbreviated story about it, and then never alluding to it again. Another path parents took to protect the child from having to deal with the concept of two sets of parents was to say that the other parents had been killed in a car accident.

As the children in these families became adults, they spoke about the shock of learning about their adoption from a neighbor, a distant relative, or from a discovered document. Adult adoptees have described the feelings of unreality that came from never having been able to fit together the pieces of their lives, sensing that there were secrets which they felt should not be discussed.

In time, adoption experts began to advise telling the child about her adoption. However, some experts advised doing it early, while others contended that revealing these facts would harm a child developmentally. Parents were caught in this debate, unable to feel comfortable with either course. The "telling" and its timing is still a source of anxiety for parents.

Adoption Today

Today adoption is more readily identified and acknowledged, especially with families whose children are from racial or ethnic groups differing from that of their parents. Multicultural and multiracial families are seen more often than before. Books are available for children and parents which narrate the adoptive process from the child's viewpoint and illustrate some of the inner struggles the child experiences within herself, and within the particular family and culture of her environment. Finally, stories about adoption are more common in the media, where tragedies of interrupted adoptions become public knowledge.

Thus, it is harder for parents to maintain the idea that there are no differences between rearing a biological child and an adopted one. Indeed, acknowledgment of the difficulties adoption poses begins much before the happy time the child is received by the family. We will therefore turn our attention first to the adoptive process as it is experienced by the parents.

Waiting to Adopt

For the parents who have decided to adopt, waiting for a baby is perhaps the most difficult time in the whole experience. For many the decision to adopt is a response to the fertility problems which could not be resolved after months or years of treatment. Would-be parents in our society face a deep loss of self-esteem when they realize they will not be able to conceive. The decision to take a child into the family is never an easy one. If the couple chooses to discuss the pros and cons of adoption with extended family or friends, it may mean exposing the fertility problems for the first time. Then, when the decision is finally made, a lawyer must be found and a legal process initiated for the home to be licensed by a social worker or the court. Now the couple feel themselves to be judged and evaluated by standards not clear to them. This may be experienced as a test of their ability to parent. This process, the home study, may be cumbersome and costly, with no clear light at the end of the tunnel because of the small number of adoptable children. However, when the final approval is given and the couple has been legally accepted into the class of licensed parents, their self esteem is restored, and they now face a second hurdle, the waiting list. They are told to expect a child any time from a few months to two or three years.*

*(This would not hold true in open adoptions or foreign adoptions.)

A pregnant couple experiences a definitive nine-month waiting period, which allows them to prepare internally and in reality for the birth. Adoptive parents do not know if the preparation time will be nine months or three years. They feel as if they are living in limbo.

"Do we buy a crib now and let it sit there empty, for an unknown time, or should we wait until we get the phone call and ask our parents to go out and get it then?" "Can we go on vacation? What if we're far away and they call us then?" "Is it bad luck to have a baby shower?"

Pregnant couples go to Lamaze classes and have a chance to share their concerns with others in the same situation. Adoptive parents often feel isolated during the waiting period, but the wished-for child is never far from their thoughts. They visit friends who have small children and they practice child rearing in their heads. The coming adoption and what it might hold for them is a recurring theme in their lives.

When the call comes the excitement and relief are palpable. The few days between the phone call and getting the baby are intense, full of hope and anticipation about the baby and how they will adjust to each other. Because the parents have surmounted so many hurdles this baby comes to them already highly prized.

Bonding and Attachment

In recent years infant research has put forth the concept that bonding is a physiological process, starting in utero and continuing in the first days after birth when mother and baby are primed to connect. The authors Brodzinsky and Schechter[1] (1992), differentiate bonding from attachment, which, they state, "grows slowly, over weeks, months and even years of living interaction, and it can grow just as well between a parent and infant who are not biologically connected as between a parent and infant who are. . . ." "Attachment," they write, "is an emotional relationship that develops gradually, after weeks and months of daily contact, conversation, caregiving, and cuddling." They call attachment the essential bond (Brodzinsky and Schechter, 1992, p. 33).

Observations confirm that babies are born with a built-in set of response capabilities and signaling systems, "But it is only after a long period of using them that attachment develops. These capabilities—crying, vocalizing, gazing, head turning—will promote close interaction between caregiver and baby, eventually this will lead to a two-way emotional bond" (Brodzinsky and Schechter, 1992, p.33). Adopted parent-infant pairs, these authors contend, form attachment relationships in a time frame that is virtually identical to that of biological parent-infant pairs.

One significant difference for adoptive parents, however, comes from the reactions of well meaning friends and family to the arrival of the baby. Unwittingly offered insensitive comments or questions often convey that adoption is a second-class form of parenthood. "It's too bad you couldn't have a baby the regular way," someone will say, or "If only you knew the joy that comes with having a baby of your own." Strangers ask questions about an adoptive child they would never ask about a biological child, such as: "What is his intelligence?" Well meaning friends ask "Where did you get her? How much did you pay for her?" These feel like hurtful intrusions into the life of the adoptive parents who are dealing with their own responses to the arrival of the child and their wishes to be successful parents.

Many factors influence the couple's growing sense of comfort in their new role as parents. One distinctive factor for them is the presence, in fantasy, of a birthmother. Adoptive mothers have told this writer that they think of her often in the first few months, and afterwards, on the child's birthday, on Mother's Day, or on the anniversary of the date the child came to them. In the first few months, especially at moments when the baby seems so wonderful and contented, thoughts of her surface: "Where is she now? Would she be pleased with how I'm taking such good care of the baby? Would she want her back? Is she still mourning? Would she be jealous of me?" The birthmother is the ghost in the nursery.*

In traditional adoptions the parents may receive information about the birthparents, their physical characteristics, educational backgrounds, talents, perhaps some hereditary history of family illnesses, and possibly other facts. But this information will never replace intimate knowledge of their own idiosyncratic development, which adults learn over time from their parents and extended family. How a dad took his first steps, as told by his mother, becomes a template for the expectation of how his son will walk. If a dad knows that he was slow to take his first steps he will not be concerned if his son is "late." The adoptive father learns to say "He'll walk when he'll walk." There will be no family antecedents to account for the manner in which an adoptive child reaches the milestones in her life.

The lack of detailed previous history may impede the parents' ability to predict how the child will develop. But the child will create her own unique, lovable characteristics and these will be the beginning of a new history, which will enter the legends of the family. Indeed, as babies become toddlers and start to imitate their parents' walk, tone of voice and other mannerisms, it appears as if the child were born into her family.

As the adoptee reaches adolescence the absence of the details of the birthparents' history may become a greater source of frustration. A girl will not know when to expect to menstruate, a boy may wonder if he will need to shave when he's fourteen. And the onset of serious physical illness, understandably, raises more unanswerable questions about heredity.

When parents are able to acknowledge their own sadness at not having the information to answer these questions, then it becomes easier for them to mirror and to be empathic with the child's wishes to know more about herself (Kirk,[2] 1964). Together, then, parents and child live through each developmental phase, with less knowledge than they would like to have, while creating a new life story which will stand on its own unique foundation.

Adoption Adjustment of the Child and Parents

Infancy

If the baby is placed in the adoptive home a short time after birth the chances for adjustment and attachment are optimal. Studies clearly show that the longer a baby remains with earlier caretakers the longer the period of adjustment to the permanent home.** Even two months makes a difference, for babies have kinesthetic, aural, olfactory and other sensory memories of their earliest caretakers. Getting used to new persons and a new physical environment takes time, in inverse proportion to the time the child has spent in previous homes.

Babies may react to the new and changed environment by experiencing distress in physiological areas such as in eating, eliminating, sleeping or motility. These difficulties create tensions in the new adoptive parents who are trying so hard to become good parents.

---

*This paper does not address the relationships between adoptive parents and birth-parents in open adoptions. Data is now being collected in this area and memoirs and personal experiences are beginning to be published. (See Watkins and Fisher,[4] pp. 178–183.)

**Justin Call, (1986). In: Lois Ruskai Melina, *Raising Adopted Children: A Manual for Adoptive Parents.* New York, Harper and Row, (p. 17).

This adjustment period also coincides with the required post placement visits of the agency or court worker before final papers are prepared for consummation of the adoption. In many states that is a six month period. Even the most confident parent has anxieties about the home visits of the worker, and if the infant is exhibiting signs of discomfort or stress, the home visit only heightens the parents' anxieties.

In this early period new adoptive mothers who meet together in groups find they gain support and guidance from each other in dealing with the babies, and with their friends and family as well as with the visits of the social workers.

Until the family goes to court to finalize the adoption the parents may feel anxieties about the possibility of losing the child. There may be a fear that one of the birthparents will try to reclaim the baby. Unfortunately, recent publicized cases have greatly increased this understandable worry. Established adoption agencies are working to decrease the opportunities for birthparents to reclaim a child by strengthening the legal structures around the consent process.

Nevertheless, mothers sometimes hesitate about taking a baby to a shopping mall, or a park, for fear that the birthmother or a close relative of hers will recognize the child and want to take her back. Some parents are wary of leaving the baby with a non-familial babysitter. This cautionary attitude usually diminishes after the finalization of the adoption.

Toddlerhood

When the child begins to walk and talk parents are faced with the dilemma of when and how to talk about the adoption. The story they choose to tell will grow out of their own acceptance of the birthmother's role and their gratitude to her for having found an intermediary who found them, and chose them as parents for the child.

An idea as complex as that, however, cannot be presented to a two-year-old. A beginning foundation for good feelings about adoption arises out of words which convey warmth and happiness about the child's arrival in the family. "I'm so glad we adopted you. That was the happiest day of our lives." If that is said at an intimate time, such as drying a child after the bath, that would be a first step in the incremental development of the rest of the story.

Later on, depending upon the child's language capacity, a parent can elaborate on the story. Its details, then, become the child's special story, and she will repeat it, ask questions, and play out the themes in her own fashion. An example follows.

"Daddy and I wanted to have a baby very much. Then one day our telephone rang. 'We have a baby girl for you,' the doctor said. 'When can we come and get her?' We asked. He said: 'Tomorrow.' We were so happy we hugged each other and cried, and then went out and bought Pampers and bottles. And the next day we drove very fast to the doctor's office and there you were, and you were the cutest little girl we had ever seen. You had a dimple right here. So we took you home and grandma and grandpa were here and everyone took pictures and there were pink balloons all over the family room, and we thought you were the best baby in the world because you went right to sleep in your crib." The child may focus on parts of the story important to her, such as the dimple, or the balloons. "Is that still my dimple?" "Who got the balloons?"

Later on, a toddler may hear other children talking about babies, or playing mommy and baby in preschool. She will also notice pregnant mothers and learn that other kids are getting new brothers or sisters at home. This is a time when an adoptive mother is faced with feelings about her child not having grown in her tummy. If the mother allows the child to express her fantasies, the child may pretend to drink from her mother's breast, or to snuggle and say she is in her mommy's tummy. If the mother can convey that it's okay to feel that way, the bonds between them will grow stronger.

Parents may not be able to determine if their young child's questions about babies relate to adoption, or birth, in general. Like sex, birth and death, adoption is a concept children try to understand and integrate into their lives at different stages. Parents who provide a receptive atmosphere for the child's questions and musings make it possible for the child to work out these concepts in a supportive environment. One can learn a great deal about the child's ideas simply by observing the play and listening to conversations with other children.*

School Age Children

When the child has grasped the concept that she grew inside another lady's tummy she will think about that. Eventually she will need to hear that her birthmother loved her, but could not take care of her, so she did the next best thing. She found a social worker, or a doctor, or . . . "Who knew that we wanted a baby very much, and so when we got you, that was the happiest day of our lives." By this time the child will have internalized the story of how her parents got her. Thus, the introduction of an intermediary who brought the parents and her together becomes another chapter added to the earlier narrative. As she grows older the child may ask questions which reflect her concern about why she was given up. Simple, factual answers provide a basis for further discussion. "Oh, so she was just a teenager, I guess she didn't have enough money to take care of me. . . . "

A seven-year-old highlighted her newfound awareness in this fashion. "Adoption means coming out of your first parents and then going to live with your second parents. The first ones are the ones who made you and the other people are your parents always. They have to take care of you and everything" (Brodzinsky[1], p. 69).

Together with this realization, however, comes sadness. Brodzinsky *et al.* have noted that between the ages of eight and eleven the child's understanding and appreciation of adoption deepens. With this, however, there is a decline in positive attitudes about adoption. The previously carefree child may become withdrawn, irritable, or sullen, and no longer want to read her favorite adoption stories. Some parents worry and wonder if they have talked too much about it, or too little.

Inwardly the child may be grieving for the parents she feels she has lost, and she may begin to think, for the first time, about the unchosen options available to the birthmother. "If she didn't know how to be a mommy, then someone should have taught her. She should have gone to school to learn—then it wouldn't have happened" (ibid. p. 69).

Children of this age want to be like everyone else, and the separateness they feel from their non-adopted peers may give them a sense of difference which is undesirable. During middle childhood, a child's self-concept and self-esteem develop at a rapid rate.

Being adopted can complicate the development of self-concept, especially if the adoptee does not look like her parents. Looking in the mirror each day and seeing one set of features, and looking at other family members and seeing a different set of features, can be disconcerting, especially for children under eight, who tend to define themselves in concrete terms. A six-year-old black child who was adopted in infancy by a white couple noticed in kindergarten that the black children in the class had black parents while the white children had white parents.

"Am I black or white?" he asked his mother one day. "What makes you ask that?" his mother replied. "Well," said James, "black kids have black skin and black parents, but I have black skin and white parents." His mother reminded him that he was adopted, and that his birthparents were black even though she and his adoptive

---

*See Watkins & Fisher,[4] *Adoptive Comments, Questions, and Play Sequences of Adopted Children in the Stories.* Arranged by age. pp. 225–238.

father were white. The child answered, "I know that, but I still don't know if I'm supposed to be black or white" (ibid, p. 64).

Biological children of mixed marriages also have this problem, and they grapple with it throughout their lives, but adopted children connect it with their understanding of adoption.

As children grow and expand their capacities to understand the world in a logical manner their picture of adoption expands as well. Here is a 12-year-old's story:

> "I was adopted when I was about three days old. My birthmother was sixteen and I don't know how old the guy was. My parents brought me home directly from the hospital. The only information I have about my background is that my birthmother was Catholic and wanted me placed with a Catholic family.
>
> "I was told I was adopted when I was about two, but I had no idea what it meant. When my parents said 'You're adopted,' I thought they were saying 'You're a doctor!' and I kept telling them 'No, I'm not a doctor!' I hated the idea of being a doctor because I hated doctors. I still hate them because I can't stand shots.
>
> "When I was three, my sister, Rebecca, was born, and that's when I realized where babies come from. My Mom explained that being adopted meant I grew up in somebody else's tummy, so it was at this time that I started asking any woman who came into the house if I had grown inside *her* tummy. I must have made a complete fool of myself.
>
> "Some of my friends asked me dumb questions, like, 'Did your parents die?' or, 'Why didn't they want you?' I think they did want me, but they were so young they would have had to drop out of school, and it would have cost a lot of money to raise me—to buy food, diapers, clothes and stuff like that. The older I get, the easier it is for me to understand. I mean, right now I'm just four years younger than she was, and it would be impossible for me to try to bring up a kid . . . " (Krementz, *How it Feels to be Adopted,* p. 19.)

Many adopted children seem very resilient and untroubled by the issues outlined above. However, one school assignment in fourth or fifth grade brings these issues to the fore. That is the assignment to draw a family tree and to write about one's ancestors. This, understandably, evokes more thinking about the question, "Who am I?" Some children choose to describe the family tree of their adopted family, while others, with the support of their parents, choose to do two family trees, and perhaps, two sets of flags, and two descriptions of countries of origin. The child's comfort with both identities is usually proportional to the interest and positive attitudes the parents have communicated about the child's birthplace and culture.

Adolescence

The issues which arose in middle childhood continue for adolescents. When looks become important to teenagers they may feel a greater wedge between themselves and their families, if they are different in appearance.

Many teenagers begin to actively imagine what their birthparents look like, as a source of clues about how they will look when they grow up. Teenagers interviewed by Krementz[3] often stated that they would have liked to know what their birthparents were like, but that they didn't necessarily have to look for them. If the adoptive parents are not threatened by the wish to know more about the birthparents and can support the youngster's desire to know more, that stance diminishes the child's fear of hurting her parents, and contributes, in the long run, to the teenager's identification with the adoptive family.

The first signs of an active search for the birthparents may show up in adolescence, although young children sometimes threaten to run away and find their "real" parents, who, they think, would not force them to eat their broccoli. (The answer to that is: "We *are* your real parents, and you have to taste the broccoli.")

It is a normal developmental task of adolescence, however, to want to separate from the family. Thinking about one's birthparents, and imagining who they are, is almost universal for adopted adolescents who have two families from which to separate, although one of those is only vaguely identifiable.

Brodzinsky and Schechter claim that all adoptees engage in an internal search process. This universal search begins during the early school years, and continues, in fantasy, or reality, throughout life, especially at times of transitions. Many of the interviews in the book *How it Feels to be Adopted* (Krementz)[3] carry passages illustrating this. "The best thing about being adopted is that I can have wonderful fantasies about my birthmother. And if you're a dreamer, which I can be, your mother can become anyone you want her to be. I happen to like opera a lot, so for a while my real mother was Maria Callas. She was such a strange and wonderful lady . . . she's dead now. She never found out what a crazy son she had," said one boy (Krementz[3] p. 67).

Another one said, "I've always had a picture in my mind of what my birthmother looks like. She's a little chubby, about thirty-seven years old . . . I think I saw her once on 79th and Broadway three years ago. I dream about her from time to time. She never changes—never gets older or anything like that" (ibid p. 70).

The adolescent stage often increases parents' insecurities about the child's attachment to them. As the adolescent talks about searching for the birthmother, the parents may worry about the repercussions of finding her. If the birthmother rejects the youngster, that itself would be a blow, but, if the birthmother wants to reconnect with the child, parents fear that they will be depreciated and diminished in importance. When one reads the interviews with teenagers in the Krementz book, however, one notes that the adoptees seem to manage with all the possible outcomes. There are accounts of older teenagers having their birthparents as "friends" of the adoptive family. There are teenagers who do not need to search, but are interested in their places of origin, and the general culture of their birthparents. In all these situations the comfort of the adoptive parents in accepting the adolescents' need to search was the critical factor in helping the adoptees make peace with what they had uncovered.

Another developmental task of teenagers is the necessity to deal with their burgeoning sexuality. Their thoughts and fantasies about the birthparents' sexual behavior may influence their ideas about how they will behave. Some girls may decide that they will not date at all until they are absolutely sure of the guy, and feel they can support a child and give it a father as well. Others may want to get pregnant early, in identification with their birthmothers. Some of these girls, however, plan to keep their babies, in an effort to do what was not done for them (Brodzinsky[1], p. 112).

The processes of pulling away from one's family, finding one's sexual pathway and peer group identity are often charged conflicts for biological adolescents. For adopted teenagers there is more bewilderment, more confusion and the possibility of greater diffusion of role models. The issues initiated during school age are reinvested with greater urgency in the adolescent period. If the adoptive parents' anxieties about losing the child's loyalty inhibit discussion of these issues at home, the teenager is likely to turn her thoughts inward, or find other sources for comfort and self-expression.

Brodzinsky[1] quotes one boy who learned not to raise adoption questions openly. He said, "She (my mother) got hysterical. That was enough for me and I never asked again. I was a zombie about adoption and I turned it off, mostly. But I thought about my mother almost every day from the age of seven on." (p. 81.) On the other hand, if parents can live through the ambiguity, the anxiety provoking family discussions, and the need for the adolescent to know as much as possible about her previous history, chances are she will find other interests capturing her attention, and, as time goes on, adoption will take on less importance in her total life.

Summary

For parents the decision to adopt is the first step in a life-long process of parenthood which has critical phases that tend to shape and reshape their thinking. Central to the parents' capacity to respond to the child's questions and musings is their acceptance of the child's need to identify the birth family and its culture, or race, if it is different. When parents communicate their positive feelings about the child's arrival in the family, and later on, about her unique heritage, the youngster will feel supported in her efforts to feel good about herself.

Children understand their own adoption stories according to their intellectual and emotional framework at any given age. Young children focus on concrete elements which make sense to them, in their world, which means that the preschooler adds fantasy to fact and wishful thinking to what she is told. School age children are capable of more abstract ideas and begin to question and compose solutions to the bigger questions, "Who was she? Why did she give me up?" If they are encouraged in looking for answers to these questions the adoption segment of their lives will be integrated into their total sense of family, culture, and community.

References

1. Brodzinsky, David, Schechter, Marshall, & Henig, Robin Marantz, *Being Adopted, The Lifelong Search for Self*, New York, Doubleday, 1992.

2. Kirk, H. David, *Shared Fate: A Theory of Adoption and Mental Health*, New York, Free Press, 1964.

3. Krementz, Jill, *How it Feels to Be Adopted*, New York, Knopf, 1987.

4. Watkins, Mary & Fisher, Susan, *Talking with Young Children about Adoption*, New Haven, Yale University Press, 1993.

Appendix: Books for Parents and Children

Is That Your Sister?, Catherine and Sherry Bunin. Pantheon Books. 1976.
> Photos of black 6-year-old telling his story in the first person, including the adoption of his 4-year-old sister. Allows for children's fantasies on why they were given up.
>
> Ages 6–10

Kati-bo, an Adoption Story, Iris L. Fisher. New York: Adams Books. 1987.
> A lovely story about adoption from a social agency. Story told by the older biological brother. Emphasis on the feelings of the siblings. Story includes post-placement visits and going to court. Highly recommended.
>
> Children up to 12

We Adopted You, Benjamin Koo, Linda Walvoord Girard. Niles, IL; Whitman & Co., 1989.
> Told in the first person by a 9-year-old Korean boy. Illustrations are realistic. Covers the trip from Korea; adjustment to the family and typical conflicts of adoption.
>
> Age 9–15

How It Feels to be Adopted, Jill Krementz. New York: Knopf (Distrib. By Random House), 1982.
> Photos of adopted children telling their fantasies about their birth parents. Actual words of the children, illuminating their innermost wishes and thoughts about the unknown parents. A most revealing book. Recommended for parent to read, when appropriate for teenagers. The book would evoke feelings in all adoptive persons and can be used as a basis for discussion.
>
> Parents, young adults

And Now We Are a Family, Judith C. Meredith. Boston: Beacon Press, 1971.
> A simple, nicely illustrated story.
>
> Ages 2–4

Families are Different, Nina Pellegrini. New York: Holiday House, 1991.
　　　Story told by a 4-year-old about herself and her adopted sister.

Age 3–6

Being Adopted, Maxine Rosenberg. New York: Lothrop Lee & Shepard, 1984.
　　　Photos and realistic story of adoption of children from other cultures, acknowledges
　　　difference in appearance, allows child to dream of other parents, to be confused.

Age 5–8

19

Children's lives are affected by the historical events of their generation. In recent history, a whole generation of children has the tragic events of September 11, 2001, seared in their memories. For those who lost family members, the trauma is even greater. Half a century ago, a generation of Jewish children lost their families, and lost their childhoods, in the Nazi Holocaust. The experience of separation, according to attachment theorists, shakes the very foundation of our emotional well-being. The attachment theorist Bowlby (1960, 1980) believed that the emotional bond of attachment was fundamental for infants' sense of themselves and others. Without the emotional security of this bond, infants were at risk to conclude to believe that they were unlovable or that other people were not trustworthy. He was very concerned by situations in which infants were separated from caregivers by illness or death, and argued that infants would experience three phases of grief in response to such separations: protest (crying, searching), despair (withdrawal, depression), and detachment (may ignore the caregiver if reunited, as if fearful of being hurt again). Upon repeated separations, the infant might enter a fourth phase, of withdrawal from all human relationships. When we reflect on the long-term experiences of child survivors of the Holocaust, we are reminded of the foundational role that attachments play in our development, and of the resilience of the human spirit.

Overview Questions

1. From an attachment perspective, explain why the separation of children from their parents when they were evacuated to safety before 1939 would be traumatic.

2. Give examples of "play, creativity, resourcefulness, and some ability to dissociate from their surroundings" as coping mechanisms for children in the ghettos.

3. Describe how the experience of hiding affected the development of identity and self-control. What is "psychic numbing," how might it relate to attachment theory, and why may it have been useful?

4. How was the relationship with parents prior to the Holocaust important to children's coping? How did their experiences affect their attitudes toward their parents and feelings about their own children?

Focus Question

1. What are important therapeutic objectives with this population? Counter-transference is the therapist's attribution of traits or reactions to the patient/client that are appropriate to someone else. How have therapists' anxieties interfered with successful therapy for survivors?

"Lost Childhood"—Lessons from the Holocaust: Implications for Adult Adjustment

Malka Sternberg and Maria Rosenbloom

This paper was written in memoriam to the one and a half million children murdered during the Holocaust; in celebration of the tiny percentage who survived; in honor of their rescuers, the "Righteous Christians"; and in meeting our own responsibility as survivors to "bear witness."

The purpose of this paper is to highlight the dysfunctional and adaptive impacts of massive traumatization on one segment of Holocaust survivors, namely those who were children during the Nazi era, 1939–1945. The nature of their suffering, their coping mechanisms, and the lifelong consequences of their tragic childhood are explored, and clinical and self-healing approaches are delineated. Study of this population can help social work professionals develop methods of prevention and/or intervention applicable to survivors of a variety of childhood traumas.

Of the six million Jews killed in the Holocaust, between 1933 and 1945, one and a half million were children. The German Nazi government made the Jewish child the foremost target in its process of annihilation. By state policy, every Jewish child was to be murdered to ensure there would be no Jewish future in Europe. It is estimated that at the end of World War II, 1,500, or 1 percent, of the prewar population of 1.5 million Jewish children were left alive in German-occupied Europe (Maxwell 1993). Survival of this group is a miracle, a cause for celebration, and the theme of this paper.

While adult Holocaust survivors and their children born after the war—the "second generation"—have been the subject of scholarly and clinical attention for the last two or three decades, the story of those who were children during the Holocaust has been taboo to historians, professionals, and the media. Child survivors did not think their story was of particular interest or importance, and the older survivors considered the younger ones lucky to have been too young to remember.

Wars, massacres, and genocides have always brought extreme suffering to children, yet social work professional interests hardly ever extend to the ongoing suffering of starving, abandoned, and orphaned children caught in the crossfire of geopolitical, racial, religious or ethnic conflicts. A review of social work journals of the last fifteen years reveals few writings relevant to these populations.

Child survivors of the Holocaust are reaching the age where they have to consider issues facing all elderly: the indignities of aging and mortality, their own as well as that of significant friends and family members. This group gives professionals a unique opportunity to reach a better understanding of the lifetime impact of severe wartime traumas on the functioning of survivors. As children, these survivors suffered the unique trauma of being condemned to total extermination for one reason only: they were Jews. Study of these children, their early life traumas and subsequent lifetime adjustments may be helpful in understanding and serving other victims of early childhood in traumas.

State of Knowledge

An informal discussion following the screening of a film *"As if it Were Yesterday"* (M. Abramowicz; E. Offenberg, 1982), about the rescue of Jewish children in Belgium, led to a conference to which child survivors and their families were invited in order to share their experiences during and since the Holocaust. The initial meeting was held in New York City in 1991, followed by another two years later in Jerusalem. The authors, both survivors, led workshops on each occasion. This paper incorporates the knowledge derived from observing, listening to, and interacting with the participants.

They came from all over the world: Europe, North America, South America, and Australia. They were well-dressed, poised, often multilingual, and obviously proud of their spouses and children. In the plenary sessions they listened politely to the speakers. Generally, they were indistinguishable from other groups that attend conventions.

But hell broke loose once they found themselves in the small groups of selected workshops. Emotions ran high and the pain was palpable as they recalled events and details of their Holocaust childhood—how they were abused, abandoned, starved, and subjected to repeated traumas. Many cried, others sat motionless, some walked out to "cool off" for a few moments. For most, it was the first time they had talked openly about their early lives, how it had affected their later lives, how they measured up as parents, grandparents, and mainly as human beings. They bonded immediately.

Contacts among survivors have continued beyond the initial gatherings, and networks have been established in many places around the globe. The silence has been broken. Stimulated by society's current interest in the Nazi era and by an awareness of their special role as the last witnesses to the Holocaust, these men and women, now in their sixties and seventies, are ready to probe into their painful past, retrieve fragments of memory, and try to complete the picture of their families and communities.

At the meetings and in the newsletters of their organizations, there are always pathetic appeals for *any* information about long-lost kin, neighbors, schoolmates. Child survivors often visit faraway places in search of *any* knowledge about their past or in an effort to meet and pay tribute to their rescuers.

Child Survivors—Who Are They?

Prior to the rise of Nazism in Germany, Jewish families lived relatively normal lives. True, there were pogroms, persecutions, and poverty, but the children were part of a cohesive Jewish society; they had friends, went to school, engaged in study and play. Traditionally, Jewish children were cherished by their families and the surrounding Jewish community. Children were well provided for physically, religiously and educationally. It was taken for granted that parents should deprive themselves, and sacrifice for the sake of their children's future (Maxwell 1993).

Child survivors of the Holocaust are Jews who lived in Europe and were under the age of sixteen between 1933 and 1945, and who have miraculously escaped the sentence of death imposed on *all* Jewish children by the Nazis. By Nazi racial doctrines, all Jews were considered inferior, and not worthy of life. This philosophy, backed by political power and military might, gradually led to implementation of legal policies against Jews, starting with a series of discriminatory laws and ending in the *Final Solution*, a code for the annihilation of six million Jews, including one and a half million children.

In the earlier years of Nazism (1933–38) Jews still had some opportunities to escape. Jewish children often managed to leave Germany with their families intact. For those who remained, loss of jobs and citizenship, arrests, street violence, book burning, and boycotts of Jewish stores created chaos and fear and shattered any sense of security. Jewish children in Germany were banned from attending schools and subjected to open hostility and derision. German children were taught both in school and at home not to associate with their Jewish contemporaries.

In response to these actions, the Jewish community organized alternative forms of learning and opened schools staffed solely by Jewish teachers. Dr. Paul Schreiber, the first Dean of the Hunter College School of Social Work, was among those Jewish teachers. Naturally, such education was interrupted with the welcome arrival of a foreign visa and an opportunity to emigrate.

In the late 1930s a series of events, particularly the violence of *Kristallnacht*, signaled approaching doom. Many remaining German Jewish families made the painful decision to send their children to safety in other countries, particularly the United Kingdom. Ten thousand children were thus transported, including some Jewish children from Austria, where annexation by Germany in 1938 immediately led to severe actions against Jews.

The later memories of these children are often focused on the agonizing moments of separation from parents at a railway station in Germany, Austria, or France. All painfully recall the fear of the unknown during the long ride across countries of Western Europe, the torturous wait for news about family, and the fading hope of ever seeing their parents again. Although some reunions eventually took place, many children were orphaned when their parents were murdered in the *Final Solution* (Whiteman 1954).

Coping and Adaptation During the Holocaust

The fate of the vast majority of Jewish children was sealed with the outbreak of World War II in 1939 and the German occupation of most of the European continent. Emigration was no longer possible. While a few children survived in the camps their survival was exceptional.

Upon arrival to the camps, they usually were sent straight to the gas chambers. There are many tragic descriptions of children torn from young mothers' arms, and destined for execution. The mothers were left alive if they were considered young enough for slave labor. The children were subjected to a process of degradation and destruction that challenged the human capacity to grasp and believe.

Herded into the *ghettos*, children were gradually starved, and exposed to deadly diseases, such as typhoid fever and dysentery. Parents whose children were still alive often envied these youngsters' death by such "natural" causes. Others were not so lucky. They were often shot or hanged on lanterns in the streets of the ghettos, exposed for kin, neighbors, young schoolmates to see (Rosenbloom 1995).

Astonishingly, children in the ghettos and concentration camps continued to engage in play and games. These activities offered a modicum of normalcy and helped children integrate terrifying experiences. In play they enacted scenes of German brutality, such as raids on the ghettos, forced removal of people from their hiding places, massacres, and marches toward the deportation trains. Often the games children played reflected the entire tragedy, start to finish. They would play at gravedigging. They would dig a pit, put a child inside, and call him Hitler (Levin 1993: 249).

Children also occupied themselves by writing poems or drawing pictures expressing their suffering and longing to return to normal life. The children were killed, but some of their memoirs (Anne Frank 1971) and drawings from Terezin (Auerbacher 1986) have survived.

Unusually resilient in the struggle for their own and their families' survival, these children would beg in the street for a chunk of bread or potato. The smallest children would often crawl beneath the barbed wire of the ghetto to smuggle in some food from the outside. Discovery meant instant death, but a little food also meant survival for another day.

Play, creativity, resourcefulness, and some ability to dissociate from their surroundings helped the children cope with extreme deprivation and a constant sense of terror. They used their imagination to express emotions, and engaged in drawing and writing. But such efforts usually could not overcome starvation or being discovered in their hiding places. Those who were old enough to remember would hope for the war to end, or that at least for their deaths to be remembered (Eisen 1988).

Most children were dragged from the ghettos with their families. There were specially organized raids on children, usually at night, to round them up for execution by firing squad or deportation to the extermination camps. The atrocities committed are well recorded. According to eyewitnesses, "At the Umschlagplatz [place where the victims were forced to assemble prior to deportation] terrible scenes were recorded. A child's eyes were gouged out by a German who desired to make two rings of them. The child's screaming pierced the laughter of the guard. A little boy asked his mother why Hitler hated him since he did not know him at all" (Levin 1993: 126).

"An infant's shrill cry pierced the air. The mother, seeing danger, covered the child with her shawl, desperately trying to quiet him. Instantly an impatient German grabbed the unruly bundle and dumped it in the nearest ditch. Then he forced the sobbing mother into a row of marchers and when she protested, he struck her with his rifle butt and threw her unconscious body into another ditch" (Gilbert 1985: 480). Children who were forced with their families into detention centers or assembly places were marched or driven to their places of death. This involved mass executions by firing squads (Einsatzgruppen) or gassing in the specially designed extermination camps.

The news about a prospective "Action" against children was devastating to the ghetto inhabitants. In desperation some parents succeeded in obtaining poison for their children, to ease the horror of death. Heart-wrenching descriptions of such merciful interventions can be found in the memoirs of a pediatrician in an orphanage of the Warsaw ghetto. As the S. S. was storming the building demanding delivery of the children, she quietly put them to sleep by giving each a vial of poison. She was not able to talk about that night for decades that followed (Szwajger-Blady).

When the German intent of killing each Jewish child became clearly evident, parents took desperate measures to find *hiding places* among Christians. Naturally, such arrangements required the utmost secrecy, for a death penalty awaited those who provided a safe place to a Jewish child. "Hiding" took a variety of forms: efforts to stay together as a family in a cellar or an attic (Frank 1971); a hayloft in a barn (Heller 1993); in specially built hideouts under floorboards, in a grave, even in sewers (Marks 1993). About 200,000 Jewish children were hidden at some point during the war (Dwork 1991).

At times, orphanages, convents, and monasteries would secretly take in Jewish children (Ruth-Hano 1988), often converting them or preparing them for careers in service of the Church (Friedlander 1979). Except for one or two people in the highest hierarchy, no one was told about the children's Jewish background. Living incognito as Christians, the children learned to lie about their family histories and deny their earlier religious practices. Even the very young ones internalized the parental warning that they must not complain or cry. Their lives depended on it (Heifetz 1989).

The children were in danger of betrayal by neighbors or staff members in the institutions (Malle 1974). This would lead to experiences of extreme suffering, and finally death. Naturally, boys were more at risk, inasmuch as circumcision, a religious ritual practiced only among Jews in Europe, was an immediate giveaway. At times, boys dressed as girls to avoid detection. Dark-haired teenagers of both sexes attempted to bleach their hair in order to appear more "Aryan" (Eisenberg 1981; Perel 1997).

Many children had to fend for themselves after the murder of their parents. Some suffered unbelievably as they wandered around the countryside, orphaned and abandoned, tormented by hunger and freezing weather. Occasionally, adolescents succeeded in escaping to the forests and joining the *partisan groups*. However, they were often mistreated and betrayed by the local peasants, and even by the partisans themselves.

Children Who Survived

The survival of an entire family was an oddity. Throughout the years of war, children who were old enough to remember dreamed of being reunited with their families. But when reunions actually took place, they were not always happy. The parents could seem like strangers, almost beyond recognition, and many children had already bonded with their "Hiding" parents (Greenfield 1993).

At the time of liberation, the very young did not know their real names, countries of origin, or native languages. Through efforts of international agencies, those whom no one claimed were adopted by families abroad. Unlike adult survivors who gravitated toward the same communities and kept in touch with each other, child survivors were scattered and did not know of each other. Characteristically, they wanted to lead ordinary, normal lives. In a way, they continued to live in "hiding" and for decades remained an invisible group in the larger population of Holocaust survivors.

Follow-up studies on these children are limited. Social agencies that were involved in their resettlement and placement arrangements rarely documented the children's subsequent experiences. A notable exception is a follow-up study by a psychologist (Moskowitz 1984) who interviewed 24 children, former residents of Liengfield House in Surrey, England. These children were brought to this halfway house immediately after the end of the war from the camps of Terezin and Auschwitz. Some remained there for years, undergoing physical and psychological rehabilitation, including sessions with Anna Freud and her colleagues at the Hampstead Clinic. Decades later, children treated at Liengfield House remembered this period of their lives with mixed emotions. Some suggested that being in therapy with others, as a group, would have been preferable to sessions alone.

Adults at the time of the follow-up interviews, living in countries scattered around the world, these child survivors seemed to have coped well with the demands of life in the decades following their stay in Liengfield House. Most had completed college, married, and had children; did not think about their early lives, and were determined to build a future for themselves and their families. They emphasized the healing power derived from having created their own families. Many have shown unusual flexibility and resilience in adjusting to changes in their environment (Moskowitz 1984).

Building new lives was facilitated by conscious and unconscious efforts to "bury" the past. In a follow-up study of a group of child survivors forty years after the Holocaust, Israeli researchers found that the defense of "psychic numbing" helped in functioning and adaptation (Mazor et al. 1990). An important, longitudinal, ongoing study conducted by Kestenberg (1995) established that many child survivors demonstrated amazing strength and resilience. Among them are successful scientists, artists, professionals, and business people. Memories or fragments of memories retrieved during these research-focused interviews were important to the child survivors in helping them feel connected to their early experiences. Several of the interviewees were chronically depressed. This was seen as a sign of incomplete mourning and unacknowledged anger, not a manifestation of clinical depression.

Many child survivors reached world wide prominence. Of two siblings, the youngest to survive the camps, the younger grew up to be the Chief Rabbi of Israel and the older became the Israeli Consel General in New York City. Eli Wiesel, another child survivor, is a Nobel prize winner. Trust in a good world could not be completely destroyed. Many child survivors wanted to live up to what they thought were the expectations of their murdered parents, and thus perpetuate their memory (*New York Times* 1997).

Many child survivors credit their "hiding parents" or their postwar adoptive parents for their present success and stability. In contrast, some say that memory of murdered parents who loved and nurtured them played the most significant role in their later development and adaptation. "These early experiences of empathy and trust left a lasting trace on character. The longer and more beneficial the pre-Holocaust period, the more strength children had to cope with the traumata" (Kestenberg 1985).

Despite their unique strength and achievements, child survivors commonly bear *vulnerabilities* and psychological problems, also a direct legacy of the Holocaust trauma. Evidence emerges from writings of psychotherapists and researchers, but primarily from the autobiographical material expressed at gatherings or recorded in memoirs or videotaped interviews.

One of the authors recalls her own war experiences as having a strong impact on her feelings of security and belief in parental omnipotence.

> After weeks on the run, living in bombed-out buildings and having belongings stolen, the police caught up with us. We were rounded up and brought into an open sports arena. We were surrounded by police. Behind them and around was a large group of local police [Po, France]. They stared at us in silence, with hostile, closed faces. They were not faces of villains. As a child I could not understand why ordinary looking people could be so full of hate.
>
> We were sent to Gurs, a transit concentration camp. It was a desolate, muddy place, riddled with disease. Twenty thousand people had lived there under inhuman conditions. I remember barracks with forty people in a room. I remember separation from my father who was interned in another part of the camp. My recollections are hazy; like other child survivors, I now wish I could remember more. (Sternberg 1997)

Child survivors often claim that a sense of sadness has never left them. Despite overwhelming historical evidence of parents' total helplessness to protect their children, many still express deep feelings of hurt and anger at what they experienced as a parental rejection and abandonment (Marks 1993).

"Conflicts over religious identity and loyalty are reported since many owe their lives to Christian families who rescued them from the fires of the Holocaust. As their own children now leave for separate lives, the painful memories come back about the 'goodbyes' they themselves never said" (Rosenbloom 1995: 6). It should be noted that child survivors have particularly strong bonds with their own children, and separation evokes powerful emotional reactions. A struggle to fill gaps in memory has recently become a strong dynamic force among many who were children during the Holocaust. They search for *any* information about the past with much rigor.

Robert Krell, child survivor and a professor of psychiatry at the University of British Columbia asks himself how it is possible that after a lifetime of raising families, achieving success in business and professions, child survivors still suffer from what happened "then." "We were so little, and it was so long ago."

Children born during or soon after the war have only fragments of memory. These fragments are traumatic but may also serve as a healing function. Adult survivors who endured unspeakable atrocities consider these children to be lucky since they had little memory of what happened. Krell goes on to say that much psychological evidence points to the contrary.

> Since a child's foundation for adulthood is predicated on developing feelings of security and trust—based on parental love, the provision of shelter, nourishment and a predictable life—all of which unfolds in the first two to three years, a dramatic disruption is devastating and long-lasting. If the trauma lasts for several years, as it did for so many, and then does not abate because of new traumas endured in the immediate post-war years, the structures required for an integrated, mature personality are shaken to the core. Even the pre-verbal memories of a vulnerable existence are engraved along with those recollections that reappear readily. They require only a sound, a smell, a touch.

He hypothesizes about the source of their strength.

> Perhaps we simply bypassed our traumatic beginnings for these many years with immersion in work, intense commitments to family and friends, busying ourselves with travels and adventures in order to contain the secret, mysterious core of shame and rage. Why shame? In response to a child's feeling that something is wrong with oneself to be treated so badly. Why rage? In response to the unfathomable experience of persecution so intense that there is no other response but to be enraged.

Krell indicates he functions well, he has a career and a loving family. Yet at one point when he was trying to tell his story in a logical manner, he was only able to weep for two hours. He wonders whether the buried feelings will ever reappear. He is sure they will.

> For as we age and reflect nostalgically on our past, unlike those whose past was normal in the sense of a good beginning, our recollections take us straight back into the nightmare that was life then. It is better to face it—and not in the presence of strangers, in the presence of us.
>   Is the situation hopeless? Far from it. Considering the fragile underpinning of our existence, what a miracle to have come this far. Should any of us have made it? Perhaps not. The usual prognosis for children entirely deprived of childhood is not promising. We have defied even the conventions of modern developmental psychology.

He cites other examples; one of a "hard nosed" professional who flaunted his achievement and did not feel in need of help. Yet, when somebody asked him to tell about his survival he started to tell and could only cry. This was the first time in fifty-two years that he cried.

Psychotherapeutic Interventions

Psychotherapy with this population must integrate the themes of separation and mourning over a lost childhood, and the search for knowledge about the past. It is important to focus on evidence of mastery and coping throughout these patients' unusually complicated lives. Enhancing self-esteem and assertiveness and combating the fear of "making waves" is another therapeutic objective.

As the last surviving witnesses to the Holocaust, many evidence a strong wish to bear witness. This should be supported and facilitated. The act of giving testimony helps link fragments of memory and put life events in chronological order. This may give some cohesiveness to a complicated life history and thus serve an ego-strengthening function.

Countertransference issues must be considered. For a long time, there has been a conspiracy of "silence" between the therapist and survivor-patient. Therapists tried to avoid their own anxieties, even shame or guilt, stirred up by listening to patients' stories of Holocaust horrors. Thus, the therapist often had difficulty conveying empathy and tended to minimize the impact of the childhood experiences on the patients' adult lives. Limitation of conceptual knowledge about victims and survivors contributed to the problem.

For all survivors who have lived through the extremes of human experience, limitations of psychotherapeutic intervention must be considered. In the words of a child survivor, now a psychiatrist, "Hard as we may try, the story remains only partially told. The closure will take many years if ever to come" (Rotenberg 1985). There is indication that membership in a group with others of similar background is of emotional benefit. In meetings and gatherings, survivors have an opportunity for collective memory and focus on issues relevant to their histories. They experience freedom to share a deeper understanding of their earlier trauma, and a sense of an extended family (Fogelman 1993). For those who wish and need therapeutic intervention, the group method may offer a uniquely meaningful experience.

The problem of "traumatic memory" has received much attention in the post-Vietnam era, and new philosophies and treatment approaches have emerged. One recent theory postulates that the early memories of childhood trauma are lodged in the primitive cells of the amygdala, and may permanently change the pathways in the brain (Le Doux 1996). A psychologist-researcher at Mt. Sinai Hospital in New York City claims that there is a biological, cortisol-related dimension to the transmission of the Holocaust trauma from survivors to the second generation (Yemuda 1995).

Engagement in Holocaust-related activities and the current intentional efforts to "remember" offers an opportunity to mourn at this difficult stage of life, when separation from children can reactivate the earlier pain of survivors' separation from their own parents.

The older survivor derives important meaning from remembering the dead. Poignant manifestations of this can be found in the ever-increasing number of memoirs about survivors and their families' fate during the Holocaust and their lives before the trauma. These paper monuments represent an effort to rescue the victims from oblivion, from melting into the amorphous six million. Creating such a monument may also represent in a symbolic way the rituals of mourning, replacing the graves, headstones, and burial places that were denied the Holocaust victims (Rosenbloom 1994). For those survivors who were children in the Holocaust, "remembrance" may meet a more basic need: to know their roots, to feel a sense of belonging and identity.

It is evident that survivors have developed a range of responses for coping with their traumatic past. The "self-healing" approaches discussed in this paper need to be understood, accepted, and integrated into our clinical framework for working with these and other victims of major disasters and catastrophes. Students in the Holocaust course at the Hunter College School of Social Work have successfully applied selected aspects of this knowledge to their work with others: victims of war, uprooting, terrorism and AIDS. It is evident that lessons derived from studies of survivors are applicable to a broad spectrum of other victims of severe childhood traumas.

References

Abramowicz, Myriam & Ofenberg, Esther. 1982. *As I f It Were Yesterday* Film, Belgium.
Auerbacher, Inge. 1986. *I am a Star—Child of the Holocaust*. New York: Simon & Schuster.
Dwork, Deborah. 1991. *Children with a Star*. New Haven: Yale University Press.
Eisen, George. 1988. *Coping with Adversity—Children and Play in the Holocaust*. Amherst: The University of Mass. Press.
Eisenberg, A. 1982. *The Last Generation*. New York: Pilgrim Press.

Fogelman, Eva. 1993. "The Psychology Behind Being a Hidden Child" in Jane Marks, *The Hidden Children: The Secret Survivors of the Holocaust* New York: Ballantine Books.

Frank, Anne. 1971. *The Diary of a Young Girl.* New York: Pocket Books.

Friedlander, Saul. 1979. *When Memory Comes.* New York: Farrar, Straus and Giroux.

Gilbert, Martin. 1985. *The Holocaust.* New York: Holt, Rinehart and Winston.

Greenfield, Howard. 1993. *The Hidden Children.* New York: Ticknor and Fields.

Heifetz, Julie. 1989. *Too Young to Remember.* Detroit: Wayne State University Press.

Heller Gottesfeld, Fanya. 1993. *Strange and Unexpected Love.* Hoboken, N.J.: KTAV.

Kestenberg, Judith. 1985. "Child Survivors of the Holocaust—40 Years Later." *Journal of the American Academy of Child Psychiatry* 24:408–409.

Krell, Robert. (1985). "Child Survivors of the Holocaust—40 Years Later." *Journal of the American Academy of Child Psychiatry* 24:378–380.

Le Doux, Joseph. 1996. *The Emotional Brain.* New York: Simon and Schuster.

Levin, Norma. 1993. *The Destruction of European Jewry.* New York: Schocken Books.

Malle, Louis. 1986. *Au Revoir Les Enfants* Film, Medium Belgium.

Marks, Jane. 1993. *The Hidden Children-Secret Holocaust Survivors.* New York: Fawcett.

Mazor, A.; Gampel, Y.; Enright, R. D., & Orenstein, R. 1990. "Holocaust Survivors: Coping With Post-Traumatic Memories in Childhood and 40 Years Later." *Journal of Traumatic Stress* 1(3):11.

Maxwell, Elizabeth. 1993. "Butterflies Don't Live Here in the Ghetto." *The British Journal of Holocaust Education* 2(1):2.

Moskowitz, Sarah. 1984. *Love Despite Hate: Child Survivors of the Holocaust.* New York: Schocken.

Perel, Solomon. 1997. *Europa-Europa.* New York: John Wiley and Sons.

Rosenbloom, Maria. 1995. Personal recollection.

Rosenbloom Hirsch, Maria. 1995. *What Can We Learn from the Holocaust?* Occasional Papers in Jewish History and Thought, No. 3, The Hunter College Jewish Social Studies Program. New York: Hunter College of the City of New York.

Roth-Hano, Renee. 1988. *Touch Wood—A Girlhood in Occupied France.* New York: Macmillan.

Rotenberg, Larry. 1985. "A Child Survivor Psychiatrist's Personal Adaptation." *Journal of the American Academy of Child Psychiatry* 24(4):385–389.

Sternberg, Malka. 1997. Personal recollections.

Szwajger-Blady, Adina. 1990. *I Remember Nothing More.* New York: Pantheon Books.

Whiteman, Dorit Bader. 1993. *The Uprooted: A Hitler Legacy.* New York: Insight Books.

Yehuda, Rachel, Kahana-Boar, Southurck, Steven M., Gillin-Earl L. 1994. Depressive features in Holocaust Survivors with Post-traumatic Stress disorders. *Journal of Traumatic Stress* 17(4):699–704.

20

■ Our well-being is intimately related to the health of our bodies. Poor health undermines our ability to think efficiently and relate positively with others. Children's health is important because good health and nutrition will help them master their developmental challenges, such as succeeding in school (Sigman, 1995). It is also important because poor health habits in childhood can lead to problems in adulthood (Boodman, 1995). Children's access to adequate nutrition and health care, as well as their exposure to factors that place them at risk, depends on many factors at several levels of their environments. Some examples include: risks in their immediate environment such as guns or lead paint, availability in the community of mass transportation to health care providers, and presence or absence of a nationalized system of health care insurance. In this article, the authors provide the example of how geographic setting, specifically rural environment, creates particular vulnerabilities for children's health.

Overview Questions

1. Approximately what percentage of U.S. children lives in rural areas? How do they generally compare to urban children in terms of ethnicity, family structure, and socioeconomic status? Name and give examples of the primary focus of children's health care.

2. When you read about rural children's lack of health insurance, dental problems, failure to complete immunization series, lack of care by pediatricians, and vulnerability to fatal accidents, what specific aspects of living in a rural environment do the authors suggest are probably responsible for these outcomes? Certainly some of these problems are due to poverty, but what special problems arise for poor people who live in rural areas?

3. What are the recent trends in HIV-infection and substance abuse for rural versus urban children and adolescents? What do you think may be responsible for these trends?

Focus Questions

1. What risks arise for rural children due to non-public water and sewage systems?

2. Compared to urban children, how likely are rural children to lack health insurance? How likely are they to belong to an HMO? What health care provider is a rural child unlikely to see? How do they compare to urban children in terms of having a regular source of care? Is this a private practitioner—why or why not? How does this relate to rural children's immunization rates?

3. What is the primary focus of children's health care—give examples. According to the most recent available data, how do urban versus rural children compare in terms of completing their immunization series? In what specific aspect of health care were they most likely to have unmet medical need (see Table 20.4)?

4. Are rural children over- or underrepresented in child mortality, compared to their proportion of the general population? Rural children and adolescents are more likely than their urban counterparts to die of what causes?

5. What trends from 1990–1995 did AIDS rates show among urban and rural children?

6. How do urban versus rural areas overall compare in crime rate? Among youths, how do rural versus urban areas compare? With what exception? Did these statistics surprise you?

7. Did the rural versus urban drug use gap show an increase or a decrease in the 1990s? Which substance are rural children more likely to use than urban children?

Rural Children's Health

Sarah J. Clark, Lucy A. Savitz, and Randy K. Randolph

We profile rural children's health in the 1990s, using recent national data, rather than single-area or -state studies. Our intent is to describe the current situation, suggest recent trends, and inform policy decisions concerning child and adolescent health in rural America. The analyses of rural child health used for this article are shown in the first box.

Demographics

As of 1996, 16 million children (<21 years) resided in nonmetropolitan areas, a significant decrease from the 1984–1985 estimate of 21 million.[1] Rural children account for 21% of all US children and represent 31% of the total nonmetropolitan population.

Rural children continue to reside predominantly in the South and Midwest. In contrast, the Northeast and West comprise small rural populations, and their proportions have decreased considerably over the past decade.

Demographic Differences Between Rural and Urban Populations

Rural and urban populations differ in several important demographic aspects (see box 20.2).

Socioeconomic Status

Rural families are, on the whole, poorer than urban families. Overall, 23.2% of rural children younger than 18 years live in poverty, compared with 21.0% of urban children. This difference is consistent across all categories of age, sex, and family status (table 20.1).

Housing Characteristics and Health

Several housing characteristics relate to health issues in the daily lives of children (table 20.2). Rural families are less likely to obtain water for residential use from a public system or private company and more likely to obtain their water from a well

BOX 20.1 • *The Data Sets Used in Framing This Article*

- National Health Interview Survey US Census
- National Survey of Family Growth
- Area Resource File
- National Crime Survey
- American Hospital Association's annual survey of hospitals
- Unpublished data provided by the Centers for Disease Control and Prevention and the National Center for Health Statistics

BOX 20.2 • *Demographic Differences between Children in Rural and Urban Populations*

- A greater proportion of rural children are white
- Whereas black children and children of Asian and Hispanic descent constitute a greater proportion of the urban child population, the rural population includes a larger proportion of Native American children
- Rural children are more likely to reside in larger families with married parents, whereas a greater proportion of urban children live in families headed by a single mother
- Rural preschool-aged children are more likely to have both or their only parent working

or another source. This may place rural children at a disadvantage in the need for fluoride supplementation, the availability of safe water for mixing infant formula, and the potential for bacterial contamination of drinking water. Rural families are also significantly more likely to use a septic tank or other sewage source, rather than a public system, and to have incomplete plumbing facilities; again, this may have a direct effect on health related to the transmission of bacteria and waterborne diseases.

Health Insurance

Insurance status is a strong predictor of the adequacy of children's health care. Uninsured children experience problems with access to medical care, delays in necessary treatment, and inadequate immunization.[2–4] Being uninsured is more prevalent among rural (15%) than urban (13.6%) children. Urban children were somewhat more likely than rural children to have private insurance coverage (65% vs 63%). Of those privately insured, a greater proportion of rural than urban children were covered by a self-purchased policy, whereas more urban children were covered under an employer-sponsored group plan. The proportion of Medicaid-enrolled children was roughly equal, even though a higher proportion of rural children live in poverty.

In the past 2 decades, the most prominent change in the area of health insurance has been the dramatic increase in managed care organizations. Although more than 80% of rural counties are presently included in the service area of at least 1 commercial health maintenance organization, actual enrollment rates are low.[5]

TABLE 20.1 *Percentage of Children Younger Than 18 Years Living in Poverty, 1996*

Category	Children, %	
	Metropolitan	Nonmetropolitan
Age, yr		
<1	23.8	29.7
1 to 5	24.1	27.3
6 to 17	19.4	21.2
Sex		
Male	20.5	23.1
Female	21.5	23.4
Family status		
Married parents	9.5	12.2
Single, female-headed	49.1	52.7
Single, male-headed	30.2	33.9

Source: 1996 Current Population Survey.

TABLE 20.2 *Health-Related Characteristics of Family Dwellings, 1990*

Variable	Distribution, %		Population, no. × 10³	
	Metropolitan	Nonmetroplitan	Metropolitan	Nonmetroplitan
Water source				
Public or private	89.5	64.4	72,076	13,993
Drilled well	9.0	28.6	7,244	6,224
Dug well	1.0	3.9	813	852
Other	0.5	3.1	387	676
Sewage source				
Public system	81.8	48.6	65,891	10,564
Septic tank or cesspool	17.5	48.5	14,121	10,550
Other	0.6	2.9	506	631
Plumbing				
Complete	99.5	98.5	57,766	13,174
Incomplete	0.5	1.5	317	205

Source: US Census of Population and Housing, Standard Tape File 3C, 1990.

Availability of Health Care Providers and Services

The presence of primary care providers in a community is an important marker of availability of health care for children. Trends in the supply of primary care providers have been discussed previously in this journal.[6]

Family physicians and general practitioners continue to provide care for many rural children; more than 20% of these physicians practice in rural areas, whereas pediatricians are predominantly concentrated in metropolitan areas. This likely creates a reliance on family physicians and general practitioners, as well as midlevel providers—physician assistants and licensed nurse practitioners—-for pediatric care of rural children.

Hospital-based services for children and adolescents are considered specialty services and as such are less available in rural than in urban areas (table 20.3). However, an encouraging trend is that half of all rural hospitals are providing inpatient surgical services for general pediatric cases. Increases in outpatient child wellness and teen outreach services in both rural and urban areas are an important expansion of health care delivery offered in hospital-based settings.

Children's Health Status and Source of Care

Differences in child health status or health outcomes are difficult to detect using the measures of function typically used with adults. Furthermore, the primary focus of children's health care is prevention: immunization, growth monitoring, vision and hearing screening, blood lead levels screening, developmental assessment, and counseling for parents. These components of preventive care usually are provided during well-child visits, recommended at scheduled intervals during the first years of a child's life.[7]

Immunization rates

Because many aspects of preventive care are not recorded in the medical record or collected in national or state data sets, immunization rates have historically served as a proxy for the overall delivery of children's well-child care. Data from the Centers for Disease Control and Prevention (CDC) from 1994 for the primary immunization series showed that 66% of rural children received appropriate vaccinations compared with 71% of suburban children and 62% of urban children.[8] National immunization rates for the primary series have risen considerably in the past 5 years, but recent data published by the CDC have not included national rural-urban trends. The ability to

TABLE 20.3 *Percentage of Hospitals Providing Child and Adolescent Services, 1995*

	Hospitals, %	
Services	*Metropolitan*	*Nonmetroplitan*
Inpatient		
Pediatric general medical surgery	63	50
Pediatric intensive care	23	6
Child and adolescent psychiatry	45	18
Outpatient services		
Child wellness	24	11
Teen outreach	22	7

Source: Annual survey of Hospitals, American Hospital Association, 1995.

analyze trends in rural areas is limited. Furthermore, computerized immunization registry systems that can generate small-area immunization rates (and enable providers to determine which children are behind schedule on immunization) are being developed almost exclusively in urban areas.

Risk of Unmet Medical Need

Another indicator of the adequacy of children's health care pertains to the ability to obtain needed medical care. Rural children are at increased risk of unmet medical need (table 20.4).[9] Overall, rural children were more likely to need but not receive dental care and were more likely to delay care because of cost.

Regular Source of Care

Having a regular source of medical care—often referred to as a "medical home"—enhances the likelihood that children receive recommended well-child care and appropriate follow-up for acute and chronic conditions.[9] In 1993, 6% of US children (4.2 million) had no regular source of care. Overall, poor and black and Hispanic children were at increased risk of having no source of care. Most insured children have a regular source of medical care, but fewer uninsured children have a regular source of care. However, rural children are as likely as urban children to have a regular source of care. In fact, among children who are uninsured or enrolled in Medicaid, rural children are more likely than urban and suburban children to have a regular source of care. Nationally, the most common reasons for having no source of care were not being able to afford care (34%), not needing a physician (31%), and care being unavailable or not convenient (17%).[9]

Medical Care Setting

Rural children, particularly those who are uninsured or enrolled in Medicaid, are substantially more likely than urban children to name a private practitioner as their

TABLE 20.4   *Percentage of Children Aged 0 to 17 Years with Unmet Medical Needs, 1993*

	Children, %		
Unmet need	*Metropolitan central city*	*Metropolitan noncentral city*	*Nonmetroplitan*
Any	10.3	9.8	13.4
Not able to get care	2.2	1.8	1.8
Care delayed due to cost	3.8	3.7	5.4
Needed dental care	6.1	5.3	8.4
Needed prescription	1.5	1.3	1.2
Needed glasses	1.4	1.2	1.6
Needed mental health care	0.4	0.5	0.3

From National Center for Health Statistics.[9]

regular source of care. Margolis and associates found that rural physicians are more likely to accept patients of varying insurance status,[10] possibly because they must retain a high proportion of the available patient pool to remain financially viable, whereas urban physicians "self-select" their patient population by limiting the number of Medicaid-covered or uninsured children.

Although rural physicians are more likely to accept a broad patient base, they are less likely to offer immunizations.[11] Those who provide immunization services are more likely to refer uninsured and Medicaid-enrolled children to a health department for immunizations.[12] Such referrals may be attributed to the high cost of vaccines, or rural physicians may not see enough children to warrant offering costly immunization services.[13, 14]

Generally, any disruption of the medical home is thought to create additional barriers to care related to increased waiting time, problems with transportation, and parental loss of work. However, in an analysis of public health department immunization data from 11 states, health departments in rural areas were highly effective in providing timely immunizations, often more so than urban health departments and private practitioners.[15]

In addition, the federal Vaccines For Children program and several state programs aim specifically to reduce the referral of children for immunizations only by decreasing patient charges for vaccines. Some evidence indicates that such programs are effective for this purpose.[11, 16, 17]

Death and Injury among Children

Mortality rates among children older than 1 year reflect both the quality of children's health care and societal problems such as violence and substance abuse. In 1992, more than 84,000 children younger than 25 years died. Twenty-three percent of deaths were among rural children.

For children older than 1 year, mortality is associated primarily with injury: motor vehicle crashes, firearm injuries, drowning, burning, suffocation, and poisoning. Morality data is from the National Vital Statistics System[18] are shown in box 20.3.

BOX 20.3 • *Important Rural-Urban Differences in Child Mortality*

- In 1992, the incidence of fatal injuries was 44% higher among rural children aged 1 to 19 years than among their urban counterparts
- Among children aged 1 to 14 years, death rates for all races were at least 20% higher in rural than urban areas
- For children aged 15 to 19 years, mortality among urban black children was 50% higher than that among rural black children; for all other ethnicities, mortality rates were higher in rural areas
- Homicide rates were 4 times higher among urban male adolescents aged 15 to 19 years, but suicide rates were higher among rural male adolescents of the same age group
- In all age groups, mortality from motor vehicle crashes is higher in rural areas, reflecting the increased travel time and distance required of rural populations
- During 1985 to 1992, rural injury mortality rates remained consistently higher than urban rates, with 1 exception: the mortality rate for rural and urban male adolescents aged 15 to 19 years is equal[18]

Human Immunodeficiency Virus Infection And/Or AIDS

Through June 1997, a cumulative total of 612,078 cases of the acquired immunodeficiency syndrome (AIDS) were reported in the United States: nearly 1% of these cases were in children younger than 13 years.[19] Between 1990 and 1995, the incidence of AIDS in children decreased 19% despite an increase of 30% in the overall incidence of the disease nationwide. Furthermore, although the incidence of AIDS in children declined 24% in urban areas, in rural areas it increased 5%.[19]

Crime and Violence

Detailed data on victims of criminal activity are collected through the National Crime Survey.[20] In the past 20 years, victimization of rural residents to violent crime has increased, but crimes of theft and household crimes have decreased. Overall victimization rates are lowest in rural areas and highest in urban areas. However, in all areas, rates are substantially increased among youths aged 12 to 19 years. In each of the 3 criminal categories, the victimization rate for rural youths is higher than that for the overall urban population. Furthermore, the urban-rural rate ratio is 1.9 for all categories of the total population; among youths, that gap narrows, with a rate ratio of 1.4 for crimes of theft and 1.2 for household crimes.

In 1989, a special supplement to the National Crime Survey contained questions on youths' victimization experiences at school, their opinions about crime, the availability of drugs, and the awareness of gangs (table 20.5).[21] Only a narrow difference existed in crime experiences among students in rural versus urban locations—a stark contrast to the larger rural-urban differences found in the regular National Crime Survey data.

TABLE 20.5   *Percentage Reporting Various Criminal Activity in the School Setting, 1989*

	Children, %		
Unmet need	*Metropolitan central city*	*Metropolitan noncentral city*	*Nonmetropolitan*
Being a victim of property crime	8	7	7
Being a victim of violent crime	2	2	2
Drugs available at school	66	67	71
Have attended drug education classes	40	35	44
Gangs active in school	25	14	8
Avoid certain places at school	8	5	6
Fear being attacked at school	24	20	20
Fear being attacked going to or from school	19	12	13

From Bureau of Justice Statistics, Office of Justice Programs, Washington, DC.[21]

Gang activity in school was cited 3 times more frequently by urban than rural youths. However, a substantial number of rural students exhibited fear about violence at school. These results indicate that rural youth are experiencing crime at a level and in ways similar to youth from the cities and suburbs.

Substance Abuse

Criminal activity is often linked to drug use, particularly among children. A 1992–1993 survey of rural and urban 8th and 12th graders showed that rural-urban differences in drug use have decreased nationwide. More rural students reported that drugs were readily available at their school, and rural students were more likely to have attended drug education classes. Of the overall trends demonstrated, most surprising was that inhalant use was more common than marijuana use among 8th graders. It appears that during the 1990s, inhalants, which are inexpensive and easily accessible, have replaced marijuana as the "gateway drug."[22] For all other drugs, lifetime prevalence among 12th graders was higher than for 8th graders. With respect to rural-urban differences, urban youths are more likely to have used marijuana, cocaine, and LSD whereas rural youths are more likely to have used smokeless tobacco. The use of alcohol and cigarettes is high in both groups.

Summary Points

- Rural children account for 21% of all US children and represent 31% of the total nonmetropolitan population
- Rural children are more likely than urban children to be uninsured, putting them more at risk of poor access to medical care, delays in necessary treatment, and inadequate immunization
- Trends in many aspects of children's health status cannot be determined, largely because of inadequacies of available data
- Despite these inadequacies, the health of rural children appears to be deteriorating with regard to crime, substance abuse, and infection with the human immunodeficiency virus or AIDS
- Fatal injuries continue to affect a disproportionate number of rural children

Conclusion

Rural areas appear to be experiencing an increase in the availability of health care services and health care providers. A provision in the 1997 Balanced Budget Act that allocated funds to states to offer coverage to uninsured children holds great potential. However, because eligibility and implementation will vary from state to state, the effects of this policy for rural children remain unclear.

References

1. McManus MA, Newacheck PW. Rural maternal, child, and adolescent health. *Health Serv Res* 1989;23:807–848.

2. Holl JL, Szilagyi PG, Rodewald LE, Byrd RS, Weitzman ML. Profile of uninsured children in the United States. *Arch Pediatr Adolesc Med* 1995;149:398–406 [published erratum appears in *Arch Pediatr Adolesc Med* 1995;149:763].

3. Newacheck PW, Hughes DC, Stoddard JJ. Children's access to primary care: differences by race, income, and insurance status. *Pediatrics* 1996;97:26–32.

4. Himmelstein DU, Woolhandler S. Care denied: US residents who are unable to obtain needed medical services. *Am J Public Health* 1995;85:341–344.

5. University of Minnesota Rural Health Research Center. *Rural Managed Care: Patterns & Prospects.* Minneapolis: University of Minnesota; April 1997.

6. Rosenblatt RA, Hart LG. Physicians and rural America. *West J Med* 2000;173:348–351.

7. American Academy of Pediatrics Committee on Psychosocial Aspects of Child and Family Health. *Guidelines for Health Supervision II.* Elk Grove Village, IL: American Academy of Pediatrics; 1988.

8. Centers for Disease Control and Prevention. Vaccination coverage of 2-year-old children-United States, 1993. *MMWR Morb Mortal Wkly Rep* 1994;43:705–709.

9. National Center for Health Statistics. *Vital Statistics of the United States, 1993: Access to Health Care Part 1: Children.* Hyattsville, MD: National Center for Health Statistics; 1997.

10. Margolis PA, Cook RL, Earp JA, Lannon CM, Keyes LL, Klein JD. Factors associated with pediatricians' participation in Medicaid in North Carolina. *JAMA* 1992;267:1942–1946.

11. Hueston WJ, Mainous AG III, Farrell JB. Childhood immunization availability in primary care practices: effects of programs providing free vaccines to physicians. *Arch Fam Med* 1994;3:605–609.

12. Ruch-Ross HS, O'Connor KG. Immunization referral practices of pediatricians in the United States. *Pediatrics* 1994;94(pt 1):508–513.

13. Bordley WC, Freed GL, Garrett JM, Byrd CA, Meriwether R. Factors responsible for immunization referrals to health departments in North Carolina. *Pediatrics* 1994;94 (pt 1):376–380.

14. Szilagyi PA, Rodewald LE, Humiston SG, et al. Immunization practices of pediatricians and family physicians in the United States. *Pediatrics* 1994;94(pt 1):517–523.

15. Slifkin RT, Clark SJ, Strandhoy SE, Konrad TR. Public-sector immunization coverage in 11 states: the status of rural areas. *J Rural Health* 1997;13:334–341.

16. Freed GL, Clark SJ, Pathman DE, Konrad TR, Biddle AK, Schectman RM. Impact of a new universal purchase vaccine program in North Carolina. *Arch Pediatr Adolesc Med* 1997;151:1117–1124.

17. Zimmerman RK, Medsger AR, Ricci EM, Raymund M, Mieczkowski TA, Grufferman S. Impact of free vaccine and insurance status on physician referral of children to public vaccine clinics. *JAMA* 1997;278:996–1000.

18. Fingerhut LA, Gunderson P. Rural children and injury: lessons from the data. Presented at: Child and Adolescent Rural Injury Control, Madison, WI, March 1995.

19. Centers for Disease Control and Prevention. HIV/AIDS Surveillance report. *Morb Mortal Wkly Rep CDC Surveill Summ* 1997;9:3–37.

20. Donnermeyer JF. Crime and violence in rural communities. In: Blaser SM, Blaser J, Pantoja K, eds. *Perspectives on Violence and Substance Use in Rural America.* Oak Brook, IL: North Central Regional Educational Laboratory, Midwest Regional Center for Drug-Free Schools and Communities; 1995.

21. Bastian LD, Taylor BM. *School Crime: A National Crime Victimization Survey Report.* Washington, DC: Office of Justice Programs, Bureau of Justice Statistics; 1991. NCJ-131645.

22. Edwards RW. Drug use among 8th grade students is increasing. *Int J Addict* 1993; 28:1621–1623.

21

A fundamental cognitive process is that of seeking regularities in our experience and classifying objects and events into categories of similar things. Conceptual development involves changes with age in the types of categories that we form and how these are organized and used in thinking. In recent years, psychologists have been fascinated with children's understanding of living things. They have been asking questions such as, "Do children classify both plants and animals as living things?" (Carey, 1985), "Do children infer that a new kind of bird will have properties like other birds, even if it resembles a bat?" (Gelman & Markman, 1986), "Do children believe that you can make a raccoon into a skunk by changing its fur color?" (Keil, 1989). Many researchers believe that children's answers to questions like these depend on theories that children are forming about the biological world, such as how properties are transmitted from parents to offspring (e.g., Wellman & Gelman, 1992). In this article, Coley argues that we cannot really answer questions about the nature and course of conceptual development by only studying one age group or one culture. His argument underscores the major themes of this book, that development must be understood in terms of the transactions between children and their social and physical environments; and that it is only by comparing differences among people that we come to understand fundamental developmental processes.

Overview Questions

1. What are the three major types of comparative research that Coley argues are needed for an understanding of the range and complexity of human conceptual development?

2. Be able to distinguish the two major views about the development of folkbiology: radical conceptual change versus knowledge enrichment. List three predictions made by the radical conceptual change theory, and provide examples of what research shows that children know in each of these areas. Why does Coley say that in order to really resolve this issue, research is needed with adults?

3. What is the diversity (similarity/coverage) principle in reasoning about categories? This principle was derived in studies of what group? What kinds of alternatives are used by other adults? What does this mean about the endstate of development?

4. What does Carey mean by an "anthropocentric" pattern of reasoning about living things? What are two reasons, Coley believes, to question the generality of this reasoning pattern? How do the results from the Menominee children support Coley's argument?

On the Importance of Comparative Research: The Case of Folkbiology

John D. Coley

Introduction

Over the last decade and a half, a central theme in research on conceptual development has been the idea that children acquire informal folk theories that allow them to explain and predict phenomena in important domains of experience (e.g., Carey, 1985; Gopnik & Wellman, 1994; Keil, 1989; Wellman & Gelman, 1992; Wellman & Inagaki, 1997). In this essay I argue that comparative research is essential for a full understanding of human conceptual development, especially in theory-rich domains. Careful comparative work is needed in at least three areas. First, more research is needed on the adult models and theories that children are presumably in the process of acquiring. To characterize the process of conceptual development, we need to understand the adult model, the modal "endstate" of development in a given society. We must be especially careful not to assume that adult cognition is necessarily normative or "correct." For example, adult judgment and decision making is rife with biases and heuristics (e.g, Tversky & Kahneman, 1974). An account of the development of decision making must have as its endpoint this adult system; an account taking optimal decision making as its endpoint would be misguided. In general, an accurate characterization of conceptual development is not possible without careful consideration of adult models.

Second, we need comparative studies of adult models and theories in different populations. Clearly there is no single ideal developmental endpoint; without some sense of the variability in possible endstates of development, we cannot hope to accurately understand the process. For example, if adults in different societies have very different explanatory theories in a domain, developmental accounts would need to explain the source of this variability. In contrast, cross-cultural consensus might call for a very different developmental account. The truth, of course, is most likely "in the gray"; comparative research is likely to reveal both cognitive universals and cultural particulars. The specifics of these emergent patterns would then serve as a target for developmentalists to explain.

Finally, we need comparative studies of development in different populations of children. By now the rationale should be obvious: we cannot presume to understand processes of conceptual development generally when the issues have been studied almost exclusively among children in middle- to upper-class relatively urban settings. Such a truncated sample leaves us with almost no idea whether we are studying universal or particular patterns of development. Comparative work carries the promise of addressing this question. If a particular developmental pattern is observed in several different populations, it becomes a candidate for a universal. If different patterns emerge, then the search is on for correlates and causes of that pattern. Either way, the results have informed developmental research.

Comparative research along these three lines is necessary to present a more complete picture of the process of human conceptual development. I will use research in the domain of folkbiology to illustrate my point here, but the point applies to other domains as well. First, I review the current debate on the nature of conceptual development in folkbiology, and argue that the resolution of this debate awaits the specification of the adult model. Next, I briefly review comparative work on folkbiological thought in adults that suggests divergent adult endstates and I consider the developmental implications of that work. Finally, I argue for the importance of comparative work with children, and present some preliminary findings indicating the value and potential informativeness of such research.

Acquisition of Folkbiology: What Is the Endpoint?

The study of children's developing conceptions of living things has been an extremely fertile area of research in the last 15 years for at least two reasons. First, folkbiology is an intrinsically interesting domain of human experience; the natural world of plants and animals is pervasive and salient in our present and in our past, both historic and prehistoric. Second, folkbiology provides a test case for more general ideas about how conceptual development takes place. In this section I argue that although this line of research has provided important insights into the nature of preschool thought, it hasn't necessarily taught us much about the process of conceptual development because there is a dearth of research on the adult endstate. To make this argument, I briefly consider the debate on the acquisition of folkbiology. This is not intended as an exhaustive review, but rather to give a sense of the debate and ultimately to underscore the point that resolution of the debate requires an understanding of the adult model.

Two competing views about the nature of conceptual change in the domain of folkbiology have been put forward. The first is the idea of *radical conceptual change*. In this view, children's conceptions of living things undergo radical revision during the early school years, to the extent that preschoolers' understanding of basic biological concepts such as life, death, and living things are incommensurate with those of adults, they belong to a completely different conceptual framework. An alternative view, *knowledge enrichment,* argues that the basic distinctions made by adults are in place early. In this view, children conceive of living things in essentially the same way that adults do, although much elaboration of these conceptions takes place during development.

The resolution of this debate has ramifications for how we characterize the process of conceptual development, in the domain of folkbiology and perhaps more generally. The radical conceptual change view portrays the preschooler's conceptual system as discontinuous with that of the adult, posits the overthrow of one system by another, and requires the specification of mechanisms by which conceptual reorganization takes place. In contrast, the gradual conceptual change view portrays the child's conceptual system as continuous with the adult's, posits the gradual elaboration of a single system, and thus requires no mechanism or trigger for radical reorganization.

The beginning of concerted developmental interest in the nature of children's folkbiology was Susan Carey's 1985 book, *Conceptual Change in Childhood.* Therein she argued that children's conceptions of living things undergo radical reorganization during the first decade, and that an intuitive biology emerges from an intuitive psychology. Although this view has been amended more recently (Carey, 1995, 1999), the central tenet—that children organize knowledge of plants and animals in a way that is incommensurate with that of adults—remains unchanged.

This radical theory change view has a number of implications for how "prebiological" children (i.e., children younger than 10 who have yet to construct an autonomous folkbiology) should see the world. First, if their conceptions of living things are essentially psychological and behavior-based, pre-biological children should see animals and plants as fundamentally different kinds of things, in part because "living thing" means nothing apart from "behaving being," and plants don't behave. Second, pre-biological children should not be able to differentiate biological from psychological construals of living things because these do not yet represent distinct systems of explanation for them. Third, pre-biological children should not appeal to any specifically biological causal mechanisms to explain biological phenomena, because they have not yet constructed folkbiology as an autonomous domain.

Since Carey's book, there has been a great deal of research on children's conceptions of biology, the bulk of which shows that children reason about living things in ways distinct from how they reason about other kinds of objects. In particular, there have been empirical demonstrations of violations of all three of the implications of the radical conceptual change view.

Plants versus animals. A number of recent studies have shown that preschoolers know quite a bit about the commonalities between animals and plants. For example, 4-year-olds reliably report that plants and animals, but not human-made artifacts, can spontaneously heal or regrow injured parts (Backscheider, Shatz, & Gelman, 1993). Four-year-olds also show an impressive understanding of seeds and plant growth and of the underlying similarities between growth in plants and in animals (Hickling & Gelman, 1995). Inagaki and Hatano (1996) present evidence that 4- and 5-year-olds believe that animals and plants, but not artifacts, spontaneously change over time; 5-year-olds also projected biological properties such as growing and needing water on both plants and animals and coherently explained biological processes (taking in nutrients, growth, death) for plants by drawing on analogous properties for animals. Taken together, these results suggest that preschoolers have begun to form a rich category of living things that unites plants and animals.

Biological versus psychological construals. Likewise, it has been demonstrated in several ways that children possess distinct biological and psychological understandings of living things. Inagaki and Hatano (1993) showed that 4- and 5-year-olds clearly differentiate biological from psychological cause; children understand that mental effort is required to influence mental outcomes like improving one's memory, but is irrelevant for biological outcomes like digestion. Coley (1995) demonstrated that 8-year-olds, and to some extent kindergartners, show clearly different patterns of projections for biological (e.g., "has blood") versus psychological (e.g., "is smart") properties over the same set of animals. These results directly contradict the claim that preschoolers cannot in principle differentiate between biological and psychological construals of animals.

Biological causal mechanisms. Finally, a number of lines of research suggest candidates for explicitly biological causal mechanisms used by preschoolers to explain biological phenomena. These include *growth and natural change* (Backscheider, Shatz, & Gelman, 1993; Rosengren, Gelman, Kalish, & McCormick, 1991; Springer, Ngyuen, & Samaniego, 1996), *inheritance* (Hirschfeld, 1995; Springer, 1992; Springer & Keil, 1991; but see Solomon, Johnson, Zaitchik, & Carey, 1996, for an alternative view), and *illness and contagion* (Kalish, 1996a, 1996b, 1997; Solomon & Cassamites, 1999). In addition to these specific causal mechanisms, several independent proposals have been put forward to characterize early folkbiological framework theories. One of these is *teleology* (Keil, 1994, p. 237), which is the idea that "Properties have a purpose for biological kinds. There is a compelling, albeit sometimes mistaken sense . . . that the properties of biological kinds are there for reasons, that they solve design problems for the kinds that possess them." The other is *vitalism* (Hatano & Inagaki, 1994, 1999; Inagaki & Hatano, 1993, 1996; Miller & Bartsch, 1997) which, briefly, is the notion that living things take in vital energy from the environment and use it to grow and function properly.

Taken together, this large and growing body of research documents violations of the aforementioned implications of the radical theory change view. Preschoolers acknowledge important commonalities between animals and plants. They distinguish biological and psychological construals of living things. And although the evidence is not yet decisive, candidates for biological causal mechanisms and framework theories have been put forward. Thus, several important implications of the radical theory change view are violated, casting doubt on radical restructuring as a mechanism of conceptual change and suggesting that the acquisition of folkbiology may be a more gradual process. Children's folkbiological belief systems may not be incommensurate with those of adults after all.

The response of proponents of radical theory change (e.g., Carey, 1995, 1999) has been to acknowledge that children have distinct ways of thinking about living things, to push the age at which an autonomous intuitive biology emerges from 10 down to 6 or 7, and to acknowledge that a strong version of the radical conceptual change claim does not hold. However this should not be taken as a surrender. Proponents of radical conceptual change have argued that the understanding of animals/living things revealed by the aforementioned body of research is not a *biological* understanding. Rather it springs from an understanding of behavior and intuitive psychology. For instance, Carey (1995) argues that "We know that children have the concept *animal*; what is at issue is whether *animal* is a biological concept" (p. 291) and " . . . preschool children think that one person can 'catch' such symptoms as rashes and watery eyes through physical contact with a person who has them, but not weird beliefs or behaviors . . . the question is whether the child has any knowledge of any biological mechanism underlying such 'catching' " (p. 291). Likewise, Solomon et al. (1996, p. 169) summarize their results on inheritance by saying "The present studies challenge the claim that preschoolers' understanding of inheritance is biological."

Whether children's early thinking about living things is "biological" depends, of course, on one's definition of "biological." If by biological we mean "utilizing the same explanatory mechanisms as scientific biology," then children's early understanding of living things is obviously not biological. Clearly, preschool children do not yet understand the mechanisms underlying many biological processes (e.g., the viral transmissions of AIDS, Au & Romo, 1996). Young children are terrible at specifying details of genetic inheritance or disease transmission or the functions of various internal organs. Nor do they seem to have a clear notion about the kinds of things that are inside animals (Simons & Keil, 1995). At the other extreme, if by "biological" we mean "about living things," then the answer is trivially yes. By age 4 children have accumulated a great deal of encyclopedic knowledge about animals and plants. Obviously, neither of these definitions will do. Furthermore, I don't believe that the question of whether young children's conceptions of living things may properly be called "biological" is the most central question facing us. To the degree that we are truly interested in understanding conceptual development in the domain of folkbiology, the central questions facing researchers in this area are three: First, what are children's conceptions of living things like? Second, what are adults' conceptions of living things like? And third, how do we best characterize the process by which children's conceptions come to resemble those of adults in their culture? Indeed, the question of whether children's understanding of living things is biological is perhaps more profitably rendered as "Is children's understanding of living things like adults' understanding of living things?"

At present we cannot answer this question because we lack detailed research on the nature of adults' folkbiological conceptual systems, especially with respect to their understanding of biological causal mechanism. The research briefly mentioned above yields a rich picture of children's conceptions of living things. We know very little, however, about adults' conceptions of folkbiology beyond their responses as a comparison group on tasks designed for preschoolers. For example, consider recent research on children's understandings of inheritance and contagion. Children appear to understand that offspring resemble their parents, but are not always clear on exactly how or why. Children appear to understand that germs can make you sick and that you can catch germs from physical contact, but they're not always clear on exactly how or why. Before these patterns of partial understanding are dismissed as nonbiological, it is crucial to assess whether the understanding of the average adult in our culture is significantly more detailed or sophisticated. To what degree do adults demonstrate detailed knowledge of the mechanisms of inheritance or disease transmission? We cannot simply assume that adults' understanding of underlying biological mechanisms is significantly more sophisticated; indeed, adults may have a surprisingly tenuous grasp of biological causality, at least with respect to disease (Au & Romo, 1999; Keil, Levin, Richman, & Gutheil, 1999).

Thus, in order to characterize the nature of conceptual change in the domain of folkbiology, we must first understand the nature of the adult endpoint. If adults do possess sophisticated knowledge of biological mechanisms, then perhaps radical conceptual change does take place. In contrast, adult models may amount to little more than elaborated versions of the input–output relations understood by children (Au & Romo, 1999). Either way, to understand development we need a detailed description of the adult conceptual system that preschoolers are presumably in the midst of acquiring. Without a relatively detailed characterization of adult folkbiological conceptual systems in a particular culture, the trajectory of development cannot be adequately understood. Before we can understand the *process* of development, we must understand the *endstate*. Without some sense of endstate, we cannot hope to resolve the debate on the nature of conceptual development in this, or any, domain.

Variations in Adult Folkbiological Thought

In the previous section I argued that understanding conceptual development requires specification of the adult endstates. This is an oversimplification; conceptual development proceeds toward a range of possible outcomes rather than a single ideal. As pointed out by Super (1980), general theories of development are not possible without comparative research on the range of variation among adult endpoints. Moreover, such research reveals conceptual universals and cultural particulars that would then constrain possible accounts of development. Recent comparative research on adult folkbiological thought reveals both universal patterns and group differences that are attributable to cultural beliefs about the natural world, personal experience with flora and fauna, and other factors (Atran, 1998). Importantly, although we can perhaps point to a consensual "adult model" that represents knowledge shared by most adults in a given culture, recent comparative research has begun to uncover variability in adult models between and within cultures (e.g., Atran et al, 1999; Coley, Medin, & Atran, 1997; Coley, Medin, Proffitt, Lynch, & Atran, 1999; López, Atran, Coley, Medin, & Smith, 1997; Medin, Lynch, Coley, & Atran, 1997; Walker, 1992, 1999). This variability has important implications for accounts of conceptual development.

For example, different populations use animal categories differently in inductive reasoning. The similarity–coverage model of Osherson, Smith, Wilkie, López, and Shafir (1990) predicts that an argument whose premises are more diverse will be judged stronger than an argument whose premises are similar. For example, one should be more willing to generalize to all birds from sparrows and flamingos than from sparrows and robins. Osherson et al. attribute this finding to *coverage;* reasoners compare the taxonomic similarity of the premise categories to sampled members of the more general conclusion category. The premise set with better coverage—that is, higher taxonomic similarity to sampled instances—makes for the stronger argument. For the most part, undergraduate research participants reason in accordance with this diversity principle, based on taxonomic similarity. This finding has provided the foundation for several studies of the development of category-based induction which in general reveal that children through age 10 have difficulty grasping this phenomenon when reasoning about living things (Gutheil & Gelman, 1997; López, Gutheil, Gelman, & Smith, 1992). So far, this appears to be a straightforward developmental story; diversity is a complex inductive reasoning principle, and is relatively late in developing (but see Heit & Hahn, 1999, for evidence that by age 5 children can successfully reason according to diversity when reasoning involves familiar properties).

Comparative research, however, reveals that this diversity phenomenon is by no means a universal feature of folkbiological reasoning. The Itzaj Maya, native to the Peten region of Guatemala, do not use diversity in evaluating arguments about local mammals. Instead of computing taxonomic distance in evaluating possible inductions, they use expansive specific knowledge on the species in question (López et al., 1997). Nor is this simply a difference between urbanized and traditional thinkers; when the subject matter is trees, some Chicago-area tree experts use diversity-based reasoning like the undergraduates do (taxonomists and landscapers), whereas others (parks maintenance workers) prefer alternative strategies, like the Itzaj (Coley et al., 1999). Indeed, it appears that for experts, diversity is one reasoning strategy among many available, and one that often loses out when pitted against domain-specific knowledge about ecological propensities and causal principles. For relative folkbiological novices (such as the participants in the original experiments by Osherson et al., 1990), diversity may be the only reasoning strategy available.

In this case, comparative work on adult patterns of induction recasts the developmental findings and the phenomenon that a developmental account must explain. Diversity-reasoning adults are not necessarily the endstate of development, but may represent instead an intermediate stage wherein one has sufficient taxonomic knowledge to use diversity, but perhaps little specific knowledge to go beyond it. Moreover, comparative adult work suggests that the content of what is learned may differ by culture. Diversity is based on taxonomic relations among categories; perhaps children in the United States learn primarily about taxonomic relations among living kinds (indeed, recent evidence suggests that parental input to children in the United States focuses on the importance of taxonomic relations, Gelman, Coley, Rosengren, Hartman, & Pappas, 1998). In contrast, Itzaj children, growing up in an environment where plants and animals are salient and important, may be more likely to learn about causal–ecological relations. More generally, as this case study demonstrates, the "adult model" of folkbiological thought is influenced by culture, experience, and probably many other factors. We are only beginning to understand the nature and complexity of this model. Still, the range of variation we see in adult folkbiological cognition, as well as apparent universals, represents important constraints on possible accounts of development.

Conceptual Development in Neglected Populations

In the preceding sections I have argued that to characterize the process of conceptual development, we must better understand the adult models that children are in the process of acquiring, and better assess the variation among different possible adult endstates. It is equally crucial to examine conceptual development among different populations of children, especially those that differ along dimensions relevant to the domain in question. In the domain of folkbiology, these dimensions include daily experience with the natural world, and cultural beliefs about the relations between humans and the rest of the biological world. Most research in the domain of conceptual development has been done using predominantly White, predominantly middle- and upper-class urban or suburban children of relatively well-educated parents.[1] The population is remarkably uniform with respect to cultural beliefs about the natural world and human beings' rightful place therein, and with respect to their (relative lack of) direct experience with, and dependence on, plants and animals. As such, this population might be a good one in which to observe the acquisition of a relatively impoverished folkbiology, but a remarkably bad one from which to glean any sense of the range of variation in patterns of conceptual development in the domain of folkbiology. From this research we have learned much about how young children in this population conceptualize plants and animals, but almost nothing about the different paths that conceptual development may take. One example from an ongoing research project with a Native American population in Wisconsin illustrates the potential value of comparative developmental research.

Carey (1985, 1995) argues that children's early understanding of plants and animals is anthropocentric. In other words, prototypicality of humans is central to children's conceptions of the biological world; children's understanding of other living things is largely in reference to, or by analogy to, human beings. One source of support for this view is a property projection task where children are taught a new fact about a given biological kind (e.g., a dog "has an omentum") and asked whether other kinds (a bird, a fish, a plant) share that property. Carey (1985) reports a pattern of results consistent with the view that 4- and 6-year-old children's conceptions of the natural world are indeed anthropocentric. First, overall projections from humans were stronger than projections from other living things. Second, specific asymmetries in projection emerged, such that (for example) inferences from *human* to *dog* were stronger than from *dog* to *human*. Finally, children's reasoning followed striking violations of similarity, such that (for example) inferences from *human* to *bug* were stronger than from *bee* to *bug*. These patterns suggest that human is a privileged inferential base for the children Carey studied. As discussed above, this pattern of reasoning has been interpreted as demonstrating that young children possess an understanding of biological phenomenona incommensurate with that of adults, and that pervasive conceptual change is necessary for children to acquire the adult model in which humans are seen as one animal among many.

It is important, however, to examine the generality of this anthropocentric pattern of reasoning on at least two grounds. First, rather than being diagnostic of deep conceptual commitments, this anthropocentric folkbiology may reflect a lack of knowledge about the biological world. Carey's subject population, in Cambridge, Massachusetts, may be relative folkbiological novices. Indeed, some evidence suggests that children who are more familiar with certain living kinds prefer to use knowledge of those kinds in reasoning. Specifically, Inagaki (1990) shows that children who raised goldfish reasoned about a novel aquatic animal (a frog) by analogy to the goldfish, not to humans. So, perhaps Carey's population (and that studied by most developmental researchers) did not have sufficient knowledge of nonhuman living kinds to use them as an inferential base. Increased knowledge might provide more salient biological exemplars which could in turn mitigate anthropocentrism.

---

[1]Not all research on the development of folkbiology has focused on this population. The work of Inagaki and Hatano—although it is not explicitly comparative—examines emerging biological knowledge among Japanese children. Hatano et al. (1993) compare biological reasoning among children in Japan, the United States, and Israel, and find striking commonalities along with some specific differences. While valuable, this work is conducted with primarily urban samples from industrialized societies that presumably have little contact with plants and animals, and therefore may not be as broad as it initally appears. Another exception is the research done by Walker (1999) among the Nigerian Yoruba. This work looks at the preservation of identity over superficial transformations, and reveals different developmental courses for rural, urban, and elite populations. Despite the existence of these studies, comparative work is nevertheless the exception rather than the rule.

Second, an anthropocentric folkbiology may reflect cultural assumptions about relations between humans and nature. Again, in the population studied by Carey (and most others), the differences between humans and nonhumans is very sharply drawn. Direct interaction with and dependence on nature is relatively rare. In Western culture, humans are seen as distinct from nature. However, in a culture where humans are perceived as an integral part of nature, people might be less likely to make anthropocentric construals.

In an ongoing comparative study of members of the Menominee Indian Tribe of Wisconsin, we are currently addressing some of these questions. This population is interesting for a number of reasons. First, on the traditional Native American view, humans are an integral part of the natural world (Bierhorst, 1994; Suzuki & Knudtson, 1992). This contrasts sharply with the Western view. Second, traditional folkbiological knowledge is especially salient to the Menominee. Unlike many woodland tribes, the Menominee reservation occupies (a small fraction of) their traditional range; thus, traditional knowledge of local plant and animal species is still very relevant today. Moreover, the Menominee run a successful logging operation that employs traditional ecological knowledge to guide forest management; thus, many Menominee depend in part on traditional knowledge for their livelihood. Children spend time fishing and hunting and in general have a very high degree of contact with plants and animals. Thus, Menominee children differ from a typical urban or suburban sample in terms of both having a cultural tradition of viewing humans as an integral part of the natural world and having a great deal of experience with plants and animals. In this work we ask whether these differences might lead to variant patterns of folkbiological reasoning.

As part of this project, we examined inductive inferences among Native American children using a property projection task. Contrary to results with middle-class urban children, Menominee children aged 6 years and above show no evidence of anthropocentric folkbiological reasoning (Coley, Medin, & James, 1999). Specifically, we find no evidence that *human* functions as well as a privileged inductive base, little evidence of asymmetries in projections, and no evidence for violations of similarity. Rather, Menominee children's projections were largely based on similarity among living things, and to some extent on causal/ecological relations.

These results raise several intriguing possibilities about the shift in reasoning reported by Carey (1985). First, the shift away from anthropocentric folkbiological reasoning may take place earlier in this population. In order to answer this question, the next step is to examine property projection in younger (4-year-old) Menominee children. Another possibility is that this population may never adopt anthropocentric reasoning patterns at all. Either of these patterns reflects a departure from what has been reported in the literature and provides a challenge to current explanations of conceptual development by providing an alternative developmental trajectory in need of explanation. These preliminary results are far from conclusive, but they broaden our view of the process of conceptual development, and raise clear questions about the generality of the process as currently described in the literature. Furthermore, they demonstrate the potential value of documenting patterns of development in populations that differ substantially from mainstream developmental research participants on relevant dimensions.

Conclusions

Using the domain of folkbiology as a demonstration case, I have argued that the study of conceptual development stands to benefit greatly by increased comparative research in several ways. First, we need comparisons between children and adults within a given society. I have argued that it is essentially impossible to understand the process of conceptual development without a detailed look at adult conceptions of folkbiology. Without such research, we cannot hope to specify how children's models come to resemble those of adults in their culture. Second, we need comparisons between adults' endstates in different contexts. A complete understanding of conceptual development demands that we understand the variability of adult conceptual systems, including the differences attributable to experience and cultural beliefs, among other factors. Conceptual development proceeds toward a range of possible outcomes, not toward a single ideal. Documenting this range is necessary for understanding development and would shed light on conceptual universals and cultural particulars that would then constrain possible accounts of development. Finally, we need comparisons among children developing in different contexts. To understand conceptual development broadly construed, comparative research needs to be conducted on the process of development in groups of children other than the standard research population. This research is needed especially among groups that differ from standard populations on a relevant dimension such as habitual experience or specific cultural beliefs. Such research goes hand-in-hand with comparative adult work and would serve to distinguish universal from particular patterns of development and thus to inform and constrain accounts of conceptual development.

It is important to acknowledge that comparative research is by no means a panacea. Like any other research paradigm, comparative studies have limitations. By definition, comparative studies violate a cardinal rule of experimental method by leaving many differences between groups uncontrolled (Cole & Means, 1981). So whereas similar patterns of development in disparate populations indicate potential cognitive universals, different patterns of development in such groups indicate the need to search further for an explanation of those differences. But the search might never have seemed necessary without the comparative findings. Thus, comparative research can be seen as a tool for raising cone questions about conceptual development as well as for answering those questions. As such, comparative research is absolutely essential for deepening our understanding of the range and complexity of human conceptual development.

Acknowledgments

This essay is based in part on a talk presented at the Biennial Meetings of the Society for Research in Child Development, April 6, 1997, in Washington, DC, as part of a symposium entitled *Flexibility in Early Reasoning about Living Things*, chaired by John Coley and Giyoo Hatano. I thank Larry Hirschfeld for encouraging my thinking along these lines, and Rebekah Levine Coley, Gregg Solomon, and Fei Xu for comments and discussion. I am deeply indebted to my major collaborators, Doug Medin and Scott Atran, for their continued support and for their efforts in pioneering comparative interdisciplinary research on folkbiological thought.

References

Atran, S. (1998). Folk biology and the anthropology of science: Cognitive universals and cultural particulars. *Behavioral and Brain Sciences, 21,* 547–609.

Atran, S., Medin, D., Ross, N., Lynch, E., Coley, J., Ucan Ek', E., & Vapnarsky, V (1999). Folkecology and commons management in the Maya Lowlands. *Proceedings of the National Academy of Sciences U.S.A., 96,* 7598–7603.

Au, T. K., & Romo, L. F. (1996). Building a coherent conception of HIV transmission: A new approach to AIDS education. In D. L. Medin (Ed.), *The psychology of learning and motivation, 35,* 193–242.

Au, T. K., & Romo, L. F. (1999). Mechanical causality in children's "folkbiology." In D. L. Medin & S. Atran (Eds.), *Folkbiology* (pp. 355–401). Cambridge, MA: MIT Press.

Backscheider, A. B., Shatz, M., & Gelman, S. A. (1993). Preschoolers' ability to distinguish living kinds as a function of regrowth. *Child Development, 64,* 1242–1257.

Bierhorst, J. (1994). *The way of the earth: Native America and the environment.* New York: Wm. Morrow & Co.

Carey, S. (1985). *Conceptual change in childhood.* Cambridge, MA: MIT Press.

Carey, S. (1995). On the origin of causal understanding. In D. Sperber, D. Premack, & A. J. Premack (Eds.), *Causal cognition: A multidisciplinary debate* (pp. 268–308). New York: Oxford University Press.

Carey, S. (1999). Sources of conceptual change. In E. Scholnick, K. Nelson, S. Gelman, & P. Miller (Eds.), *Conceptual development: Piaget's legacy* (pp. 293–326). Mahwah, NJ: Erlbaum.

Cole, M., & Means, B. (1981). *Comparative studies of how people think.* Cambridge, MA: Harvard University Press.

Coley J. D. (1995). Emerging differentiation of folkbiology and folkpsychology: Attributions of biological and psychological properties to living things. *Child Development, 66,* 1856–1874.

Coley, J. D., Medin, D. L., & Atran, S. (1997). Does rank have its privilege? Inductive inferences within folkbiological taxonomies. *Cognition, 64*(1), 73–112.

Coley, J. D., Medin, D. L., & James, L. (1999). *Folk biological induction among Native American children.* Paper presented at the Biennial Meetings of the Society for Research in Child Development, Albuquerque, NM, April, 1999.

Coley, J. D., Medin, D. L., Proffitt, J. B., Lynch, E. B., & Atran, S. (1999). Inductive reasoning in folkbiological thought. In D. L. Medin & S. Atran (Eds.), *Folkbiology.* Cambridge, MA: MIT Press.

Gelman, S. A., Coley, J. D., Rosengren, K. R., Hartman, E. E., & Pappas, A. S. (1998). Beyond labeling: The role of parental input in the acquisition of richly-structured categories. *Monographs of the Society for Research in Child Development, 63*(1, Serial No. 253).

Gopnik A., & Wellman, H. M. (1994). The theory theory. In L. A. Hirschfeld & S. A. Gelman (Eds.), *Mapping the mind: Domain specificity in cognition and culture* (pp. 257–293). Cambridge, UK: Cambridge University Press.

Gutheil, G., & Gelman, S. A. (1997). Children's use of sample size and diversity information within basic-level categories. *Journal of Experimental Child Psychology, 64*(2), 154–179.

Hatano, G., & Inagaki, K. (1994). Young children's naive theory of biology. *Cognition, 50,* 171–188.

Hatano, G., & Inagaki, K. (1999). A developmental perspective on informal biology. In D. L. Medin & S. Atran (Eds.), *Folkbiology.* Cambridge, MA: MIT Press.

Hatano, G., Siegler, R. S., Richards, D. D., Inagaki, K., Stavy, R., & Wax, N. (1993). The development of biological knowledge: A multinational study. *Cognitive Development, 8,* 47–62.

Heit, E., & Hahn, U. (1999). Diversity-based reasoning in children age 5 to 8. *Proceedings of the 21st Annual Conference of the Cognitive Science Society* (pp. 212–217). New Jersey, Erlbaum.

Hickling, A. K., & Gelman, S. A. (1995). How does your garden grow? Early conceptualization of seeds and their place in the plant growth cycle. *Child Development, 66,* 856–876.

Hirschfeld, L. A. (1995). Do children have a theory of race? *Cognition, 54,* 209–252.

Inagaki, K. (1990). The effects of raising animals on children's biological knowledge. *British Journal of Developmental Psychology, 8,* 119–129.

Inagaki, K., & Hatano, G. (1993). Young children's understanding of the mind-body distinction. *Child Development, 64,* 1534–1549.

Inagaki, K., & Hatano, G. (1996). Young children's recognition of commonalities between animals and plants. *Child Development, 67,* 2823–2840.

Kalish, C. W. (1996a). Causes and symptoms in preschoolers' conceptions of illness. *Child Development, 67,* 1647–1670.

Kalish, C. W. (1996b). Preschoolers' understanding of germs as invisible mechanisms. *Cognitive Development, 11,* 83–106.

Kalish, C. W. (1997). Preschoolers' understanding of mental and bodily reactions to contamination: What you don't see can hurt you, but cannot sadden you. *Developmental Psychology, 33*(1), 79–91.

Keil, F. C. (1989). *Concepts, kinds, and cognitive development.* Cambridge, MA: MIT Press.

Keil, F. C. (1994). The birth and nurturance of concepts by domains: The origins of concepts of living things. In L. Hirschfeld & S. Gelman (Eds.), *Domain specificity in cognition and culture* (pp. 234–254). New York: Cambridge University Press.

Keil, F. C., Levin, D. T., Richman, B. A., & Gutheil, G. (1999). Mechanism and explanation in the development of biological thought: The case of disease. In D. L. Medin & S. Atran (Eds.), *Folkbiology* (pp. 285–319). Cambridge, MA: MIT Press.

López, A., Atran, S., Coley, J. D., Medin, D., & Smith, E. E. (1997). The tree of life: Universal and cultural features of folkbiological taxonomies and inductions. *Cognitive Psychology, 32,* 251–295.

López, A., Gutheil, G., Gelman, S. A., & Smith, E. E. (1992). The development of category-based induction. *Child Development, 63,* 1070–1090.

Medin, D. L., Lynch, E. B., Coley, J. D., & Atran, S. (1997). Categorization and reasoning among tree experts: Do all roads lead to Rome? *Cognitive Psychology, 32,* 49–96.

Miller, J. L., & Bartsch, K. (1997). The development of biological explanation: Are children vitalists? *Developmental Psychology, 33*(1), 156–164.

Osherson, D. N., Smith, E. E., Wilkie, C., López, A., & Shafir, E. (1990). Category-based induction. *Psychological Review, 97,* 185–200.

Rosengren, K. S., Gelman, S. A., Kalish, C. W., & McCormick, M. (1991). As time goes by: Children's early understanding of growth in animals. *Child Development, 62,* 1302–1320.

Simons, D. J., & Keil, F. C. (1995). An abstract to concrete shift in the development of biological thought: The inside story. *Cognition, 56,* 129–163.

Solomon, G. E. A., & Cassamites, N. L. (1999). On facts and conceptual systems: Young children s integration of their understanding of germs and contagion. *Developmental Psychology, 35,* 113–126.

Solomon, G. E. A., Johnson, S. C., Zaitchik D., & Carey, S. (1996). Like father, like son: Young children's understanding of how and why offspring resemble their parents. *Child Development, 67,* 151–171.

Springer, K. (1992). Children's awareness of the biological implications of kinship. *Child Development, 63,* 950–959.

Springer, K., & Keil, F. C. (1991). Early differentiation of causal mechanisms appropriate to biological and nonbiological kinds. *Child Development, 62,* 767–781.

Springer, K., Ngyuen, T., & Samaniego, R. (1996). Early understanding of age- and environment-related noxiousness in biological kinds: Evidence for a naive theory. *Cognitive Development, 11,* 65–82.

Super, C. M. (1980). Cognitive development Looking across at growing up. *New Directions for Child Development, 8,* 59–70.

Suzuki, D., & Knudtson, P. (1992). *Wisdom of the elders: Sacred native stories of nature.* New York: Bantam Books.

Tversky, A., & Kahneman, D. (1974). Judgement under uncertainty: Heuristics and biases. *Science, 185,* 1124–1131.

Walker, S. J. (1992). Supernatural beliefs, natural kinds, and conceptual structure. *Memory & Cognition, 20*(6), 655–662.

Walker, S. J. (1999). Culture, domain-specificity and conceptual change: Natural kind and artifact concepts. *British Journal of Developmental Psychology, 17,* 203–219.

Wellman, H. M., & Gelman, S. A. (1992). Cognitive development: Foundational theories of core domains. *Annual Review of Psychology, 43,* 337–375.

Wellman, H. M., & Inagaki, K. (Eds.). (1997). The emergence of core domains of thought: Children's reasoning about physical, psychological and biological phenomena. *New Directions for Child Development, 75.*

References for Introductory Information and Critical Thinking Exercises

Ainsworth, M. D. S. (1967). *Infancy in Uganda: Infant care and the growth of love.* Baltimore, MD: Johns Hopkins Press.

Ainsworth, M. D. S., Blehar, M., Waters, E., & Wall, S. (1978). *Patterns of attachment.* Hillsdale, NJ: Erlbaum.

American Psychiatric Association. (1994). *Quick reference to the diagnostic criteria from DSM-IV.* Washington, DC: American Psychiatric Association.

Baumrind, D. (1967). Child care practices anteceding three patterns of preschool behavior. *Genetic Psychology Monographs, 75,* 43–88.

Berry, J. W., Kim, U., Power, S., Young, M., Bujaki, M. (1989). Acculturation attitudes in plural societies, *Applied Psychology: An International Review, 38,*(2), 185–206.

Boodman, S. G. (1995, June 13). Researchers study obesity in children. *Washington Post Health,* 10–15.

Bowlby, J. (1960). Separation anxiety. *International Journal of Psychoanalysis, 41,* 89–113.

Bowlby, J. (1969). *Attachment and Loss: Vol. 1. Attachment.* New York: Basic Books.

Bowlby, J. (1980). *Attachment and Loss: Vol. 3. Loss, Sadness and Depression.* New York: Basic Books.

Bronfenbrenner, U. (1979). *The ecology of human development: Experiments by nature and design.* Cambridge, MA: Harvard University Press.

Carey, S. (1985). *Conceptual change in childhood.* Cambridge, MA: MIT Press.

Cooley, C. H. (1902). *Human nature and the social order.* New York: Scribner's.

Dennis, W. & Dennis, M. G. (1940). The effect of cradling practices upon the onset of walking in Hopi children. *Journal of Genetic Psychology, 56,* 77–86.

Duvall, E. M. (1977). *Marriage and family development* (5th ed.). Philadelphia: J. B. Lippincott.

Dweck, C. S. & Leggett, E. L. (1988). A social-cognitive approach to motivation and personality. *Psychological Review, 95,* 256–273.

Garmezy, N. (1991). Resiliency and vulnerability to adverse developmental outcomes associated with poverty. *American Behavioral Scientist, 34,* 416–430.

Gelman, S., & Markman, E. (1986). Categories and induction in young children. *Cognition, 23,* 183–208.

Harris, M. (1992). *Language experience and early language development: From input to uptake.* Hove, UK: Erlbaum.

Helms, J. E. (1992). Why is there no study of cultural equivalence in standardized cognitive-ability testing? *American Psychologist, 47,* 1083–1101.

Hopkins, B. (1991). Facilitating early motor development: An intracultural study of West Indian mothers and their infants living in Britain. In J. K. Nugent, B. M. Lester, & T. B. Brazelton (Eds.), *The cultural context of infancy: Vol. 2. Multicultural and interdisciplinary approaches to parent-infant relations.* Norwood, NJ: Ablex.

Keil, F. (1989). *Concepts, kinds and cognitive development.* Cambridge, MA: MIT Press.

Lewis, M., & Brooks-Gunn, J. (1979). *Social cognition and the acquisition of self.* New York: Plenum.

Lovett, A. (1998). An Adoptee's Advice to Prospective Adoptive Parents. Philadelphia Area Resolve Conference, Sunday April 26th 1998. [Online]. Available: http://www.adoption-forum.org/ap/advice.htm

Meier, R. P. (1991). Language acquisition by deaf children. *American Scientist, 79,* 69–70.

Nelson, K. (1973). Structure and strategy in learning to talk. *Monographs of the Society for Research in Child Development, 38*(Serial No. 149).

Rogoff, B. (1990). *Apprenticeship in thinking: Cognitive development in social context.* NY: Oxford University Press.

Sigman, M. (1995). Nutrition and child development: More food for thought. *Current Directions in Psychological Science, 4,* 52–55.

Trickett, P. K., & McBride-Chang, C. (1995). The developmental impact of different forms of child abuse and neglect. *Developmental Review, 15,* 311–337.

Verschueren, K., Marcoen, A., & Schoefs, V. (1996). The internal working model of self, attachment, and competence in five-year-olds. *Child Development, 67,* 2493–2511.

Vygotsky, L. S. (1978). *Mind in society: The development of higher psychological processes.* Cambridge, MA: Harvard University Press.

Wellman, H., & Gelman, S. (1992). Cognitive development: Foundational theories in core domains. *Annual Review of Psychology, 43,* 337–375.

Werner, E. E., & Smith, R. S. (1992). *Overcoming the odds: High-risk children from birth to adulthood.* Ithaca, NY: Cornell University Press.

Wolfner G. D., & Gelles, R. J. (1993). A profile of violence toward children: A national study. *Child Abuse and Neglect, 17,* 197–212.

Credits

Overview

Reading 1   Lerner, R. M. (1991). Changing organism-context relations as the basic process of development: A developmental contextual perspective. *Developmental Psychology, 27*(1), 27–32. Copyright © 1991 by the American Psychological Association. Reprinted with permission. Figure 1 from R. M. Lerner (1984) *On the Nature of Human Plasticity,* Figure 5, used by permission of Cambridge University Press. Permission obtained from R. M. Lerner for use of article and use of Figure 1.

Birth, Infancy, and Toddlerhood

Reading 2   Crowe, T. K., McClain, C., & Provost, B. (1999). Motor development of Native American children on the Peabody Developmental Motor Scales. *American Journal of Occupational Therapy, 53*(5), 514–518. Copyright (1999) by the American Occupational Therapy Association Inc. Reprinted with permission by Sage Publications.

Reading 3   Hughes, M., Dote-Kwan, J., & Dolendo, J. (1999). Characteristics of maternal directiveness and responsiveness with young children with visual impairments. *Child: Care, Health and Development, 25*(4), 285–298. Used by permission of Blackwell Science Ltd.

Reading 4   Zach, U., & Keller, H. (1999). Patterns of the attachment-exploration balance of 1-year-old infants from the United States and Northern Germany. *Journal of Cross-Cultural Psychology, 30*(3), pp. 381–388. Copyright © 1999 by Western Washington University. Reprinted by Permission of Sage Publications, Inc.

Preschool

Reading 5   Finton, L. (1996). Living in a bilingual-bicultural family. In I. Parasnis, (Ed) (Ed.), *Cultural and language diversity and the deaf experience.* (pp. 258–271): Cambridge University Press, New York, NY, US. Reprinted with the permission of Cambridge University Press.

Reading 6   Mundy, P., & Markus, J. (1997). On the nature of communication and language impairment in autism. *Mental Retardation and Developmental Disabilities Research Reviews, 3*(4), 343–349. Copyright © 1997 Wiley-Liss, Inc. This material is used by permission of Wiley-Liss, Inc., a subsidiary of John Wiley & Sons, Inc.

Reading 7   Rutter, M. & the English and Romanian Adoptees (ERA) Study Team. (1998). Developmental catch-up, and deficit, following adoption after severe global early privation. *Journal of Child Psychology and Psychiatry, 39*(4) 465–476. Used by permission of Blackwell Publishing, Ltd.

Middle Childhood/School Age

Childhood (across age groupings)

Reading 19   Sternberg, M., & Rosenbloom, M. (2000). "Lost childhood"—Lessons
              from the Holocaust: Implications for adult adjustment. *Child and Ado-
              lescent Social Work Journal, 17*(1), 5–17. Used by permission of Kluwer
              Academic/Plenum Publishers.

Reading 20   Clark, S. J., Savitz, L. A., & Randolph, R. K. (2001). Rural children's
              health. *Western Journal of Medicine, 174,* 142–147. Used with permis-
              sion of the BMJ Publishing Group.

Reading 21   Coley, J. (2000). On the importance of comparative research: The case
              of folkbiology. *Child Development, 71*(1) 82–90. Used by permission of
              Society for Research in Child Development.